Discourse Studies Reader

BLOOMSBURY DISCOURSE

Series Editor:
Professor Ken Hyland, University of Hong Kong

Discourse is one of the most significant concepts of contemporary thinking in the humanities and social sciences as it concerns the ways language mediates and shapes our interactions with each other and with the social, political and cultural formations of our society. The *Bloomsbury Discourse* aims to capture the fast-developing interest in discourse to provide students, new and experienced teachers and researchers in applied linguistics, ELT and English language with an essential bookshelf. Each book deals with a core topic in discourse studies to give an in-depth, structured and readable introduction to an aspect of the way language is used in real life.

OTHER TITLES IN THE SERIES:

Academic Discourse, Ken Hyland
Discourse Analysis, Brian Paltridge
Discourse Analysis (2nd edition), Brian Paltridge
The Discourse of Blogs and Wikis, Greg Myers
The Discourse of Online Consumer Reviews, Camilla Vásquez
The Discourse of Text Messaging, Caroline Tagg
The Discourse of Twitter and Social Media, Michele Zappavigna
Historical Discourse, Caroline Coffin
Metadiscourse, Ken Hyland
News Discourse, Monika Bednarek and Helen Caple
Professional Discourse, Britt-Louise Gunnarsson
School Discourse, Frances Christie
Using Corpora in Discourse Analysis, Paul Baker
Workplace Discourse, Almut Koester

Discourse Studies Reader

Essential excerpts

Edited by

KEN HYLAND

BLOOMSBURY DISCOURSE

BLOOMSBURY

LONDON · NEW DELHI · NEW YORK · SYDNEY

Bloomsbury Academic

An imprint of Bloomsbury Publishing Plc

50 Bedford Square   175 Fifth Avenue
London   New York
WC1B 3DP   NY 10010
UK   USA

www.bloomsbury.com

This Collection first published 2013

British Library Cataloguing-in-Publication Data

A catalogue record for this book is available from the British Library.

ISBN: HB: 9781441179821
PB: 9781441154972
PDF: 9781441192653
ePub: 9781441172693

Library of Congress Cataloging-in-Publication Data

A catalogue record for this book is available from the Library of Congress.

Typeset by Newgen Imaging Systems Pvt Ltd, Chennai, India
Printed and bound in India

Contents

1

Introduction

Ken Hyland

Discourse and discourse analysis

Discourse is one of the most significant concepts of modern thinking in a range of disciplines across the humanities and social sciences. Applied linguists originally took an interest in the idea to study language beyond the sentence, extending their traditional concerns with the constraints on morphemes, words and syntax to look for the patterns which seemed to distinguish *texts* from random collections of *sentences*. Today, however, discourse analysis is used to understand *language in the world*. It is the principle means to explore how language functions in potentially all aspects of human life; how it works to create and sustain social relationships among individuals, and so shape our identities and our interactions with society. So while the analysis of discourse begins with linguistic study, it takes us far beyond texts, helping us to understand how language is used to construct ourselves, our communities and our political and cultural formations. It has, in other words, become an inescapably important concept for understanding all aspects of society and human responses to it.

The study of discourse is therefore the study of language in action: how language works in relation to particular social contexts. The fact that language is connected to almost everything that goes on in the world, means that discourse analysis has become central to those disciplines which study humans and society scientifically, such as anthropology, sociology, philosophy, psychology and so on. Thus, sociologists attempt to find principles of social organization in conversational interaction and communication theorists look for, among other things, the ways we persuade each other to buy products or buy into ideas. 'Discourse' is therefore something of an overloaded term, covering a range of meanings and with several distinct uses in play, and its complexities do not allow it to be carved up neatly between disciplines.

People who study discourse might therefore focus on the analysis of speech and writing to bring out the dynamics and conventions of social situations, or take a more theoretical and critical point of view to consider the institutionalized ways of thinking which define our social lives. Discourse analysis, to take some liberties with simplification, can be seen to spread between two poles, giving more-or-less emphasis to concrete texts or to institutional practices, to either particular cases or talk or to how social structures are formed by it.

There is, for example, a long tradition of treating discourse in linguistic terms, informed by both pragmatics and a maturing, activity-centred linguistic perspective on language. This take on discourse recognizes 'language-in-use' as a legitimate object of analysis and sets out to discover grammatical and structural features of language operating at levels higher than the sentence. Many different frameworks have been developed for this purpose, crossing a number of disciplines and drawing on a broad variety of assumptions and analytical methods. Halliday's (1994) Systemic Functional Linguistics is perhaps the most elaborated and sophisticated of these models, but they all regard linguistic signalling and organization patterns as potential resources for interpreting text meanings and as contributing to our understanding of how texts are produced and used.

Many social scientists, however, particularly those influenced by Foucault (1972), pay very little attention to textual features. Instead they focus on the 'socially constructive effects' of discourse, or on the ways it functions to create social, cultural and institutional developments and to influence how we understand the world. This is what we might describe as discourse as form-of-life: the stuff of our everyday world of activities and institutions which is created by our routine uses of language, together with other aspects of social practices. It is through discourses, for example, that we build meanings for things in the world such as lectures, meetings and celebrity; it is the ways that we construct identities for ourselves and relationships with others; it is how we distribute prestige and value to ideas and behaviours and it is the ways we make connections to the past and to the future.

This difference is neatly encapsulated in Gee's (1999) distinction between 'big D' and 'little d' discourse. Gee defines discourse (with a little 'd') as 'language-in-use', that is, language as we use it to enact our identities as teachers, discourse analysts, taxi drivers or particle physicists and how we get things done in the world. Discourse (with a big 'D'), on the other hand, is a wider concept involving both language and other elements. It highlights the fact that our displays of who we are and what we are doing when we act as members of particular groups, always involves more than just language. As Gee observes:

> It involves acting-interacting-thinking-valuing-talking in the 'appropriate way' with the 'appropriate' props at the 'appropriate' times in the 'appropriate' places. Such socially accepted associations among ways of using language, of thinking, valuing, acting, and interacting in the 'right' places and at the 'right' times with the 'right' objects (associations that can be used to identify oneself as a member of a socially meaningful group or 'social network'), I will refer to as 'Discourses' with a capital 'D'. (1999: 17)

Discourse, then, is a way of being. It is the institutions, activities and values which we constantly recreate through discourse as members of social groups.

Fairclough (2003), like Gee, is just one among many analysts who see no opposition between the two views of discourse and its analysis. He observes that:

> Text analysis is an essential part of discourse analysis, but discourse analysis is not merely the linguistic analysis of texts. I see discourses analysis as 'oscillating' between a focus on specific texts and a focus on what I shall call the 'orders of discourse', the relatively durable social structuring of language which is itself one element of the relatively durable structuring and networking of social practices. (2003: 3)

For Fairclough, then, this 'oscillation' between texts and the structures which support them is needed to understand how language is used to conduct interactions and how it is embedded in social and cultural practices.

The point here is that we do not only use discourse to express our attitudes, ideas and understandings, but that these are themselves shaped by discourse. Authorized and valued ways of using language make certain possibilities available to us and exclude others, thereby constraining what can be said and how it can be said. The topics we discuss, how we approach them and the ways we see the world are all influenced by the language we have available to us.

Domains and methods

These different aspects of discourse and discourse analysis are illustrated in the pages of this book, which is composed of chapters compiled from my *Bloomsbury Discourse*. This is something of an innovative publishing move, a sampler which is more often found in music genres or Penguin fiction, but it is one which has more than a simple marketing motive. The chapters were selected to offer a broad and accessible flavour of current issues in discourse, exemplifying some of the ways it is studied, the areas that are studied and the findings that such studies produce. Together they not only offer a taste of the series, but also stand alone in their own right to offer a wide-ranging and structured introduction to discourse issues for students, researchers, teachers and others interested in language use and how communication is accomplished.

The volume is divided into three broad sections dealing, respectively, with some key methodological approaches, with the analysis of central institutional and social domains and with emergent electronic discourses. The first deals with three of the main approaches to researching discourse which inform the analyses conducted in the book together with a broad introduction to research issues. The second section illustrates a range of analytical approaches to discourse studies and some central areas of interest, focusing on the ways language is used in education, the media and the professions. The final section looks at the characteristics of emergent electronic genres, showing both the challenges to discourse analysis these present and its potential to describe these genres.

The collection suggests some of the varied ways that discourse analysis has been helpful in addressing a range of questions to do with language use, offering new ways of understanding domains such as language learning, language change and language variation. They also exemplify some of the ways that discourse studies have opened up new ways of exploring areas which have traditionally been associated with fields that focus on human life and communication, where research has provided insights into such issues as solidarity and oppression, identity and community. More specifically, these studies offer concrete examples of Gee's assertion that language functions in every aspect of human endeavour, 'scaffolding the performance of social activities and social affiliations within culture, groups and institutions' (Gee, 1999: 1). The study of discourse thus reaches into every corner of social life, telling us more about gender and ethnicity, media and politics, aging and disability and persuasion and ideology, while contributing to our understanding of how we argue and inform, tell jokes and sell things.

The chapters included here therefore introduce some of the questions that discourse analysts ask and which they help answer. These are questions such as: What role does grammar play in constructing meaning (Chapters 2 and 5)? How does the discourse used in a particular domain differ over time (Chapter 7)? How do individuals enact social relations in a range of different contexts (Chapters 3, 6, 8 and 12)? How do images and text interact in presenting an argument (Chapters 5 and 9)? How do learners acquire different genres (Chapters 2, 5 and 8)? How does language work to construct identities for users in different contexts (Chapters 10 and 11)? And how does language do many of these things in the confined spaces of new electronic genres (Chapters 10, 11 and 12)? The chapters also illustrate some of the different ways that analysts approach these questions. Chapter 4, for example, speaks to students and novice researchers to raise issues that need to be considered when planning and conducting a discourse analysis project, while Chapters 1, 2 and 3 provide accessible introductions to a number of central contemporary methodologies for analyzing discourse: Corpus analysis, Systemic Linguistics and Metadiscourse.

Corpus analysis, using collections of electronically encoded text, draws on frequency information about the occurrence and co-occurrence of particular linguistic items to draw inferences about how particular groups use language. Corpora of various kinds are employed in many of the chapters (particularly 6, 8, 11 and 12) but corpus techniques are most explicitly discussed in Chapter 2. Here Paul Baker uses a small corpus of holiday leaflets written for young adults to explore some basic principles of corpus analysis and how its procedures can be carried out on texts. By showing how lists of frequently occurring words and measures such as dispersion and type-token ratios help to give an account of the meaning and complexity of a text, he illustrates some of the ways corpus analyses can be valuable to discourse analysts and inform their work. Another key approach is Systemic Functional Linguistics, adopted in the analyses in Chapters 5 and 9 and discussed more fully in Chapter 3. This model seeks to offer a comprehensive account of how language users create meanings in discourse by drawing on Halliday's multifunctional model of language (e.g. Halliday and Mathiessen, 2004) . Other approaches discussed are that of Metadiscourse, which attempts to map the interactional resources of language (Chapter 4), and the sociohistorical perspective, illustrated in Chapter 7, which shows how discourse is temporally situated and changes over time.

Although it cannot claim to be comprehensive, the collection offers some interesting analyses and fascinating insights into the ways language is used in a variety of different contexts.

Threads and themes

In addition to revealing aspects of these genres and exemplify methods of analysis, these chapters have been selected as they embody a number of key principles of discourse analysis.

The first is that they all see discourse as contextualized activities rather than simply as objects of study. While dealing with linguistic materials, taking words as raw data, they are words which are recognized as coming from a wider set in a particular situation and which help to construct that situation. The underlying assumption in all these chapters is therefore that the study of language should be the study of society; it is part of a wider landscape of approaches to appreciating the workings of everyday life, whether it is initiating young children into the ways of understanding and talking about the natural world through school science texts (Chapter 5), the communicative functions of images in the presentation of news stories (Chapter 9) or how colleagues use small talk to oil the wheels of the transactionally oriented workplace (Chapter 6). In all these cases, what counts for authors is the ways that words act as semiotic resources to get things done in particular contexts and circumstances and how they are seen as meaningful by those who use them.

A sensitivity to context means showing how discourses are socially situated in institutional and social environments and, often, taking seriously the constructionist idea that things are only true for a particular group at a particular time. This is perhaps most obvious in the 'new discourses' of the electronic age such as blogs and wikis (Chapter 10), electronic texts (Chapter 11) and microblogging on Twitter (Chapter 12). In these contexts, actors redefine demarcations between the personal and the public to forge social bonds and construct new communities using a variety of rhetorical and technical resources (respellings, abbreviations, multimedia links, etc.) not previously possible on the same scale or in the same way. In Chapter 7, Britt-Louise Gunnarsson demonstrates quite starkly the importance of situating cultural practices in their wider social contexts by showing how writers have used language to construct a world of medical research facts at different periods of history. Studies such as this reveal the historical circumstance in which current discourses emerge and become relatively stabilized in certain periods, showing how the writing conventions familiar to us today are not timeless and self-evident means of establishing knowledge but have been consciously developed over time in response to particular social situations.

The second theme which emerges from these chapters is the fact that discourse matters to people. Discourse is firmly anchored in our daily lives as we go about our business in the workplace, in the classroom and in the mall, and in how we keep in touch with our non-present friends and members of our communities. This is perhaps best illustrated in the ways that colleagues use humour to facilitate cooperation and shared ways of doing things in the workplace (Chapter 6) and how microbloggers both express meanings and create a community through the particular features of tweets (Chapter 12). It is, however, also apparent in the care that bloggers take to construct an argument which can effectively interact with an audience and convey the complexity, interest and novelty of the views they are expressing (Chapter 10) and in the at lectures, seminars and undergraduate textbooks students encounter and engage with new knowledge and was of acquiring it in Higher Education (Chapter 8).

The third thread running through this selection is that language users have repertoires of language through which they engage with others in different situations. These repertoires both constrain and facilitate communication so making meaning possible, but they are unevenly distributed in a society so that they signal both membership and exclusion: they mark insider status and identify outsiders.

Several chapters (e.g. 3, 6 and 8) explore genres which relate to the acquisition of prestige discourses –those of education, but others illustrate how we draw on particular discourses to engage with others or cope in the situations in which we find ourselves. Most of us are able to gossip and make small talk while going about our daily business (Chapter 6), for example, and have relatively little difficulty in adjusting to other kinds of narrative when it is presented as televised news (Chapter 9). Engaging in more specialized discourses such as contributing to a blog (Chapter 10), manipulating spelling conventions to text friends (Chapter 11), tweeting to an unknown audience of followers (Chapter 12), or being happy to be constructed by holiday leaflets as a potential Club 18–30 member (Chapter 1), however, involve drawing on discoursal repertoires which display in-group competencies which mark us out as certain kinds of people. Just as linguistic and semiotic repertoires are conditioned by differential access, facilitating or denying access to particular groups, they also facilitate and deny access to particular identities – of enacting certain statuses and presentations of particular selves.

The analysis of electronic discourses is important here for as new genres have emerged and flourished analysts have been able to see past the technology and gee whiz of these applications to what bloggers and Facebook friends actually do. These electronic genres are interesting to analysts for another reason. The innovations that we find in such rapidly evolving discourses as blogs, sms messaging and social networking sites can help us to focus more clearly on aspects of language we often take for granted in more stable genres.

Here, then, is a new kind of book; a collection of chapters lifted from their original contexts to illustrate something of the range of topics and variety of methods to be found in the field of discourse analysis. More than this, however, in these pages we find how key principles and understandings are made concrete in actual analyses of texts and corpora: the ways speakers and writers use a variety of patterns and resources to shape their texts, engage with others, display membership and solidarity and construct themselves as particular kinds of people.

PART ONE

Discourse research methods

2

Corpora and discourse analysis

Paul Baker

Introduction

Frequency is one of the most central concepts underpinning the analysis of corpora. However, its importance to this field of research has resulted in one of the most oft-heard misconceptions of corpus linguistics – that it is 'only' a quantitative methodology, leading to a list of objections: frequencies can be reductive and generalizing, they can oversimplify and their focus on comparing differences can obscure more interesting interpretations of data. It is the intention of this chapter to introduce the reader to the uses (and potential dangers) of frequency lists – as one of the most basic tools of the corpus linguist, they are a good starting point for the analysis of any type of corpus. Used sensitively, they can illuminate a variety of interesting phenomena. This chapter examines how frequency lists can be employed to direct the researcher to investigate various parts of a corpus, how measures of dispersion can reveal trends across texts and how, with the right corpus, frequency data can help to give the user a sociological profile of a given word or phrase enabling greater understanding of its use in particular contexts. None of these processes are without problems, however, so the potential shortcomings of frequency data, and possible ways to overcome them, are also discussed here. This chapter also provides a good grounding for the later methodological chapters – without discussing frequency it is more difficult to understand the concepts of collocation and key words

Why is frequency of interest to discourse analysis? It is important because language is not a random affair. Words tend to occur in relationship to other words, with a remarkable degree of predictability. Languages are rule-based – they consist of thousands of patterns governing what can and can not be said or written at any given point. However, despite these rules, people usually have some sort of choice about the sort of language that they can use. This argument is summed up by Stubbs (1996: 107), who writes 'No terms are neutral. Choice of words expresses an ideological position.'

It is the tension between these two states – language as a set of rules vs. language as free choice – that makes the concept of frequency so important. If people speak or write in an unexpected way, or make one linguistic choice over another, more obvious one, then that reveals something about their intentions, whether conscious or not.

For example, as Zwicky (1997: 22) points out, one contested choice is between the use of *gay* as opposed to *homosexual*. Other choices could include the use of euphemisms (*that way inclined, confirmed bachelor,* etc.), derogatory terms (*faggot, sissy*) or reclaimings of such terms (*queer, dyke*). Danet (1980) describes a case where a doctor who carried out a late abortion was tried for manslaughter. The language used in the courtroom was an explicit concern of the trial, with lawyers negotiating the different connotations of terms such as *products of conception, fetus, male human being, male child* and *baby boy*. The choice of such terms assume different frames of reference, e.g. *baby boy* suggests helplessness, whereas *fetus* expresses a medical position. However, choice need not be lexical. Another type of choice relates to grammatical uses of words: the use of *gay* as a noun or *gay* as an adjective. Most people would (hopefully) argue that 'he is gay' is somewhat less negatively biased than 'he is a gay'. Here the adjectival usage suggests a person is described as possessing one trait among many possible attributes, whereas the noun usage implies that a person is merely the sum total of their sexuality and no more. More specifically, we could consider *gay* as an attributive adjective (occurring before a noun), e.g. 'the gay man' or *gay* as a predicative adjective (occurring after a link verb), e.g. 'he is gay'.

In describing the analysis of texts using critical discourse analysis, Fairclough (1989: 110–11) lists ten sets of questions relating to formal linguistic features, each one indicating that a choice has been made by the author – e.g. pronoun use, modality, metaphors, agency, passivization, nominalization, etc. While Fairclough frames his questions in terms of appearing within 'a specific text', there is no reason why such an analysis of linguistic choices cannot be carried out on a corpus in order to uncover evidence for preference which occurs across a genre or language variety. However, as Sherrard (1991) argues, such a view of choice presupposes that language users feel that they actually *have* a choice or are aware that one exists. She points out that speakers will always be restricted in their ways of using language – for example, people in the 1950s would not have used a term like *Ms* because such a choice was not available to them. It is therefore important that as researchers we are aware of the range of possible choices open to language users and interpret their decisions accordingly.

Related to the concept of frequency is that of dispersion. As well as knowing that something is (or isn't) frequent in a text or corpus, being able to determine *where* it occurs can also be extremely important. Again, language is not random; texts have beginnings, middles and ends. Narrative structures are usually imposed on them.[1] It may be relevant to know that a particular word form is more frequent at the start of a text than at the end. It may be useful to ascertain whether its occurrences are all clumped together in one small section of the corpus, or whether the word is a constant feature, cropping up every now and again with regularity. Dispersion analyses are one way that we can take into account the fact that texts are discrete entities within themselves, and they also allow us to begin to consider the relevance of context.

Join the club

In order to demonstrate some possible uses of frequency and dispersion I am going to describe how they can be employed on a small corpus of data which consists of 12 leaflets advertising holidays. These leaflets were produced by the British tour operator Club 18–30, which was established in the 1960s and describes itself in its website as being 'all about having a positive attitude. It's about the clothes that you wear, the music you listen to and the places you go but more importantly it's about you.'[2]

The holiday leaflets were all published in 2005 and my goal in collecting them was to investigate discourses of tourism within them. As well as considering the leaflets as a single corpus, I was also interested in whether there was any variation between them – so were there different discourses to be found or was this a relatively homogenous corpus with a great deal of lexical and discursive repetition?

Morgan and Pritchard (2001: 165) report how in 1995 (ten years prior to my study) Club 18–30 used a campaign of

> sun fun and sex . . . Posters were launched carrying slogans such as "Discover your erogenous zone", "Summer of 69" and "Girls, can we interest you in a package holiday?" with a picture of a man, described by *The Times* as wearing "a well-padded pair of boxer shorts". In addition to this high profile poster campaign (which was later extended to cinemas), the company continued the sexual theme in the pages of their brochures.

However, Club 18–30 holidays have more recently been criticized in the media. For example, in August 2005, in the UK, Channel 5 broadcast a television programme called 'The Curse of Club 18–30' which featured interviews by people who had not enjoyed their holiday, including a man who had been temporarily blinded at a foam party and a girl who had had her head shaved by a gang of drunken men. The Telegraph reported a story in 2003 about a Club 18–30 resort in Faliraki that had been reviewed by holiday goers as being a place to avoid if you are over 30, teetotal or not promiscuous.

Perhaps as a response to these and other criticisms, at the Club 18–30 website is a section on 'myths' about the holiday operator.[3] One such myth reads: 'All Club 18–30 holidays are about being forced to drink too much and having sex. I've heard that the reps shove drink down your throat and make sexual innuendos all the time!' The Club 18–30 response is: 'We are not moral guardians – what you do on your holiday is 100 per cent down to you. If you want to drink on holiday, you drink, if you don't, you don't – simple as that! Young people drinking abroad is not exclusive to Club 18–30.' It would therefore be interesting to see the extent to which Club 18–30 holiday brochures currently refute or support the 'myths' of alcohol consumption and promiscuity.

Holiday brochures are an interesting text type to analyse because they are an inherently persuasive form of discourse. Their main aim is to ensure that potential customers will be sufficiently impressed to book a holiday: 'The drive to create impactful *and* effective advertising still remains a major advertising challenge, despite the development of sophisticated advertising tracking and evaluation techniques' (Morgan and Pritchard 2001: 17).

However, as with most advertising texts, writers must take care to engage with what can be a diverse audience in an appropriate way. For example, by deciding what aspects of the holiday are foregrounded (or backgrounded) and what assumptions are made about the interests and lifestyles of the target audience. Language, therefore is one of the most salient aspects of persuasive discourses. The message must be sufficiently attractive for the potential audience to want to engage in something that will essentially result in a financial exchange.

With that in mind, Table 2.1 shows the filenames and word counts of the 12 leaflets used in the holiday corpus. It should be noted from the filenames of the leaflets (which are derived from their titles), that the leaflets mainly advertise holidays on Spanish and Greek islands.

While the analysis of this corpus focuses on the language used in the leaflets, it should be noted that there is a visual aspect to the holiday leaflets which also plays an important role in how the leaflets are understood and the discourses contained in them. As Hunston (2002: 23) points out, a corpus

TABLE 2.1 Holiday leaflets

Filename	Words
cancun.txt	756
corfu.txt	1258
crete.txt	1995
cyprus.txt	1146
gran.txt	1089
ibiza.txt	2273
intro.txt	3639
kos.txt	1126
mallorca.txt	1764
rhodes.txt	1206
tenerife.txt	918
zante.txt	695

cannot show that a text does not consist of words alone but is encountered by audiences within its visual and social context (see Kress 1994; Kress and van Leeuwen 1996). As well as drawings, diagrams and photographs the text itself is not 'plain'. The font, colour, size and positions of text also play a role in how tourist discourses are likely to be interpreted. Therefore, although this chapter focuses on the analysis of the electronically encoded text in the corpus of leaflets, visuals are also an important part of these leaflets and ought to be examined in conjunction with the corpus-based findings (something I return to at the end of this chapter).

Frequency counts

Using the corpus analysis software WordSmith, a word list of the 12 text files was obtained. A word list is simply a list of all of the words in a corpus along with their frequencies and the percentage contribution that each word makes towards the corpus. Considering frequencies in terms of standardized percentages is often a more sensible way of making sense of data, particularly when comparisons between two or more data sets of different sizes are made. Figure 2.1 shows how the word list is represented by WordSmith. The output consists of three windows (F), (A) and (S), only the top window (F) is shown in Figure 2.1. The (F) window shows frequencies in terms of the highest first, whereas the (A) window re-orders the word list alphabetically. The (S) window gives statistical information about the corpus, including the total number of words (tokens), in this case 17,865 (this is only a very small corpus), the number of *original* words (types) and the type/token ratio, which is simply the number of types divided by the number of tokens expressed as a percentage. For example, the word *you* occurs 348 times in the corpus, although it only consists of one *type* of word. We could also refer to the type/token ratio as 'the average number of tokens per type'. A corpus or file with a low type/token ratio will contain a great deal of repetition – the same words occurring again and again, whereas a high type/token ratio suggests that a more diverse form of language is being employed. Type/token ratios tend to be useful when looking at relatively small text files (say under 5,000 words). However, as the size of a corpus grows, the type/token ratio will almost always shrink, because high frequency grammatical words like *the*

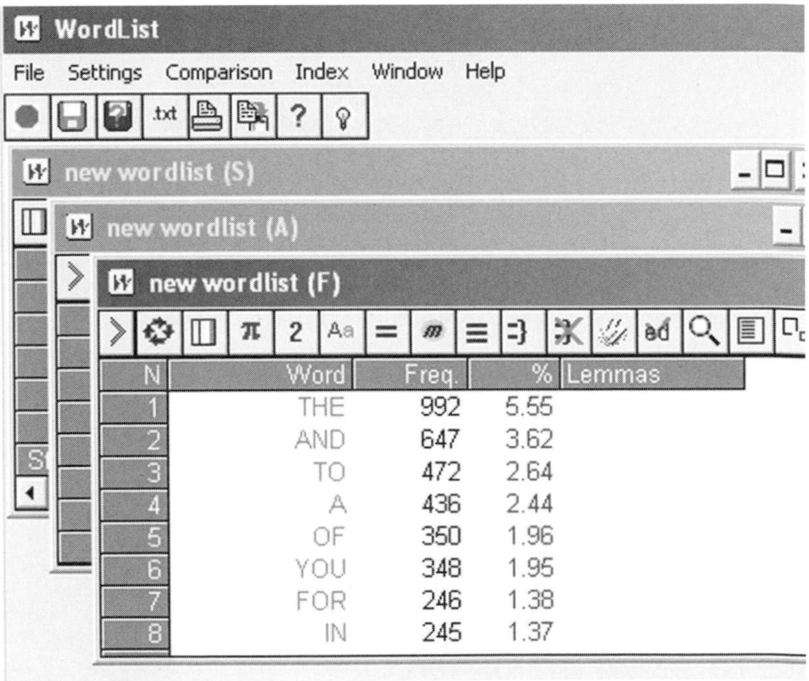

FIGURE 2.1 *Word list output of WordSmith*

and *to* tend to be repeated no matter what the size of the corpus is. Because of this, large corpora almost always have very low type/token ratios and comparisons between them become difficult. Therefore WordSmith also calculates a standardized type/token ratio which is based on taking the type/token ratio of the first 2,000 words in the corpus, then the type/token ratio of the next 2,000 words and the next 2,000 words after that, and so on, and then working out the mean of all of these individual type/token ratios. This standardized type/token ratio is almost invariably higher as a result and a better measure of comparison between corpora. For example, the type/token ratio of our corpus is 12.16, whereas the standardized type/token ratio is 40.03.

Why is the type/token ratio useful? It can give an indication of the linguistic complexity or specificity of a file or corpus. A low type/token ratio is likely to indicate that a relatively narrow range of subjects are being discussed, which can sometimes (but not always) suggest that the language being used is relatively simplistic. For example, the standardized type/token ratio in the FLOB corpus of British English (which contains a range of written texts from different genres) is 45.53, where the same figure in a sample of transcribed informal spoken conversations from the British National Corpus is 32.96, reflecting the fact that written language tends to contain a higher proportion of unique words, whereas informal spoken language is more lexically repetitive. Comparing this to the standarized type/token ratio of the holiday leaflets (40.03), we find that it falls somewhere in between spoken and written language, a fact we may want to keep in mind for later. Clearly, however, the type/token ratio merely gives only the briefest indication of lexical complexity or specificity and further investigations are necessary.

Looking at Figure 2.1 again, there are two columns of numbers. The 'Freq.' column gives raw frequencies, whereas the per cent column gives the overall proportion that a particular word contributes towards the whole corpus. So the word *you* occurs 348 times and occurrences of this word contribute to 1.95 per cent of the corpus overall. When comparing multiple corpora of different sizes it is useful to refer to the per cent column as this presents a standardized value. However, for the purposes of this chapter, where we are only using one corpus, we will simply use raw frequencies.

From Figure 2.1 it becomes apparent that the most frequent words in the corpus are grammatical words (also known as function words). Such words belong to a closed grammatical class each consisting of a small number of high frequency words (pronouns, determiners, conjunctions, prepositions), these categories tend not to be subject to linguistic innovation – we don't normally invent new conjunctions or pronouns as a matter of course.

With few exceptions, almost all forms of language have a high proportion of grammatical words. However, in order to determine whether any of these words occur more often than we would expect, it can be useful to compare our holiday corpus to a corpus of general language like the British National Corpus. Table 2.2 shows the top ten words in the holiday corpus and their equivalent proportions in the whole BNC and its written and spoken components.

TABLE 2.2 Percentage frequencies of the ten most frequently occurring words in the holiday corpus and their equivalencies in the BNC

	Word	% Frequency in holiday leaflets	% Frequency in BNC	% Frequency in BNC (written texts only)	% Frequency in BNC (spoken texts only)
1	the	5.55	6.20	6.46	3.97
2	and	3.62	2.68	2.70	2.53
3	To	2.64	2.66	2.70	2.26
4	A	2.44	2.21	2.24	1.99
5	Of	1.96	3.12	3.29	1.69
6	you	1.95	0.68	0.45	2.59
7	for	1.38	0.90	0.93	0.64
8	In	1.37	1.97	2.05	1.37
9	On	1.15	0.74	0.74	0.78
10	all	1.04	0.28	0.26	0.42

Comparing the frequencies in the holiday corpus with their equivalencies in the BNC reveals some interesting findings. Some words in the holiday corpus have similar rates of occurrence in the spoken section of the BNC (*to, of, in*), other words have higher rates compared to the BNC, including those which generally occur more in the written section (*and, for*) or the spoken section (*on, all*). The use of *you* in the holiday corpus is closer to the figure for the spoken section of the BNC than it is for the written. This suggests that although the texts consist of written documents, there are at least some aspects of the language within them that are similar to spoken language. The high use of *you* (the only pronoun to appear in the top ten) also suggests a personal style of writing, where the writer is directly addressing the reader.

Comparing frequencies of function words can be useful in terms of discerning the register of a text. For example, Biber, Conrad and Reppen (1998) show how frequencies of different function words (among other things) can be used to categorize texts across a range of five stylistic dimensions (for example dimension 1 is 'involved vs. information production'). However, perhaps we can get a better idea of *discourses* within the corpus if we put the grammatical words to one side for the moment, and only consider the most frequent lexical words and terms (e.g. the nouns, verbs, adjectives and lexical adverbs). Table 2.3 shows what the top ten looks like if we do this.

This table gives us a much better idea of what the corpus is *about*. There are words describing holiday residences (*studios, facilities, apartments*) and other attractions (*beach, pool, club, bar*). One aspect of the table worth noting is that *bar* and *bars* both appear in the top ten list. Added together, their total frequency is 173, meaning that the noun lemma BAR would potentially be the most common lexical term in the corpus. A lemma is the canonical form of a word. Francis and Kučera (1982: 1) define it as a 'set of lexical forms having the same stem and belonging to the same major word class, differing only in inflection and/or spelling'. Lemmatized forms are sometimes written as small capitals, e.g. the verb lemma WALK consists of the lexemes *walk, walked, walking* and *walks*.

TABLE 2.3 The most frequent ten lexical words in the holiday corpus

	Word	Frequency
1	beach	124
2	pool	122
3	studios	116
4	sleep	107
5	club	99
6	facilities	96
7	bar	94
8	private	87
9	bars	79
10	apartments	78

Considering that the lemma BAR is so frequent, it is possible that other lemmas may have important roles to play in the corpus. Therefore, Table 2.4 shows the top ten recalculated to take into account the most frequent lexical lemmas.

The ordering of the lexical lemmas list is rather different to the simple frequency list. Now the two most frequent items are BAR and CLUB which give us an idea about the focus of the holiday brochure. The other words in Table 2.4 are similar to those in Table 2.3, although we now also find DAY and NIGHT appearing as frequent lexical lemmas. Obviously, at this stage, while we can make educated guesses as to why and in what contexts these terms appear (for example, we would expect BAR to usually, if not always, refer to contexts of consuming alcohol, rather than say, an iron bar), it is always useful to verify these guesses, using other techniques. In this chapter I'm going to focus on frequent clusters (see below).

So now that we have a list of frequent terms, what can we do with them, and how can this information be used to tell us anything about discourses within the corpus? Let us examine the most frequent term, BAR, in more detail.

TABLE 2.4 The most frequent lexical lemmas in the holiday corpus

Rank	Lemma	Frequency
1	BAR	173
2	CLUB	144
3	BEACH	136
4	POOL	128
5	STUDIO	116
6	FACILITY	96
7	APARTMENT	80
8=	BALCONY	78
8=	DAY	78
10	NIGHT	70

Considering clusters

How are bars described in the corpus? In order to do this we need to consider frequencies beyond single words. Using WordSmith it is possible to derive frequency lists for *clusters* of words. For example, by specifying the cluster size as 3, the word list in Figure 2.2 is found.

Using this word list, it is possible to search for clusters which contain the term *bar* or *bars* in order to uncover the ways that they are used. An examination of three word clusters reveals some of the most common patterns: *bars and clubs* (21 occurrences), *loads of bars* (6), *the best bars* (6), *bar serving snacks* (6), *pool and bar* (4). There are a number of other clusters which emphasize the amount of bars: *heaps of bars*, *plenty of bars*, *never-ending stream of bars*, *tons of bars*, *variety of bars*. How else are bars described? Some two-word clusters include *well-stocked bar* (4), *vibrant bars* (2), *lively bars* (3), *24-hour bar* (3), *excellent bars* (4) and *great bars* (3).

What about the second most popular lexical lemma, CLUB? The most common two word cluster is *Club 18–30* (53 occurrences or about 37 per cent of cases of the word *club*). Other frequent clusters include *bars and clubs* (21), *club tickets* (10), *club nights* (3) and *club scene* (3). Two word clusters that involve evaluation include: *great club* (3), *best clubs* (2), *lively club* (1), *hottest club* (1) and *greatest clubs* (1).

At this stage, we can say with certainty that places where alcohol can be consumed are the most frequent concept in the Club 18–30 brochures (taking

N	Word	Freq.	%	Lemmas
1	ALL HAVE PRIVATE	135	0.76	
2	HAVE PRIVATE FACILITIES	62	0.35	
3	PRIVATE FACILITIES AND	34	0.19	
4	MINUTES FROM THE	27	0.15	
5	COM OR TEXT	26	0.15	
6	AND APARTMENTS SLEEP	24	0.13	
7	MINUTE STROLL FROM	22	0.12	
8	BARS AND CLUBS	21	0.12	
9	AND ALL HAVE	20	0.11	
10	METRES FROM THE	20	0.11	

FIGURE 2.2 *Wordlist of three word clusters*

priority to other places such as the beach or the apartment where people will be staying). We also know that bars are repeatedly evaluated positively (great, excellent, vibrant, lively) as well as being plentiful (heaps, plenty, never-ending, tons). The frequency of such terms coupled with the use of evaluations suggests a process of normalization: readers of the brochures will be encouraged to believe that bars are an important part of their holiday.

However, we need to be careful about jumping to conclusions too early in our analysis. While BAR and CLUB are the most frequent lexical lemmas in the holiday corpus, they are also the *only* lemmas in the top ten that relate to alcohol. We would perhaps expect other alcohol-related words to be reasonably frequent. And sometimes what is not present in a frequency list can be as revealing as what is frequent. With this in mind, I scanned the remainder of the frequency list to see where (if at all) other alcohol-related words appeared: *cocktail* (3 occurrences), *cocktails* (3), *daiquiri* (1), *margaritas* (1), *hungover* (1). The single use of *hungover* was interesting, and I examined its occurrence in the corpus: 'If you're too lazy (or hungover!) to cross the road to the beach you can chill out and lounge on a sunbed round the pool area.' However, despite this statement, which carries an assumption on the behalf of the reader (that they might be hungover), the list of other alcohol-related terms is very small, while words like *beer*, *lager*, *wine* and *alcohol* do not appear at all. Perhaps then, it is the case that encouragement to consume alcohol is a Club 18–30 myth and the high frequency of BAR is due to other reasons, concerned with say, the social function of bars.

So while the findings so far are somewhat suggestive, we can not say at this stage that the brochures actively advocate consumption of alcohol (or if they do, to what degree). In order to begin to answer this question, we need to consider another class of words: verbs. Verbs play a particularly interesting role in tourist discourses as they can often be instructional, giving advice on the sort of activities and behaviours that tourists should and should not engage in while on holiday. Omoniyi (1998: 6) refers to imperative verb phrases as invitational imperatives, the reader is invited to partake of an activity, but under no obligation to do so. However, invitational imperatives are another way that norms are imposed in tourist discourses.

What verbs, then, are the most frequently occurring in the holiday corpus? Here it is helpful to have carried out a prior part-of-speech annotation of the corpus, so that it is possible to distinguish words which can belong to multiple grammatical categories (e.g. *hits* can be a noun or a verb). Table 2.5 shows the most frequent lexical verb forms in the corpus.

Here, overwhelmingly, it looks as if the most frequent verb is concerned with sleeping, a curious and unexpected finding. However, an examination of clusters reveals that all cases of *sleep* involve the phrase *studios/rooms sleep 2–3/3–4* which are used to detail how many people can book an apartment or room.

TABLE 2.5 The most frequent lexical verbs in the holiday corpus

Rank	Verb	Frequency
1	sleep	107
2	book	34
3	want	30
4	cost	29
5	work	26
6	miss	24
7	make	23
8	chill	29
9	find	18
10	relax	17

Similarly, the verbs *book* and *cost* are also concerned with aspects of booking a holiday or flight, rather than activities to do on the holiday. The remaining seven verbs in Table 2.5 are more interesting to examine. Frequent imperative verb clusters include *don't miss out* (16), *chill out* (15) and *make sure* (12). A closer examination of *chill* and *relax* may be useful here. There are seven references in the corpus to 'chilling out during the day'. The following sentences taken from the corpus illustrate the main pattern of 'chilling' as an invitational imperative:

'The hotel pool is a great place to chill-out during the day before starting your night with a drink in Bar Vistanova.'

'The swimming pool is a great place to chill-out during the hot sunny days and the hotel bar is the ideal choice for your first drink before heading into the vibrant bars of Rhodes Town.'

'The Partit Apartments are right on the doorstep of Club base Casita Blanca where you can have a swim in the pool, chill out with a cold drink and grab some snacks at the bar or just lounge around in the sun and re-charge your batteries!'

'The 24 hour bar, Petrino's, is usually rammed at 5am as everyone gets together to chill out after a heavy night partying!'

The verb *relax* also follows a similar pattern:

> 'The Green Ocean has all the qualities of a great Club 18–30 property, with the added bonus of being the ideal place to relax and catch up on some well-earned snoozing!'
>
> 'The pool area is the perfect place to hang out whether you want to be active or simply relax and recover.'
>
> 'There is also a fantastic Vital Wellness Centre where you can relax and recharge in the spa or sauna before heading into the vibrant nightlife of Playa Del Ingles.'

Chilling/relaxing is therefore suggested as a precursor before 'starting the night' or after a 'heavy night partying'. It is also used to catch up on sleep, recover or recharge batteries. Therefore, the frequent use of the verbs *chill* and *relax* are attached to the presupposition that such activities will be required, due to the fact that holidaymakers are expected to be out all night partying. Despite the fact that we do not find frequent imperative phrases to the reader to party or get drunk, the relatively high number of 'recovery' imperatives suggests a more subtle way that alcohol consumption is normalized to the reader.

Dispersion plots

One word in Table 2.5 is somewhat unexpected: the verb *work* which occurs 26 times in the corpus. We would perhaps not expect work to feature too often in a corpus about holidays. So it is interesting to explore this word further.

Interestingly, not all of the citations of work actually refer to paid work. The phrase *work on your tan* occurs three times, for example, while *work out cheaper* occurs twice (referring to different holiday packages). However, the phrase *work 2 live* occurs 14 times in the corpus. So far we have considered the term *work* simply in terms of the clusters which it tends to be most (and least) often embedded in. However, another way of looking at the word is to think about where it occurs within individual texts and within the corpus as a whole. Does it generally occur at the beginning of each pamphlet, towards the end or is it evenly spread out throughout each pamphlet? Also, does it occur more often in certain pamphlets than others?

In order to answer these questions it is useful to carry out a dispersion plot of the phrase *work 2 live* across the whole corpus. A dispersion plot gives a visual representation of where a search term occurs (see Figure 2.3).

N	File	Words	Hits	per 1,000	Plot
1	corfu.txt	1,242	2	1.61	
2	zante.txt	689	1	1.45	
3	mallorca.txt	1,750	2	1.14	
4	tenerife.txt	910	1	1.10	
5	kos.txt	1,117	1	0.90	
6	cyprus.txt	1,126	1	0.89	
7	rhodes.txt	1,185	1	0.84	
8	intro.txt	3,574	3	0.84	
9	crete.txt	1,962	1	0.51	
10	ibiza.txt	2,265	1	0.44	

WORKxLIVE: 14 entries (sort: File,File)
dispersion plot (F)

FIGURE 2.3 *Dispersion plot of the phrase work 2 live in the holiday corpus*

The dispersion plot shows ten of the files in the corpus, each represented by a single row. Two of the files, cancun.txt and gran.txt did not contain any references to *work 2 live*, so do not appear on the dispersion plot. As well as giving the file name, we are also told the total number of words in each file, the number of 'hits' (occurrences of the phrase *work 2 live*) and the number of occurrences per 1,000 words in the corpus. Then we are given a visual representation of where each occurrence of the phrase *work 2 live* occurs in the corpus. Each vertical black line represents one occurrence. The plot has also been standardized, so that each file in the corpus appears to be of the same length. This is useful, in that it allows us to compare where occurrences of the search term appears, across multiple files.

Looking at the plot, we can see then that for nine of the files, the term *work 2 live* occurs very close to the beginning of each individual text. Why is this the case? An investigation of the texts themselves is required. By taking a closer look at the beginnings of the pamphlets it becomes apparent that the majority of them begin with a short description of a (possibly fictional) holidaymaker:

Clare, Bank Clerk: just worked the last 3 Saturdays – this Saturday she's having a laugh on the beach . . . don't miss out, work 2 live

Thea, Waitress: fed-up with serving food and drink to everyone else. Up for being the customer herself . . . don't miss out, work 2 live

Matt, Chef: the pressure of 80 covers a night has done his swede in, now he's letting off steam . . . don't miss out, work 2 live

Therefore, the beginning of each brochure follows the same pattern:

> [Name of person] [Occupation] [Description of undesirable working conditions] [Description of preferable holiday] don't miss out, work 2 live.

The importance of this pattern, occurring as it does at the beginning of most of the brochures, and having the same structure, illustrates the over-arching ideology of Club 18–30, as a holiday destination that offers escapism from the mundanity and grind of everyday working life. The pattern ends with two imperatives: *don't miss out* and *work 2 live*. The phrase *work 2 live* therefore implies that working is somehow not living, but a means to living – and that a Club 18–30 holiday constitutes living.

So that gives us an idea about discourses of tourism in the Club 18–30 holiday leaflets. However, a further aspect of discourses is that they help to construct the identity of both the producer and consumer of a text. For example, the descriptions of characters employed in unfulfilling jobs, escaping to a holiday, sets up a process of identification for the reader, constructing expectations about why readers may want to go on holiday and what activities they will engage in on arrival. Identity construction and identitification are important processes in advertising discourses. Readers may be encouraged to identify with aspirational ideals or with identity constructions who are more realistic, e.g. less aspirational but similar to themselves. In what other ways can reader identity be constructed? Blommaert (2005: 15) suggests:

> Language users have repertoires containing different sets of varieties . . . People, consequently are not entirely free when they communicate, they are restrained by the range and structure of their repertoires, and the distribution of elements of the repertoires in any society is unequal. . . What people actually produce as discourse will be conditioned by their sociolinguistic background.

Therefore, we could argue that lexical choices here are related in some way to identity.

On reading this chapter, you may have noticed a number of informal terms and phrases which have appeared in the holiday corpus: *heaps of bars* or *chill out* for example. At this stage we may want to inquire why such terms are so popular in the corpus, and what contribution they make towards identity construction.

In order to determine how and why this is the case, it is useful to carry out an exploration of these informal lexis, both in the holiday corpus and in a general corpus of spoken English in more detail.

Comparing demographic frequencies

By examining the frequency list again, the most frequent informal terms in the corpus were collected and are presented in Table 2.6.

Clearly, in compiling this table it was necessary to explore the contexts of some of these words in detail, in order to remove occurrences that were not used in a colloquial or informal way. In addition, the categorization of a word as being 'informal' is somewhat subjective. For example, the most frequent informal word *action* occurred in phrases like 'There's always plenty of action here during the day' rather than in phrases like 'The government took action to establish her whereabouts.' So in the holiday corpus, *action* refers to general excitement, activity and fun.

The table also shows the frequencies per million words of the terms in the written and spoken sections of the British National Corpus. Perhaps surprisingly, most of the terms occurred proportionally more often in written, rather than spoken British English (the exceptions being *loads* and *mates*). However, this is due to the fact that most of the colloquial terms in the list are derived from non-colloquial words, so would be expected to occur more often in formal, written English. For example, *tons of steel* (formal) vs. *tons*

TABLE 2.6 The most frequent informal terms in the holiday corpus

Rank	Verb	Frequency in holiday corpus	Frequency in written BNC	Frequency in spoken BNC
1	action	30	239.78	87.9
2	chill	29	8.73	2.22
3	loads	25	9.15	64.21
4	mates	15	7.42	9.67
5	cool	12	41.69	17.7
6	chilled	11	3.9	0.58
7	massive	11	45.48	32.49
8	fab	10	1.29	0.58
9	info	10	2.26	0.97
10	tons	10	12.33	7.06

of fun (informal). The spoken texts tend to contain many of the more informal meanings of the words in Table 2.6. And when the words occurred as informal in the written texts in the BNC, a high proportion of these cases referred to reported speech in novels. So why do we find a reasonably high proportion of informal lexis in the holiday corpus? One line of enquiry I want to explore is to consider which sorts of people are more likely to use informal language in their speech, by referring to a reference corpus.

Using the spoken section of the BNC, I explored the demographic frequencies of the words *loads*, *mates*, *cool*, *massive*, *fab*, *info* and *tons*. I did not look at *chill*, *chilled* and *action* as these words did not occur very often in their colloquial form in the BNC, even in spoken British English. Therefore the data would need a great deal of combing through and editing before any conclusions could be made. Table 2.7 shows the combined frequencies per million words for these three words in terms of sex, age and social class.[4]

From this table it can be seen that in terms of age, the 15–24 group use these terms most often, males use these terms slightly more than females,

TABLE 2.7 Combined frequencies per million words of loads, mates, cool, massive, fab, info and tons in the BNC for age, sex and social class

Demographic	Group	Frequency per million
Age	0–14	538.85
	15–24	615.88
	25–34	304.19
	35–44	371.6
	45–59	235.02
	60+	225.32
Sex	Male	376.75
	Female	334.65
Social Class	AB	268.63
	C1	369.39
	C2	311.74
	DE	347.8

and social class C1 use the terms more than other social class grouping. The strongest influence on usage seems to be age, whereas the weakest appears to be gender. However, it is important at this stage not to conclude that the most typical speaker of these sorts of words is a composite of these three demographics, e.g. a male aged 15–24 from social class C1. Different demographic factors can cause interaction effects – for example, hypothetically the high proportion of C1 speakers in the table could be due to the fact the these words are very commonly used by C1 females rather than C1 males, whereas the combined occurrences of these words from social groupings AB, C2 and DE could all consist of males only. It is therefore useful to cross tabulate the demographics in order to get a clearer picture of how they interact together (see Table 2.8).

Table 2.8 gives a much more sophisticated and complex picture of the frequencies of these informal words in society. While males aged 15–24 from social class C1 use these words quite often (263.44 occurrences per million words) they are by no means the most frequent users. This distinction goes to males aged 15–24 from social class AB (702.76 occurrences per million words). Other high users are males aged 0–14 from social class C1 and females aged 15–24 from social class C2.

TABLE 2.8 Combined frequencies per million words of loads, mates, cool, massive, fab, info and tons in the BNC, cross-tabulated for sex, age and social class

	Males				Females			
	AB	C1	C2	DE	AB	C1	C2	DE
0–14	187.72	559.69	367.95	417.01	216	56.64	319.71	0
15–24	702.76	263.44	313.17	680.59	422.42	417.81	587.9	406.91
25–34	0	214.4	171.8	178.52	218.48	155.38	201.11	365.21
35–44	125.37	106.52	177.61	0	128.21	119.68	122.73	125.39
45–49	182.07	127.22	45.77	63.75	77.77	138.92	130.3	118.9
60+	43.07	0	54.05	107.24	140.02	60.47	74.4	210.73

How can we then link these findings to the presence of these sorts of terms in the holiday corpus? There are a number of possible answers. First, perhaps the texts were written by males aged between 15–24. This is possible, but unlikely.

More likely then, is that the leaflets were written with certain social groups in mind, emulating the typical language that those groups would use themselves and therefore be familiar with. Unsurprisingly, Club 18–30 specifically target their age demographic in their own name, so it makes sense for them to aim the language in their brochures at a young age group – this is confirmed by the high use of colloquial terms found in the 15–24 group in the BNC and in the holiday corpus. Although AB speakers, on the whole, tend to use fewer colloquial words than other groups, the exception to this are AB males aged 15–24, who, interestingly, use more colloquial terms than anyone else. Perhaps this is an attempt to over-compensate, with young middle-class men desirous to appear more streetwise.

It perhaps should also be noted that some of the cells in Table 2.8 contained frequencies of zero. This shows up one of the potential limitations of this sort of analysis. We should not conclude that males from social group AB instantly stop using colloquialisms once they reach the age of 25, but rather, the refined data sets of different sorts of speakers are perhaps too small to draw accurate conclusions.

So when looking at demographic frequency data it is important to take care before drawing strong conclusions as there are many possible factors at play. When considering different types of demographic data (e.g. age *and* sex *and* social class) it should be borne in mind that individual categories may become quite small or in some cases non-existent, meaning that results may be due to the eccentricities of a small range of speakers. It may also be necessary to take into account context such as the location of the speech (at home vs. outside) or the audience (are young people more likely to use informal language around other young people? Will the presence of older people inhibit their informal language?) Additionally, it may be necessary to take into account issues such as reported speech. One example from a young woman in the BNC illustrates this: 'she said there are loads of them on the cycle path without lights on!' Should this use of *loads* count in the same way as non-reported speech?

Finally, just because words like *loads* occur with a higher frequency in certain social groups than others, that doesn't mean that all people from that social group use words like that all the time, or that people from other groups don't use those words. Instead, high or low frequencies simply tell us about the typical (even stereotypical) language of a particular group. They do not tell us *why* a particular group uses language often (or not) in that way. It may not always be necessary for us to fully explore reasons for that and some sociolinguists do not go beyond descriptions of incidences. If we do try to offer explanations (and as discourse analysts it is generally important to answer the *why* question) we should also try to avoid tautologies: 'young people say *loads* because they are young'. A better (although still somewhat circular) explanation would be 'young people say *loads* because by using informal language they are constructing/performing their identity as distinct to people who do not use this word'. However, in order for such a hypothesis to make sense, we need to assume that people somehow know (consciously or not) what sort of language is typical of different types of identities. People's intuitions about actual language can be quite poor, e.g. generally people think that more words in English start with 'k', than have 'k' as their third letter (Tversky and Kahneman 1973). However, estimating frequencies of different types of words may be different from estimating stereotypical usage between different social demographics, and people may be more attuned to do the latter.

In any case, for the authors of the holiday leaflets to use informal language in order to index youthful identities we need to assume that they believed that such language was typical of this identity and that the target audience would also 'read' the leaflets in the same way. We may have to find other examples to support our case (for example – does this type of informal language occur very frequently in magazines or television programmes aimed at young people?), and also use our judgement of the author's own linguistic competence (will a highly literate L1 speaker be a better judge of the social nuances and stereotypical demographic distributions of language than an L2 speaker?)

So I do not therefore advocate over-reliance on demographic frequency data, nor would I recommend using it to make bald statements about absolute 'differences' in language use between social groups. What is more useful, however, is by investigating how a particular word or phrase may be used in order to index a stereotypical social identity based on age, sex or class or a combination of all three, or other factors (bearing in mind that writers/ speakers and audiences may or may not all have access to the same sort of stereotypical notions of language and social identity).

What we should be able to glean from the BNC spoken data though, is that the colloquialisms which co-occur in the holiday corpus are most strongly associated with young adults and have clearly been used as a means of creating identification and making the message attractive to its target audience. By using a form of language which is strongly associated with youthful identities, the audience may feel that they are been spoken to in a narrative voice that they would find desirable (the voice of a potential friend or partner) or at least are comfortable with. Here it is perhaps useful to bring in additional non-corpus-based evidence, by looking at the visual aspects of the leaflets.

An examination of the images used in many of the leaflets seems to support this hypothesis – many of them depict young, attractive men and women having fun, either in swimming pools or the sea, or at nightclubs or bars. Several of the pictures show young people enjoying a drink together, while one of the brochures contains a full page advertisement for the vodka-based drink WKD. Another advertisement advises holidaymakers to 'pack some condoms and always choose to use one', while there is also a full page 'Model search' contest, looking for '3 gorgeous girls and 3 fit fellas to be our models of the year . . . All you have to do is send a full-length picture in swimwear'. The images of happy holidaymakers in the leaflets are perhaps somewhat idealized, everyone is happy, healthy and attractive; the women are all slender, the men muscular; there are no people who are overweight or wearing glasses. So while these images may not reflect the physical appearances of many of the potential readers of the leaflets, they do show desirable identities, suggesting to readers that these will be the types of people they will meet while on holiday, or even the types of people that they could *become* if they take the holiday.

In addition, the use of colloquialisms also contributes to normalization of certain types of youthful identities. It suggests a shared way of speaking for young people, which may not even be noticed by those who it aims to target. However, young people who do not use informal language may be alerted to a discrepancy between their linguistic identities and those of the people featured in the brochure (and the narrative voice). In a similar way, young people reading the Club 18–30 brochure will be made aware of the expectations placed on them, if they are to take a holiday with the tour operator. They may decide not to go, but if they do, they may face pressure to conform to the over-arching ideology of clubbing, chilling and more clubbing that the brochures put forward, particularly as this ideology is represented as both attractive (through the use of positive evaluation) and hegemonic (due to its repetition and high frequency in the brochures).

Conclusion

To summarize, what has the corpus analysis of the Club 18–30 leaflets revealed about discourses of tourism? The analysis of frequent lexical lemmas revealed some of the most important concepts in the corpus (*bar, club,* etc.) and a more detailed analysis of clusters and individual incidences containing these terms revealed some of the ways that holidaymakers were constructed, for example, as being interested in information about the variety and number of places to drink which are near their holiday accommodation, and likely to need periods of 'chilling' to recover from the excesses of the previous evening. The analysis of the dispersion plot for *work 2 live* revealed how this term constituted a salient part of the overall discourse in the leaflets, being used at the start of each brochure in a repetitive structure which emphasized how working is a means to living which can be achieved by being on holiday.

Interestingly, the leaflets did not explicitly advise holidaymakers to get drunk (and elsewhere in the Club 18–30 website, accusations that tourists are encouraged to drink are dismissed as a myth). However, the frequency analysis does suggest that there are more subtle messages at work. References to sex (another 'myth' according to the Club 18–30 website) also do not appear to be frequent in the leaflets, however, an analysis of the visual content suggests that the leaflets are somewhat sexualized, again with implicit messages. As Morgan and Pritchard (2001: 165) note 'The sheer dominance of these images – many of them taking up a whole page – creates the brochures' atmosphere of sexuality.' Perhaps, in reacting to criticism, Club 18–30 have changed the tone of their leaflets, but at the same time used more oblique references to ensure that certain types of tourist discourses remain intact.

Finally, by investigating how high frequency informal language occurred in a reference corpus of spoken British English, we were able to gain evidence in order to create hypotheses about how the readership of the holiday leaflets were constructed.

Frequency counts can be useful, but as we have seen, their functionality is limited. Their main use is in directing the reader towards aspects of a corpus or text which occur often and therefore may or may not show evidence of the author making a specific lexical choice over others, which could relate to the presentation of a particular discourse or attempts to construct identity in some way. Comparing the relative frequencies in a text or smaller corpus to a reference corpus is one good way of denoting whether a word occurs more or less often than expected. Examining frequent clusters of words or their dispersions across a text (or set of texts) may be more revealing than just looking at words in isolation, and as the course of this chapter developed it became clear that context plays an important role in the analysis of particular words, something which is difficult to achieve from looking at frequencies alone.

Notes

1 Exceptions could include extremely restricted forms of language which do not adhere to usual grammatical rules, such as shopping lists.

2 www.club18–30.biz/attitude.asp.

3 www.club18–30.com/ab_myths.php.

4 The social classifications in the BNC are based on occupation and are as follows
   AB: higher and intermediate managerial, administrative and professional. C1:
   Supervisory, clerical and junior management, administrative and professional.
   C2: Skilled manual. DE: Semi-skilled and unskilled manual, casual labourers,
   state pensioners and the unemployed.

3

Systemic functional linguistics and discourse analysis

Caroline Coffin

. . . if we simply approach each text with an ad hoc do-it-yourself kit of private commentary, we have no way of explaining their similarities and differences – the aesthetic and functional values that differentiate one text from another.

(HALLIDAY, 2002, p. 187)

There are several aspects of the discourse of school history that merit further exploration, especially if a central aim is to understand the particular demands of learning to read and write history. I argued there that discourse analysis can help to:

- overturn the common-sense classification of history writing as either narrative or argument and provide a richer understanding of the range of texts that operate in (school) history; and
- extend our understanding of areas of meaning central to historical thinking and writing – namely time, cause-and-effect and the judgement/ assessment of past events.

To investigate these areas requires a linguistic framework that has a focus on meaning and function rather than simply form and structure. The framework also needs to take into account the situated nature of language use and how it varies depending on its context. In this chapter, I explain how systemic functional linguistics (SFL) does this, and I show how its tools of analysis can provide some fascinating insights into key areas of historical discourse such as those identified above. First, I set out one of the most important principles underpinning SFL's theory of language (a view of language as both system and instance) and then I introduce aspects of the theory of particular relevance to this book. Throughout the chapter, I will use extracts from student writing and history textbooks in order to help those of you unfamiliar with SFL to ground the theory. I should like to emphasize, however, that some readers may want to treat this chapter as a reference resource that can be returned to at point of need. You may also wish to consult one of the books that serve as introductions to SFL theory (e.g. Bloor and Bloor, 2004; Butt *et al.*, 2000; Eggins, 2004; Humphrey and Droga, 2002; Thompson, 2004; Martin and Rose, 2003).

A systemic functional linguistic view of language: system and instance

In this section, I provide an overview of a key theoretical principle underpinning systemic functional linguistics in order to show how it informs SFL analysts' approach to analysing and interpreting discourse. Specifically, I shall show how a *system* perspective on language influences the way analysts interpret each individual text as an *instance* both of an overall language system (in this case English) and a particular discourse or 'discourse domain' (in this case school history).

A system perspective on discourse and language

While a *structural* perspective on language looks at the ordering of elements in terms of what goes together with what, a *system* perspective looks at the options available to speakers of a language, that is, patterns in what *could* go together with what. These differences are illustrated at clause level in Figure 3.1. Thus, we can look at the following sentence in terms of

	Orderings				
	This	is	her	DVD	case
	That	was	his	video	collection
Options	These	are	its	water	supplies
	Those	were	our	computer	printouts
			their	press	releases
			your	media	events

FIGURE 3.1 *Ordering and options*

the ordering of its elements noting that in English the inversion of verb and subject creates an interrogative mood or question form:

a) Should the arrival of the white Europeans in Australian be seen as invasion?
(interrogative – subject follows auxiliary verb, *should*)

Equally, however, we could examine the same clause from the perspective of why the speaker or writer chose the interrogative form rather than, say, the declarative form with appropriate intonation or punctuation (or indeed a negative or positive question tag form) to indicate a question function:

b) So, the arrival of the white Europeans in Australia should be seen as invasion?
(declarative – verb follows subject)

c) The arrival of the white Europeans in Australia should be seen as invasion, should it?
(declarative + positive question tag, *should it*)

d) The arrival of the white Europeans in Australia should be seen as invasion, shouldn't it?
(declarative + negative question tag, *shouldn't it*)

Once we start asking these types of questions as to why one structure rather than another, we can begin to see how speakers and writers make different 'choices' in grammar (albeit often unconsciously) and how these are influenced by the context in which they are using language. Thus, in the examples above, one reason for choosing one form rather than another may be related to whether the context is spoken or written. In spoken text, for example, a question that is clearly signalled through an interrogative structure may be less ambiguous than one that relies on intonation. Equally, another reason may lie in the relationship between the interactants. While sentence a) suggests an open dialogue, the use of the negative tag in sentence d) suggests the speaker already has a preferred interpretation of events in mind and expects agreement from their audience.

Although in SFL priority is given to options, and structure is not seen as the defining characteristic of language, this does not mean that it is an unimportant part of the theory. Rather, it means that structure needs to be 'interpreted as the outward form taken by systemic choices' (Halliday and Matthiessen, 2004, p. 23). Language, in other words, is primarily conceptualized as a system of choices, a 'meaning potential', and each act or instance of meaning derives its meaning from what could have been selected but was not.

There is an important point to make in relation to language as a system of options. Within a language and grammatical system as a whole (such as English) there are a set of options. However, depending on the context of a text there are differences in the choices that are typically taken up. Returning to our examples above, for instance, we saw how the specific social context of language use might play an important role in explaining these choices. The following two (longer) examples provide further illustration. Each was produced in a different context for a different purpose, and you will see that this has affected the choices that the writers have made in relation to grammar and lexis (vocabulary) as well as the overall organization or structure of each text. As you read through the pieces of writing, you will see that some of the choices are similar in both texts (e.g. the use of the past tense) but other choices are quite distinct in line with their different contexts. You may wish to consider the likely context for each text and the influence it has exerted on the writer.

TEXT 3.1 The Hero of Geduldig

The snow began to fall, the winds began to howl and the temperature began to drop.

Santina poked her head out of the window. Her face did not flinch when the snow rose to head height. This was not unusual weather on the planet of Geduldig; these snowstorms were about as common as rain is in England. Santina felt a flood of relief when she saw the temperature had dropped to −500°.

She had been worried that the weather was going to get warmer. The forecaster on Ice-vision last night had looked very worried. With a slight tremble in his voice, he had warned that the planet was getting perilously close to the sun. The protective blanket of white cloud surrounding Geduldig was in danger of being destroyed by the sun's heat.

That would be more than just a bad spell of weather; it would be the end of her planet, her home, her life. She tried to picture in her mind what it would be like if the temperature rose. The ice cold, bitterness of the planet would be destroyed. The vapour, rising mysteriously up from the crystal-white floor would no longer exist. The world would no longer be peaceful and airy, with only the colour white and the gold of the peoples' eyes.

. . .

Santina, her heart finally at rest, went over to her bed (made of ice), slid back in between the ice sheets and went back to sleep. She started sweating, and felt hot and clammy. She woke up and once again looked out of the window. She was horrified to see that the whole world was beginning to melt. Drip, drip, drip. CRASH, the cathedral spire had collapsed into a slushy mess. People everywhere were running, screaming, shouting, praying for the temperature to drop. Santina looked up and saw the ball of the sun getting ever closer, red, blazing, angry.

She ran into her closest friend Eaon. He looked at Santina, saw her golden eyes staring fearfully out of that pale face, and they both understood. They knew that they had to do something. They ran out into the square, and looked at the remains of the cathedral. They stood in horror, their silver hair blowing in the strangely warm breeze.

'We must find Iceana' said Eaon determinedly. 'Only he can save us.'

. . .

She heard a terrifying, thundering sound. She looked up and saw a massive chunk of blazing rock broken off from the sun. It was hurtling, like a shooting star, straight towards Santina. She could feel its heat, boiling her blood . . .

Santina, as if in slow motion saw Eaon forcing the massive fireball down the hill into the raging torrent. With a final cry, he hit the fireball. They vanished together in a huge explosion of steam. Steam rose up clouding the whole of Goduldig, forming new, fresh clouds, to protect her world from the cruel heat of the sun. Geduldig was saved.

TEXT 3.2 Eora Resistance to Europeans 1790–1816

The Eora people had lived in the Sydney area for at least 40,000 years before the Europeans arrived. They had lived by hunting, fishing and gathering and believed that they were the guardians of the land. This lifestyle did not last.

When the Europeans arrived in 1788 they occupied sacred land and destroyed Eora hunting and fishing grounds. In 1790 the Eora people began a guerrilla war against the Europeans.

In 1794 the Eora, whose leader was Pemulwuy, attacked the European settlement of Brickfield. Thirty six British and fourteen Eora were killed during this attack. In the same year the Eora killed a British settler. Then the British ordered that six of the tribe be killed.

The Aborigines continued to resist the European invaders by burning their crops and houses, taking food, destroying cattle and killing some settlers. In 1797 they attacked Toongabbie and within a week the farmers had to retreat and the farms were burned. In that year their leader, Pemulwuy, was captured by the British but later escaped.

By 1801 many settlers lived in fear of the Eora and the British started a campaign to destroy Aboriginal resistance. Troopers were sent to kill Aboriginal fighters and capture Pemulwuy. One year later settlers killed the leader in an ambush.

> *Other great Aboriginal leaders continued fighting against the white settlers. However, the guns of the British were more powerful than the Aboriginal spears. The British shot many of the Aboriginals and many others died of the diseases that the British brought.*
>
> *This period of black resistance in Sydney finally ended in 1816. It is a significant period in Australian history as it showed the determination of the Aboriginal people to resist the invasion. It also demonstrated how unjustly the Aboriginal people were treated by the White invaders.*

No doubt you had no difficulty in identifying that Text 3.1 was produced within the context of school English and Text 3.2 within school history. That is, even though both texts use English grammar and lexis and even though both might be described as a 'narrative' – in that they are both concerned with an unfolding of events over time – it is also apparent that there are a number of differences between the two.

Significantly, these differences lie not only in the subject matter: the texts are also organized differently in terms of their beginning, middle and end structures and these function to create quite different types of meaning. Text 3.1, which was written by Jessica, a Year 7 British girl, has a beginning stage that orients the reader to what is to follow by establishing a setting and introducing characters. Then follows a stage where the main character, Santina, is confronted with a problem – the heating up of her planet. The next stage deals with Santina's and Eaon's reactions to the problem, which is resolved in the final stage of the text. In Rothery's terms this is a story genre (Rothery, 1996). Text 3.2, on the other hand (which was written collectively by a Year 8 Australian history class), has a beginning stage that provides a background – a summary of previous historical events that are of significance to the rest of the text. This background stage is followed by a sequence of chronologically ordered, past events. The final stage draws out the historical significance of the events. In my terms, this is a historical recount genre.

Another difference between the two texts, apart from the way they are structured, is one that you may have picked up 'impressionistically': Text 3.1 is likely to have come across as more emotionally charged, whereas Text 3.2 may have seemed somewhat flat and impersonal. Looking more closely at the language, we can detect some of the features that create such an impression. First, Text 3.1 deals with *Santina* and *Eaon*, named (fictional) individuals (or specific participants) who are easier to identify with than the more remote, generalized (or 'generic') participants of Text 3.2 (*the Eora people, the Europeans, the British, settlers*). Second, there is a difference in the way in which each student writer gives meaning to the events recorded. In Text 3.1 it is the characters' thoughts, feelings and emotional reactions to the problem they must solve that give particular significance to the events and serve to create suspense by slowing down the action (the words marked in bold below). You will notice, in particular, that feelings are often intensified (e.g. *felt a flood of relief* as opposed to *felt relieved*).

> Santina felt **a flood of relief**
>
> He looked at Santina, saw her golden eyes staring **fearfully** out of that pale face, and they both understood
>
> They stood **in horror**, their silver hair blowing in the strangely warm breeze

In Text 3.2, rather than highlighting people's emotional responses to events, the writer foregrounds the ethical dimension of people's behaviour and makes judgements in terms of Aboriginal resolve and European immorality (the words marked in bold):

> it showed the **determination** of the Aboriginal people to resist the invasion
>
> it also demonstrated how **unjustly** the Aboriginal people were treated by the White invaders

The above are only some of the features that distinguish the two texts. However, it is these sorts of differences that, from an educational perspective, are useful to make explicit to students. Too often students produce a piece of writing that may be effective in its own terms but is not appropriate to the history classroom, therefore receiving low marks and a comment such as: 'This reads more like something you'd write for your English teacher. Too much imagination and not enough fact.'

Meaning potential and cultural purpose

We have seen that narratives, in which plot and suspense are vital ingredients and where fictional characters must face, emotionally respond to, and deal with a problem, may be at the heart of English, but are not what history is about.[1] Rather, history is concerned with the chronological ordering of past events and their historical (often social or political) significance. We must now ask what is the significance of these different choices? Why do different learning areas value different types of text and meaning? These are important questions for both educators and students.

In the SFL model, differences in systems of options (whether in terms of genres or grammatical and lexical choices) can partly be accounted for by the different cultural and social purposes that underlie different discourse domains. While one of the ultimate goals of the school subject of English is to develop in students a sensibility for appreciating literary works (see Christie, 1999), a key disciplinary purpose of school history is to develop students' ability to sequence and explain past events and in so doing, develop their understanding of who they are and where they come from (both as individuals and as members of a society). As a consequence, English and history select and value quite different types of text that fulfil these distinct goals. We have already seen these goals exemplified in the two pieces of writing (Texts 3.1 and 3.2). At one level, they both might be described as narrative but, at another level, the more specific purpose of 3.1 is to create a fictional story, whereas 3.2's goal is to record historically significant past events.

English tends to place importance on texts such as the type of 'story' genre exemplified in Text 3.1 in order to develop students' understanding of plot and their appreciation of character development (through the construal of feelings, thoughts and responses). Another important text type or genre that students learn to produce in English is the interpretation genre, a genre that is designed to develop students' skills in reading the message of a literary work and responding to its cultural values (see Rothery, 1994, pp. 156–70). Both the story and the interpretation genres are pivotal in achieving the disciplinary goals of the subject area of English. In contrast, the very different approach to knowledge taken by history means that texts such as that exemplified in Text 3.2, where the focus is on building a chronological record of the past in order to develop an understanding of the historical significance of events, are central to meaning making. We will also see that texts that argue why events happened in the way they did, play an important role in history and are, in fact, the texts that are given the greatest value in the later years of secondary school.

In sum, a system perspective on a discourse domain enables us to see what choices are common or 'typical' in a particular domain in relation to other domains. (This does not, however, preclude variation or even 'departure' from the way individuals take up or instantiate the meaning potential.) Such a perspective encourages the analyst to consider what it is about the cultural and social purposes operating in a domain such as school history or English that establish particular 'meaning potentials' and why these may change over time. In relation to contemporary approaches to history teaching and learning in Western-style education systems, analysts may consider why texts that frame reconstructions of the past as a matter of perspective and argument are generally more highly valued than texts that merely record past events. Is it the case, for example, that an approach that trains students to weigh up the validity of different viewpoints in relation to different forms of evidence provides useful preparation for participation in Western-style administrative, legal and democratic systems?

Having looked at discourse from the perspective of system and considered how different contexts make available different sets of meanings, I shall go on to consider why it is useful to take an instance as well as a system view of language. First I shall discuss the theoretical principle underpinning such a perspective and then I shall consider the insights that can be derived from looking at instances of language, that is, the particular texts or utterances that are produced or 'chosen' by writers and speakers, in this case, secondary school history students.

System and instance: two complementary perspectives

SFL's dual focus on the complementary perspectives of language as system and language as instance is what distinguishes it from many other approaches to language and discourse analysis, and therefore it is worthwhile elaborating the theoretical principle. To do this, an analogy of the climate and weather is useful. Following Halliday (2004, pp. 26–9), climate and weather, rather than being distinct phenomena, are two different ways of looking at the same phenomenon. While climate is based on the observation and modelling of long-term, and possibly quantitative, patterns of hours of sunshine and centimetres of rainfall, weather is an immediate and direct experience of 'rain falling' or 'the sun shining'. Language can be conceptualized in a similar manner. On the one hand, in the same way that weather is a kind of 'event', language can be seen as an event, with words unfolding in a particular context (the instance perspective). But, equally, we can stand back and look at language from a greater depth of time and observe it as a whole system of meanings or resources that are available to speakers of a particular language (the system perspective). This is comparable to seeing climate as the same phenomenon as weather but viewed from an increased temporal perspective.

History as a system of meanings

The systemic approach proposes that to fully understand and make useful observations about language, it is helpful to look at it from both ends (that is, take both a 'weather' and a 'climate' perspective). In other words, rather than treating the language system as one phenomenon and focusing on instances of language as another, we always need to bring both halves of the picture together. Earlier, we explored the notion of historical discourse as an overall pattern of meanings associated with a given type of context (i.e. a school subject area where the overall aim is to record and argue about past events). Looked at from the perspective of the overall system of the English language, these patterns of meaning can be interpreted as a particular sub-system of meaning potential whereby contextual factors lead to adjustments in the systemic probabilities of the English language. Thus, to take an example, lexis associated with moral judgements as opposed to a personal, emotional response is more likely to occur in the discourse of school history than in English (see Matthiessen, 2005, for further examples of specific domains or in SFL terms 'registers' as particular settings of systemic probabilities).

History as instance

By mapping the typical choices in a particular discourse domain, we are able to identify when a particular instance or a specific text does or does not fit with the usual patterns. The following piece of writing, for example, would generally not be regarded as typical, 'standard' history, even though it was written by a 12-year-old boy as a history assessment task.

TEXT 3.3

Many years ago I was the leader of a tribe, I looked after my family I made sure we travelled to places where food was plentiful and there was plenty to drink and no one ever went hungry, we were all happy we had each other and a great mother in our land our religious beliefs kept out minds strong and our teachings righteous, the most wonderful part of my life that I foolishly took for granted was my freedom. I assumed that I would always have it. Then one day the white people dressed in fancy clothes came upon our shores, I sat silently in the bushes with the men from my tribe and men from about nine other tribes in the area, it was the first time that all the tribes in the area at the same time meet with each other.

When we heard the first couple of gun shots we thought the men may have been gods, and we thought that explained why they were dressed also strangely.

Soon a few of the men including me found the courage to show themselves to the white's and they slowly walked down to the land that the white men were building on, when they reached the whites they asked what are you doing here!

Read out of context, it is likely that many readers would locate Text 3.3 as belonging to the curriculum area of English. For example, there is the use of the authorial *I* and a high frequency of affective meanings (*we were all **happy**, most **wonderful** part of my life, I **foolishly***). In addition, there is almost a complete absence, or low frequency, of language features associated with history. For instance, there is an absence both of temporal resources to create a chronological framework and of causal language to explain connections between events. Readers may also have noticed that the structure of the text is more akin to that found in English (as opposed to historical) narratives, i.e. a problem (the arrival of the white people) and a resolution (confronting the white men).

It is important to remember, of course, that in some approaches to history the boundary between history and English is relatively weak and some teachers may encourage imaginative, empathetic writing of the type illustrated here (albeit that history teachers would expect the story aspect to be more clearly rooted in historical facts and understanding). It is perhaps worth reflecting at this point as to whether the types of writing tasks that teachers set for students always provide practice in what would be unproblematically regarded as historical discourse (of the type, for example, represented by Text 3.2, *Eora Resistance to Europeans 1790–1816*). Certainly, the increasing trend for teachers to set students a wide range of writing tasks such as news reports, diaries, dialogue and speeches (among others) may be increasing the demands made on students. While teachers' motives for setting such tasks may be to provide a more engaging and stimulating writing environment, and while a common belief is that such tasks are less demanding than traditional history essays, it is also worth considering that students may be denied sufficient practice in developing the writing skills that will earn them high marks in public exams.

To sum up, we have now considered the way in which SFL analysts conceptualize language from a system and instance perspective. In relation to system, we have considered not only how specific languages (such as English) offer particular meaning potentials, but how different discourse domains offer distinct meaning potentials (sub-systems) providing us with insight into wider cultural and social questions. We have also seen how a system perspective enables us to regard the degree to which instances of discourse represent more or less typical patterns of a discourse domain. Whereas most history teachers would regard *Eora Resistance to Europeans 1790–1816* as successful historical discourse, the account of the tribal leader would not be so highly valued.

In the following two sections, I develop further the idea that different meaning potentials and therefore different discourse domains both shape, and are shaped by, their cultural and social context. First I consider the concept of genre. This concept has influenced a number of approaches to literacy and subject learning as well as literacy strategies in both Australia and the UK. However, the concept has often been considerably 'watered down', so it is useful to locate it within a broader theory of how language works. Most importantly, it gives us insight into how history texts are 'put together' in order to achieve a writer's goals.

The cultural context and the notion of genre

Within SFL, the cultural context is seen as playing an important role in shaping meanings. Indeed the 'context of culture', as it is more technically referred to, is sometimes described as the sum of all the meanings it is possible to mean in a particular culture (see Butt *et al.*, 2000, p. 3) or 'sub'-culture, such as an academic discipline or school subject. In particular, it is proposed that a culture's purposes and goals and how members set about achieving such goals lead to predictable text structures or 'genres' (see Martin, 1997; Ventola, 1987, 1995). That is, the different purposes involved in *chatting with friends*, *recording personal experiences* or *explaining why a particular historical event occurred* will all result in distinct types of spoken or written text. Text 3.4 illustrates how a common purpose in history – chronicling past events – results in a three-part structure: *Background*, *Record of events* and *Deduction*. This is a structure that we first came across at the beginning of the chapter in relation to Text 3.2, which I am now describing more technically using the functional vocabulary of SFL genre analysis. Each element or part of the structure is referred to as a generic stage and is labelled according to its distinct function in achieving the overall purpose of the text, in this case recording past events. The genre is referred to as a historical recount.

TEXT 3.4 Eora Resistance to Europeans 1790–1816

Background
provides summary of previous historical events that are of significance

The Eora people had lived in the Sydney area for at least 40,000 years before the Europeans arrived. They had lived by hunting, fishing and gathering and believed that they were the guardians of the land. This lifestyle did not last.

Record of events
provides a record of main events as they unfolded over time

When the Europeans arrived in 1788 they occupied sacred land and destroyed Eora hunting and fishing grounds. In 1790 the Eora people began a guerrilla war against the Europeans.

In 1794 the Eora, whose leader was Pemulwuy, attacked the European settlement of Brickfield. Thirty six British and fourteen Eora were killed during this attack. In the same year the Eora killed a British settler. Then the British ordered that six of the tribe be killed.

The Aborigines continued to resist the European invaders by burning their crops and houses, taking food, destroying cattle and killing some settlers. In 1797 they attacked Toongabbie and within a week the farmers had to retreat and the farms were burned. In that year their leader, Pemulwuy, was captured by the British but later escaped.

By 1801 many settlers lived in fear of the Eora and the British started a campaign to destroy Aboriginal resistance. Troopers were sent to kill Aboriginal fighters and capture Pemulwuy. One year later settlers killed the leader in an ambush.

Other great Aboriginal leaders continued fighting against the white settlers. However, the guns of the British were more powerful than the Aboriginal spears. The British shot many of the Aboriginals and many others died of the diseases that the British brought.

Deduction
draws out the historical significance of the events that have been recorded

This period of black resistance in Sydney finally ended in 1816. It is a significant period in Australian history as it showed the determination of the Aboriginal people to resist the invasion. It also demonstrated how unjustly the Aboriginal people were treated by the White invaders.

Genre, within SFL, has a distinct definition – it is 'a staged, goal oriented, social process' (Martin, 1992, p. 505) and the emphasis is on the social and cultural dimension. That is, rather than being conceptualized in psychological terms, as the realisation of speakers' intentions, genres are seen as systems of social processes, operating within the culture at large. In this book, you will gain insight into the relationship between the system of written history genres that operate within secondary school history, and the wider academic discipline of history and Western educational culture in which they are set. From the perspective of understanding how discourse works (including historical discourse), a focus on the social as well as cultural context is important. It can, for example, open our eyes as to why some texts are dense and abstract and others more colourful and immediate. In the next section, I shall introduce Context of Situation and include examples of spoken language used in the history classroom as well as a variety of primary sources. Therefore my focus will expand beyond written texts produced by historians or students of history to include those that inform and influence student writers.

The social context and the notion of register

In the opening section of this chapter, in examples a) to d), we saw that grammatical choices are selected from the language system as an outcome of the specific social context in which an interaction is embedded (for example, whether an interaction is spoken or written and what kind of relationship holds between the interactants). In this section, we see how the notion of register serves to tighten up and systematize the relationship between key aspects of the social context and the grammatical and lexical (or 'lexicogrammatical') choices made by speakers and writers. Register therefore helps to explain variation within a discourse domain such as that of history.

Within SFL, the specific Context of Situation is an extralinguistic category for defining the situation type in which a text is embedded. Its conceptualization traces its genealogy through the linguist J. R. Firth back to the anthropological writings of Branislaw Malinowski. In Malinowski's work (e.g. 1935), describing the Context of Situation was a necessary part of the effective translation and interpretation of the spoken texts of the peoples of the Trobriand Islands. In this early work, the main focus was the ethnographic description of the observable, material circumstances of the people under study. Since then, Context of Situation has evolved into a more generalized and abstract model whose purpose is to define the social variables that have an effect on language choice. These contextual variables turn on:

a) the type of social activity taking place;

b) the social roles and relationships between the participants; and

c) aspects of the channel of communication such as whether the text is monologic or dialogic, spoken or written, or close or distant in time to the event represented.

These three variables are referred to (respectively) as *field, tenor* and *mode*, and collectively they are referred to as register (see Figure 3.2).

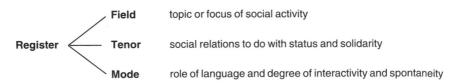

Field   topic or focus of social activity

Register   **Tenor**   social relations to do with status and solidarity

Mode   role of language and degree of interactivity and spontaneity

FIGURE 3.2 *The register variables*

The register variables of field, tenor and mode capture in a systematic manner the links between the main facets of a social situation and the language choices we make. In teaching history, these three elements can be used as 'pegs' for helping students to interpret as well as produce texts. In particular, they can facilitate an understanding of how changing register variables result in language variation as students move through the school curriculum, as well as the fact that textbook writers may make rather different language choices to student writers. In the following sections, each of the three variables is discussed in greater detail.

The topic or activity of the text: field

Field refers to the topic or social activity in which language plays a part. At a broad level, we can talk about the field of history. At this most general level, although it would be hard to predict with any specificity the types of participants and activities we might come across in actual historical texts (i.e. instances of historical discourse), we would expect them to be quite different to those found in other learning areas such as physics or mathematics. Thus, while in mathematics we would not be surprised to encounter *cosine ratios*, *acute angles* and *hypotenuses* alongside processes of *dividing*, *calculating*, *solving equations*, and so on, in history we would expect to come across a very different set of participants (e.g. *kings and queens*, *soldiers*, *politicians*, *explorers*) engaged in quite different types of activities (such as *ruling*, *invading*, *governing*, *exploring*). And most likely, these activities would be set in particular (often temporally specified) circumstances (such as *in the tenth century*, *100 years ago*, *two decades later*).

Within the broad field of history, there are, of course, many more, narrowly defined, fields such as *military history*, *the history of film*, *constitutional history*, *heritage*, and so on, and within each of these there are specific topics such as the *War of the Roses*, *the development of talking movies*, *democratic government*, *Aboriginal artefacts*, etc. It is also important to recognize that some topics can be viewed from outside a historical field. For example, if we take the topic of *migration*, we can examine it from an everyday, common-sense perspective based on direct personal experience of family or neighbourhood migration. But equally we can investigate migration from a historical perspective, conceptualizing it in generalized, abstract terms and investigating worldwide patterns of movement at different points in history. The movement from personal, common-sense experience and knowledge, to less familiar, increasingly more sophisticated 'educational' knowledge is one of the purposes of school history and schooling generally (see Bernstein, 1975, for further discussion of 'common-sense' and 'educational' knowledge) and is an important theme throughout this book. Figure 3.3 illustrates the

Heritage construed as part of an everyday field (familiar to students)	Heritage construed as part of a historical field (new to many students)
Expected Participants and Processes things in students' home, what their family looks like, the languages they speak, local street names and buildings	**Expected Participants and Processes** Aboriginal sites, artefacts, the Dreaming, preservation, archaeological evidence

FIGURE 3.3 *Heritage – moving from an everyday to a historical field*

process of re-contextualization of a field. In the figure, everyday heritage (drawing on students' first-hand experience and knowledge) is reworked as historical knowledge (using specialized lexis), thus extending students' experience beyond the personal and familiar.

We can also see this movement in the following two texts. Both of them deal with the same field: the Holocaust. The first is a primary source and the other is an extract from a popular history textbook. Both are texts that students would be likely to come across in any study of the Second World War. In the first text (3.5), the writer, Victor Greenberg, uses everyday language to describe his first-hand, personal experience of the gas chambers. He is the main participant and therefore there is repeated use of the *I* personal pronoun. Events are recounted in everyday terms. He tells how he was *punched*, *locked into* a barrack but *managed to climb out* (all concrete, physical processes). The circumstances of the events are mainly to do with place – he was locked *into a barrack*, he climbed *through a narrow window*, etc.

TEXT 3.5 An account by a Holocaust survivor, Victor Greenberg

They punched me until I was in a state of collapse. I was eventually locked into a barrack full of people who had been selected to be taken to the gas chambers. Realising the consequences, I was determined to escape and managed to climb out at night through a narrow window with a colleague. (Beechener *et al.*, 2004, p. 141)

In the following text, the same event (i.e. the Holocaust) is described with increased distance in time and space and a historical rather than personal perspective is developed. The participants are groups of people – *the Nazis, the Jews* – and events are set in time – *after the outbreak of the Second World War, in 1941*. There is also use of specialist terms such as the *'Jewish problem'*, *the Final Solution*, *policy*, *extermination* and *labour camps*.

TEXT 3.6 Hitler's Final Solution

After the outbreak of the Second World War the Nazis changed their policy towards the Jews. They wanted to get rid of as many Jews as possible, and began to make plans for how to deal effectively with what they called the 'Jewish problem'. In 1941 they came up with a plan which was known as the Final Solution. The Jews would be dealt with in two ways: they would either be worked to death or executed. Extermination and labour camps were therefore set up throughout Europe in order to exterminate the estimated eleven million European Jews. (Beechener *et al.*, 2004, p. 138)

In sum, some aspects of language (namely what are referred to in SFL as the Participants, Processes and Circumstances[2]) will be determined by the contextual variable of field – that is to say, the subject matter or the aspect of human experience referred to (for example, law enforcement, news reporting, medicine and public health, or history). We have seen, however, that field is not simply a matter of 'subject matter' but also includes the way in which the field is made sense of, or interpreted i.e. the degree to which specialist knowledge extends common-sense understanding of phenomena. As you proceed through the book you will see that this is particularly pertinent in a study of school history where, as students move from the earlier to later years, they learn to see the past through increasingly specialized eyes – the eyes of a historian.

The relationship between users of language: tenor

Tenor refers to the nature of the relationship between users of language in a particular social context. Language will vary according to factors such as:

- how often the interlocutors have contact;
- how well they know each other;
- their social roles (e.g. *teacher/student*);
- their relative social status (e.g. *expert/novice*);
- the degree to which their values are perceived to be aligned (i.e. the degree of *solidarity*).

Thus, just by looking at a piece of dialogue and its linguistic patterns, we can deduce a great deal of information about the interlocutors. In the following piece of dialogue, for example, it would not take long to figure out the social roles and relative status of the interlocutors.

Peter: Ok, everybody, now everybody if you can have a look at the
           overhead that's up there now [pause] Ali? [pause]. We can see that,
           um, we have some of, what we have here, are aspects of warfare.
           In other words, the 'input'. So, for instance, first of all, we have an
           unavailability of goods here. That means that people couldn't get
           certain things at the end of the war. Now, how do you think that
           might have affected Australian society at that time? What would the
           consequences be of that? Katina?
Katina: They had to produce their own?
Peter: Very good. They had to produce their own goods.

In conventional history classrooms, patterns in dialogue between teacher and
students often resemble those illustrated above. Frequently, they indicate:

- the roles of assessor and appraised (in addition to those of teacher
  and student);

- unequal status – the teacher is in a more powerful institutional
  position both as subject expert and arbiter of classroom behaviour;

- regular contact – students and teachers meet regularly each week
  during school term;

- alignment – students may often align their values with those of the
  authoritative teacher (though this does, of course, depend on the
  nature of the pedagogic task and type of interaction).

In the dialogue, where the history teacher, Peter, addressed his whole class
(Year 10) on the topic of the effects of the Second World War on Australian
society, we can see how the teacher's status and authority are construed
through his asymmetrical use of commands and questions (underlined below)
and his lengthier turns. The role of teacher/assessor is constructed through
his use of evaluative language (*very good*) and the degree of alignment is
indicated by the student's compliance in answering his question and providing
the expected/historically valued answer.

Teacher: Ok, everybody, now everybody if you can have a look at the
           overhead that's up there now [pause] Ali? [pause]. We can see that,
           um, we have some of, what we have here, are aspects of warfare.
           In other words, the 'input'. So, for instance, first of all, we have an
           unavailability of goods here. That means that people couldn't get
           certain things at the end of the war. Now, how do you think that
           might have affected Australian society at that time? What would the
           consequences be of that? Katina?
Katina: They had to produce their own?

Teacher: Very good. They had to produce their own goods.

(Data recorded during a Year 10 history lesson in a Sydney school – as part of the WIR project)

Tenor in history textbooks may sometimes be more difficult to identify and describe, since, although authors often adopt an overall authoritative tone thus creating an unequal status relationship between textbook writer and student reader, there may be shifts from a more authoritative impersonal style to a more casual, friendly one in which the writer directly engages with the reader. This is illustrated in the following textbook extract where the writer, Walsh, uses the pronoun *you* and the interrogative (underlined) to create a friendly relationship with his audience. However, at the end of the extract, Walsh resumes his teacher role by telling the student what they will do next – *To find out, you are going to look back at the final stages of the war.*

TEXT 3.7 The impact of the First World War

In 1914 the Germans were a proud people. Their Kaiser – virtually a dictator – was celebrated for his achievements. Their army was probably the finest in the world. A journey through the streets of Berlin in 1914 would have revealed prospering businesses and a well-educated and well-fed force. There was a great deal of optimism about the power and strength of Germany.

Four years later a similar journey would have revealed a very different picture. Although little fighting had taken place in Germany itself, the war had still destroyed much of the old Germany. The proud German army was defeated. The German people were surviving on turnips and bread, and even the flour for the bread was mixed with sawdust to make it go further. A flu epidemic was sweeping the country, killing thousands of people already weakened by rations.

This may not surprise **you**, given the suffering of the First World War. What might surprise **you** is that five years later the situation for many people in Germany was still very grim indeed.

Whatever had gone wrong in Germany? To find out, **you** are going to look back at the final stages of the First World War. (Walsh, 2001, p. 137)

In history textbooks there is a wide array of tenor relationships other than those that hold between textbook writer and student, since many books are made up of a range of primary sources in which social status varies immensely, as does the degree of distance/closeness between interlocutors. For example, a politician addressing the general public entails a very different tenor to that of a soldier writing home to his wife. The following two primary sources illustrate the sorts of differences that can hold between writer and reader. Text 3.8 is a diary entry and therefore, presumably, the writer, Doreen Ellis, did not have a wider audience in mind. For this reason there is no need for her to signal or negotiate status and roles. Consequently, there is no use of the *you* pronoun and no questions or commands. In other words, there is no explicit dialogic engagement.

TEXT 3.8 Doreen Ellis, writing in her diary about life during the Second World War

A friend of mine was caught in the blast from a nearby bomb and was taken to hospital with several shrapnel wounds. The all-clear went at about 6am and we were able to go home to bed. Two hours later, I got up and went to work. (Beechener *et al.*, 2004, p. 215)

Text 3.9, in contrast, is a letter written in the early nineteenth century in which the writer, Ned Ludd, sets up a dialogue with his addressee, Frederick Smith (a mill owner), through the use of the personal pronouns *I* and *you*. He makes clear his status by setting down a series of conditions (*if they are not taken down*, *if we come*, etc.) concluding with a command in the form of an imperative (*Inform your neighbours* . . .).

TEXT 3.9 A letter to Frederick Smith, a mill owner, from Ned Ludd, 1812

Sir,
Information has just been given in that you are an owner of those detestable shearing frames, and I was asked by my men to write to you and warn you to pull them down.

If they are not taken down by the end of next week, I will send one of my lieutenants with at least 300 men to destroy them. If we come, we will increase your misfortune by burning your buildings to ashes. If you fire upon any of my men, they have orders to murder you and burn all your housing.

Inform your neighbours that the same fate awaits them if their shearing frames are not speedily taken down, as I understand there are several in your neighbourhood. (Beechener *et al.*, 2004, p. 41)

While tenor relations may vary considerably in the texts history students need to read, the general expectation is that, in their own writing, students should adopt an impersonal tenor. Text 3.10 (an introduction to a student essay) is fairly typical in this regard – there is no use of the personal *I* pro-noun to draw attention to the fact that the student is making an interpretation. Nor is modality used (words such as *may, perhaps, it is possible*) to soften or open up her interpretation to negotiation. Rather, the use of categorical declaratives construes an authoritative stance and assumes alignment between writer and reader.

TEXT 3.10

It is only to a small extent that discontent among the peasants and proletariat contribute to the outbreak of revolution. The grievances of these groups are a part of the overthrow but there are many other factors more significant than their discontent. These include economic and social factors, as well as disillusionment with the monarchy. (Board of Studies, 1997, p.112)

If you look at my reworked alternative to Text 3.10, Text 3.11, you will see that the different choices there construe a rather different tenor. The use of overt authorial intrusion (*in my view, in my opinion, I*) and modality (*probably, I think, may, could*) develops a dialogue with potential readers. The writer 'persona' does not assume a shared interpretation of past events.

TEXT 3.11

In my view, it is probably only to a small extent that discontent among the peasants and proletariat contribute to the outbreak of revolution. I think it's very likely that the grievances of these groups are a part of the overthrow but I think there may be other factors more significant than their discontent. In my opinion, these could include economic and social factors, as well as disillusionment with the monarchy.

Later in the book we will explore more fully how different styles in interpreting and arguing about the past are influenced by the degree to which the reader is construed as being in agreement or disagreement.

Before we move to considering mode, it is worth bearing in mind the point that I have made before. You have just seen that writing a diary and a letter both require quite different uses of language and that, in turn, these are quite different to those of the traditional history essay. It is therefore worth returning to the issue of writing tasks which require students to compose fictional diary entries, letters and dialogues, amongst others. To what extent might students benefit from practising these uses of language as opposed to those more typical of historical discourse? What balance should there be between the different types of writing?

The channel of communication: mode

Mode is the channel of communication, with speaking and writing being the two most basic channels. In a spoken text, the speaker and listener are often close to each other and are frequently concerned with 'here and now' situations with the result that gestures, facial expressions and shared observations do a great amount of work in communicating meanings. The interactivity and spontaneity of the spoken mode is something that children have considerable experience of when they begin school. However, at school, whilst the dialogic spoken mode remains important, the less directly interactive (and more reflective) mode of writing becomes particularly valued. This is because it serves to synthesize, compress and store information. Making the shift from the spoken to the written mode is a major feature of all school literacy. The following classroom dialogue and essay extract, both concerning the impact of the Second World War on Australia, illustrate some of the differences between the two modes. In the classroom interaction, for example, the teacher and student jointly construct the consequences of war through the technique of question and answer. Certain points are emphasized through pauses and repetition (underlined) and the ideas are packaged in accessible language.

> Teacher: Another aspect of war was that aeroplanes, ammunition and machinery were needed. [pause]. Badly. [pause]. So, what did the Australians do?
> Student: They <u>made their own.</u>
> Teacher: That's right. They <u>made their own.</u>
>
> (Data recorded
> during a Year 10 history lesson in
> a Sydney school as part of the WIR project)

In the following essay extract, the everyday language of the dialogue is absent. Rather, ideas are packaged in more abstract language, e.g. *a restructuring of the Australian economy, industrial production, the momentum*, and the writer's thoughts are formulated as complete clauses that move the argument forward.

TEXT 3.12 What was the effect of World War II on Australian society?

One major effect of World War II was a restructuring of the Australian economy: the unavailability of goods meant that Australia had to begin to produce its own. In addition, because better equipment, such as aeroplanes, machinery and ammunition, was needed during the war, industries such as the iron and steel ones, as well as ship building, were greatly boosted. In fact between 1937 and 1945 the value of industrial production almost doubled. This increase was faster than would otherwise have occurred and the momentum was maintained in the post war years.

In order to be successful writers, history students need to move towards producing highly reflective and abstract representations of the past, of the sort illustrated in Text 3.12. In order to be successful readers, however, they need to be able to deal with a range of modes (as well as manage variation in tenor and field). This is because of the interweaving of secondary and primary sources in history textbooks and worksheets. Thus students need to be able to handle everyday, spoken text (such as a recorded, spontaneous conversation), more formal spoken text (such as a political speech) and all types of written texts (including dense, abstract legal documents). The variation of mode in primary sources and its influence on language choices are illustrated in the following three primary sources, all of which concern the Cuban missile crisis of 1962. The annotations to the right of the sources indicate some of the shifts in style and indicate why the second and third source, Texts 3.14 and 3.15, might be less accessible to students than Text 3.13.

More spoken, everyday ↑	Text 3.13 Kennedy speaking after a meeting with Khrushchev in 1961. Khrushchev had been very aggressive towards Kennedy.	Language use
	I think he [Khrushchev] did it because of the Bay of Pigs. He thought that anyone who was so young and inexperienced as to get into that mess could be beaten; and anyone who got into it and didn't see it through had no guts. So he just beat the hell out of me. If he thinks I'm inexperienced and have no guts, until we remove those ideas we won't get anywhere with him. (Walsh, 2001, p. 347)	Use of I pronoun, contraction (*didn't, I'm, won't*) everyday, colloquial language (*that mess, guts, beat the hell*)

Text 3.14 President Kennedy speaking in 1963

I believe there is no country in the world . . . whose economic colonisation, humiliation and exploitation were worse than in Cuba, partly as a consequence of US policy during the Batista regime. I believe that, without being aware of it, we conceived and created the Castro movement, starting from scratch.
(Walsh, 2001, p. 347)

Use of I pronoun and colloquial language (starting from scratch). But also abstract nouns (colonisation, humiliation, exploitation, consequence, policy)

More written, abstract

Text 3.15 Written by Robert Kennedy in *13 days*

Even after it was all over (the President) made no statement to take credit for himself or for his administration for what had occurred. He instructed all (his staff) that no interview should be given, no statement made, which would claim any kind of victory. He respected Khrushchev for properly determining what was in his own country's interests and in the interests of mankind. If it was a triumph, it was a triumph for the next generation and not for any particular government or people.
(Walsh, 2001, p. 352)

Third person pronouns (he, it), abstract nouns (statement, credit, administration, victory, triumph, generation)

Mode is also concerned with the role that language plays in a text and whether it does all the work or, alternatively, interacts with another semiotic mode. For example, in the primary source shown in Figure 3.4, a propaganda war poster, language interacts with an image (that of a smiling woman at work in a factory). In combination, the verbal text and the visual image create the message that women can find happiness in war-related industries. This interplay of modes is now commonplace in history textbooks, CD ROMs and DVDs but may create difficulties for some students. Kress and van Leeuwen (1996), for example, have argued that visual images are socially and culturally constructed products and have their own culturally specific grammar. As a consequence, the meanings are not always transparent, obvious and accessible to all students (see also Coffin and Derewianka, forthcoming).

FIGURE 3.4 *World War II propaganda poster encouraging women to work outside the home. Courtesy of the Library of Congress (website: www.ualr.edu/arwomen/timeline.htm, accessed July 2006)*

Register, meaning and language

So far we have considered, in rather general terms, how the register variables of field, tenor and mode have an impact on how people use language within the context of school history. In this section I will show how, within the SFL model, register is used to systematically link the three aspects of social context we have now discussed with three general areas of meaning which, in turn, link to specific areas of the language system.

In order to explain what I mean by three *general areas of meaning*, I need to introduce another key theoretical principle underlying the SFL model – the notion that language has three main functional orientations which have evolved to represent three areas of meaning. Referred to as *metafunctions*, these three primary functions of language enable users to:

- model or represent the world – referred to as the *ideational* metafunction;
- engage interpersonally and exchange points of view – referred to as the *interpersonal* metafunction;
- engender or create cohesive text – referred to as the *textual* metafunction.

Thus, in the extract from Text 3.4,

> *It also demonstrated how unjustly the Aboriginal people were treated by the White invaders.*

we can say that language is simultaneously working to:

a) represent past events: Aboriginal people were treated unjustly by the White invaders;

b) present a point of view: the behaviour of the White invaders was unethical;

c) link different parts of the message together: the conjunction *also* signals that the writer has already drawn a deduction about the significance of the events.

Each of the three general areas of meaning (ideational, interpersonal and textual) – as represented by the metafunctions – is associated with particular systems of language. Thus areas of language such as Participants (*Aboriginal people, the White invaders*) and Processes (*treated*) are fundamental to the building of propositional or ideational content whereas attitudinal lexis (*unjustly*), alongside systems of modality (e.g. *may, probably*), are connected to the exchange of views and attitudes and therefore are interpersonal in orientation. Finally, there are language systems such as conjunction (*also*) and reference (***these*** events) which function to build cohesive texts and are therefore textual in orientation.

The notion that the internal organisation of language is not accidental but embodies the functions that language has evolved to serve in the life of social beings (Halliday, 1973, pp. 43–4) provides a basis for construing the relationship between context and language as dialectical. The SFL model posits that there is a two-way relationship between the social and cultural environment and linguistic choices. That is, the social context in terms of its field (e.g. war), tenor (e.g. teacher to student) and mode (e.g. written as opposed to spoken) will affect language choices. But equally, by making certain language choices, writers and speakers can influence their relationship with their audience as well as shaping the degree to which their text sounds written or spoken. This is a principle that may need to be taught explicitly to students to ward off comments on their written work such as:

> This is too informal. It gives the impression that you're chatting with friends rather than writing an essay.

> This reads like a harangue rather than an essay.

The two extracts below, which are both taken from a chapter on Pompeii in the textbook *Living through History*, provide further illustration of the principle that there is a two-way relationship between the social context and language choices. In the two extracts, even though the writer and assumed readership remain the same throughout the book, there is a distinct shift in tenor relations: in the first extract the writer construes a distant and authoritative persona and develops an expert-to-novice relationship, whereas in the later extract a more collaborative, equal relationship is created, primarily through the collective personal pronoun *we*. This shift in tenor relations can perhaps be explained by the fact that, in the first extract, the writer's expertise regarding the historical facts (i.e. 'what happened' to Pompeii) is not contestable, whereas in Extract 2, the writer, other historians and the student reader are equal in their lack of knowledge of how many people died.

Extract 1
On 5 February AD 62 the Italian town of Pompeii was rocked by an earthquake. Almost all the buildings in the town were damaged and a flock of six hundred sheep is said to have been swallowed into a huge crack in the ground. After the earthquake the town was repaired and life returned to normal. (Kelly *et al.*, 1997, p. 34)

Extract 2
We don't know exactly how many people died at Pompeii, or in the neighbouring town of Herculaneum which was totally engulfed in boiling volcanic mud. We do know, however, that thousands of men, women and animals died a terrible death. (Kelly *et al.*, 1997, p. 35)

As discussed earlier, in the case of student writing, a typical tenor relation constructed between student writer and teacher is akin to that of Extract 1. That is, even though in general, the student writer's teacher/assessor will, in reality, be more expert than their student, pupils are encouraged to emulate the voice of an authoritative and objective historian. However, there are also shifts in tenor as students move through secondary school, particularly in terms of the degree to which they can assume convergence and alignment in the interpretation of past events.

In order to explain the context–language relationship in a systematic way, each register variable is posited as interrelating with one of the three metafunctions and with particular areas of language. The relationship between register variables, metafunctions and language is displayed in Figure 3.5. At this point, therefore, Figure 3.5 serves as both a review of the Hallidayan model of language I have introduced (i.e. one that highlights the context–meaning–language 'hook-up') and a preview of areas of language I shall go on to introduce and explore.

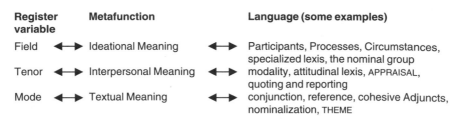

Register variable		Metafunction		Language (some examples)
Field	←→	Ideational Meaning	←→	Participants, Processes, Circumstances, specialized lexis, the nominal group
Tenor	←→	Interpersonal Meaning	←→	modality, attitudinal lexis, APPRAISAL, quoting and reporting
Mode	←→	Textual Meaning	←→	conjunction, reference, cohesive Adjuncts, nominalization, THEME

FIGURE 3.5 *Register–metafunction–language relationship*

Ideology and the development of social subjectivities

The main focus of this chapter has been to consider the overall 'architecture' of SFL and to provide an overview of its particular approach to language and discourse analysis. You will have seen that its general orientation towards language is to theorize it as a social phenomenon. Thus it links, in a systematic manner, specific language systems with particular types of meaning (ideational, interpersonal and textual) that in turn relate to variables in the social context (the subject matter, social relations and channel of communication) and the cultural context (namely the overall goal or purpose of an interaction).

Given the focus on language as a social phenomenon, it is not surprising that SFL discourse analysts take the view that the examination of any discourse domain or register increases our awareness of the ideology that is enshrined in the way in which the discourse (such as that of school history) construes the world (see, for example, Halliday, 1993, p. 132, in relation to science). It is important to emphasize, therefore, that ideology in this book refers not to 'false or distorted consciousness' but to a theory or system of beliefs which has come to be constructed as a way of comprehending the world (cf. Carter, 1987, p. 92).

In particular, the book takes the view that fundamental to the question of ideology is the way in which social subjects position and are positioned within a culture (in relation to their age and gender and cultural, political and social values) and the way in which this positioning engenders social subjectivities. One way of approaching social positioning is to examine the environments in which individuals learn to develop linguistic resources and expand their meaning potential, an ontogenetic process (see Painter, 2003). Another is to examine the way in which such positioning occurs through the unfolding of a text (a logogenetic perspective). Both approaches give insight into the positioning strategies deployed by, and across, different texts or genres. As Martin (1997) asserts, a logogenetic and ontogenetic perspective (a 'semohistory' across two different time frames) makes it possible to:

foreground the ways in which subjects engage dynamically with texts as they unfold (logogenesis), the ways in which they are positioned and repositioned socially throughout their life (ontogenesis) . . . In a model of this kind, it would be more natural to interpret language, register and genre as the projection of semohistory. (Martin, 1997, p. 10)

This book, by examining the shifts in the language, register and genres of school history, as students move from the earlier to later years of secondary schooling, can be seen as providing an ontogenetically oriented 'semohistory' and thus as providing insight into the (ideological) evolution of a social subjectivity as shaped through school learning (in this case, school history). Equally, analyses of typical evaluative patterning in history discourse and how these unfold across specific instances of text can be seen as providing insight into the persuasive power of different rhetorical strategies.

Summary

In this chapter, we have seen how SFL as a framework for contextually based linguistic analysis has the potential to provide some interesting insights into the discourse of history. Already we have seen that:

- history makes available a set of meanings quite distinct from those in other subject areas;
- these meanings are influenced by the overall disciplinary purpose of history;
- by becoming aware of the typical meanings and realizations in school history we can recognize and explain why some instances of historical discourse might not be viewed as 'standard' history and may be less highly valued than others;
- different purposes in writing about the past result in different ways of structuring texts, i.e. different genres;
- particular features in the social context (the field, tenor and mode) within which school history is embedded influence grammar and lexis (or 'lexicogrammar'); and
- different register variables and therefore different lexicogrammatical patterns operate at different points in secondary school history.

Notes

1 It has been argued that some forms of professional written history can be viewed as developing similar plot lines to literary fiction. Hayden White (1973), for example, suggested that historical narratives follow four basic plots: comedy, tragedy, satire and romance.

2 Following the SFL tradition, function labels have initial capitals.

4

Metadiscourse

Ken Hyland

Conflicting definitions and ambiguity surrounding the term 'metadiscourse' has led to uncertainty about what features to include in analyses and how to categorize these. More significantly, this lack of clarity has seriously undermined confidence in the concept itself and frustrated attempts to operationalize it consistently as a means of describing discourse. In this chapter, I propose a more theoretically robust and analytically reliable model of metadiscourse, based on a number of core principles and offering clear criteria for identifying and coding features. The key assumption here is that rhetorical features can be understood and seen as meaningful only in the contexts where they occur, and as a result metadiscourse must be analysed as part of a community's practices, values and ideals. This kind of analysis can then reveal, and help explain, why discourses are structured in a particular way among a particular group of users.

This chapter spells out what it means to take this view of metadiscourse seriously. I begin by briefly discussing three basic principles of metadiscourse, and then go on to suggest a functional framework which characterises metadiscourse as a means of conceptualising interpersonal relations.

4.1 Key principles of metadiscourse

The first place to start is with a clear definition:

Metadiscourse is the cover term for the self-reflective expressions used to negotiate interactional meanings in a text, assisting the writer (or speaker) to express a viewpoint and engage with readers as members of a particular community.

While this definition relates to some of the earlier work on metadiscourse, it is also clear that it differs from it in important ways, overlapping with other views of language use which emphasize the interpersonal, such as *evaluation, stance* and *engagement*. Essentially it sees metadiscourse as a system of meanings realized by an open-ended set of language items. These items can also perform non-metadiscoursal roles and so are recognized only in actual instances of realization. Underpinning this conception of metadiscourse is a functionally oriented perspective, which sees writers as conducting interaction with their readers, and three key principles of metadiscourse (Hyland and Tse, 2004). These are:

1   that metadiscourse is distinct from propositional aspects of discourse

2   that metadiscourse refers to aspects of the text that embody writer–reader interactions

3   that metadiscourse refers only to relations which are internal to the discourse

i. Metadiscourse is distinct from propositional aspects of discourse

Central to definitions of metadiscourse is the line they draw between propositional material, or the 'communicative content' of discourse, on one hand and material which organizes this content and conveys the writer's beliefs and attitudes to it on the other. To oversimplify this distinction slightly, we might suggest that writers have something to say and the ways they choose to say it are influenced by their expectations of how it will be received by a particular audience. That is, the main purpose of a text is to be read, and the writer's anticipation of this reading has a backwash effect on the composition of the text, influencing how it is set out and the position the writer takes towards it. We can see these two dimensions as two simultaneously enacted aspects of language in use, referring to two main types of entity: things in the world and things in the discourse, propositions and metadiscourse.

This division is an essential starting point for both theory building and analysis, but because the idea of 'proposition' is under-theorized and rarely elaborated, it has not provided researchers with an infallible means of identifying what is propositional and what is not. The two statements in example (1), for instance, could be seen as discussing something going on in the world (propositional matter) or reports on such matters in the discourse (non-propositional material):

(1) A taxonomic scheme such as the one I present below is not just a neutral description of diversity but a theory in itself.

(Science textbook)

"Political correctness" is a tired old expression, not used much nowadays by anybody but the Daily Mail, which employs it as a weapon with which to castigate the left.

(Newspaper column)

The 'taxonomic scheme' in the first utterance might be *a specific example*, something referred to and discussed in the text itself, or a reference to *all* such schemes existing in the world beyond the text. Similarly, the newspaper columnist might be evaluating *the expression* 'political correctness' as part of the discourse, or its actual manifestation in real-world behaviours. The fact that the first writer refers to the scheme as 'presented below' and that 'political correctness' is enclosed in quotes and anaphorically referred to as 'a tired old expression' and 'it', suggests a discourse-internal reading for both examples. The point of such examples is that a propositional/content distinction is required for exploring metadiscourse, but we need clear principles for identifying actual instance in practice.

It is true that many professional and academic texts are concerned with issues other than themselves. They seek to inform or persuade readers of activities, objects, or people in the world. Equally though, a large proportion of every text is not concerned with the world, but with its internal argument and its readers. It is also important to note that one is not 'primary' and one 'secondary' to the meaning of a text. Metadiscourse does not simply support propositional content: it is the means by which propositional content is made coherent, intelligible and persuasive to a particular audience. As Malinowski (1923) argued when discussing 'phatic communion' 80 years ago, language does not exist only to reflect thought, but to also satisfy other communicative needs. In particular we employ it to express social relations and establish bonds with others. Following Malinowski, then, we can say that metadiscourse is not *secondary* but *specialized*. It is how we organize out texts and construct a stance to what we say. It is what engages receivers and encourages them to accept our positions.

Essentially, this position is implied in Sinclair's (1981) discussion of 'planes of discourse' mentioned in Chapter 1. Sinclair's account offers a dynamic view of how language works by suggesting how we create text by setting out our material and negotiating relationships so others will understand it. In addition to the propositional, transactional, informative or ideational dimension of language, Sinclair argues that language performs important work in structuring and shaping the writer's understandings of the world for readers. This is a model of recipient design.

He offers a model of text which rests on two basic components. One is the expressive, attitudinal, interactional or interpersonal plane which reflects 'the need of language users to negotiate their affairs with one another'; and the other is the textual, organizational and text-maintenance plane where speakers or writers transform the world outside to the world of language. Sinclair explains the distinction like this:

> As we put language to use, we make text by negotiating our affairs with each other. At any one point, the decisions about what effect utterances should aim at, what acts they should perform, or what features of the world they should incorporate, are decisions on the interactive plane. Each segment of activity thus has an existential quality. But at the same time it is building up from text which has gone before, readjusting, working in the new material with the old, and maintaining records, moment by moment. Decisions in this intra-textual area are made on the autonomous plane.

So on the autonomous plane language works to organize and share relevant experiences and is 'concerned with language only and not with the means by which language is related to the world outside the text'. On the interactive plane, it seeks to negotiate and engage readers with those experiences. Sinclair represents these planes diagrammatically as in Figure 4.1. The curved lines suggest a portion of a circle where everything inside has to do with language and outside is the real world. The interactive plane is the interface between the two.

Hunston (2000: 183) sees the distinction in terms of the roles of writer and reader. At any point the writer is an informer and the reader is informed by the structure and nature of the text, this is the autonomous plane. At the same time, on the interactive plane, the writer is acting as a text constructor and the reader is informed through moment-by-moment negotiation. In terms of the present discussion, the model presents a view of discourse which

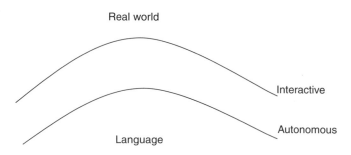

FIGURE 4.1 *Sinclair's planes of discourse model*

distinguishes metadiscourse from propositional content with no separate 'textual' function.

We also need to remember, however, that both propositional and metadiscoursal elements occur together in texts, often in the same sentences, and that both elements are crucial to coherence and meaning. Such integration is common, with each element expressing its own content: one concerned with the world and the other with the text and its reception. Like propositional discourse, metadiscourse conveys the writer's intended meaning – it is part of the message, not an entirely different one. In other words, we have to see metadiscourse as integral to the process of communication and not mere commentary on propositions. It is not simply the 'glue' that holds the more important parts of the text together, but is itself a crucial element of its meaning – that which helps relate a text to its context, taking readers' needs, understandings, existing knowledge, intertextual experiences and relative status into account. Metadiscourse is therefore an important concept for analysing the ways writers engage with their subject matter and readers, allowing us to compare the strategies used by members of different social groups.

ii. Metadiscourse expresses writer–reader interactions

A second principle of metadiscourse is that it must be seen as embodying the interactions necessary for successful communication. As such, definitions and coding schemes have to reject the duality of textual and interpersonal functions found in much of the metadiscourse literature. Instead, I suggest that **all** metadiscourse is interpersonal in that it takes account of the reader's knowledge, textual experiences and processing needs and that it provides writers with an armoury of rhetorical appeals to achieve this (Hyland and Tse, 2004).

As we saw in the previous chapter, there are difficulties in distinguishing a purely textual function for metadiscourse. Most 'textual metadiscourse' is realized by conjuncts (*so, because, and*) and adverbials (*subsequently, first, therefore*), together with their respective metaphorical or paraphrasing expressions (*as a result, on the other hand, needless to say*). For many metadiscourse analysts, these conjunctive relations (called 'text connectives' by Vande Kopple, 1985 and 'logical connectives' by Crismore et al., 1993), are treated as "straightforward and unproblematic" textual markers (Crismore et al., 1993: 48). But like other features of 'textual metadiscourse', the transitions and links that conjunctions mark between clauses can be oriented towards **either** the experiential **or** the interpersonal, to either propositional or interactional meanings. Our tendency to see conjunctions as expressing connections between ideas is perhaps a result of our primarily *ideational* orientation to the world, but we can also see conjunctions as interactionally motivated, contributing to the creation and maintenance of shifting *interpersonal* orientations.

In some cases, then, so-called textual devices deal with the logic of discourse: they work to cement the text together. In other cases they concern the logic of life: they function to extend, elaborate or enhance propositional meanings. These distinct functions can be seen in the following examples. In (2a) the conjunctions *but*, *then* and *first* function *ideationally*, connecting propositions and signalling the writer's understanding of the relations between ideas by creating links with statements about the *world*. In (2b), however, they function *interactionally* to engage the reader as a participant in the discourse, recognizing his or need for explicit signalling of links in the *argument*:

(2a) Harmison returns to the attack, *but* he overpitches and Jacobs punches him straight down the ground for four lovely runs.

(Cricket over-by-over commentary)

I met one guy who was forced to play piano accompaniment, for these kinda plays, for several years and *then* was forced to do very hard labor and he said he enjoyed the hard labor.

(University seminar)

A marketing research project is undertaken to help resolve a specific marketing problem but *first* the problem must be clearly defined.

(Marketing textbook)

(2b) The city is a great place to visit, *but* would you want to bank there?

(Advertisement)

If it is said that the individual constituent should dominate over the social one, *then* the desirable political arrangements will be those that foster individual autonomy at the expense of social authority.

(Philosophy article)

First, preheat the oven to 190 degrees C. Lightly grease 10 muffin cups, or line with muffin papers.

(Banana muffin recipe)

The *interpersonal* use of conjunctions is perhaps most apparent in the use of concessive forms as these both mark what the writer anticipates will be unexpected and also monitor the reader's response to the discourse (e.g. Martin and Rose, 2003). In academic writing in particular, tracking readers' expectations is a vital interpersonal strategy. Concessives rhetorically acknowledge voices other than the writer's by demonstrating a sensitivity to audience understandings and explicitly attempting to engage with these. In the examples below, for instance, the writers are doing more than creating a textually cohesive text; they are manoeuvring themselves into line with community expectations and shaping the reader's role to gain a more sympathetic hearing for their views (3). This is especially important when writers seek to head off potentially detracting information or competing interpretations (4):

(3) *Verbal Hygiene* is worth reading, *even if* it is sometimes irritating in its extreme views and expressions.

(Book review)

Admittedly, the data collection of the present study may be classified as 'opportunistic', rendering the representativeness of the research findings very limited.

(Ph.D. dissertation)

(4) *Of course*, these survey findings provided a more objective and independent perspective on police performance, *but* the findings are relevant to the service as a whole and cannot be reduced to individual and team performance.

(MA dissertation)

As suggested by Ortmeyer, Quelch, and Salmon (1991), the EDLP store basket price attracts time constrained consumers, and the PROMO store's deals attract the potential cherry pickers. *However*, positioning involves more than pricing.

(Research paper)

In other words, unlike propositional and interpersonal meanings, both of which orient to non-linguistic phenomena, the textual function is intrinsic to language. It exists to construe **both** propositional and interpersonal aspects of texts into a coherent whole. We should, then, see textuality as a general property of the realization of discourse itself, perhaps analogous to syntax. This interpretation corresponds to that of other writers. Halliday (1994), for instance, refers to textual elements as having an *enabling* role, facilitating the creation of discourse by allowing writers to generate texts which make sense within their context.

In sum, so-called textual devices organize texts as propositions by relating statements about the world and as metadiscourse by relating statements to readers, they do not function independently of these two functions. Figure 4.2 illustrates this relationship.

An important characterization of interactions relevant to this discussion is provided by Thompson (2001) and Thompson and Thetela (1995) who, like Sinclair in his model of *planes of discourse*, not only separate the ideational and interactive aspects of texts but also distinguish two main types of interaction. These they call the *interactive* and the *interactional*. *Interactive* resources

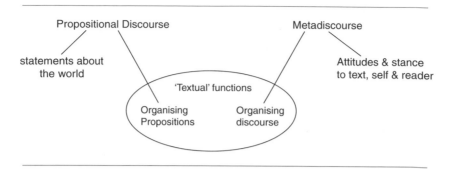

FIGURE 4.2 *The role of 'textual' devices in texts*

concern the ways writers signal the arrangement of their texts based on their appreciation of the reader's likely knowledge and understandings. This influences the 'reader friendliness' of a text and primarily involves the management of information flow, addressing how writers guide readers by anticipating their likely reactions and needs. *Interactional* resources, however, are more personal and involve the reader collaboratively in the development of the text. These concern the writer's explicit interventions to comment on and evaluate material, and so relate more directly to Halliday's interpersonal metafunction which

> is concerned with the social, expressive and conative functions of language, with expressing the speaker's angle: his attitudes and judgments, his encoding of the role relationships in the situation, and his motive in saying anything at all. (Halliday and Hasan, 1989: 26)

Thompson (2001: 61) points out that these two aspects of interaction, the interactive and the interactional, 'are essentially, the two sides of the same coin'. This is because an overt intervention to elicit a response, such as a question or directive which might be seen as primarily having an interactional purpose, can also signal where the text is going next, and so function interactively as well. Similarly, interactive resources such as conjunctions not only create structural links which assist comprehension, but also serve important interactional functions by anticipating, and perhaps deflecting, possible reader objections or counterclaims (cf. Barton, 1995).

The *interactional* thus represent the writer's overt performance in the text while the *interactive* more discreetly embodies it. As Thompson (2001: 61) puts it:

> Rather than simply moulding the text interactively to fit the readers, writers may choose at any point to bring their management of the unfolding of the text to the surface and to engage themselves and their readers explicitly

in the process.. . . . The reasons why this option might be selected are very varied but typically reflect an attempt to involve the reader in some way.

Such involvement displays solidarity with readers, showing concern for their processing of the text, and the stance of the writer. It also, as we shall see, works to position readers by manipulating their understanding of propositional matter and encouraging them to accept it.

In sum, we should see the explicit signalling of connections and relationships between elements in an argument as related to the writer's awareness of self and of the reader when writing. By making reference to the text, the audience, or the message, the writer indicates his or her sensitivity to the context of the discourse, by making predictions about what the audience is likely to know and how it is likely to respond. So-called *textual metadiscourse* is therefore actually another aspect of the *interpersonal* features of a text. It concerns decisions by the writer to highlight certain relationships and aspects of organisation to accommodate readers' understandings, guide their reading and make them aware of the writer's preferred interpretations. We can, then, say that **all** metadiscourse refers to interactions between the writer and reader.

iii. Metadiscourse distinguishes external and internal relations

If we accept that many so-called textual items can realize either interpersonal or propositional purposes depending on their context, then we need a means of distinguishing their primary function in the discourse. This brings us to the third key feature of metadiscourse, and one I have alluded to several times already, the distinction between 'internal' and 'external' reference.

Once again, connective items offer a clear example of this division as they can function to either connect steps in an exposition (internal), organising the *discourse* as an argument, or they can connect activities in the world outside the text (external), representing *experiences* as a series of events (Martin, 1992). An internal relation thus connects events in the account and is solely communicative, while an external relation refers to those situations themselves. Halliday (1994: 325) provides an unambiguous statement of this difference when discussing temporal connectors:

Many temporal conjunctives have an 'internal' as well as an 'external' interpretation; that is, the time they refer to is the temporal unfolding of the discourse itself, not the temporal sequence of the processes referred to. In terms of the functional components of semantics, it is interpersonal not experiential time.

For example, the connecting devices in (5) express a relation between activities and processes and so are experientially oriented. In these utterances *therefore* signals a consequence concerning how something will happen in the world, *in contrast* compares the characteristics of two cultures, and *then* tells us that events follow in time:

> (5) We understand that the idea of moving your account to us may be daunting *therefore* we will do most of it for you.
>
> (Bank advertisement)
>
> *In contrast* to Western culture, Asian societies put emphasis on an interdependent view of self and collectivism.
>
> (Textbook)
>
> So Moses finished the work. *Then* a cloud covered the tent of the congregation, and the glory of the LORD filled the tabernacle.
>
> (The Bible)

In contrast, the examples in (6) set up relations between aspects of the discourse and express metadiscoursal functions. They construct logical relations which are internal to the steps in their arguments. Here *therefore* signals that the writer is drawing a conclusion from the preceding argument, *in contrast* flags a disjunctive relation, alerting the reader to a move away from the expectancies set up by the prior text, and *then* realizes a logical condition in an argument:

> (6) The poll was taken just after this month's messy reshuffle and puts the Tories on 33 points, Labour on 32 and the Liberal Democrats on 25. *Therefore*, on today's results the Tories would gain an extra 41 seats and the Lib Dems 20 in the next election, leaving Blair with an uncomfortably narrow majority.
>
> (Newspaper article)
>
> *In contrast*, these findings were not found among the low collectivists.
>
> (Ph.D. dissertation)
>
> If you link the swipe card to your mobile number *then* you can use it at any one of over 60,000 TopUp points where you see the green TopUp sign.
>
> (Mobile phone SIM brochure)

The function of discourse features to refer to either relationships internal to the discourse or to events in the world can also be seen in the use of sequencing devices. These resources can be employed to arrange the argument and inform readers of how the interaction itself is being organized (7), or to the how events unfold as steps in a particular process, relating one real-world event to another (8):

(7) *Firstly*, the importance of complete images in compression is described in section one. *Secondly*, predictors used for lossless image coding are introduced. *Thirdly*, the results and analysis are used to show the performance of the proposed compression.

(Ph.D. dissertation)

First, seloot the picture and double click on it. *Second*, click on the arrow buttons to go forward or backward. *Finally*, click 'OK' on the operation panel to return to the previous display.

(Camera manual)

(8) *Firstly*, the number of observations in the first segment (Nj) and the second segment (N2) were combined and a 'pooled' regression conducted. *Secondly*, individual regressions of the two periods were carried out. *Then*, finally, the F test was applied . . .

(Ph.D. dissertation)

In assigning either propositional or metadiscoursal values to items, the distinction between internal and external reference differentiates two writer roles, reflecting Bunton's (1999: S47) view of *research acts* and *writer acts*. The former concerns events which occur in the research process itself and which form part of the subject matter of the text, such as the steps used to describe the experiment in example (8) above. Here the researcher is acting as a researcher, not as writer, reporting processes that would be carried out irrespective of how the research is eventually written up. Describing an experiment in the hard sciences or a theoretical model in the humanities involves the writer in reporting events in the world. In contrast, by constructing an argument, the writer is making choices about presentation and how best to fashion material for a particular readership and this is where metadiscourse is used.

The internal/external distinction is analogous to that made in modal logic between *de re* and *de dicto* modality, concerning the roles of linguistic items in referring to either the reality denoted by propositions or the propositions themselves. Palmer (1990: 185) recognizes this distinction as epistemic and dynamic modality, the latter 'concerned with the ability or volition of the subject of the sentence, rather than the opinions of the writer' (1990: 36). That is, items such as *might* and *possible* can be regarded as interpersonal features where they express writers' inferences about the likelihood of something, and as propositional where they are referring to real-world enabling conditions which can affect outcomes (Coates, 1983: 113; Hyland, 1998: 110).

The determining factor is therefore the objectivity of the event, whether the outcome is related to the speaker's assessments of possibility about something happening or to external circumstances which might make it possible. The clearest cases are those where such objective enabling conditions are made explicit. Thus (9) comments on the writer's estimation of possibilities, and is thus an example of metadiscourse, while (10) is propositional as it represents an outcome as depending on certain circumstances.

(9) The poor market performance *could be* due to customers switching to alternative on-line sources for their groceries.

(Business report)

It is *possible* that Strauss will also pull out of the tour to Zimbabwe this winter.

(Newspaper)

(10) Of our small British birds, *perhaps* this is the most common and well-known, as it frequents the dwellings of man and even lives in the heart of great cities.

(Bird guide)

A Travelcard makes it *possible* to visit all these sites in one day.

(London Guide)

In some cases both epistemic and dynamic readings are possible, but coding is rarely problematic.

There are, then, good reasons for distinguishing metadiscourse from the propositional content of a text and for seeing it more broadly as encompassing the interactional aspects of discourse, using the criteria of external and internal relations. If the term is to have any coherence as a means of conceptualizing and understanding the ways writers create meanings and negotiate their ideas with others, then the distinction between matters in the world and those in the discourse are central.

4.2 A classification of metadiscourse

The classification scheme summarised in Table 4.1 embodies these principles. It is based on a functional approach which regards metadiscourse as the ways writers refer to the text, the writer or the reader. It acknowledges the contextual specificity of metadiscourse and, at a finer degree of delicacy, employs Thompson and Thetela's (1995) distinction between *interactive* and *interactional* resources to acknowledge the organisational and evaluative features of interaction (Hyland, 2001a; Hyland and Tse, 2004). But while the model owes a great deal to Thompson and Thetela's conception, it takes a wider focus by including both stance and engagement features (Hyland, 2001a) and by building on earlier models of metadiscourse (Hyland, 1998 and 2000).

TABLE 4.1 An Interpersonal model of metadiscourse

Category	Function	Examples
Interactive	**Help to guide reader through the text**	**Resources**
Transitions	express relations between main clauses	in addition/but/thus/and
Frame markers	refer to discourse acts, sequences, or stages	finally/to conclude/my purpose is
Endophoric markers	refer to information in other parts of the text	noted above/see Figure/in section 2
Evidentials	refer to information from other texts	according to X/Z states
Code glosses	elaborate propositional meanings	namely/e.g./such as/in other words
Interactional	**Involve the reader in the text**	**Resources**
Hedges	withhold commitment and open dialogue	might/perhaps/possible/about
Boosters	emphasize certainty or close dialogue	in fact/definitely/it is clear that
Attitude markers	express writer's attitude to proposition	unfortunately/I agree/surprisingly
Engagement markers	explicitly build relationship with reader	consider/note/you can see that
Self-mentions	explicit reference to author(s)	I/we/my/me/my/our

The model recognizes that metadiscourse is comprised of the two dimensions of interaction:

The interactive dimension. This concerns the writer's awareness of a participating audience and the ways they seek to accommodate its probable knowledge, interests, rhetorical expectations, and processing abilities. The writer's purpose here is to shape and constrain a text to meet the needs of particular readers, setting out arguments so that they will recover the writer's preferred interpretations and goals. The use of resources in this category therefore address ways of organising discourse, rather than experience, and reveal the extent to which the text is constructed with the reader's needs in mind.

The interactional dimension. This concerns the ways writers conduct interaction by intruding and commenting on their message. The writer's goal here is to make his or her views explicit and to involve readers by allowing them to respond to the unfolding text. This is the writer's expression of a textual 'voice', or community recognized personality and includes the ways they convey their judgements and overtly align themselves with readers. Metadiscourse here is essentially evaluative and engaging, expressing solidarity, anticipating objections, and responding to an imagined dialogue with others. It reveals the extent to which the writer works to jointly construct the text with readers.

4.3 Metadiscourse resources

These two dimensions are defining characteristics of any communication, whether spoken or written, and are expressed through a range of rhetorical features which themselves perform more specific functions. I will briefly discuss these below.

i. Interactive resources

As discussed above, these features are used to organize propositional information in ways that a projected target audience is likely to find coherent and convincing. They are clearly not simply text-organizing as their deployment depends on what the writer knows of his or her readers. They are a consequence of the writer's assessment of the reader's assumed comprehension capacities, understandings of related texts and need for interpretative guidance, as well as the relationship between the writer and reader. There are five broad sub categories:

- *Transition markers* are mainly conjunctions and adverbial phrases which help readers interpret pragmatic connections between steps in an argument. They signal additive, causative and contrastive relations in the writer's thinking, expressing relationships between stretches of discourse. It is unimportant whether items here contribute to syntactic coordination or subordination, but to count as metadiscourse they must perform a role internal to the

TABLE 4.2 Different roles for internal and external transitions

Relation	External	Internal
Addition	adding activities	adding arguments
Comparison	comparing and contrasting events, things and qualities	comparing and contrasting arguments and evidence
Consequence	explaining why and how things happen	drawing conclusions or countering arguments

discourse rather than the outside world, helping the reader interpret links between ideas. Martin and Rose (2003: 127) summarize the different discourse roles played by internal and external transitions (Table 4.2) like this:

- **Addition** adds elements to an argument and potentially consists of items such as *and, furthermore, moreover, by the way,* and so on. **Comparison** marks arguments as either similar (*similarly, likewise, equally, in the same way, correspondingly,* etc.) or different (*in contrast, however, but, on the contrary, on the other hand,* etc.). **Consequence** relations either tell readers that a conclusion is being drawn or justified (*thus, therefore consequently, in conclusion,* etc.) or that an arguments is being countered (*admittedly, nevertheless, anyway, in any case, of course*).

- **Frame markers** signal text boundaries or elements of schematic text structure. Once again, care needs to be taken to identify features which order arguments in the text rather than events in time. Items included here function to sequence, label, predict and shift arguments, making the discourse clear to readers or listeners. Frame markers can therefore be used to sequence parts of the text or to internally order an argument, often acting as more explicit additive relations (*first, then, 1, 2, a, b, at the same time, next*). They can explicitly label text stages (*to summarize, in sum, by way of introduction*). They announce discourse goals (*I argue here, my purpose is, the paper proposes, I hope to persuade, there are several reasons why*). In addition, they can indicate topic shifts (*well, right, OK, now, let us return to*). Items in this category therefore provide framing information about elements of the discourse.

- **Endophoric markers** are expressions which refer to other parts of the text (*see Figure 2, refer to the next section, as noted above*).

These make additional ideational material salient and therefore available to the reader in aiding the recovery of the writer's meanings, often facilitating comprehension and supporting arguments by referring to earlier material or anticipating something yet to come. By guiding readers through the discussion, they help steer them to a preferred interpretation or reading of the discourse.

- **Evidentials** are 'metalinguistic representations of an idea from another source' (Thomas and Hawes, 1994: 129) which guide the reader's interpretation and establish an authorial command of the subject. In some genres this may involve hearsay or attribution to a reliable source; in academic writing, it refers to a community-based literature and provides important support for arguments. Evidentials distinguish *who* is responsible for a position and while this may contribute to a persuasive goal, it needs to be distinguished from the writer's *stance* towards the view, which is coded as an interpersonal feature.

- **Code glosses** supply additional information, by rephrasing, explaining or elaborating what has been said, to ensure the reader is able to recover the writer's intended meaning. They reflect the writer's predictions about the reader's knowledge-base and are introduced by phrases like *this is called*, *in other words*, *that is*, *this can be defined as*, *for example*, and so on. Alternatively, they are marked off by parenthesis.

ii. Interactional resources

These features involve readers and open opportunities for them to contribute to the discourse by alerting them to the author's perspective towards both propositional information and readers themselves. They help control the level of personality in a text as writers acknowledge and connect to others, pulling them along with their argument, focusing their attention, acknowledging their uncertainties and guiding them to interpretations. But these resources are not only the means by which writers express their views, but how they engage with the socially determined positions of others. They therefore act to anticipate, acknowledge, challenge or suppress alternative, potentially divergent positions and so work to expand or restrict opportunities for such views (White, 2003). Once again, there are five subcategories.

- **Hedges** are devices like *possible*, *might* and *perhaps*, which indicate the writer's decision to recognize alternative voices and viewpoints and so withhold complete commitment to a proposition. Hedges emphasize the subjectivity of a position by allowing information to be presented as an opinion rather than a fact and therefore open that position to negotiation. Writers must calculate what weight to give to an assertion, considering the degree of precision or reliability that they want it to carry and perhaps claiming protection in the event of its eventual overthrow (Hyland, 1998). Hedges therefore imply that a statement is based on the writer's plausible reasoning rather than certain knowledge, indicating the degree of confidence it is prudent to attribute to it.

- **Boosters**, however, are words like *clearly*, *obviously* and *demonstrate*, which allow writers to close down alternatives, head off conflicting views and express their certainty in what they say. Boosters suggest that the writer recognizes potentially diverse positions but has chosen to narrow this diversity rather than enlarge it, confronting alternatives with a single, confident voice. By closing down possible alternatives, boosters emphasize certainty and construct rapport by marking involvement with the topic and solidarity with an audience, taking a joint position against other voices (Hyland, 1999). Their use strengthens an argument by emphasising the mutual experiences needed to draw the same conclusions as the writer. The balance of hedges and boosters in a text thus indicates the extent the writer is willing to entertain alternatives and so plays an important role in conveying commitment to text content and respect for readers.

- **Attitude markers** indicate the writer's affective, rather than epistemic, attitude to propositions. Instead of commenting on the status of information, it's probable relevance, reliability or truth, attitude markers convey surprise, agreement, importance, obligation, frustration and so on, rather than commitment. While attitude is expressed by the use of subordination, comparatives, progressive particles, punctuation, text location and so on, it is most explicitly signalled metadicoursally by attitude verbs (e.g. *agree*, *prefer*), sentence adverbs (*unfortunately*, *hopefully*) and adjectives (*appropriate*, *logical*, *remarkable*).

- **Self-mention** refers to the degree of explicit author presence in the text measured by the frequency of first person pronouns and possessive adjectives (*I, me, mine, exclusive we, our, ours*). All writing carries information about the writer, but the convention of personal projection through first person pronouns is perhaps the most powerful means of self-representation (Ivanic, 1998). Writers cannot avoid projecting an impression of themselves and how they stand in relation to their arguments, their community and their readers. The presence or absence of explicit author reference is generally a conscious choice by writers to adopt a particular stance and a contextually situated authorial identity (Hyland, 2001b).

- **Engagement markers** are devices that explicitly address readers, either to focus their attention or include them as discourse participants. So in addition to creating an impression of authority, integrity and credibility through choices of *hedges*, *boosters*, *self-mention* and *attitude*, writers are able to either highlight or downplay the presence of their readers in the text. As affective devices can also have relational implications, attitude and engagement markers are often difficult to distinguish in practice. The latter, however, focus on reader participation with two main purposes:

- The first acknowledges the need to adequately meet readers' expectations of inclusion and disciplinary solidarity, addressing them as participants in an argument with reader pronouns (*you, your, inclusive we*) and interjections (*by the way, you may notice*).

- The second purpose involves rhetorically positioning the audience; pulling readers into the discourse at critical points, predicting possible objections and guiding them to particular interpretations. These functions are mainly performed by questions, directives (*mainly imperatives such as see, note and consider and obligation modals like should, must, have to*, etc.), and references to shared knowledge.

In any communicative situation, an orientation to the reader is crucial in securing social and rhetorical objectives. Readers always have the option of reinterpreting propositional information and rejecting the writer's viewpoint, which means that writers have to anticipate and respond to potential objections to their views. Metadiscourse is the way they do this: drawing on the rhetorical resources it provides to galvanise support, express collegiality, resolve difficulties and avoid disputes. Choices of *interactive* devices address readers' expectations that an argument will conform to conventional text patterns and predictable directions, enabling them to process the text by encoding relationships and ordering material in ways that they will find appropriate and convincing. *Interactional* choices focus more directly on the participants of the interaction, with the writer adopting an acceptable persona and a tenor consistent with the norms of the community. In academic writing, this mainly involves establishing a judicious, discipline-defined balance of tentativeness and assertion, and a suitable relationship to one's data, arguments and audience.

4.4 An illustration: metadiscourse in postgraduate writing

To illustrate the model and show how these resources are used to facilitate effective, community-specific interactions in academic writing, I will briefly describe a study of metadiscourse use in graduate research writing (Hyland, 2004a; Hyland and Tse, 2004). Metadiscourse is particularly important at this advanced level of academic writing as it is represents novice writers' attempts to negotiate propositional information in ways that are meaningful and appropriate to a particular disciplinary community. On one hand, metadiscourse reveals writers' assumptions about the processing abilities, contextual resources, and intertextual experiences of their readers, and on the other, writers' abilities to adopt an appropriate disciplinary persona by revealing a suitable relationship to their data, arguments and audience.

The importance of metadiscourse in advanced postgraduate writing is shown by the fact that there were over 184,000 cases in a four million word corpus of 240 masters and doctoral dissertations written by EFL students in Hong Kong. This is a frequency of 1 in every 21 words. It is important to note that because metadiscourse often has clause or sentence length realization, these standardized figures are not meant to convey the overall *amount* of metadiscourse in the corpus, but simply to allow comparison of different patterns of *occurrence* of metadiscourse in different genre and disciplinary sub-corpora. A concordance programme searched the texts for some 300 potential expressions of metadiscourse and a large sample was analysed manually to ensure each was functioning as metadiscourse. Table 4.3 shows that writers

TABLE 4.3 Metadiscourse in postgraduate dissertations (per 10,000 words)

Category	Master	Doctoral	All	Category	Master	Doctoral	All
Transitions	75.8	95.6	89.0	Hedges	86.1	95.6	92.4
Evidentials	40.0	76.2	64.1	Engagement markers	39.7	51.9	47.8
Code glosses	27.4	40.6	36.2	Boosters	31.7	35.3	34.1
Frame markers	20.7	30.3	27.1	Attitude markers	20.4	18.5	19.2
Endophorics	22.3	24.0	23.4	Self-mentions	14.2	40.2	31.5
Interactive	**186.1**	**266.7**	**239.8**	**Interactional**	**192.2**	**241.5**	**225.0**

used slightly more interactive than interactional forms, and that hedges and transitions were the most frequent devices followed by engagement markers and evidentials.

The significance of these frequencies are perhaps more clearly understood when compared to other common features of published academic writing. A large corpus-based study for the Longman Grammar, for instance, for instance, give figures of 18.5 cases per 1,000 words for passive voice constructions and 20 per 1,000 words for past tense verbs (Biber et al., 1999). These metadiscourse signals are therefore important components of academic prose.

The high use of transitions, representing internal connections in the discourse, is clearly an important feature of academic argument. Transitions represent over a fifth of all metadiscourse in the corpus, demonstrating writers' concerns that readers are able to recover their reasoning unambiguously. The most frequent sub-category however is hedges, which constitute 41 per cent of all interactional uses. This frequency reflects the critical importance of distinguishing fact from opinion in academic writing and the need for writers to evaluate their assertions in ways which recognize potential alternative voices. In fact, *may*, *could* and *would* were among the highest frequency items in the corpus, presenting claims with both caution and with deference to the views of readers/examiners. In general, then, the use these students made of metadiscourse demonstrates a principal concern with expressing arguments explicitly and with due circumspection.

We can also see that the use of metadiscourse varied considerably across the two corpora of dissertations. There was an overall balance between interactive and interactional forms in the Master's theses, with slightly more interactional uses, while the doctoral texts contained 10 per cent more interactive forms. The Ph.D. dissertations however contained far more metadiscourse, with 73 per cent of all cases. This may have something to do with the fact that Ph.D. theses are often twice as long as the masters dissertations, so students have to make greater use of interactive devices to structure more discursively complex arguments. However, the higher frequencies in the Ph.D.s also seem to represent more determined and sophisticated attempts by writers to engage with readers and to present themselves as competent and credible academics immersed in the ideologies and practices of their disciplines.

In the **interactive categories**, for instance, doctoral writers made far more use of *evidentials*, with over four times the number of intertextual references. Citation is central to the social context of persuasion, as it not only helps provide justification for arguments and demonstrates the novelty of the writer's position, but it also allows students to display an allegiance to a particular community and establish a credible writer identity, showing a familiarity with the literature and with an ethos that values a disciplinary research tradition. The writers of masters' theses, however, are unlikely to be so concerned about establishing their academic credentials. Not only are their texts much shorter, but they are also completed fairly quickly and in addition to substantial coursework, while many of their writers are often studying part time and are looking forward to returning to their professional workplaces rather than a career in academia. Consequently their reading of the literature, and their desire to demonstrate their familiarity with it, may be less pressing.

Similarly, doctoral students employed far more **interactional metadiscourse** markers per 10,000 words, with much higher use of *engagement markers* and *self-mentions*. Self-mention is a key way which writers are able to promote a competent scholarly identity and gain approval for their research claims. While many students are taught to shun the use of first person, it plays a crucial interactional role in mediating the relationship between writers' arguments and their discourse communities, allowing them to create an identity as both disciplinary servant and creative originator (Hyland, 2001b). The points at which writers choose to metadiscoursally announce their presence in the discourse tend to be those where they are best able to promote themselves and their individual contributions. Engagement features are also far more common in the doctoral texts, particularly imperatives and obligation modals which direct the reader to some thought or action. These are important means of bringing readers into the text as participants in an unfolding dialogue.

There were also substantial variations in the use of metadiscourse across **disciplinary communities.** The corpus contained equal numbers of dissertations from six disciplines in the natural and social sciences, and Table 4.4 shows that the more discursive 'soft' fields employed more metadiscourse overall and almost two-thirds of the interactional features. Hedges were well over twice as common in the soft fields and self-mentions almost four times more frequent (before norming for text length).

The figures reflect the greater role that explicit personal interpretation plays in the humanities and social sciences where interpretations are typically more explicit and the conditions for establishing proof less reliable than in the hard fields (e.g. Hyland, 2000). Dealing with human subjects and data is altogether more uncertain and writers are unable to draw to the same extent on empirical demonstration or trusted quantitative methods. Consequently persuasion lies far more in the efficacy of argument and the role of language to build a relationship with readers, positioning them, persuading them and including them in the argument.

Overall, these results suggest the extent to which metadiscourse is related to the socio-rhetorical contexts in which it used. As it enables text producers to frame and organize propositions, to position and engage readers and to express a stance and enter relationships with their interlocutors, metadiscourse

TABLE 4.4 Metadiscourse in dissertations by discipline
(per 10,000 words)

Category	Applied Linguistics	Public Admin	Business Studies	Computer Science	Electronic Engineering	Biology
Transitions	95.1	97.8	89.1	74.3	76.9	86.6
Frame markers	25.5	29.5	25.3	35.4	24.7	22.5
Endophorics	22.0	15.5	19.6	25.9	43.1	23.0
Evidentials	82.2	55.6	60.7	31.1	20.1	99.5
Code glosses	41.1	36.6	30.0	32.3	30.7	36.0
Interactive	**265.9**	**240.5**	**224.7**	**199.0**	**195.5**	**267.6**
Hedges	111.4	109.7	93.3	55.8	61.5	82.1
Boosters	37.9	39.5	29.8	29.4	28.0	30.5
Attitude markers	20.3	26.1	20.7	16.2	10.6	15.5
Engagement markers	66.1	42.0	35.8	59.2	32.7	15.4
Self-mentions	50.0	22.4	31.6	29.3	18.1	5.7
Interactional	**285.7**	**239.8**	**211.1**	**190.0**	**150.9**	**149.2**
Totals	**551.6**	**474.9**	**435.8**	**389.0**	**346.5**	**416.8**

provides a link between texts and cultures. It thus helps to characterize the rhetorical context by revealing some of the expectations and understandings of the audience for whom a text was written. As metadiscourse is the way writers construe their readers, its study enables us to explore writers' perceptions of the communities for which they are writing. This, in turn, helps to reveal not only readers' preferred discourse patterns, but also something of their social practices, values and ways of thinking.

4.5 The limits of description

It should be borne in mind that no taxonomy or description will ever be able to do more than partially represent a fuzzy reality. This is partly because metadiscourse studies deal only with *explicit* devices which can be clearly identified in the text (see Hyland, 2005 chapter 2 for discussion). The decision to focus on overt surface features is due, to some extent, to the practical purposes of identification, but equally importantly, this explicitness is itself textually and rhetorically interesting as it represents the writer's conscious choice to indicate a presence in the discourse. Explicitness is therefore related to the author's awareness of both self and audience: it signals a point where the writer has reflected on the process of text creation, and this induces a similar awareness in the reader. Explicitness therefore represents the writer or speaker's overt attempt to create a particular pragmatic or discoursal effect, and while explicitness may be a matter of degree, it does not alter the principle of excluding implicit authorial presence from analyses.

Clearly, however, dichotomizing authorial presence into high and low explicitness does not do full justice to the writer's intervention in a text, as any textual choice is a non-explicit signal of such a presence. But metadiscourse analysis is indicative rather than comprehensive. It helps us to understand the extent of authorial self-awareness, how far writers are able to see their texts as an outcome of writing (rather than as a study or theory in the world) and to compare the ways writers employ this awareness in crafting texts in different genres, cultures and communities.

A further limitation of the description, however, is the fact that the imposition of discrete categories on the fluidity of actual language use inevitably conceals its multifunctionality, blurring simultaneous meanings in an 'all-or-nothing' interpretation of how particular devices are used. Writing effectively means anticipating the needs of readers, both to follow an exposition and to participate in a dialogue, and occasionally devices are used to perform both functions at once so there will inevitably be some overlap between categories. Not only are metadiscourse functions often confused with propositional ones, as we have seen, but contrastive connectives like *but* and *however*, which principally play interactive roles by organizing the discourse, can also act interactionally by shifting from a positive to a negative judgement (Hood and Forey, 1999) or by mitigating the introduction of a counter claim (Barton, 1995). Similarly, code glosses not only reveal the writer's assessments of shared subject matter, but also imply an authoritative position vis-a-vis the reader.

A classification scheme can therefore only approximate the complexity of natural language use. But while it may give no firm evidence about author intentions, it is a useful means of revealing the meanings available in the text and perhaps some of the assumptions writers hold about the issues they address and the ways they see their audiences. Interacting effectively means anticipating the needs of readers, both to follow an exposition and to participate in a dialogue; it should be no surprise that many devices are used to perform both functions at once.

4.6 Summary and conclusions

This chapter has presented a model of metadiscourse based on its primary function of negotiating interactions in texts. Essentially my argument has been that metadiscourse offers a way of understanding the interpersonal resources writers use to organize texts coherently and to convey their personality, credibility, reader sensitivity and relationship to the message. There is often a tendency in the metadiscourse literature to focus on surface forms and the effects created by writers, especially in pedagogic materials, but metadiscourse should not be seen as an independent stylistic device which authors can vary at will. I hope the model described here overcomes many of these limitations and offers a comprehensive and pragmatically grounded means of investigating the interpersonal resources in texts.

The importance of metadiscourse lies in its underlying rhetorical dynamics which relate it to the contexts in which it occurs. In most of our communications that matter, such as the writing we do for academic or professional purposes, interaction involves 'positioning', or adopting a point of view in relation to both the issues discussed in the text and to others who hold views on those issues. In claiming a right to be heard, and to have our views taken seriously, we must display a competence as community insiders. This competence is, at least in part, achieved through establishing an appropriate writer-reader dialogue which situates both our arguments and ourselves, establishing relationships between people, and between people and ideas. Successful writing thus depends on the individual writer's projection of a shared community context. Metadiscourse emphasizes that in pursuing their goals, writers seek to create a recognizable social world through rhetorical choices which allow them to conduct interpersonal negotiations and balance claims for the significance, originality and plausibility of their work against the convictions and expectations of their readers.

To the analyst, metadiscourse is a useful concept because it reveals the presence of the author in the text and his or her awareness of a reader. It is a specialized form of discourse which allows writers to engage with and influence their interlocutors and assist them to interpret and evaluate the text in a way they will see as credible and convincing. As a result, metadiscourse is intimately linked to the norms and expectations of particular communities through the writer's need to supply as many cues as needed to secure the reader's understanding and acceptance of the propositional content. Central to this conception of metadiscourse, then, is the view that it must be located in the settings which influence its use and give it meaning. These functions and connections will be elaborated in the following chapters.

5

Critical discourse analysis

Brian Paltridge

The norms and values which underlie texts are often 'out of sight' rather than overtly stated. As Hyland (2005: 4) observes, acts of meaning making (and in turn discourse), are 'always engaged in that they realize the interests, the positions, the perspectives and the values of those who enact them'. The aim of a critical approach to discourse analysis is to help reveal some of these hidden and 'often out of sight' values, positions and perspectives. As Rogers (2004: 6) puts it, discourses 'are always socially, politically, racially and economically loaded'. Critical discourse analysis examines the use of discourse in relation to social and cultural issues such as race, politics, gender and identity and asks why the discourse is used in a particular way and what the implications are of this kind of use.

Critical discourse analysis explores the connections between the use of language and the social and political contexts in which it occurs. It explores issues such as gender, ethnicity, cultural difference, ideology and identity and how these are both constructed and reflected in texts. It also investigates ways in which language constructs and is constructed by social relationships. A critical analysis may include a detailed textual analysis and move from there to an explanation and interpretation of the analysis. It might proceed from there to deconstruct and challenge the text/s being examined. This may include tracing underlying ideologies from the linguistic features of a text, unpacking particular biases and ideological presuppositions underlying the text, and relating the text to other texts and to people's experiences and beliefs.

Critical discourse analysis starts with the assumption that language use is always social and that discourse both 'reflects and constructs the social world' (Rogers, 2011: 1). A critical analysis might explore issues such as gender, ideology and identity and how these are reflected in particular texts. This might commence with an analysis of the use of discourse and move from there to an explanation and interpretation of the discourse. From here, the analysis might proceed to deconstruct and challenge the texts, tracing ideologies and assumptions underlying the use of discourse, and relating these to different views of the world, experiences and beliefs (Clark, 1995).

5.1 Principles of critical discourse analysis

There is no single view of what critical discourse analysis actually is, so it is difficult to present a complete, unified view on this. Fairclough and Wodak (1997), however, describe a number of principles for critical discourse analysis· which underlie many of the studies done in this area. These include:

- social and political issues are constructed and reflected in discourse;
- power relations are negotiated and performed through discourse;
- discourse both reflects and reproduces social relations;
- ideologies are produced and reflected in the use of discourse.

Each of these is discussed in the sections which follow.

i. Social and political issues are constructed and reflected in discourse

The first of Fairclough and Wodak's principles is that critical discourse analysis addresses social and political issues and examines ways in which these are constructed and reflected in the use of certain discourse strategies and choices.

Recently, I received mail in my letterbox about a proposal to build 125 apartments on top of a shopping mall which is very near where I live. There was a letter from the local council, and a pamphlet from a local protest group, each of which expressed very different views on the development. One was very factual (the letter from the council) which aimed to remain 'neutral' on the topic in that it did not express a particular point of view on the project. It just outlined the procedures for the development, and how the public would be consulted about it, largely through written submissions and a public meeting that would be held in the near future. The pamphlet from the protest group, by contrast, outlined the problems the development would create for the neighbourhood such as over-shadowing of properties, increased demand for on-street parking and lack of privacy from windows in the apartments that would overlook people's back gardens. Both texts, then, referred to the same event but chose very different ways of approaching it which were, in turn, reflected in their discourse. One gave the impression it was neutral on the topic whereas the other had a very particular take on the new development and what it would mean for people living in the area.

A further example of this is Teo's (2005) study of slogans for Singapore's 'Speak Mandarin' campaign. In this campaign, there is clearly a view that Singaporeans of Chinese decent should speak Chinese, despite the fact that, at the time of the launch of the campaign, only a small percentage of them actually spoke Mandarin as their first language. The aim of the campaign was to connect Chinese Singaporeans with Chinese cultural traditions as well as help counter 'negative effects of westernisation' (Teo, 2005: 123). The campaign was also motivated by an economic policy which aimed at attracting foreign investment, especially from China. These arguments were captured in slogans such as *Mandarin: Window to Chinese Culture*, *Speak Mandarin, It's an Asset* and *Speak Mandarin: Your Children's Future Depends on Your Effort*. Mandarin was also presented as cool and of contemporary relevance, as well as a 'stepping-stone to greater business opportunities' with the Chairman of the Promote Mandarin Council saying that Mandarin is ' "cool" in more ways than one', 'Mandarin is definitely "in" ' and Mandarin is 'a store of linguistic and cultural treasure waiting to be explored' (Teo, 2005: 134). The discourse of the campaign, thus, constructs the view of Mandarin as a language that has both cultural, social and, in particular, economic value for the people of Singapore.

ii. Power relations are negotiated and performed through discourse

The next principle of critical discourse analysis is that power relations are both negotiated and performed through discourse. One way in which this can be looked at is through an analysis of who controls conversational interactions, who allows a person to speak and how they do this.

In the case of the building of the apartments near my house, the two different texts I received gave very different impressions of how people were encouraged to speak on the topic and negotiate different points of view on the development. The letter from the Council said that people would be free to speak at the public meeting, but that they would be required to register their intention to speak at the start of the meeting. The letter did not mention that the full Council would be at the meeting, plus representatives of the developers who had put forward the proposal. The pamphlet encouraged residents to write to their local councillors about the issue and gave the names and address of each of the members of the local council. The area in which I live however is very multicultural. I am not certain the elderly Vietnamese couple who live next door to me would have written to the councillors, or would have felt their voices would have been heard, had they gone to the meeting. They would most likely not have felt they had the power to change things, nor were they in a position to influence the outcomes of this discussion. The 90-year-old woman who lives by herself on the other side of my property may also not have felt comfortable going to the meeting and standing up in front of everyone to have her say, as unhappy as she was about the development.

Hutchby (1996) examined issues of power in his study of arguments in British radio talk shows. As Hutchby and Wooffitt (2008) point out, the person who speaks first in an argument is often in a weaker position than the person who speaks next. The first person has to set their opinion on the line whereas the second speaker merely has to challenge their opponent to expand on, or account for their claims. In a radio talk back programme it is normally the host that comes in the second position and has the power to challenge the caller's claim, or to ask them to justify what they have just said. The following example shows how a talk back show host does this simply by saying *Yes* and *So*:

> Caller: I: have got three appeals letters here this week. (0.4) All a:skin' for
>   donations. (0.2). hh Two: from tho:se that I: always contribute to
>   anywa:y,
> Host: *Yes?*
> Caller: .hh But I expect to get a lot mo:re.
> Host: So?
> Caller: .h Now the point is there is a limi[t to …
> Host: [What's that got to do – what's that got to do with telethons though.
> Caller: hh Because telethons … (Hutchby, 1996: 489)

The host does this again in the next example where *What's that got to do with it?* challenges the caller and requires them to account for what they just said:

> Caller: When you look at e:r the childcare facilities in this country, hh we're
>   very very low, (.) i-on the league table in Europe of (.) you know of you
>   try to get a child into a nursery it's very difficult in this country.. hh An'
>   in fa:ct it's getting wor::se.

Host: *What's that got to do with it.*
Caller: .phh Well I think whu- what 'at's gotta d-do with it is ... (Hutchby,
         1996: 490)

The caller can take the second speaking part in this kind of interaction only
when the host has moved, or been manoeuvred, into first position by giving
an opinion of their own. If this does not happen, it is hard for the caller to
take control of the conversation, and challenge the control of the host. This
kind of analysis, then, shows how power is brought into play, and performed,
through discourse (Hutchby, 1996).

iii. Discourse both reflects and reproduces social relations

A further principle of critical discourse analysis is that discourse not only
reflects social relations but is also part of, and reproduces, social relations.
That is, social relations are both established and maintained through the use
of discourse.

The letter from my Council that I referred to earlier was written with authority
and contained a lot of technical detail, setting up a very clear power imbalance
between the writer and readers of the text. It was signed 'Director – Planning
and Development', and it gave no actual name for people to call to speak to.
The pamphlet from the protest group, however, was much more informal and
gave an email address to write to for further information and advice on what
to do to change the situation. The social relations produced (and reproduced)
through the two texts were, thus, quite different.

Page's (2003) study of representations in the media of Cherie Blair, wife
of the British Prime Minister Tony Blair, illustrates this further. Page shows
how representations of Cherie Blair in the media as a lawyer, a wife and,
especially, a working mother aim to establish a certain relationship between
her and the public and, in particular, other working mothers. While Cherie Blair
is largely presented by the media as a success story for managing her role
as a working mother, as Page points out, working mothers are more typically
presented in negative terms in everyday discourse, in a way that produces
quite different readings of the term, and in turn, different views of women
with children who work. Stokoe's (2003) study of neighbourhood disputes
shows, equally, how terms such as *mother* and *single women* can be used
to make moral assessments about women as well as perpetuate 'taken-for-
granted "facts" about women's appropriate behaviour' (p. 339) and social
relations with other people. The use of language in this way both reflects and
reproduces certain social views and relations. It, equally, reinforces social and
gendered stereotypes and inequalities (Page, 2003).

iv. Ideologies are produced and reflected in the use of discourse

Another key principle of critical discourse analysis is that ideologies are produced and reflected in the use of discourse. This includes ways of representing and constructing society such as relations of power, and relations based on gender, class and ethnicity.

The mail I received on the development project near my house were each quite different. The letter from the Council presented the addition of 125 new apartments (plus additional retail and commercial floor space and three 8 storey residential towers on top of the already five storey mall) at the end of my street as a neutral event that would have no consequences for me or for where I am living. The pamphlet from the protest group made it clear what the consequences of this would be, outlining them in detail, and strongly voiced its opposition to the project.

Mallinson and Brewster's (2005) study of how stereotypes are formed in everyday spoken discourse is a further illustration of the ways in which ideologies are produced and reflected in the use of discourse. As Mallinson and Brewster point out, negative attitudes towards non-standard social dialects of English are often transferred to negative views of the people who speak these dialects. A job applicant who speaks a non-standard dialect, for example, may not be hired when an employer uses this use of discourse as a way of predicting the applicant's future occupational performance; that is, the view that 'good workers' speak standard English and 'bad workers' do not.

In their study of US restaurant workers' views of their customers, Mallinson and Brewster found that the (white) workers viewed all black customers as the same, in negative terms, using stereotypes to form their expectations about future interactions with black customers, and the broader social group of African Americans. This was clear in the 'discourse of difference' (Wodak, 1997) that they used as they spoke about their black customers and distanced themselves from them. The workers' views of rural white Southerner customers were similarly stereotyped, although they talked about this group in somewhat different ways, referring to where they lived, the ways they dressed and their food and drink preferences as a way of justifying their claims about them. In both cases, the workers' use of discourse privileged their own race and social class, reflecting their ideological, stereotyped views of both groups of customer.

Fairclough and Wodak also argue that all texts need to be considered in relation to the texts that have preceded then and those that will follow them. They also need to be understood by taking sociocultural knowledges of the texts and the matter at hand, more broadly, into consideration. In the letter from my Council, there was no mention that this was the third time the development company was attempting to have their proposal approved, and that there had been two previous public meetings on the topic where the application had been rejected. The pamphlet from the protest group, however, made this very clear. A critical analysis of these communications then, is a form of social action in that it attempts to intervene and bring about change in both communicative and sociopolitical practices (Fairclough and Wodak 1997).

Critical discourse studies, then, aim to make connections between social and cultural practices and the values and assumptions that underlie the discourse. That is, it aims to unpack what people say and do in their use of discourse in relation to their views of the world, themselves and relationships with each other. Critical discourse analysis takes the view that the relationship between language and meaning is never arbitrary in that the choice of a particular genre or rhetorical strategy brings with it particular presuppositions, meanings, ideologies and intentions (Kress, 1991). As Eggins (1994: 10) argues:

> Whatever genre we are involved in, and whatever the register of the situation, our use of language will also be influenced by our ideological positions: the values we hold (consciously or unconsciously), the biases and perspectives we adopt.

Thus, if we wish to complain about a neighbour we may chose a genre such as a neighbour mediation session, or we may decide to air our complaint in a television chat show, as some of the speakers did in Stokoe's (2003) study of neighbour complaints. We may also do this by complaining to another neighbour about them. Our intention in speaking to the other neighbour may be to build up a 'neighbourhood case' against the person we are unhappy with. If the neighbour we are complaining about is a single mother we may draw on other people's prejudices against single mothers, and our own biases and moral judgements about them as an added rationale for complaining about the neighbour. The woman being complained about may pick up on this, as did one of Stokoe's subjects, Macy, in a neighbour mediation session where she says 'if I had a big bloke living with me ... none of this would happen' (Stokoe, 2003: 329). Macy does not allow her single status to be used as a reason to complain about her.

In a further extract, Stokoe shows how speakers may draw on the fact that their neighbour has boyfriends (more than one) as added ammunition against her; that is, the view that women should be monogamous (but not men) and if a woman breaches this rule, she should be held morally accountable for her behaviour. The following example illustrates this. In this example Terry (T) is the chat show host and Margaret (M) is a member of the audience who is complaining about her neighbour:

T: I want to know (.) what happened to you
        (0.5)
M: after living very happily (.) in my (.) one bedroom flat for thirteen years (.)
        it was a *three* storey block of flats and I was on the top floor (.) and the
        young woman was put in the flat below me (0.5) I them had (.) seven
        and a half ye:ars (.) of sheer hell
T: *what* sort of hell?
M: loud music (.) night *and* day (.) it just depended=
T: =well that wasn't the worst was it?
M: = (0.5) it was boyfriends (.) and lovemaking that ... (Stokoe, 2003: 333)

The rhetorical strategy here, then, is to draw on a moralizing discourse about women (and especially, single women who have sex) as a way of legitimating complaints about female neighbours, as well as building a defence for making the complaint (Stokoe, 2003).

Resende (2009) provides a similar example of how, through the use of discourse, groups of people are framed in particular ways. She examines a report of a meeting on homeless people which was sent, as a circular, to residents of a middle-class apartment building in Brazil. The circular reported on a meeting that had been convened by a local restaurant owner who was concerned about homeless people living in the area and the financial impact it was having on his business. What she found was the genre of 'apartment circulars' which normally addresses issues such as building maintenance had been appropriated to make a case for the removal of people from the area. It used terms such as 'government authorities' and 'public security representative' to give it authority so that the views expressed in the circular would be taken as given and not open for discussion. Views were expressed categorically and disguised the main issue, the problem of living on the streets. The issue was reframed in terms of individual and community comfort and avoided the underlying social cause of the problem.

Meadows (2009) employed *ethnographically sensitive critical discourse analysis* to examine the relationship between nationalism and language learning in an English language classroom on the Mexico–US border. The students in the classes he examined were all Mexican management-level employees who held positions of economic and social privilege in their particular community. The data he collected included participant-observations, interviews, questionnaires, classroom activities and emails. The data was collected was then examined from a critical discourse perspective with the aim of exploring how the relationship between nationalism and language learning played out in the classroom. Meadowns found that the classroom provided a site for the reproduction of nationalist border practices as well as a place in which hierarchies of privilege were reinforced. This was revealed through the ways in which the students discussed border categories using, for example, polar categories such as *americano* and *mexicano*, and negative attitudes to categories which blurred these boundaries, such as *Spanglish*, *Mexican-American* and *paisano*. The teacher, further, often used nationalist categories in the classroom which the students positively responded to. His study shows how language classrooms are not only about developing language proficiency. They are also often closely linked to students' investment in their worlds outside the classroom.

A key focus, then, of critical discourse studies is the uniting of texts with the discourse and sociocultural practices that the text reflects, reinforces and produces (Fairclough, 1995). The chart in Figure 5.1 summarizes this. Discourse, in this view, simultaneously involves each of these dimensions.

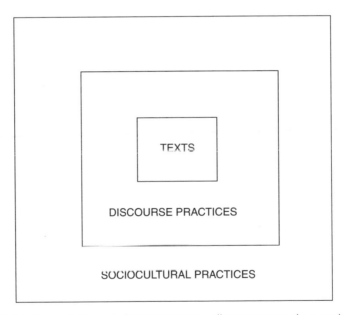

FIGURE 5.1 *The relationship between texts, discourse practices and sociocultural practices in a critical perspective (adapted from Fairclough 1992: 73)*

5.2 Doing critical discourse analysis

Critical discourse analysis 'includes not only a description and interpretation of discourse in context, but also offers an explanation of why and how discourses work' (Rogers, 2004: 2). Researchers working within this perspective:

are concerned with a critical theory of the social world, the relationship
of language and discourse in the construction and representation of the
social world, and a methodology that allows them to describe, interpret
and explain such relationships. (Rogers, 2011: 3)

A critical analysis, then, might commence by deciding what discourse type,
or genre, the text represents and to what extent and in what way the text
conforms to it (or not). It may also consider to what extent the producer of
the text has gone beyond the normal boundaries for the genre to create a
particular effect.

The analysis may consider the *framing* of the text; that is, how the content
of the text is presented, and the sort of angle or perspective the writer, or
speaker, is taking. Closely related to framing is the notion of *foregrounding*;
that is, what concepts and issues are emphasized, as well as what concepts
and issues are played down or *backgrounded* in the text. Equally important
to the analysis are the background knowledge, assumptions, attitudes and
points of view that the text presupposes (Huckin, 1997).

At the sentence level, the analyst might consider what has been *topicalized*
in each of the sentences in the text; that is, what has been put at the front of
each sentence to indicate what it is 'about'. The analysis may also consider
who is doing what to whom; that is, *agent-patient relations* in the discourse,
and who has the most authority and power in the discourse. It may also
consider what agents have been left out of sentences, such as when the
passive voice is used, and why this has been done (Huckin, 1997).

At the word and phrase level, connotations of particular words and phrases
might be considered as well as the text's degree of formality or informality,
degree of technicality and what this means for other participants in the text.
The choice of words which express degrees of certainty and attitude may
also be considered and whether the intended audience of the text might be
expected to share the views expressed in the text, or not (Huckin, 1997).

The procedure an analyst follows in this kind of analysis depends on the
research situation, the research question and the texts that are being studied.
What is essential, however, is that there is some attention to the *critical,
discourse* and *analysis* in whatever focus is taken up in the analysis (Rogers,
2011).

Critical discourse analysis, then, takes us beyond the level of description
to a deeper understanding of texts and provides, as far as might be possible,
some kind of explanation of why a text is as it is and what it is aiming to do. It
looks at the relationship between discourse and society and aims to describe,
interpret and explain this relationship (Rogers, 2011). As van Dijk (1998) has
argued, it is through discourse that many ideologies are formulated, reinforced
and reproduced. Critical discourse analysis aims to provide a way of exploring

this and, in turn, challenging some of the hidden and 'out of sight' social, cultural and political ideologies and values that underlie texts.

5.3 Critical discourse analysis and genre

One way in which a question might be approached from a critical perspective is by considering the genres that have been chosen for achieving a particular discourse goal. Flowerdew (2004) did this in his study of the Hong Kong government's promotion campaign of Hong Kong as a 'world-class city'. He discusses the various genres that were involved in constructing this view of Hong Kong. These included committee meetings, policy speeches, commission reports, an inception report, public fora, exhibitions, focus group discussions, presentations, a website, consultation documents, information leaflets, consultation digests and videos. He discusses how each of these genres played a role in the construction of this particular view of Hong Kong. He then carries out an analysis of three different genres which made this claim: a public consultation document, the Hong Kong annual yearbook and a video that was produced to promote Hong Kong as 'Asia's World City'.

Flowerdew shows how the Hong Kong bureaucracy developed and constructed this particular view, from the generation of an initial idea through to the public presentation of this view. He also shows that while the official aim of the consultation process was to gain feedback on the proposal, it was as much designed to win over the public to this view. The public consultation document, Flowerdew shows, used a language of 'telling' rather than a language of 'asking' (or indeed consulting). The tone of the text was prescriptive in its use of the modal verb will, for example, as in *every Hong Kong resident will, HK 2030 will involve* and *This will ensure.* The voice of authority, thus, was dominant in the use of the genre and discouraged dissent from the view that it promoted.

The yearbook that Flowerdew examined extolled the virtues of Hong Kong and was overtly promotional in nature. Other voices were brought in to give authority to this view such as 'perceptions of Hong Kong internationally' and 'our review on international perspectives of Hong Kong'. Who these views actually belong to was not stated. This text, interestingly, was produced before the actual public consultation process commenced and suggests the government had already decided on the outcome of its consultation, before it had actually commenced.

The voice on the video that was examined, as with the yearbook, was overwhelmingly promotional. The difference between this and the yearbook was that the video used the discourse of advertising and public relations to make its point, rather than the discourse of bureaucracy. The video used short sharp pieces of text such as *The pace quickens* and *Horizons expand*. These statements were accompanied by series of images of technology, architecture and night-life that presented Hong Kong as a vibrant and fast-paced modern city. The mix of traditional Chinese and Western music on the soundtrack of the video gave both an Asian and an international feel to the video. The video was also produced before the public consultation actually took place. As Flowerdew points out, this is consistent with branding theory which emphasizes the importance of gaining support and the belief of the public in the promotion of a brand, or product. It is not, however, the sequence of genres that might be expected to conform with a public consultation process. Flowerdew, then, shows how the voices of three very different genres come together to impose, rather than negotiate, a certain point of view on the readers and viewers of the texts that formed part of the campaign.

5.4 Critical discourse analysis and framing

A further way of doing a critical analysis is to examine the way in which the content of a text is framed; that is, the way in which the content of the text is presented to its audience, and the sort of perspective, angle and slant the writer or speaker is taking. Related to this is what is foregrounded and what is backgrounded in the text; that is, what the author has chosen to emphasize, de-emphasize or, indeed, leave out of the text (Huckin, 1997).

Huckin (1997) looks at a newspaper report on a demonstration at a nuclear test site in the United States in just this way. Figure 5.2 is the opening section of the text he examined.

The demonstration described in this report is framed as a confrontation between the group of protesters and law-officials. The report does not discuss the issue that motivated the protest. The protesters and how many were arrested is presented to the readers. The protesters are presented negatively, as trespassers, rather than as people with a concern for the environmental future of their country. A 'police versus protesters' frame is foregrounded, and also presented, rather than the social, public health or environmental issues they are protesting about. There is much that is backgrounded, or omitted from the text. Information on nuclear testing planned for the site is left out, nor is anything mentioned of the health issues faced by people living near the site. The role of the government is also omitted from the text. The story, thus, presupposes that the most interesting and important aspect of the story is the number of protesters that were arrested, not the issues they were protesting about (Huckin, 1997).

Huckin goes on to examine topicalization in the text. As he shows, the topic of the sentences support his claim that the text is 'about' protesters versus

Nevada Officials Arrest 700 At Test-Site Gulf Protest

MERCURY, NV (AP) – More than 700 people were arrested Saturday during an anti-nuclear, anti-Persian Gulf buildup protest at the Nevada Test Site, an official said.

Thousands turned out for the demonstration. Those arrested on misdemeanour trespass charges were taken to holding pens, then transported by bus it Beatty, 54 miles north of the remote nuclear proving ground.

An Energy Department spokesman estimated the crowd at 2,200 to2,500 people. A sponsor of the protest, American Peace Test, said the crowd was 3,000 to 4,000 strong.

The turnout was one of the largest since anti-nuclear demonstrations began at the test site nearly a decade ago, but it failed to match a turnout of5,000 demonstrators in 1987, when 2,000 people were arrested on trespass charges.

The DOE spokesman, Darwin Morgan, said more than 700 people werearrested and would be released in their own recognizance.'Some of the demonstrators were a bit more aggressive, kicking at the guards when they were brought out of the pens' Morgan said. . . .

FIGURE 5.2 *A newspaper report on an anti-nuclear demonstration (Huckin 1997: 85). Used with permission of the Associated Press Copyright © 2011*

officials, not the issues that prompted the demonstration. In the following examples the topic of each sentence is in italics:

More than 700 people were arrested Saturday during an anti-nuclear, anti-Persian Gulf buildup protest at the Nevada Test Site.

Thousands turned out for the demonstration.

A sponsor of the protest, American Peace Test, said the crowd was 3,000 to 4,000 strong.

Throughout the text, it is the officials that largely have the agency; that is, it is they who initiate the action. They do the arresting and decide if the protestors will be released. The protesters only have agency when they are engaged in antisocial behaviour, such as kicking the guards.

The text is mostly written in the semi-formal register of 'objective' news reporting. Events are presented as factual, 'without the slightest trace of uncertainty'. This has the effect of making the issues that underlie the protest 'completely closed to discussion and negotiation' (Huckin, 1997: 89–90). As Huckin shows, the tactics used by the writer put a particular slant on the text and encourage the reading of the text in a particular way. Analyses of this kind, thus, aim to bring hidden meanings to the surface by unpacking the assumptions, priorities and values that underlie texts.

5.5 Critical discourse analysis and larger data sets

Much of the work in critical discourse analysis draws its discussion from the analysis of often only a few texts which have sometimes been criticized for being overly selective and lacking in objectivity. One way in which the scale of texts used for a critical analysis can be expanded is through the use of texts that are available on the World Wide Web. Using material from the WWW is not without its problems, however. It is not always possible to identify the source of texts on the web. It is also not always possible to determine which texts have more authority on a topic than others on the web. It is also difficult to see sometimes who in fact is writing on the web. Texts on the web, further, also often rely on more than just words to get their message across. Their multimodal nature, thus, needs to be taken account of in any analysis of material from the web. Texts on the web are also more subject to change than many other pieces of writing. Each of these issues needs to be considered when using data from the WWW for a critical (or indeed any kind of) discourse study (Mautner, 2005a).

The WWW has, however, been used productively to carry out critical discourse studies which draw on the strengths of the web's capacity to collect a lot of relevant data. Mautner's (2005b) study of 'the entrepreneurial university' is an example of this. Mautner did a search of the web for the term 'entrepreneurial university' to see who is using this term, what genres it typically occurs in, and how it is typically used. She used a search engine to do this as well as carried out a trawl through the websites of 30 top UK universities to find further uses of the term. She also used a reference corpus to see what words 'entrepreneurial' typically collocated with, outside of her particular area of interest.

Mautner observes that the use of the term entrepreneurial university brings together the discourses of business and economics with the discourse of the university. It is not just the newer, seemingly more commercially driven universities, however, that are doing this. The following example from the Oxford University website illustrates this:

> Oxford is one of Europe's most innovative and *entrepreneurial universities*. Drawing on an 800-year tradition of discovery and invention, modern Oxford leads the way in creating jobs, skills and innovation for the 21st century. (Mautner, 2005b: 109)

The term 'entrepreneurial university' was not, however, used positively in all the texts that Mautner examined. On occasions writers purposely distanced themselves from the term by putting scare quotes around these words. Even those who are advocates of the entrepreneurial university also showed they are aware of the potentially contentious nature of the term by adding qualifying statements to their use of it, such as 'we still care about eduction and society' and 'it isn't about commercialisation' (Mautner, 2005b: 111). Studies such as this, then, show the enormous potential of using the WWW for the critical study of the use of discourse.

5.6 Criticisms of critical discourse analysis

Critical discourse analysis has not been without its critics, however. One argument against critical discourse analysis has been that it is very similar to earlier stylistic analyses that took place in the area of literary criticism. Widdowson (1998, 2004) for example, argues that a critical analysis should include discussions with the producers and consumers of texts, and not just rest on the analyst's view of what a text might mean alone. Others have suggested that critical discourse analysis does not always consider the role of the reader in the consumption and interpretation of a text, sometimes mistaking themselves for a member of the audience the text is aimed at (van Noppen, 2004). Critical discourse analysis has also been criticized for not always providing sufficiently detailed, and systematic, analyses of the texts that it examines (Schegloff, 1997).

There have been calls for critical discourse analysts to be more critical and demanding of their tools of analysis, as well as aim for more thoroughness and strength of evidence for the claims that they make (Toolan, 1997). Others, however, have come to the defence of critical discourse analysis arguing that its agenda is important and of considerable social significance but that there are important details and arguments that still need to be carefully worked out (Stubbs, 1997).

Writers such as Cameron (2001) discuss textual interpretation in critical discourse analysis saying it is an exaggeration to say that any reading of a text is a possible or valid one. She does, however, agree with the view that a weakness in critical discourse analysis is its reliance on just the analyst's interpretation of the texts. She suggests drawing more on recipients' interpretations in the analysis and interpretation of the discourse as a way of countering this. As Cameron (2001: 140) suggests, a critical discourse analysis:

> is enriched, and the risk of making overly subjective or sweeping claims reduced, by going beyond the single text to examine other related texts and to explore the actual interpretations recipients make of them.

As she points out, all discourse and all communication is interactive, and this needs to be accounted for in the analysis.

Benwell (2005) aimed to deal with this in her study of the ways in which men respond to the discourse of men's lifestyle magazines. Drawing on a textual *culture* approach, two groups of readers were interviewed about their reading habits, practices and dispositions with reference to issues such as gender, sexism, humour and irony in articles and images in the magazines. *Conversation Analysis* and *membership categorization analysis* were used for the analysis of the data. One of the interviewees said, laughing, *Lucky this is anonymous!* when admitting that he had responded to the influence of an advertisement in a magazine and had gone and bought a skin care product, more commonly associated with women. In his hesitation in revealing this, he also showed his alignment with the constructions of masculinity promoted by the magazine as well as his affiliation with the view that '"real" men do not use grooming products' (Benwell, 2005: 164). The combination, thus, of Benwell's reading of the texts, with readers' views in relation to the texts, tells us more about the texts themselves, as well as about how many men may read them.

A further way in which critical discourse studies could be enhanced is through a more detailed linguistic analysis of its texts than sometimes occurs. Systemic functional linguistics has been proposed as a tool for one way in which this could be done (Fairclough, 2003; Martin, 2000a). Corpus approaches have also been proposed as a way of increasing the quantitative dimension of critical discourse analyses (Mautner, 2005a). Others have proposed expanding critical discourse studies by drawing on work such as schema theory and work in the area of language and cognition (McKenna, 2004).

Threadgold (2003) proposes a greater bringing together of work in the area of cultural studies with work in the area of critical discourse analysis, suggesting the issue of *performativity* (see Chapters 1 and 2 of this book) be given greater prominence in this work to give greater explanation and understandings of what people 'do' in their use of spoken and written discourse. Trautner (2005) did this in her examination of how exotic dancers do both gender and social class in their presentations of themselves to their clients. She found that gender and social class are a central feature of the interactions that take place in dance clubs. They are reflected, she found, 'in very concrete ways: in the appearance of dancers and other staff, dancing and performance styles, and the interactions that take place between dancers and customers' (Trautner, 2005: 786). The notion of performativity, thus, provides an important way for thinking about language, identity, class, social memberships and, in turn, the critical analysis of discourse.

5.7 Summary

This chapter has discussed key issues and principles in critical discourse analysis. It has given examples of studies that have been carried out from this perspective, all of which have aimed to uncover out of sight norms and values which underlie texts which are key to understanding the roles that texts play in particular social, cultural and political contexts. Suggestions have then been made for ways of doing critical discourse analysis. Criticisms of critical discourse analysis have also been discussed and ways of responding to these criticisms have been suggested.

5.8 Discussion questions

1   To what extent do you think texts reflect hidden and 'often out of sight' values? Choose a text which you think illustrates this and explain in what way you think this is done through the use of the discourse.

2   To what extent do you think that the way a text is 'framed' encourages a certain reading of it. Choose a text which you think illustrates this. Discuss framing, foregrounding, backgrounding and the presuppositions that underlie the way the text is presented to its audience.

3   Choose a text which you feel encourages a certain reading from its use of illustrations, pictures, layout and design, etc. How do you feel each of these resources aim to 'position' the reader in a particular way?

5.9 Data analysis projects

1   Choose a text which you feel would be useful to examine from a critical perspective. Analyse it from the point of view of genre and framing. Link your analysis to a discussion of how you feel the text aims to 'position' its readers. Read Huckin (1997) on critical discourse analysis to help with this.

2   Choose a text which you feel uses multimodal discourse such as layout, design and images to communicate its message to its audience. Analyse your text highlighting the ways in which it does this. Look at van Leeuwen's (2005) *Introducing Social Semiotics* for suggestions on how to do this.

5.10 Exercises

i. Textual silences

Huckin (2002), in his article 'Textual silence and the discourse of homelessness', examines newspaper reporting on homelessness in the United States. He defines textual silence as 'the omission of some piece of information that is pertinent to the topic at hand' (p. 348). One of the silences he discusses is *manipulative silences*, a strategy of deliberately concealing relevant information from readers to the advantage of the writer. The writer, thus, decides 'what to say and what not to say about the topic' (p. 356). In his study of 163 newspaper articles and editorials on this topic he found the most common themes were *causes* of homelessness, *effects* of homelessness, *public responses* to homelessness and *demographics* such as number and types of homelessness. That is, these were the topics that were foregrounded (Huckin 1997) in the texts. Topics such as treatment of the causes of homelessness, for example, were omitted, or generally 'textually silent'.

Look at the following extracts from one of the editorials Huckin analyses in his article. Which of the themes Huckin lists are represented on this text? What are some of the issues that are not mentioned, but could have been in this text?

Sunday, 3 January 1999 – Final edition
Editorial – page B6 (Editorial)

Off-Ramp Etiquette
YOU see them at the highway on- and off-ramps. These freeway destitutes, with their imploring eyes and scribbled signs of woe, make passers-by uncomfortable. 'Homeless single mom', waits at one exit. 'Need gas money' and 'Will work for food' huddle in the rain and wind at other locations. Where to stop the car, especially if you don't plan to give?

Due to a combination of necessity, pluck and success, an increasing number of panhandlers place themselves prominently in your daily path: freeway exits, the grocery store, the post office. Cruel as it sounds, don't roll down the window, salve your conscience and offer a five-spot. Give the time or money to recognized organizations catering to the homeless . . .

Saying no to the guy on the off-ramp holding a hard-luck sign and leaning on a pair of crutches may seem cold, mean-spirited. But good citizens can still give generously to a recognized shelter or food bank. Give the panhandler a coupon to a fast-food restaurant. Buy the Real Change newspaper. Some proceeds go to the sellers. That at least shows some initiative and dignity. Volunteer time at a food bank or shelter.

Give gifts that feed, clothe and attempt to break the cycle of chronic homelessness. In the long run, such acts of kindness are far more helpful and meaningful.

ii. Migration and identity

Krzyzanowski and Wodak (2008), in a chapter titled 'Multiple identities, migration and belonging', discuss ways in which belonging in relation to migration is constructed through discourse. The data they analyse is based on focus group discussions held in eight European countries (Austria, Cyprus, France, Germany, Italy, Sweden, Poland and the United Kingdom). Look at the following extracts from their data. In what way is belonging (and not belonging) constructed in their discourse? What is the point of difference between where the speaker is living and their home country in each of these extracts?

(i) And since 7 years (.) I've been standing astride, one leg here and another there. We want to be at home because we have nothing to live on, no work and here we are fine (1.0) but it is not our home, I mean, not fully ours. Not because we are not fine here but because our roots are there (.) in the Ukraine. We have friends there, a family . . . (Female speaker living in Poland)

(ii) I know my religion keeps me apart from the English people because nearly every English person was a protestant. (Female speaker living in the United Kingdom)

(iii) Having another culture is useful . . . it is important to know where one is from . . . many don't know. I like to talk about it, because if you don't know your origins and your roots, it has no sense. (Female speaker living in Italy)

(iv) Because you see other people with other ideas different from you. (Female speaker living in Italy)

iii. Gender, identity and online chat rooms

In their paper 'Constructing sexuality and identity in an online teen chat room', Subrahmanyam, Greenfield and Tynes (2004) discuss ways in which gender roles and expectations can become blurred, and indeed resisted, in online chat rooms. The following data is an example of what they term 'cyber-pickup', where one of the participants identifies a potential partner with whom they will 'pair off'. They will then go off with that person into a private instant message space.

In what ways do these extracts show resistance of traditional gendered expectations? (The numbers refer to lines from the data set. FoxyR and Breethebrat are teenage girls. DEREKH101 is a teenage boy).

210.	FoxyR:	wassssssssssup yallllllllllll
212.	FoxyR:	anybody here like 50 cent press 1234
214.	FoxyR:	1234
221.	FoxyR:	Wasssssssssssup
222.	FoxyR:	wanna chat
262.	FoxyR:	any body wanna chat with a hot chick
264.	FoxyR:	press 1234
265.	Breethebrat:	if there r any m/13/Tx in here if so im me
266.	DEREKH01:	1234
304.	FoxyR:	any body wanna chat

5.11 Directions for further reading

M. Bloor and T. Bloor (2007), *The Practice of Critical Discourse Analysis*. London: Hodder Arnold.
Bloor and Bloor's book contains many useful exercises and activities. Sample texts are drawn from history, advertising, literature, newspapers and television. Specialized terminology is explained and there is a glossary and grammar appendix which outlines systemic functional terms used in the text.

J. Flowerdew (2008), 'Critical discourse analysis and strategies for resistance', in V. K. Bhatia, J. Flowerdew and R. Jones (eds), *Advances in Discourse Analysis*. London: Routledge, pp. 195–210.
This chapter gives details of linguistic features that critical discourse analysis might examine as part of its overall project. Future directions of critical discourse analysis are also discussed.

R. Rogers (ed.) (2011), *An Introduction to Critical Discourse Analysis in Education*. Second edition. London: Routledge.
This second edition of Rogers's book contains a wide range of chapters that are useful for understanding what critical discourse analysis is and how to do it. The book explains key concepts and issues in critical discourse analysis and provides many examples of critically oriented discourse studies.

T. van Leeuwen (2008), *Discourse and Practice: New Tools for Critical Discourse Analysis*. Oxford: Oxford University Press.

This book brings together van Leeuwen's work in the area of critical discourse analysis, drawing on the work of Foucault, Bernstein and Halliday. There are examples and sample analyses in each of the chapters.

R. Wodak (2011), 'Critical discourse analysis', in K. Hyland and B. Paltridge (eds), *Continuum Companion to Discourse Analysis*. London: Continuum, pp. 38–53.

Wodak's chapter reviews current approaches and developments in critical discourse analysis. She also provides a sample study as an example of how to do critical discourse analysis.

For an extended list of references and further readings see the companion website to *Discourse Analysis: An Introduction* by Brian Paltridge: http://www.continuumbooks.com/CompanionWebsites/book-homepage.aspx?BookId=158033.

PART TWO

Analyses of institutional discourses

6

School discourse

Frances Christie and Beverly Derewianka

Introduction

School science seeks to initiate the young into an understanding of scientific knowledge and scientific methods, and this has consequences for the scientific discourses that students learn to write, for it involves learning a technical language and a set of written text types or genres which encode scientific principles and procedures. In the latter half of the 20th century various progressivist and/or constructivist pedagogies had considerable influence on the teaching and learning of science (and other subjects) in the English speaking world, with often deleterious consequences. That is because they frequently failed to develop an appropriate knowledge of science, its methods or its writing practices, leaving students unskilled. The impact of such pedagogies was still apparent in some Australian curricula at the time of writing this book, though it had also become clear that some reassessment had commenced, and that science education was being promoted in a more ordered way, at least in some states. The two New South Science school syllabus statements for school years *Kindergarten to Year 6* (New South Wales Board of Studies 1991)[1] and *Years 7–10* (New South Wales Board of Studies 2003), for example, provide evidence of a more systematic approach to the teaching of scientific knowledge, including some of its history, while they aim to develop skills said to be distinctive to the discipline. Thus, the rationale statement for the 7–10 Syllabus reads in part:

> Science provides a distinctive view and way of thinking about the world. The study of science has led to an evolving body of knowledge organized

as an interrelated set of models, theories, laws, systems, structures and interactions. It is through this body of knowledge that science provides explanations for a variety of phenomena and enables sense to be made of the biological, physical and technological world. An understanding of science and its social and cultural contexts provides a basis for future choices and ethical decisions about local and global applications and implications of science. *Years 7–10 Science Syllabus* (New South Wales Board of Studies 2003: 8).

Science deals with the phenomena of the natural world, involving careful observations of the phenomena concerned, and documentation of the methods used to make the observations, as well as conclusions reached. An important feature of science is that it builds on its traditions, so that various theories, methods and practices that have informed the emergence of science in the past are part of the knowledge that is taught and learned in its name in schools. In this sense, its knowledge structures are 'hierarchical' (Bernstein 2000: 155–74), meaning that they expand by subsuming various theories and principles, integrating these into a coherent body of knowledge having a logic and internal unity. While physics is typically cited as the paradigm case with such a knowledge structure, the other branches of science – biology and chemistry for example – function similarly. This is not to suggest that scientists all agree, or that that there are not significant issues always up for debate. However, it is to suggest that science functions with reasonably stable knowledge bases, that these are understood by members of the scientific community, and that even where scientists disagree – indeed, particularly where they disagree – they do so in the light of considerable consensus about what constitute established ideas and principles for working scientifically and for building scientific argument. Bazerman (1988) has offered an account of the history of scientific English from the 17th century on, tracing the evolution of the 'experimental article' in particular. Relatedly, Halliday and Martin (1993) discuss the emergence of scientific language in the English speaking tradition, using systemic functional linguistic theory to draw attention, among other matters, to its particular discourse features and the challenges these can pose for children learning science. O'Halloran (2007) offers a recent discussion of knowledge in science and mathematics, tracing aspects of the emergence of hierarchical knowledge structures in science.

Veel (1997),[2] reporting the findings of a genre-based study in secondary science classrooms in Sydney, argued that school science, while intimately related to science in the wider community, nonetheless differs from it. In wider contexts, including universities and and/or industrial and technological sites, science is practised, but also often challenged, as part of the process of building and applying scientific knowledge. In schools, Veel suggested, challenge is less common, and children spend a great deal of time reproducing science in their various activities, including writing. Science education is sometimes criticized for such a tendency, just as it is sometimes criticized for its apparently arcane uses of language, which can alienate, leaving students unable to access the discourses of science. While acknowledging the potential sources of difficulty, Veel (1997: 109) also noted, however, that a function of school science is that it necessarily simplifies and reduces the knowledge of science, in the interests of making it learnable by children: hence some of the genres of school science often do involve reproducing scientific knowledge and principles. Indeed, the very repetition of experimental procedures is in any case part of learning that they are replicable, and hence capable of validation, so that anyone following the same steps will get the same results, and hence reach the same conclusions. As for scientific terminology, a function of science will be that children learn to manipulate often unfamiliar technical language, as a necessary part of mastering the subject. These things are part of the process of recontextualization of knowledge that Bernstein (1990, 2000) argued is a feature of all school teaching and learning.

Veel (1997), Unsworth (2000) and Martin and Rose (2008) have all offered discussions of science genres, providing both typological and topological perspectives, and while we shall not consider all types, nor discuss those we select with the detail they employ, we shall draw on their descriptions in examining the texts we have collected, while also proposing at least two genres they do not propose. Our discussions are also informed by consultation with practising scientists, referred to below. The genres discussed are selected for their relevance in tracing the developmental trajectory involved when children learn to write science, and no attempt is made to consider all those potentially found in schools. What is constant to all the genres we shall identify in this chapter is careful attention to the study of natural phenomena, whether these are observed and recorded, experimented with, classified, described, explained or discussed.

In this chapter we shall consider *procedural recounts, demonstration genres, research articles* and *field studies,* all to do with observing, experimenting with, and documenting natural phenomena, where such phenomena are investigated either in the laboratory, or in the field. These contrast with other school genres such as *reports*, to do with classifying and describing natural phenomena, and *explanations*, to do with explaining how or why natural phenomena occur.

Though the developmental processes in learning to write science are similar, there are differences, many to do with attitudinal expression. The movement is from the congruent to the non-congruent and from the immediate and 'concrete' to the increasingly abstract. Modality emerges in late childhood to early adolescence, and modal verbs in particular occur in school science texts, involved in writing statements about the likelihood/probability of some phenomenon occurring. Many science texts, however, offer no overt attitudinal expression, and this is a principal source of difference compared with either English or history. Scientific methods and procedures require that matters be reported in a disinterested fashion, where it is the phenomenon itself that requires consideration, and the object – ideally – is to arrive at some truth in a dispassionate way. Of course, it would be false to argue that attitude and evaluative stance have no role in science writing. The decision to select one phenomenon over another for investigation in itself has some attitudinal significance, though evaluative language is nonetheless restrained. Feelings in particular are rarely expressed, even among novice writers, as children learn quite early that these are irrelevant to the meanings of science.

A topology of experimental research genres

Like Bazerman, Halliday (2004a: 145) sees 'the birth of scientific English' in the work of Isaac Newton, for example in his *Treatise on Opticks* (1704). Many of the discourse features in Newton that Halliday identifies remain evident in contemporary science writing, including the procedural recounts children learn to write. For that reason, they are worth mentioning here. Thus, Halliday notes, departing from the earlier practices of writing science found in Chaucer for example, Newton used material Processes to tell what he did (e.g. *I held/ stopped/removed the Prism*), while he used Processes of projection to tell what he found or 'observed' (*I observed the length of its refracted image to be many time greater than its breadth …*). Further, Newton used the passive voice at those points where 'the balance of the information' required that an item be placed in Theme position (*the Sun's beam which was propagated into the Room …*). Halliday suggests that the contemporary use of the passive voice favoured by science writers (in practice often not observed), is historically recent, and it was not found in Newton, for he often thematized himself. (Bazerman makes a similar observation.) Tense choices varied, involving the past, to create what Newton *did,* the future to tell what he said *will appear,* and some present tense choices to record what he said *appears* to be so. Apart from these matters, Newton used technical language, much of it built using grammatical metaphor, and while that is not a feature of the writing of young children writing science, it does emerge by late childhood to adolescence, as we have noted above. Clause complexes were 'intricate', employed in building steps taken in the experiment, reasons for these, and observations made as a result. As we have suggested in looking at developments – in the cases of stories and response genres, for example – clause complexes that are 'intricate' emerge after about the age of 8/9, becoming more varied, as children master the various clauses of expansion, as well as those of projection. They thus become a feature of children's science writing, especially from late childhood and throughout the years of adolescence, though the extent to which intricate clause relations are deployed depends on the field and the genre.

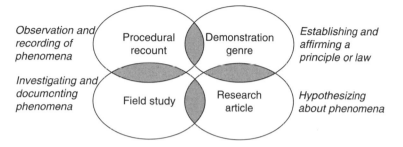

FIGURE 6.1 *A topology of experimental/investigative genres in school science*

Figure 6.1 sets out a model of the topology of these genres.

Procedural recounts, outlining an aim, a record of events observed and some conclusion, are prototypical science genres, learned in childhood and henceforth endlessly recycled by science students and scientists alike. However, by mid- to late adolescence, while procedural recounts are still employed, they are also often overtaken by developments in at least two directions. One such direction involves the appearance of *demonstration genres*, not found in Veel (1997), Unsworth (2000) or Martin and Rose (2008), which involve pursuing an experimental procedure in order to affirm a scientific principle, or even a law. No originality is claimed or sought in such a text; on the contrary, the intention is to validate, yet again, an established principle. These also outline an aim, a record of the demonstration and a discussion, where the latter affirms the principle or law. The other direction taken involves the appearance of larger genres, normally called *research articles*, which investigate by outlining background information for the study, providing an aim, a hypothesis, and discussions of results and conclusions reached (though other elements are often found).

Field studies, also not found in the genre discussions of Veel (1997), Unsworth (2000) and Martin and Rose (2008), are related to research articles, though their purposes and method are different. They are associated with several kinds of scientific studies – ecological, biological and earth sciences, to name a few – and they emerged in the 19th century in areas such as biology or geology, where investigative work in some site was required. Many of Darwin's original investigations were field studies, investigating for example the behaviour of birds and other creatures in their natural environments. Field studies involve an aim and statement of the site or context to be investigated, and an account of the procedures undertaken as part of their investigations, some of which may be experimental (e.g. testing the quality of the water in a particular location). Their object is to understand the site and its phenomena. The conclusion may recommend changes and it may also identify further problems and/or hypotheses to be explored.

While the four genres differ, they all involve some kind of problem to do with natural phenomena, and observational methods and carefully conducted procedure(s) to investigate the phenomena. Hence Figure 6.1 shows areas of overlap.

TABLE 6.1 A sample of experimental and investigative genres: procedural recounts, demonstrations, research articles and field studies

Text	Genre	Sex and age of writer
6.1 'Plants need air'	Procedural recount	Boy aged 7/8 years
6.2 'Distillation'	Procedural recount	Girl aged 12/13 years
6.3 'AC Induction Motor'	Demonstration	Boy aged 17/18 years
6.4 'First to live, last to die'	Research article	Girl aged 15/16 years
6.5 'A study of the local street'	Field study	Boy aged 8/9 years
6.6 'Mullet Creek catchment'	Field study	Boy aged 15/16 years

Table 6.1 sets out the procedural recounts, demonstration, research articles and field study to be considered in this chapter.

Procedural recounts

TABLE 6.2 Schematic structure of procedural recounts

Genre	Elements of structure
Procedural recount	Aim Record of events Conclusion

Table 6.2 displays the schematic structure of procedural recounts. The *Aim* states as clearly as possible what the purpose of the scientific experiment is to be, and it normally includes advice about materials or equipment to be used; the *Record of Events* reveals what was done in an accurate ordered way; and the *Conclusion* reveals what was established.

Texts 6.1 and 6.2, both procedural recounts, were written, respectively, by a student in early childhood, and in early adolescence. Like most genres written in school science, these texts make use of images. Traditionally, the images in science were diagrammatic, though today many types of images and diagrams are found in children's science textbooks, and they encounter various examples in websites, CDROMs and DVDs. While such images or diagrams are not necessarily the same as those in the professional publications of science, they nonetheless initiate children into many of the multimedia practices of science (Lemke 2002: 24). Images then, are very much part of the mode of communication learned and employed in writing science from the earliest years. They have an essential role in building meaning, though they are not addressed in this discussion, since our focus is on the verbal text.

Text 6.1 offers a Record and a Conclusion, revealing what has been learned or 'shown'. No aim is provided, though the title reveals the general interest. The first element identifies *materials* required, and is so labelled.

TEXT 6.1 Plants need air

Materials required	*Material: 2 pill bottles (one with a cap)*
	Beans
	Water
Record	*What we did*
	First we soaked 50 beans. Then we filled both bottles with the soaked beans and put a little water in the bottom of each.
	Next we put the cap tight on one of the bottles and left the other open. Finally we shook the water over the beans.
	What we observed
	The seeds [in the bottle with the cap off] started to sprout.
Conclusion	*Conclusion*
	Plants need air to grow.

In terms of overall textual organization, we can note firstly the series of headings (all underlined by the child), pointing directions to be taken. Under the heading *What we did,* there is a series of unmarked topical Themes, identifying class members (*we*). The pattern changes with the latter two headings, for it is the phenomena being studied that are thematized. Thus, under the heading *What we observed,* specific reference is used to identify the seeds, where an interesting early use of two embedded phrases extends the meaning:

   the seeds [in the bottle with the cap off].

Then, under the last heading *Conclusion,* the young writer uses generic reference to write of *plants* in Theme position:

   plants need air to grow,

showing he is aware he now generalizes about plants from the specific experimental activity recorded. Apart from these matters, the ordered sequence of steps in the Record is marked by a series of conjunctive relations (*first, then, next, finally*). Experientially the text uses mainly material Processes, for example:

we soaked; we filled; we shook,

and one mental Process of cognition:

we observed,

deployed much as Newton used such a process.

The same basic structure appears in Text 6.2 (whose writer was 12/13) though there are grammatical changes characteristic of a writer in early adolescence. For example, four marked Themes appear, realizing the directions taken in the experiment, and hence in the Record, while one also starts the Conclusion. Some other grammatical matters are noted below.

Where the grammar in Text 6.1 is entirely congruent, that in Text 6.2 shows non-congruent realizations. Note for example the nominal group structure:

many times of repeating this process.

The writer could have written 'After we had repeated this process many times', though the nominalization achieves a desirable outcome, in that it removes human agency, foregrounding instead the *many times* involved, making this a phenomenon of relevance to the experiment.

TEXT 6.2 Experiment: Distillation

Element of structure	Text
Aim:	*To extract oil from leaves i.e. eucalyptus oil or lemon scented tea tree oil.*
Record	*Observations:*
	After heating the contents of the flask *it started to rise and bubble (boil). We were aiming to prevent boiling, so <<**as soon as bubbles appeared**>> the Bunsen would be moved away, and so on.* **After many times of repeating this process,** *milky liquid started to drip out of the end of the condensor tube. This liquid was the lemon-scented tea tree oil, which was a milky colour. The tea tree oil had a strong scent, as it was 'lemon scented tea tree oil'.*
Conclusion	**After the condensing** *the leaves must evaporate, as the end result was free of leaves.*

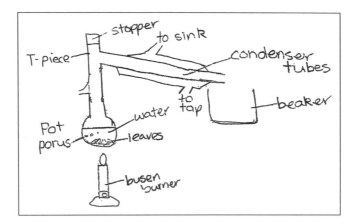

The Conclusion also involves two instances of nominalization, though the grammatical expression is rather awkward:

> After **the condensing** the leaves must evaporate, as **the end result** was free of leaves

The meaning is a little obscured here, since more congruently (and accurately) the writer actually meant: 'After the liquid had been condensed // the leaves must have evaporated // because there were no more leaves left in the condensor tube'.

Acknowledging the clumsiness of the expression, we can note that the use of *the condensing* compresses, removing human agency, while creating a phenomenon which is foregrounded. The nominalization in the last clause creates another phenomenon, *the end result*, having both temporal and causal significance.

Finally, we can note that the text is generally free of attitudinal expression.

Demonstration genres

We shall now turn to Text 6.3, an example of a demonstration, by a boy aged 17/18 and in his last year of schooling, though these can occur earlier. The text is included next because it reveals how similar many of its features are to those of a procedural recount, while it provides evidence of the developmental changes apparent in the writing of a much older student writing such a genre.

Table 6.3 displays the schematic structure of demonstrations.

The *Introduction* states the purpose of the experiment, in particular revealing the scientific principle or law which is to be demonstrated, while

TABLE 6.3 Schematic structure of demonstrations

Genre	Elements of structure
Demonstration	Introduction Demonstration record Discussion

it also indicates any materials or equipment needed; such information is typically clarified by use of a figure. In addition, it indicates the steps to be taken in pursuit of the demonstration involved. The *Demonstration Record* reveals the results obtained. The *Discussion* element discusses the result, reaffirming the principle or law that has been demonstrated.

Text 6.3 outlines an experiment demonstrating *Lenz's Law* in physics, which states that the magnetic field of any induced current opposes the changes that induced it. While the experiment is in itself simple to execute, it leads to enunciation of an abstraction: *the principle of an AC induction motor*. Such an abstraction is created using grammatical metaphor, for it depends on observing a number of events in the physical world – detailed in the text – and abstracting away from these to create a broad generalization. The language in Text 6.3 is remarkable for the absence of attitudinal expression, while there is no overt reference to the person involved in the study, a matter to which the use of the passive voice at times contributes. The effect is to foreground the phenomenon of interest. Theme choices are unmarked, and the text contains some highly abstract nominal groups.

The Introduction details the aim and the steps to be taken, while a figure is used to illustrate what is to be done. The set of steps – the *procedure* – is detailed as a series of points, using the imperative mood, and employing simple material Processes, reminiscent of the processes Halliday observed in Newton. Abstraction is introduced when reference is made to the *variables*. Things which are 'variable' are subject to change and it is important to be able to quantify the kinds of variables that may impact on a scientific experiment and its results. The very notion of a variable in this sense depends on previously established knowledge concerning what might constitute such a phenomenon. The writer of Text 6.3 thus exhibits familiarity with some reasonably abstract principles and methods, when he identifies his three variables. Effectively he defines them, for there are three implicit identifying Processes involved:

The independent variable is the direction of the magnet.

The dependent variable is the direction of movement of the plate.

The conditioned variables are the plate used, the magnet used, the wooden frame used.

TEXT 6.3 Experiment: AC Induction Motor

Introduction

Aim: To demonstrate the principle of an AC induction motor.
Method: Apparatus:

- *Horseshoe magnet*
- *Swinging plate*
- *Wooden frame for plate*

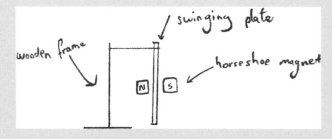

FIGURE 1 *The experimental set-up*

1 *Set up the equipment as shown in Figure.*
2 *Move the magnet quickly away from the plate, and observe and record the motion of the plate.*
3 *Move the magnet from a position away from the plate quickly towards it, to the starting position around the plate as shown in Figure 1. Observe and record the motion of the plate.*

INDEPENDENT VARIABLE: The direction of the magnet.
DEPENDENT VARIABLE: The direction of movement of the plate.
CONDITIONED VARIABLES: The plate used, the magnet used, the wooden frame used.

Demonstration record

Risk assessment: The magnet was heavy, and could be dropped on a toe. Covered footwear was used, and care was taken to reduce this risk. Also, the wooden frame consisted of a sharp, nail like object [[on which to hang the plate]]. This could cause injury, especially to the eye. To reduce this risk, care was taken.

Results:

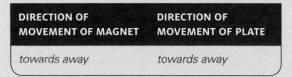

DIRECTION OF MOVEMENT OF MAGNET	DIRECTION OF MOVEMENT OF PLATE
towards away	*towards away*

Discussion	*Discussion: The experiment demonstrated Lenz's Law. The eddy current [[produced]] must have been produced in such a way [[as to oppose the motion of the magnet]].*
	The movement [[produced in the plate]] was minimal, though movement was still visible. The experiment could be Improved by increasing the strength of the magnet, or the speed [[with which it is moved]] in order to produce more movement in the plate. The experiment could also be improved by repetition.
	The principle of an AC generator was evident through the movement produced in the plate. It shows that a magnetic field can produce movement.

The Demonstration Record uses the past tense, signalling that matters are recorded after the event, and there is further compression of meaning in the nominal groups, using grammatical metaphor:

direction of movement of magnet

and

direction of movement of plate.

The notion of *risk assessment* is another abstraction. Incidentally, one practising scientist we consulted observed that a statement of risks and how they are addressed has become more commonly a feature of such genres than in the past, suggesting that it may become a recognized element of structure in the future.

Apart from these matters, there is some grammatical metaphor expressed in one Circumstance of manner, for it expresses a causal connection between events:

*The eddy current [[produced]] must have been produced **in such a way [[as to oppose the motion of the magnet]].***

More congruently this might read:

'The magnet did not move // because the eddy current opposed it.'

Finally, the Discussion uses two relational identifying Processes, among other things, to reveal what has been 'shown', and again this is reminiscent of Newton:

*The experiment **demonstrated** Lenz's Law*

and, in the last clause:

*(the movement produced in the plate**) shows [[***that a magnetic field can produce movement]].*

This is a very abstract text, marked by a level of abstraction not found in the writing of younger students, either in childhood or in early adolescence.

Research articles

Our data suggest that procedural recounts, while found in childhood, are not as common as reports, but they are the commonest of the scientific text types written in early adolescence, and they continue to be used throughout the years of adolescence. Demonstrations, such as Text 6.3, and research articles, tend to emerge by mid-adolescence. Research articles incorporate some of the elements found in procedural recounts (and indeed in demonstration genres), but they embrace a number of other elements, and they pursue those principles for mounting scientific argument, which, Bazerman (1988: 79) suggests, have been fundamental in the emergence of experimental reports or articles. Such principles constrain the manner in which the argument is constructed, so that it is a different kind of argument, for example, from that found in the expositions of history or the thematic interpretations of English. In fact the language capacities needed to write a research article, like those for writing field studies, are those that typically emerge in adolescence. They are apparent, as we noted above, both in the expansion of all resources found within clauses, and in the expanded range of clause interdependencies that develop by late childhood to mid-adolescence, contributing to the shaping of the arguments of written scientific discourse in a number of ways. There are variations in the overall structures of research or experimental articles, though some reasonably constant features emerge. The schematic structure offered here draws on the work of a group of practising scientists at the University of Technology, Sydney (personal communication), and on discussions in Martin and Rose (2008), though differing a little from that proposed by the latter. Table 6.4 displays the schematic structure we have identified.

The *Abstract* – which is optional – summarizes what is in the article. The *Introduction* explains the background to the investigation, establishing a context and the significance of the study. It normally alludes to other relevant papers, indicates why the problem is important, and outlines the aim of the particular experimental investigation, specifying the hypothesis that is to be

TABLE 6.4 Schematic structure of research articles

Genre	Elements of structure
Research article	(Abstract)
	Introduction
	Aim
	Method
	Results
	Discussion
	Conclusion
	(References)

tested by the experiment. The *Method* element details how the investigation was/is to be conducted, identifying equipment used and procedures followed, as well as any risks involved. It also identifies the observations that were to be made and how they were measured. The *Results* element identifies what was found, typically using tables, graphs, diagrams or photographs as well as the verbal text. The *Discussion* considers what inferences can be made from the data obtained, and what information can be derived from the results. It also considers new (or further) questions that emerge from the results and possible explanations. The *Conclusion* presents a summary of the outcomes of the study and their significance. The *References* element – also optional, though generally present – lists other related studies consulted.

Text 6.4, by a girl aged 15/16, is a research article, whose structure accords closely with that displayed in Table 6.3, though it shows some variations. The text is a long one (230 ranking clauses), and it was presented on a series of 12 large boards mounted in the classroom, in the manner of poster displays at the conferences professional scientists attend. The student had been asked to design and implement a research investigation, following procedures taught by her teacher, a fact made evident by the fact that all her fellow students followed similar procedures for designing and writing up their investigations, though there was considerable variation in their choices of problems examined (others included, for example, a test for measuring hearing loss in people of different ages, and a test of the water-holding properties of a number of brands of balls used in playing softball).

We shall make selective use of the text, commencing with the opening element, the *Aim*. Headings and sub-headings function as part of the textual metafunction, shaping and giving directions to the discourse. Topical Themes, with one exception, are unmarked, and their function is to facilitate the unfolding of the text and, in the first paragraphs at least, they identify algae or some features of them. The opening paragraphs are in one sense grammatically simple, in that they are built using a number of simple clauses, a number not conjunctively related: their complexity resides in the dense nominal groups in which participants are expressed. By contrast, the latter part of this element shows grammatical intricacy, in that it uses a number of interdependent clause complexes.

We should note, before displaying the text, that the student was wrong when she said that an alga is a 'single celled' plant. There are, in fact, many single-celled algal species, though many others are multicellular and therefore macroscopic, for example, the giant kelps. Furthermore, the 'black algae' she refers to may have been moulds, and therefore fungi, rather than algae. It is probable that the teacher corrected these errors, though we have no information about that.

Of the large nominal groups deployed, some identify, as in the opening clause with its relational identifying Process:

The aim is [[to determine //which household or pool products affect //and kill black-spot algae // and to determine // if the pool product [[we are currently using]] is the most effective and efficient // to kill all the algae.]]]]

while others describe:

This form of Algae is very slow growing but very hardy.

Other Processes are existential, whose function is also to identify, though in a different sense:

there are 30,000 different varieties of algae [[all containing chlorophyll]]

TEXT 6.4 First to live, last to die

Introduction/ Aim   *INTRODUCTION*
Aim: The aim of my Science Experiment is [[to determine //which household or pool products affect //and kill black-spot algae // and to determine // if the pool product [[we are currently using]] is the most effective and efficient // to kill all the algae.]]]]

Black-Spot Algae:
An alga is a microscopic single celled form of plant life which may be introduced into the water by wind and rain from the atmosphere. There are 30,000 different varieties of algae [[all containing

chlorophyll]]. They are one of the hardiest and most widespread living organisms on this planet. Black-Spot Algae is a formation of 1 to 3cm sized black (or dark blue-green) spots, which attach and adhere to pool surfaces. Black-Spot Algae form a layered structure, where the first layer (which chlorine may kill) protects under layers from further destruction. Black-Spot Algae are similar to the black Algae [[that is found on bathroom shower tiles and in silicone seams near the bath]]. It is also found in aquariums as dark blotching on the glass sides. This form of Algae is very slow growing but very hardy. It is extremely chlorine resistant.

HYPOTHESIS

<u>My hypothesis may be biased</u> as I already know the effectiveness of the pool products from past use in the pool, so they would already appear to be the most efficient. However, I believe that bleach would be more effective and I'm not completely convinced the pool products are the most successful.
I believe either Pool Clear Acid or Bleach will have the most effective impact on the algae's growth.
I believe these two products will be the most effective as acid creates such an uninhabitable environment for algae, and bleach is proven to kill algae and grime in bathrooms and laundries.

OUTLINE

In order to determine what kills blackspot algae the best and to verify my hypothesis I chose 5 different chemicals. These products included three pool chemicals and two household chemicals.
I also decided to check four environmental factors [[which may impact the growth and life of Algae]]. I thought I would test these environmental factors in an effort [[to understand //why our Spa does not have Blackspot algae //and the Pool does, //even when the chlorine level in both is the same.]] The only obvious difference is [[that the Spa is much hotter //and has a cover on most of the time.]]

TEXT 6.4—Cont'd

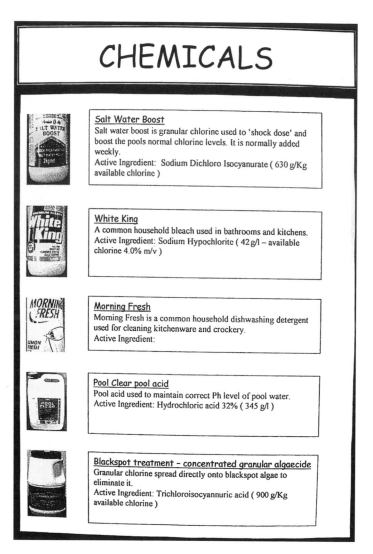

CHEMICALS

Salt Water Boost
Salt water boost is granular chlorine used to 'shock dose' and boost the pools normal chlorine levels. It is normally added weekly.
Active Ingredient: Sodium Dichloro Isocyanurate (630 g/Kg available chlorine)

White King
A common household bleach used in bathrooms and kitchens.
Active Ingredient: Sodium Hypochlorite (42 g/l – available chlorine 4.0% m/v)

Morning Fresh
Morning Fresh is a common household dishwashing detergent used for cleaning kitchenware and crockery.
Active Ingredient:

Pool Clear pool acid
Pool acid used to maintain correct Ph level of pool water.
Active Ingredient: Hydrochloric acid 32% (345 g/l)

Blackspot treatment – concentrated granular algaecide
Granular chlorine spread directly onto blackspot algae to eliminate it.
Active Ingredient: Trichloroisocyannuric acid (900 g/Kg available chlorine)

TEXT 6.4—Cont'd

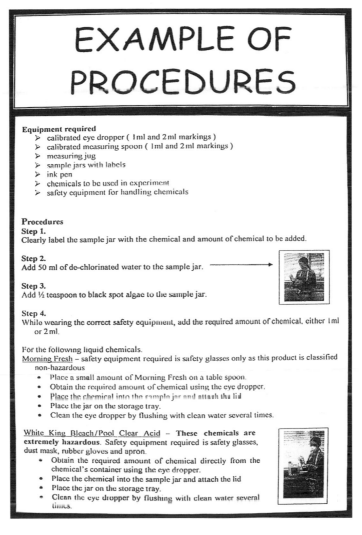

EXAMPLE OF PROCEDURES

Equipment required
➢ calibrated eye dropper (1 ml and 2 ml markings)
➢ calibrated measuring spoon (1 ml and 2 ml markings)
➢ measuring jug
➢ sample jars with labels
➢ ink pen
➢ chemicals to be used in experiment
➢ safety equipment for handling chemicals

Procedures
Step 1.
Clearly label the sample jar with the chemical and amount of chemical to be added.

Step 2.
Add 50 ml of de-chlorinated water to the sample jar.

Step 3.
Add ½ teaspoon to black spot algae to the sample jar.

Step 4.
While wearing the correct safety equipment, add the required amount of chemical, either 1 ml or 2 ml.

For the following liquid chemicals.
Morning Fresh – safety equipment required is safety glasses only as this product is classified non-hazardous
• Place a small amount of Morning Fresh on a table spoon.
• Obtain the required amount of chemical using the eye dropper.
• Place the chemical into the sample jar and attach the lid
• Place the jar on the storage tray.
• Clean the eye dropper by flushing with clean water several times.

White King Bleach / Pool Clear Acid – **These chemicals are extremely hazardous.** Safety equipment required is safety glasses, dust mask, rubber gloves and apron.
• Obtain the required amount of chemical directly from the chemical's container using the eye dropper.
• Place the chemical into the sample jar and attach the lid
• Place the jar on the storage tray.
• Clean the eye dropper by flushing with clean water several times.

Grammatical metaphor is frequently used to create the nominal groups building phenomena of various kinds, some expressed as the technical language of science. Possible congruent realizations are also displayed.

In all such cases the nominalized expressions, when realized more congruently, lead to clause complexes in which actions are expressed in verbal groups, while conjunctive relations between clauses are rendered explicit. Grammatical metaphor has a particular role in creating the technical language characteristic of scientific English (Halliday and Martin 1993). The writer of Text 6.4 shows herself well in control of many of the features of scientific English in building the technical language and/or the abstractions in

Non-congruent expression	Congruent realization
They are **one of the hardiest and most widespread living organisms on this planet.**	Algae are very hardy //and they live very widely on this planet.
Black-Spot Algae is **a formation of 1 to 3cm sized black (or dark blue-green) spots, which attach and adhere to pool surfaces**.	Black-Spot Algae consist of black or dark blur-green spots that are 1 to 3 cm long, // and they attach and adhere to the surfaces of pools.
It is also found in aquariums as **dark blotching on the glass sides**.	It also appears in aquariums// where it grows in blotches on the glass sides.

which it is expressed. But there are other ways in which the writer displays a control of the written language, found particularly in the clusters of clause interdependencies used.

Thus, echoing some of the features of Newton's language, the section devoted to the *Hypothesis* uses mental processes and various dependent clauses of enhancement, involving reason, result, purpose and time, all of them involved in building meanings relevant to the hypothesis involved. An opening clause is followed by two dependent clauses as shown:

> *My hypothesis may be biased*
>
> **as I already know the effectiveness of the pool products from past use in the pool** (clause of reason)
>
> **so they would appear to be the most efficient**. (clause of result)

Then the writer proceeds, using projecting mental Processes and another one of reason:

> *However, I believe //that bleach would be more effective*
>
> *and I'm not completely convinced //the pool products are the most successful …*
>
> *I believe // either pool Clear Acid or Bleach will have the most effective impact …. I believe // these two products will be the most effective*
>
> *as acid creates such an uninhabitable environment for algae* (clause of reason)

The *Outline* of the method is then introduced, using a clause of purpose in marked Theme position:

> **In order to determine // what kills blackspot algae the best // and to verify my hypothesis** // *I chose 5 different chemicals,*

while later clauses include two more of projection, the first of which reads:

> **I also decided** //to check four environmental factors [[which may impact the growth and life of Algae]],

and the second involves quite an intricate example of grammatical metaphor expressed in a Circumstance of purpose, in which several clauses are embedded:

> **I thought** I would test these environmental factors **in an effort [[to understand //why our spa does not have blackspot algae // and the pool does // even when the chlorine level in both is the same.]]**

Congruently this would read:

> 'I thought
> I would test these environmental factors
> because I wanted to understand
> why our spa does not have blackspot algae
> and why the pool does,
> even when the chlorine level in both is the same.'

The metaphor is useful because human agency is removed in the wording of the Circumstance.

In Appraisal terms, the hypothesis section is of interest as well. Where the opening of the element is largely free of attitudinal expression (though expressions like *very slow growing* or *extremely chlorine resistant* show intensity, building emphasis, hence high Graduation), this section offers some Appreciation of the writer's own action in hypothesizing, where a reservation is openly acknowledged:

> *My hypothesis may be biased as I already know ...,*

and a degree of negative Appreciation of the effectiveness of the pool products:

> *I'm not completely convinced the pool products are the most successful.*

Later elements show a table detailing observations made at intervals in the experimental phase, displayed here, and other matters not displayed. One small section from the Results element is displayed for its interest in terms of how the observations made are recorded. Here the grammatical intricacy noted by Halliday in Newton's work is again evident. The opening clause (using a causative Process) establishes 'what was observed', while the subsequent sets of interdependent clauses build their meanings by weaving various equal and dependent clauses.

SAMPLE OF DATA

Experiment observations
Chemicals - Variable 1 ml
NOTE: Algae appearance before chemicals added was dark green

Time period	Salt Boost	Black spot treatment	Pool Clear pool acid	White King bleach	Morning Fresh
1 minute	algae yellow to white, granules dissolved	Granules not dissolved, algae sitting on top of granules	Algae went light brown instantly	Light fading of algae	No colour change
4 hours	All algae white	All algae white, granules not dissolved	Algae light brown	Algae white, larger pieces green in centre	Algae light green
Day 2	All algae white	All algae white, granules not dissolved	Algae light brown	Algae white, larger pieces green in centre	Algae light green
Day 4	All algae white, algae breaking down	All algae white, algae breaking down, granules dissolved	Algae light brown	Algae white, flaky Only a little green in centres	Algae light green
Day 6	Algae white, flaky	Algae white, flaky	Algae brown, larger pieces olive green in centre	Algae white, flaky Only a little green in centres	Algae olive green
Day 8	Algae white, flaky	Algae white, flaky	Algae brown, larger pieces olive green in centre	Algae white, flaky Only a little green in centres	Algae olive green
Day 10	Algae white, flaky	Algae white, flaky	Algae light green	Algae white, flaky Only a little green in centres	Algae olive green
Day 12	Algae white, flaky, some clear flakes	Algae white, less flakes	Algae green, some dark green	Algae white, flaky Only a little green in centres	Algae light brown
Day 14	Algae white, flaky, some clear flakes	Algae white, less flakes	Algae mostly dark green, looks like its recovering	Algae white, flaky Only a little green in centres	Algae light brown

After outlining the results the student provides a Conclusion. In fact, the Conclusion is quite cleverly shaped, drawing on all the resources of Theme (some marked, and realized in dependent clauses), modality, several dense nominal groups (some metaphorical) realizing phenomena discussed, and a range of transitivity choices, and clause types, alluded to below. The writer offers some Appreciation of her findings, for though her hypothesis was *incorrect,* she had established *the most important thing [[I learnt from my experiment]].*

TEXT 6.4 — Cont'd

Results
(extracts only)

The Black Spot Algaecide:
The algaecide [[used for this condition]] caused a gradual but consistent deteriorating effect on the algae]]. **Once the chemical reacted with the algae //** *it lost all colour, // broke down, // and died, // which left sediment at the base of the container.* **At the end of the observation period** *the algae had died off // and didn't make a recovery.*

Conclusion
(extracts only)

After reviewing the results of my observations *it would appear [[that the Salt-Boost Chlorine and the Black-Spot Treatment Algaecide are the most effective products //to kill Black-Spot Algae // and ensure // they don't re-grow.]]*

. . . .

Hypothesis Review:
Despite the fact [[I could have based my hypothesis on previous information and past experience with the pool products]], *I believed other chemicals may have been more effective. My hypothesis [[that Pool Clear Acid or White King Bleach would have the most effective impact on the algae's appearance and growth]] was incorrect.* **As it turns out**, *the two chlorine based pool products were the most effective although the other products [[used]] still impacted the algae's health to some degree.*

. . . .

The most important thing [[I learnt from my experiment]] is [[Blackspot Algae is tough stuff to kill]]. The acid had a pH of less than 0.5, a concentration of between 8 and 17 grams/litre. Most life cannot survive in this environment but the algae re-generated. The cold, dark or heat did not kill it in the periods [[tested]]. It survived the bleach and dishwashing liquid as well.
This showed me why the alga was one of the first life forms on the planet Earth. It also proves to me that algae will also survive long after most species of life are long extinct.

Three topical Themes are significant in shaping the directions of the argument here, the first realized in a dependent clause of time, alluding in summary way to what has been observed:

After reviewing the results of my observations *it would appear [[that the Salt-Boost Chlorine and the Black-Spot Treatment Algaecide are the* *most effective products //to kill Black-Spot Algae // and ensure // it doesn't re-grow.]],*

the second expressed in a Circumstance of concession, alluding to the hypothesis, now disproved:

Despite the fact [[I could have based my hypothesis on previous information and past experience with the pool products]], *I believed other chemicals may have been more effective,*

while the third, realized in a clause of manner, alludes to what has been achieved:

as it turns out, *the two chlorine based pool products were the most effective although the other products [[used]] still impacted the algae's health to some degree.*

Most transitivity choices are relational in this element, realizing statements of what is the case, though two verbal Processes project:

*This **showed** me //why algae was one of the first life forms … It also **proves** to me // that algae will survive ….*

Various dense nominal groups identify phenomena, some used in relational Processes that appraise the qualities of phenomena, expressing some Appreciation:

The two chlorine based pool products *were the most effective,* **the most important thing [[I learnt from my experiment]]** *is* **[[Blackspot Algae is tough stuff [[to kill]]].**

Text 6.4 has many of the characteristics of a successful student in mid-adolescence in writing science, though the errors about algae we have alluded to were unfortunate.

Field studies

Table 6.5 reveals the schematic structure of field studies, though like research articles, these can vary. In the school science program, field studies are typically undertaken in ecological endeavours of some kind, tracing the relationships between biological and environmental factors. They are found in environmental science and geography. The *Introduction* provides background information about the field, as well as sources of concern or problems.

TABLE 6.5 Schematic structure
of field studies

Genre	Elements of structure
Field Study	(Abstract)
	Introduction
	Field features
	Results
	Conclusion
	(References)

It reveals what is to be investigated and why this is important. The *Field Features* element provides information about the field site, for example, natural environmental factors, or the impact of human activity, recording what is observed. The *Results* discusses the matters observed and recorded while the *Conclusion* rounds things off, normally making recommendations for action. The *References* element indicates sources of information used to inform the study. Like the research article, a field study seeks to investigate and record scientific phenomena, and while some implicit hypothesis may be involved, the object is not primarily to test any hypothesis, but to amass information that might provide a basis for future actions, including proposing hypotheses for further testing.

We shall briefly examine Text 6.5, a simple field study undertaken by a boy aged 8, included here as early evidence of the emergence of field studies. The boy had been asked by his teacher to investigate his own community, identifying and observing sources of environmental pollution, and any items that could be recycled. Text 6.5 was set out as a series of steps in a power point presentation. Extracts only are displayed. The text records observation of data, the making of some predictions over what is observed and some discussion. While the child offers occasional Judgement about people:

people shouldn't leave the autumn leaves,

The text is largely free of attitudinal expression, while the recording of observations, predictions, results and explanations all reveal an attempt to record matters in an objective fashion.

While the language is reasonably simple, characteristic of a child of 8, it is interesting that he makes use of several dependent clauses, employing them to weave together steps in the way he reasons about phenomena:

Everything was left by people even the natural things// **because people should get their droppings in bags** (clause of reason) // **to throw away** (clause of purpose)
They should put them on the garden // **to save water**. (clause of purpose)
The tissue is gone // **because they fall apart easily**. (clause of reason)
It hasn't rained yet // **so the river is still okay**. (clause of result)
Car oil spills. Still there // **because it didn't rain**. (clause of reason)
I think a chain would be good [[to have]] // **so I don't know //** *why nobody took it.* (clause of result)

TEXT 6.5—Cont'd

Field
features

Investigation
First I checked my street for pollution and drew a map in a notebook
Next I listed natural pollution and pollution left by people

NATURAL	LEFT BY PEOPLE
Autumn leaves	Tissues
	Petrol caps
	Car oil spills
	Plastic bag
	Concrete lump
	Apple core
	Scraps of foam
	Metal chain
	Bottle tops
	Drink bottle
	Lollipop stick

Everything was left by people even the natural things because people should get their droppings in bags to throw away. Another thing is [[people shouldn't leave the autumn leaves]]. They should put them on the garden to save water. That is called mulch.
Next I made predictions about [[what will happen to the rubbish]].

- *Tissue. This will rot away when it rains.*
- *Petrol cap. I will keep it I think for a souvenir.*
- *Car oil spills. Rain will wash the oil to the river and hurt pneumatophores.*
- *Plastic bag. The bag says biodegradable but it doesn't work. It is supposed to go back to nature.*
- *Concrete block. Maybe the garbage men will take it.*
- *Apple core. Birds and ants will eat it.*
- *Metal chain. Maybe it could lock up a motorbike. Bottle tops. Maybe someone will put it in the bin. Drink bottle. Same.*
- *Lollipop stick. Same.*

Results	**_Testing Predictions_**
	After two weeks I looked all round the street again. These things had changed.

- Tissue. Gone.
- Car oil spills. It hasn't rained yet so the river is still okay.
- Plastic bag. The biodegradable bag is still there
- Concrete block. Gone.
- Apple core. Gone. I think the birds and ants liked it.
- Metal chain. Still there.
- Bottle tops. Gone.
- Drink bottle. Gone.
- Lollipop stick. Gone.

Conclusion	**_Explaining what occurred_**
	The tissue is gone because they fall apart easily.
	I took the petrol cap.
	Car oil spills. Still there because it didn't rain.
	Plastic bag. I think it doesn't work.
	Concrete block. Taken by garbage truck.
	Apple core. Gone. I think the birds and ants enjoyed it.
	Metal chain. I think a chain would be good to have so I don't know why nobody took it.
	Bottle tops. People tidied up.
	Drink bottle. People tidied up.
	Lollipop stick. People tidied up.

Text 6.6, written by a boy aged 16, is a more mature instance of a field study. It is quite long (1527 ranking clauses) and was written in geography. It records a field study of the *Mullet Creek Catchment*. The creek involved, incidentally, is to be found near the Australian city of Wollongong, where some of the texts used in this book were collected. We shall examine the opening element, in which the writer provides some background information about the physical site and a statement of the aim of the investigation. Several quite dense nominal groups (some involving grammatical metaphor) are used to identify phenomena and/or entities of interest, and while several clauses are relatively simple, such as the first, which creates a single sentence, others are deployed in clause complexes relevant to building aspects of the problem or of the aim.

One marked Theme (expressed in a grammatical metaphor) establishes reference to previous events, realized in a Circumstance of time:

Before human invasion, *this ecosystem was unspoiled,* while another, realized in two dependent clauses of concession, acknowledges previous useful activity:

> **while some problems have been recognized** (clause of concession)
> **and (while) some improvements have been made by Wollongong City Council** (clause of concession)
> *more needs to be done.*

The third marked Theme introduces a clause complex in which two dependent clauses of purpose and a clause of result express the aims:

> *During a fieldtrip on Thursday 2nd June, tests were carried out*
> **in order to describe current conditions at Mullet Creek,** (clause of purpose)
> **and (in order to) identify the impacts of human activities** (clause of purpose)
> **so that extra management strategies could be formulated and recommended.** (clause of result)

TEXT 6.6 Mullet Creek Catchment (extract only)

Introduction

Introduction

Mullet Creek Catchment is the heart of the water flow of the Illawarra region. Spread across the catchment is a diverse environment, where many natural processes occur. **Before human invasion**, *this ecosystem was* <u>unspoiled</u>. *Human activities have had some* <u>very negative</u> *impacts on the catchment and its natural processes.* **While some problems have been recognised, and some improvements have been made by Wollongong City Council,** *more needs to be done.* **During a fieldtrip on Thursday 2nd June**, *tests were carried out in order to describe current conditions at Mullet Creek, and identify the impacts of human activities so that extra management strategies could be formulated and recommended.*

Location *(see Figure 2)**
The Mullet Creek Catchment is located on the south coast of NSW in the Illawarra district. It spreads through the entire Illawarra area. The site [[where the tests were carried out]] was at the Canoe Club, William Beach Park, in Brownsville, near Dapto.

The Catchment
The Mullet Creek catchment covers an area of 73 square kilometres and spreads from sea level on the shores of Lake Illawarra, all the way up to over 570 metres high onto the Illawarra Range. The upper reaches of the catchment are subject to very intense rainfall.

---

* Not reproduced.

The writer shows skill in creating an Introduction that establishes aims and purposes for the field study, where these include establishing problems needing attention and some value positions about the propriety of addressing these. The directions to be taken in later elements are thus clarified. The directions are then pursued in the Field Features element (the longest in the text), in which the student outlines information about the *Natural environment* (*habitat survey, water quality* and *soil quality*) *Human impacts (erosion, recreational activity, agriculture, residential impacts* and *vegetation*). An extract shows how the writer shapes the directions taken.

Three marked Themes are used, the first of which is realized in a dependent clause of concession:

> ***Although the right side (north side) of the creek scored well in all the sections, with good, dense vegetation cover,*** *the left side (south side) of the creek was shocking,*

the second in a dependent clause of manner:

> ***As shown in the field sketch*** *(see Figure) there is a huge man-made rock retaining wall on the left bank, ensuring that the bank remains stable,*

and the third in a Circumstance of manner:

> ***Instead of the natural vegetation,*** *there is only a field of kikiyu grass which borders onto a road, making both Bank Vegetation and Verge Vegetation, as well as Bank Erosion and Stability, poor.*

Table 6.6 giving the *Habitat Survey Text Results,* is one of three such tables in the text, the others to do with recording measures of water and soil quality. These involve use of scientific methods to arrive at the data, so that the student reveals familiarity with established procedures, learned at some earlier point, and utilized here in the field study. A developing maturity in understanding scientific procedures and the language in which to construct them is thus evident in this writer.

Two further extracts from the Field Features element will be displayed, the first of which is selected because it provides a *factorial explanation* outlining causes of a phenomenon (similar to the factorial explanation genres). Its presence provides further evidence that by mid- to late adolescence young people often show considerable facility in deploying a range of grammatical resources to control written English for subject science, including embracing more than one genre type within their written texts. Thus, the first paragraph reveals the phenomenon involved:

> *Agriculture is one of the major land uses,*

and it is said to *have a significant impact on the creek and its ecosystem.* Subsequent paragraphs go on to explain the nature of the impacts – or factors involved. These are signalled very clearly using textual Themes (*firstly, secondly, thirdly,* and *fourthly*).

The final extract we shall display from this element, addresses *Management Strategies* and a *Conclusion* follows this. The discussion of *Management Strategies* begins with a claim that there are several ways that *negative human impacts* can be addressed, while the writer goes on to itemize possible steps for *Rehabilitation.* Here negative Appreciation of the impacts of human settlement is indicated, while Judgement is expressed about what has been done in terms that state that *more will be needed.* These sections of the text are indeed the most opinionated and judgemental.

TEXT 6.6—Cont'd

Field features
(extracts only)

Natural Environment

The natural environment of William Park Beach and the Mullet Creek Catchment is unique. There are many segments of the environment which contribute to the delicate biodiversity of the area.

Habitat Survey

TABLE 6.6 Habitat survey test results

Test	Left Bank Score	Right Bank Score	Overall Score
Bank Vegetation	2 (poor)	6 (fair)	4 (poor)
Verge Vegetation	2 (poor)	6 (fair)	4 (poor)
In-stream Cover	2 (poor)	8 (good)	5 (fair)
Bank Erosion and Stability	1 (poor)	8 (good)	2.5 (poor)
Riffle, Pools and Bends	3 (fair)	3 (fair)	3 (fair)
TOTAL SCORE	10 (very poor)	31 (good)	18.5 (poor)

*The Habitat Survey was carried out on the bridge, looking down at the creek, facing west toward the weir and the golf course. **Although the right side (north side) of the creek** <u>scored well</u> **in all the sections**, **with** <u>good</u>, **dense vegetation cover,** the left side (south side) of the creek was <u>shocking</u>.*

As shown in the field sketch (see Figure)*, there is a huge man-made rock retaining wall on the left bank, ensuring that the bank remains stable. This structure had to be constructed as the ground on the left bank is <u>bare</u> of natural vegetation, making it <u>vulnerable to erosion</u>. **Instead of the natural vegetation**, there is only a field of kikiyu grass which borders onto a road, making both Bank Vegetation and Verge Vegetation, as well as Bank Erosion and Stability, <u>poor</u>.

The In-steam Cover and Riffles, Pools and Bends both <u>rated fairly</u>. The right side of the stream had good In-Stream Cover, making up for the lack of it on the left side. There were some small bends and riffles along the creek also, ensuring a <u>fair rating</u> for that section.

---

* Not reproduced.

Field features
(extract only)

Agriculture
Agriculture is one of the major land uses of the land in and around the catchment area. **As mentioned above**, the weir and irrigation have had a large impact, let alone the paddocks surrounding the area. **Near the Canoe Club,** there were several paddocks to harbour introduced species (mainly cows and horses) These paddocks and their occupants have a significant impact on the creek and its ecosystem.

Firstly, a great amount of native vegetation has had to have been cleared to make space for the paddocks. The removal of native flora would destroy the homes and food source of some of the smaller organisms in the area. **With fewer plants and trees in the area around the creek**, the soil would suffer dreadfully, and this lack of plants may be one of the sources of the lack of stability in the creek bank and the large amount of erosion.

Secondly, the introduced animals themselves could do great harm to the natural environment. The creatures would not only graze and interfere with the native plants, but at the same time be competitors for native fauna for food.

Thirdly, fertilizers used for agriculture could cause problems. As the fertilizer is placed directly onto the soil, it is quite easy for it to infiltrate the ground or become run off during the next rainfall. Fertilizer could make its way into the creek, and pollute it even more.

Fourthly, pesticides used for agricultural benefits will have negative effects. Pesticides kill not only pests, but native organisms as well. They can also easily intoxicate the creek, wreaking havoc on the ecosystem.

It is apparent that modality, attitudinally coloured lexis and other resources help build the overall values to do with environmental conservation. Thus, after identifying possible *Management Strategies*, the writer moves to establishing what should be done, using modality to express Judgement about desirable behaviours people should pursue:

> *A number of strategies **must** be used to improve the quality of the Mullet Creek Catchment and its environment*

As the element unfolds, strategies such as *weed removal* are outlined, and the writer draws his account of these matters to a close by again expressing Judgement:

> *but more is needed to make a significant difference.*

He then goes on to outline several possible steps for education, using modality and introducing Judgements about the values of these:

> *Firstly signs **could** be erected around the creek........*

> *Secondly, public meetings **could** be conducted, where environmental officers **could** educate the people of the uniqueness of the area and [[how they can care for it]].............. . .*

TEXT 6.6—Cont'd

Field features
(extract only)

Management strategies

There are a number of ways in which some of the <u>negative</u> human impacts mentioned above can be reduced. <u>A number of strategies must be used to improve</u> the quality of the Mullet Creek Catchment and its environment. Wollongong City Council have already started some programs, <u>but more will be needed</u>. These will benefit both the flora and fauna, as well as local residents.

Rehabilitation

Rehabilitation is <u>essential</u> for improving conditions at Mullet Creek. Firstly, **<<as the Bank and Verge Vegetations scored badly in the Habitat Survey (see Figure 3)>>** <u>something must be done to improve native vegetation. Weeds must be eradicated from the area so that new, native vegetation can be planted. The weeds should be removed carefully, preferably manually, as chemicals would harm the native flora that is already in the area.</u>
After weed removal, <u>the original plant species must be planted back into the area, in the correct numbers. The plant locations should be as close to [[how they were originally]] as possible.</u> **As the plants grow**, they will encourage native creatures back into the area. The roots will also improve soil and bank stability, lowering erosion. Deep rooted plants will also keep the water table down. There is already some revegetation happening around the area, near the large meander, <u>but more is needed to make a significant difference.</u>

> ## TEXT 6.6—Cont'd
>
> ### Education
> It is <u>essential</u> that the local community is aware of Mullet Creek and its unique ecosystem. Many residents are already <u>harming the creek unintentionally</u> through activities such as car washing. The education could take various forms.
> <u>Firstly, signs could be erected around the creek. These signs could both encourage people not to litter and to mind where they step, as well as informing them of the natural beauty and complex ecosystems in the area.</u>
> <u>Secondly, public meetings could be conducted, where environmental officers could educate the people of the uniqueness of the area, and [[how they can care for it]].</u>
> <u>These strategies would raise the much needed awareness [[that Mullet Creek requires]] so both local and visiting people can appreciate the Catchment without harming it.</u>
>
> **Conclusion**   The Mullet Creek Catchment is a complex ecosystem [[consisting of many types of plants and animals]]. <u>There are many human activities which occur in and around the catchment which have negative effects on it.</u> However, management strategies are being devised, so that the creek can become a <u>cleaner and healthier</u> place, benefiting both the local ecosystems and the local community.

The Conclusion opens with a relational clause of attribution which establishes an important characteristic of Mullet Creek Catchment:

> *Mullet Creek Catchment is a complex ecosystem [[consisting of many types of plants and animals]]*

while an existential clause then introduces a clause complex elaborating on this, using two dependent (non-defining relative) clauses:

> *There are many human activities // which occur in and around the catchment // which have negative effects on it.*

Finally, a further series of interdependent clauses constructs the writer's last observation, indicating grounds for optimism:

> *However, management strategies are being devised,* ***so that the creek can become a cleaner and healthier place*** (clause of result)
>
> ***benefiting both the local ecosystems and the local community.*** (clause of result)

A very short bibliography is attached to the field study, not reproduced here. An overall strong value position about the importance of conserving environmentally sensitive areas is established in Text 6.6, making it rather different from the other texts reviewed in this chapter. Such attitudinal expression is more common in texts of environmental science than in the others discussed.

Lexical density in the experimental/ investigative genres

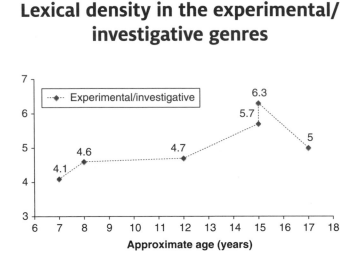

FIGURE 6.2 *Lexical density in a sample of experimental/investigative science genres*

Figure 6.2 displays the lexical density for the texts we have discussed in this chapter, arranged with respect to age. The three texts of childhood to late childhood (Texts 6.1, 6.2 and 6.5) all have densities of 4 or more, so that they show greater densities than do the stories and response genres by children of comparable ages. Beyond about the age of 11 or 12, so our texts suggest, the density increases, hovering between 5 (as in Text 6.3) by a student aged 17/18, and 6.3 (as in Text 6.4) by a 15/16 year old. Science texts, on this sample, are reasonably dense, even in the earliest years.

Conclusion

Experimental and investigative science genres are important text types for children in childhood and adolescence, for they encode fundamental scientific principles that shape a great deal of scientific knowledge and activity. The procedural recount represents the prototypical experimental genre, learned in childhood and early adolescence, and remaining important throughout adolescence, though by mid- to late adolescence it is often subsumed into the research article and/or the demonstration genre. The field study, more common in adolescence than childhood (though we did consider an early instance) has elements similar to the other genres, and its principal characteristic is that it amasses significant information about some scientific phenomenon so that it can be used to inform possible future scientific endeavour. In general, experimental/investigative genres have restrained attitudinal expression, though field studies sometimes express values. In terms of language development, the first science texts are expressed congruently, shifting towards greater abstraction after early adolescence, when the resources of grammatical metaphor and an expanded range of clause interdependencies in particular open up new areas of meaning making for apprentice scientists.

Notes

1 At the time of writing this book, this syllabus was undergoing review: http:// news. boardofstudies.nsw.edu.au/index.cfm/2007/3/15/K6-Science-and-Tech nology-syllabus-review-set-to-commence (accessed 15 November 2007).

2 The results of the study discussed by Veel are also reported in Korner, McInnes and Rose 2007.

7

Small talk at work

Almut Koester

7.1 Introduction

The important role played by relational talk and interpersonal elements of language in workplace discourse, despite its overall focus on transactional goals, has already been highlighted throughout this book. This chapter focuses specifically on relational talk in the workplace, paying particular attention to small talk and the use of humour.

The traditional dichotomy between transactional or task-oriented talk and relational talk (or 'phatic communion') has been challenged by a number of recent studies into the use of small talk in workplace and institutional settings (Holmes 2000a, McCarthy 2000, Ragan 2000, Koester 2006). While Malinowski (1923/1972) contrasts phatic communion 'used in free, aimless, social intercourse' (1972, p. 149) to more purposeful types of interaction, these studies have shown that relational talk is far too prevalent to be considered marginal in the workplace. Moreover, it is not possible neatly to separate talk that is purely instrumental from talk that has a relational or social purpose. Holmes identifies a continuum of task-orientation in interactions from the Wellington Language in the Workplace Project, with 'core business talk' and 'phatic communion' at opposite ends of the continuum, and 'work-related talk' and 'social talk' in between. In my own work investigating the ABOT corpus, I have proposed that relational talk can be found at various 'levels' of discourse from extended non-transactional conversations to shorter exchanges or sequences occurring during transactional talk: (see Koester 2004 and 2006):

1   non-transactional conversations: office gossip and small talk

2   phatic communion: small talk at the beginning or end of transactional encounters

3   relational episodes: small talk or office gossip occurring during the performance of a transactional task

4   relational sequences and turns: non-obligatory task-related talk with a relational focus

In some encounters at work, participants do not orient to any workplace concerns, and such interactions are referred to as 'non-transactional conversations'. The term 'phatic communion' is used here to refer not to relational talk in general (as Malinowski does), but in a more restricted sense, following Laver (1975), to ritual exchanges and small talk at the beginning and end of encounters. But in addition to taking place at the 'edges' of an encounters (where it most typically occurs), relational talk can also occur as a 'relational episode', which interrupts the performance of a transactional task. Non-transactional conversations and relational episodes can involve either 'office gossip' or 'small talk'. Office gossip is not task-oriented, but consists of talk about some aspect of the workplace, for example colleagues and events at work. Small talk addresses topics outside the workplace, such as the weekend and holidays, or family and friends. In this chapter, however, the term 'small talk' is mainly used in its broader meaning as a synonym for 'relational talk', in keeping with its general usage in much of the literature on relational talk.

Relational sequences and turns are woven into task-oriented talk, and, as corpus analysis reveals, are used in ways specifically adapted to the workplace context. Even relational talk which may seem quite extraneous to the business at hand, may ultimately serve transactional goals, as found for example by Coupland (2000) and Ragan (2000) in two different health care contexts (geriatric and women's health respectively). In interactions between health care providers and patients, small talk and humour were found to facilitate treatment and patient compliance, and therefore ultimately to serve a medical goal.

Further support for seeing relational talk as central, rather than peripheral, to workplace interactions comes from outside discourse analytical research. In Wenger's (1998) community of practice framework, relational aspects are considered to be an integral part of the practice. In describing the job of claims processors in a health insurance company, Wenger asserts:

Their practice ... makes the job habitable by creating an atmosphere in which the monotonous and meaningless aspects of the job are woven into the rituals, customs, stories, events, dramas, and rhythms of community life. (1998, p. 46)

His ethnographic work in this workplace setting revealed the importance of the employees' relationships with one another: they were aware of their interdependence in getting the job done efficiently and making it more meaningful and enjoyable (ibid., p. 47).

Moreover, among the list of 'indicators' which provide evidence of the existence of a community of practice, Wenger (ibid., p. 125) highlights both workplace relationships and relational talk and humour:

- 'sustained mutual relationships – harmonious or conflictual'

- 'local lore, shared stories, inside jokes, knowing laughter'

Holmes and Marra (2002) and Holmes and Stubbe (2003, pp. 122–133) use a community of practice framework to investigate humour and workplace culture. Holmes and Marra (ibid.) list two more of Wenger's indicators as particularly relevant for examining spoken interaction in general, and humour in particular:

- 'shared ways of engaging in doing things together' (Wenger 1998, p. 125)

- 'certain styles recognized as displaying membership' (ibid., p. 126)

By comparing humour across a number of dimensions in four different workplace settings from the Wellington Language in the Workplace Project, Holmes and Marra identify differences in workplace culture in the four communities of practice. Their study indicates that examining key components of discursive practice, such as humour, can reveal ways in which communities of practice can differ from one another and develop their own distinctive cultures. Comparing relational talk across different workplace settings can also give an indication of differences in workplace culture between communities of practice, as explored in this chapter by examining relational talk in the ABOT corpus.

Far from being 'purposeless', then, relational talk performs important functions in the workplace, and the chapter begins by discussing and exemplifying some of the different 'work' that such talk performs. A comparative overview of relational talk in different office settings in the ABOT Corpus then provides an indication of some of the ways in which discursive practices and workplace culture can differ.

The second part of the chapter looks more closely at humour in the workplace, reviewing studies of humour in a number of organizational settings. Holmes and Marra's (2002) comparison of the way humour is used in four different workplaces is reviewed in some detail, and the chapter concludes with an analysis of the types and functions of workplace humour found in the ABOT Corpus.

7.2 'Work' done through relational talk

Most studies agree that small talk is used in workplace contexts to perform a range of types of face work (Coupland and Ylänne-McEwen 2000, Holmes 2000a, Holmes and Stubbe 2003). In my work on data from the ABOT Corpus (Koester 2004 and 2006), I distinguish between 'solidarity' and 'politeness' functions performed by the various types of relationally oriented talk listed above. Holmes and (2000a) and Holmes and Stubbe (2003) find that small talk is frequently used to 'do collegiality', but that it can also be used to 'do power'. Thus, while managers may use small talk as a way of reducing the social distance between themselves and their subordinates, they can also exercise their power by deciding when and for how long small talk takes place.

Relational talk also contributes to forging a sense of group identity and building social cohesion (Eggins and Slade 1997, Poncini 2002 and 2004, Pullin Stark 2007). This function of small talk is particularly foregrounded in multi-national work groups or business interactions, where there is no pre-existing group allegiance, and a group identity must first be built, as illustrated in Poncini's work. Eggins and Slade (1997) show that there is also a 'darker', coercive side of small talk, as it can be used to negotiate group alignments around difference as well as solidarity, including out-groups as well as in-groups. They analyse interactions of male factory supervisors in Australia during their lunch break, and show how, through small talk, group alignment is negotiated around cultural values, such as ethnicity and gender. The dominant members of the group are able to set the agenda for the values of the group, which include, in this instance, misogyny, machismo and a particular view of what it means to be Australian (ibid., pp. 116–168). Two specific functions of relational talk are discussed in more detail here: relationship-building and identity work.

7.2.1 Relationship-building

Small talk of course contributes to relationship-building between co-workers, business partners and service providers and recipients in relation to service encounters. In the ABOT Corpus, small talk was particularly frequent between colleagues who had developed a close relationship (Koester 2006), and the few encounters between complete strangers contained little relational talk.[1]

Relationship-building in action can be seen particularly clearly in the occurrence of phatic communion – the ritual exchanges and small talk at the beginning and end of encounters. Far from being trivial, Laver (1975, p. 233,) asserts that phatic communion reveals 'the cumulative consensus about a relationship reached as the result of repeated encounters between the two participants' and that it 'constitutes the essence of that relationship' (see Koester 2006, pp. 57–58). This is illustrated nicely in some encounter-final phatic communion that occurred in the office of a printer between the office manager, Val, and a visiting platemaker, Gary, who does regular work for the company. Example 7.1 below shows the end of a discussion about a printing job and a fairly abrupt switch to relational talk occasioned by Val patting Gary's stomach (he is standing near her chair):

Example 7.1

(1) Val ⌊Well from *our* point of view, we need to get it mo:ving, because … he wants delivery … by a certain *da:y.* an' he's not approved the artwork, so …

(2) Gary Pa:r for the course. ⌊ isn't it.

(3) [Val pats Gary's stomach]

(4) Gary Leave my stomach alone!

(5) Val (Heheheh)

(6) Gary Took a lot of time, … cultivating that,

(7) Val ⌊ to build that up,

(8) Gary Longest pregnancy in history. I've got,

(9) Ally [chuckles]

　[3]

(10) Val Is it the beer,

　[5]

(11) Gary No comment.

(12) Val No comment. Okay.

　[2]

(13) Gary On the grounds it might incriminate me.

This good-natured teasing seems surprisingly intimate for a workplace relationship, particularly as it involves physical contact; but it seems clear that for the participants no boundaries are over-stepped. What this phatic communion seems to be doing is signalling that the relationship is so well-established that such intimacy is permitted.

Phatic communion occurring 'at the boundaries of interactions' is the most typical kind of small talk at work (Holmes and Stubbe 2003, p. 90); however, it is not present in every encounter. Colleagues who work together closely can often dispense with opening and closing routines, especially if they work in the same physical space. According to Laver (1975), speakers *do* engage in phatic communion when the roles they will play in the encounter are not clearly defined in advance. Evidence from the ABOT Corpus suggests that what is also important is whether or not the speakers' *relational* roles are well-established. In the few encounters between strangers (all service encounters), there are few phatic exchanges, with participants simply enacting their pre-established transactional roles of server and servee.[2] Close colleagues, on the other hand, do not need to preface all encounters with small talk, as they already have an established relationship. However, when people do not work together on a regular basis, they need to spend more time on building their relationship when they do meet up; and it is in encounters between people in this group that phatic communion occurs most in the corpus. One striking example of this is a service encounter involving a meeting between a supplier and customer, where the small talk at the beginning and end of the meeting takes up 18 and 8 turns respectively. In contrast, phatic communion between co-workers frequently consists of quite short sequences, sometimes just a single adjacency pair.

7.2.2 Identity negotiation

Relational talk can also be seen as a site for identity negotiation. In workplace interactions, speakers frequently make relevant other identities besides their institutional identities (Schenkein 1978, Greatbatch and Dingwall 1998, Benwell and Stokoe 2006), and both longer and shorter stretches of relational talk provide an opportunity for negotiating alternative identities. Gary, the platemaker, from example 7.1 above, makes such an alternative identity particularly clear when he introduces a joke by saying:

Example 7.2

Anyway, ... I'm not really a plate supplier, I'm a *joke* supplier.

By contrasting his institutional identity ('plate supplier') with a jocular alternative identity of 'joke supplier', he simultaneously provides an account for introducing a longer small talk sequence in which jokes are exchanged, and legitimates a relationship with his interlocutors which goes well beyond that of a purely transactional one.

Shorter relational sequences are frequently used during transactional talk to negotiate particular identities in relation to a task at hand. For example, in interactions where the institutional relationship is asymmetrical (e.g. manager-subordinate), more symmetrical identities may be negotiated (see Koester 2006, pp. 155–157). This may be a useful way of dealing with a problematic situation, as in example 7.3 below. Here Chris, the head of a small American advertising company, is having a meeting with his sales manager, Joe:

Example 7.3

1. Chris   Haven't seen much in the way of *sales* the last half of the week.

2. Joe   .hh Well, a lot of the media, the– the orders have been *very* difficult getting out. Stuff is– is jammed.

3. Chris   Oh they didn't go out?

4. Joe   *Yeah*. Jane's orders are *clog*ged. And … trying to get out hehch

5. Chris   └ Heheh   └ clogged orders!

6. Joe   Clogged orders! .hh they can't get out o' the system.

7. Chris   ⌊Oh no!

Chris begins by invoking his institutional identity as Joe's boss, and therefore as someone who is in a position to criticize the performance of Joe's sales team. However, Joe then slips into a joking frame by talking about 'clogged orders' in order to provide an account for the low level of sales, and Chris affiliates with him and joins in the joking. In doing this, he sets himself on a more equal footing with Joe, enabling him to back down from the 'authoritarian' identity just invoked, thus perhaps mitigating any face-threat implied in turn 1 with the direct reference to problems for which Joe is responsible.[3] Relational sequences can also reinforce, rather than downplay, institutional roles, for example when a manager, Ben, checks whether the new employee he is training is coping:

Example 7.4:

Ben   Alright, but you're sort of– getting the … getting the drift of it yeah,

By expressing concern for the employee, Ben invokes an identity as a responsible manager who cares about his staff.

Identity negotiation of course also takes place as part of transactional talk (see Cook-Gumperz and Messerman 1999). In fact, Tracy and Naughton (2000) suggest that both transactional and relational talk can be analysed in terms of 'identity work', and that this is a more fruitful endeavour than trying to distinguish between the two kinds of talk. Such an approach brings into focus the key group and professional identities that can be negotiated through seemingly marginal non-task chat or comments. For example, in analysing meetings of hospice workers, Tracy and Naughton (ibid.) found that third-party comments about patients, such as 'she's a dear soul' (p. 77), are used to construct an identity of staff as caring and concerned professionals.

7.3 The role of relational talk within a community of practice

In addition to examining the functions relational talk performs, it is also interesting to consider the role it plays within a community of practice. As discussed at the beginning of this chapter, relational talk is seen by Wenger (1998) as an important aspect of a community of practice. This section compares relational talk across the different workplace settings which provided the data for the ABOT Corpus, drawing on transcribed data, interviews and ethnographic observation. The aim of this comparison is to ascertain whether differences in the nature and frequency of relational talk, as well as participants' views about small talk, can provide any insights into the practices of the different workplace communities.

The composition of the ABOT Corpus is useful to review the various workplace settings from which the data were collected, in order to contextualize the discussion of the different communities of practice. The following workplaces in Britain and the North America were included in the study (see also Koester 2006, pp. 29–30):

1 Universities:

   ● British: departmental office for undergraduate administration and teaching

   ● American: graduate school office for postgraduate administration and teaching

2 Publishing:

   ● British: editorial office for English Language Teaching (ELT)

   ● American: editorial office for ELT

3 Private commercial sector:
British:

- Paper supplier: branch office selling (mainly on the telephone) to wholesalers and printers

- Printer: small printing company specialized in printing labels. Recordings made in the office, which dealt with orders for printing jobs.

American:

Advertising: a small family business selling specialist advertising to businesses (mainly on the telephone) in the form of postcards. Recordings made mainly in the office of the president

Food retailer: the back office of a co-operative selling organic food

In comparing relational talk across these settings, I consider the various types of relational talk detailed above, from more extended office gossip and small talk to shorter relational episodes. In addition, I draw on interviews with at least one main participant in the interactions recorded in each setting. Two of the interview questions related to small talk:

1 How often do you engage in small talk?

2 What role do you think small talk has in your work?

This is supplemented with my own participants observation based on one to several days spent in each of the workplace settings.

While relational talk occurred in all the office settings, there were substantial differences in the amount and nature of the small talk and other relational talk that occurred. The differences observed in the data and from participant observation seem to correlate with what interviewees said about small talk.

In some of the workplaces, participants engaged in quite extended small talk and office gossip, whereas in others there were few extended episodes, but frequent short relational sequences, for example in the form of banter and teasing. Overall, there was more extended relational talk in the university and publishing offices than in the workplaces in the private commercial sector (with the exception of the food cooperative). It is likely that this is linked to the nature of the work in commercial settings, where people are working to short-term targets, involving, for example, selling on the telephone, as in two of the settings. This is confirmed by comments made during the interviews, for example the office manager of the printing firm acknowledged the role that small talk plays in 'creating bonds', but said there wasn't much time for it. In contrast, one of the two secretaries working in the British university office, in which the most extended relational talk was recorded, said that up to 100 per cent of all talk might be relational, when they were not busy (whereas at busy times it would only be 0–10 per cent).

However, the lack of extended small talk did not mean that there was little relational talk. In the sales office of the British paper supplier (in which most recordings were made in the main open plan office where reps were selling over the phone) no extended small talk between reps was recorded, but there was very frequent banter and teasing, which seemed to form an integral part of the workplace culture. In fact, a number of the workplaces seem to have incorporated such humorous banter into their workplace practice. This cut right across workplace sectors, as, in addition to the paper supplier, the American editorial office, the British university office and the food retailer all exhibited such a teasing, jocular culture to a greater or lesser extent. This is nicely illustrated in the following exchange from the British university office, where one of the secretaries, Liz, interrupts a conversation Susan is having with a colleague, Fiona, to announce that she is going to take some money to the finance office. This leads her colleague, Susan, to tease her about getting mugged because she is carrying so much cash on her, and Liz to joke about making off to the airport with the money:

Example 7.5

(1) Liz	Excuse me please … I ha– I'm going to Finance.
(2) Susan	Right.
(3) Liz	If I'm /going today/
(4) Susan	Do you want a big envelope to put all that *in*.
(5) Fiona	/???/
(6) Susan	⌊ So you don't get mugged on the way up
(7) Liz	Am I going to get mugged on the way to Finance?
	Will anybody mess–
(8) Susan	⌊Won't if you do that. But you might do if you– don't.
(9) Liz	Nobody'll mess with me.
[...]	
(10) Liz	I'm going to Finance the time is now … ten … twenty:::
(11) Susan	six
(12) Liz	six seven eightish
(13) Susan	If you are not back by … ten … forty =

(14) Liz   = I'm at the airport. 'Cause that's where I'll be.

[Fiona and Susan laugh]

(15) Susan   You won't get very far on that. It's Stoke on Trent again,

(16) Liz   [leaving office] Isn't that /another/ country?

(17) Susan   Right. I'll come with you then hehe!

(18) Liz   ⌊ Hehehe!

In offices where there were interactions with customer or visitors, as well as with colleagues, it is interesting to compare the amount of small talk that occurred with each type of interlocutor. The only extended small talk or office gossip in both British companies (the paper supplier and the printer) occurred with visitors to the office. This was also the case for the American university office, in contrast to the British one, where small talk was frequent between close colleagues as well as with students, academic staff or other visitors coming into the office. This may have been due to the very close relationship the two secretaries, Liz and Susan, sharing the departmental office in the United Kingdom university seemed to have developed. However, the overall greater amount of relational talk with visitors and customers compared to that between colleagues in many of the settings confirms the importance of phatic communion for relationship-building when the relationship is not so well-established, as discussed above. That this was also recognized by the participants themselves was apparent in some of the interviews. The main speaker recorded in the American university office had the job of 'staff assistant', and was the first point of contact for anyone coming into the office with an enquiry. He remarked that students who came in were often worried about something, and that small talk was important to help put them at ease. Both the branch manager and his deputy, the office manager, of the paper supplier commented in their interviews on the importance of small talk with customers, saying that it was important for 'relationship-building' and to 'get to know customers'. They both seemed to see relational talk as an essential part of their workplace practice, and the branch manager elaborated on this in some detail in relation to a phone call he had just had with a customer on the phone:

Example 7.6

I mean that was [name], I mean I've known the guy twenty years, I know he's just come back off holiday, I know he's been to Scotland, you know; and I'll rib him, I mean I probably would have done ... more with him today– than I did today, but normally I just 'Hey what you doing up in Scotland, it's cold up there!' Uhm ... But I mean I know about him, I know his– his kids and, I mean *that's* the sort of relationship we– and quite often I can phone him up and go 'We are dead quiet down here', uhm … 'Do your old mate a favour, any orders that you'd normally give to, you know, Fred Bloggs and Joe Soap, sling them my way this week cause we're …' And you get *that* close to your customers …

The interviews showed that relational talk is seen as integral to the speakers' workplace practice to varying degrees: Some saw it as an important component of their work practice, for example the managers of the paper supplier, as shown above. Others considered it more as ancillary to the main business of work, saying, for example, that it made work more enjoyable or 'humanized' it. Again, there did seem to be a link between the frequency of relational talk and how important it was considered to be. In the British university office, in which there was a great deal of relational talk, one of the secretaries remarked in her interview that not only was small talk important to get to know the people she worked with, but that something might 'come up' during small talk which was relevant for a workplace task, such as finding the solution to a problem. In the back office of the food co-operative, where people worked in a cramped open plan office, there was a great deal of office gossip and small talk between co-workers from desk to desk, often across partitions. The two people who were interviewed (the finance manager and the bookkeeper) both accorded considerable importance to relational talk. The bookkeeper said that it was one reason people stayed a long time: 'you can make friends and have a good time'; and the finance manager felt that it helped people function in a tightly cramped space.

The combined evidence from the recorded data, the interviews and participant observation point to a clear link between the frequency and nature of relational talk and workplace culture. Individual relationships of course also play a role, and relational talk seems to occur particularly frequently between colleagues who have developed a close working relationship, such as the departmental secretaries. A particularly striking example of this occured in the American editorial office, between an editor, Paula, and her assistant, Rob. These two kept up a constant banter, typically involving good-natured teasing and mock confrontation, even when fully engaged in a workplace task, as illustrated in example 7.7, where they argue about who should deal with the payment of a research fee for a book:[4]

Example 7.7

(1) Rob   Why don't you do it.

(2) Paula   Honey …

(3) Rob   It's your book. [1] Hehehe

(4) Paula   It's ... *your* project.

(5) Rob   [Name of book] is my project? One eight hundred... alive and well I'm living in ... dream land.

(6) Paula   ⌊Hehhehe

(7) Paula   Oh, just *do* it.=

(8) Rob   =I'll give you the name and number. *You* deal with it.
[...]

(9) Paula   *Pa:y* it and be done with it.

(10) Rob   ⌊I have to call her I guess anyway and tell her– but I mean you call her and tell her we're paying it.

(11) Paula   ⌊↑No *you.*=

(12) Rob   =*I*'ll call and tell her we're paying it.

(13) Paula   Um ...

(14) Rob   [laughing] Professionalism at work. No ↑*you you you.*

Their joint practice is distinct from that of their colleagues, but it seems to flourish as a result of a general fostering of relational talk and humour in this community of practice. That this was the case is corroborated by a comment made by another editor during her interview: she remarked that the editor-in-chief took time to make small talk with the people who worked for her.

7.4 Humour

As the discussion so far has shown, much relational talk in the workplace involves the use of humour. Humour clearly plays a role in workplace interaction and has been examined in a number of studies both within organizational studies (Collinson 1988, Ackroyd and Thompson 1999, Taylor and Bain 2003) and sociolinguistics/pragmatics (Holmes 2000b and 2006, Holmes and Marra 2002, Pullin Stark 2007 and 2009). This section reviews some key finding from studies of workplace humour, focusing in particular on the functions it performs in workplace contexts and what it can reveal about workplace culture.

Interactive humour in social and workplace settings can include a wide range of linguistic and discursive activities, including personal anecdotes, jointly produced narratives, word-play and punning, teasing, joking about an absent other and self-denigration (Norrick 1993 and 2003, Boxer and Cortés-Conde 1997, Ackroyd and Thompson 1999, Norrick and Chiaro 2009). What counts as humorous is obviously dependent on contextual factors, such as setting, participants and culture (Norrick 1993), but a key characteristic is that humorous contributions are intended to be amusing or perceived as amusing by at least one of the participants (Holmes 2000b).[5] Holmes (ibid.) points out that the role of the analyst in interpreting an utterance as humorous is also important, and that laughter may be an important clue to humour, although it is not essential, and may have other functions as well.

Looking at humour as collaboratively constructed, Holmes and Marra 2002 (and Holmes 2006) distinguish between two different types and styles of humour:

1 Type of humour: supportive versus contestive

2 Style of humour: collaboratively constructed humour versus competitive (or minimally collaborative) humour

The distinction between supportive and contestive humour is based on the pragmatic orientation of its content: supportive humour agrees with or elaborates on previous contributions, whereas contestive humour disagrees with or challenges earlier propositions (Holmes and Marra 2002, pp. 1687–1688). The style of the humour refers to the way humour is discursively constructed, thus collaboratively constructed humour displays tightly integrated contributions (e.g. using echoing and utterance completion); competitive humour is characterized by loosely linked one-off quips (ibid, pp. 1688–1690).

Humour has also been found to perform a range of functions, which overlap to a great extent with those of relational talk in general: solidarity and relationship-building (Boxer and Cortés-Conde 1997, Hay 2000, Holmes 2000b), identity functions (Boxer and Cortés-Conde 1997, Hay 2000) and power (Hay 2000, Holmes 2000b). The role of humour in gender construction in both social and workplace settings has also been the topic of research (Hay 2000, Kotthoff 2000, Holmes et al. 2001, Holmes 2006, Schnurr and Holmes 2009), and some differences in the way humour is used by men and women have been identified. Looking beyond the immediate discourse at the broader social context, Eggins and Slade (1997, p. 159) assert that humour and teasing are used too convey the norms and values of the group.

Turning specifically to humour in the workplace, there seems to be a general consensus that humour may be broadly supportive or broadly contestive (e.g. Holmes 2000b, Holmes and Marra 2002, Pullin Stark 2009). Within organizational studies, the consensual role of humour has been emphasized, often being viewed as a 'safety valve' – as a way for employees to 'let off steam' – and as a tool for reinforcing corporate culture (Rodrigues and Collinson 1995, p. 739). Similarly, humour in health-care contexts has been also found to have a positive effect in interactions between health-care professionals and their patients as well as among medical staff (Ragan 2000, Åstedt-Kurki and Isola 2001). Humour can facilitate difficult or unpleasant medical procedures or examinations, for example by helping patients to relax, thus contributing to the achievement of medical goals (Ragan 2000). Rodrigues and Collinson (1995) challenge this view of organizational humour as primarily promoting harmony, arguing that workplace humour can also be oppositional and function as a tool for employee resistance. In a similar vein, Taylor and Bain (2003) examine subversive humour in call centres, showing how humour was used instrumentally in one call centre as a deliberate strategy to undermine management authority and campaign for unionization. Holmes (2000b) and Holmes and Stubbe (2003) found that humour is used both to 'do collegiality' and to 'do power', and as a subversive strategy 'to mask risky negative messages' (Holmes and Stubbe 2003, p. 117) which challenge authority.

Here the focus is on the role of humour within a workplace community of practice. I first review Holmes and Marra's (2002) study on humour and workplace culture in different types of organizations in the Wellington Language in the Workplace Corpus; and then examine the types and functions of humour found in the ABOT Corpus.

7.5 Humour and workplace culture

Holmes and Marra (2002) use a communities of practice framework to explore differences in workplace culture in four organizations from the Language in the Workplace Database. The data consist of at least two larger meetings from four contrasting workplaces:

- a factory (FAC)
- a private commercial organization (PRI)
- an organization from the voluntary 'semi-public' sector (SPU)
- a government department (GOV)

Holmes and Marra (ibid.) compared the amount of humour occurring in each of the meetings, as well as the type and style of humour (see section 7.4 above). Instances of humour were most frequent in the factory and least frequent in the semi-public organization as shown below in Figure 7.1:

Most ←——————→ Least

FAC, PRI, GOV, SPU

FIGURE 7.1 *Amount of humour by workplace (Source: adapted from Holmes and Marra 2002, p. 1694)*

The results for humour type (supportive versus contestive) showed that supportive humour was more frequent in all the settings except the PRI organization, where more contestive than supportive humour was used. The most supportive humour occurred in the SPU organization, where supportive humour was three times as frequent as contestive humour.

Two aspects of humorous contributions were examined when comparing style of humour: (1) whether it consisted of single quips or comments or extended sequences and (2) whether it was more collaborative or competitive. In the white-collar settings (PRI, GOV and SPU), extended sequences were more frequent than in the factory. This was largely due to the structure of the FAC meetings, where the manager was the main speaker, and any contributions from the floor were limited. Collaborative humour was more frequent than competitive humour in all the settings, but competitive humour occurred more frequently in PRI and FAC organizations than in the other two. A difference can be observed, therefore, between the private and public or semi-public organizations, where there is considerably less competitive humour.

Holmes and Marra (2002) conclude that the combined effect of the patterns identified for the use of humour provide insights into the workplace culture of each community of practice. Moreover the findings from the comparative analysis of humour correlate with other aspects of workplace practice identified, for example, through ethnographic observation. The way in which each team 'does humour' is indicative of how the participants construct their collegial relations within each of the workplaces. The factory team, for example, was a very cohesive group, which was mirrored in its use mostly supportive humour. In contrast, in the commercial team (PRI), members worked more independently from one another, which seemed to correlate with their more contestive use of humour. Holmes and Marra speculate that the contestive nature and competitive style of humour in PRI may well be a reflection of the more individualistic values of this organization, in contrast to the public (GOV) and semi-public (SPU) organizations, where humour was predominantly supportive and collaborative. The SPU meetings contained the fewest instances of humour of the four data sets, which was probably due to the fact that this team, which consisted of regional managers, did not meet very frequently, and therefore the participants did not know each other as well as in the other teams. However, these meetings contained three times as many supportively and collaboratively constructed sequences as competitive and contestive ones, which reflected the overall harmonious nature of the interactions, and clearly contributed to cementing relationships.

7.6 Humour in the ABOT Corpus

Holmes and Marra's (2002) study illustrates the kind of insight that can be gained into workplace communities of practice by comparing humour across different organizational settings. In this section, we continue exploring the use of humour across different workplaces by examining the different types and functions of humour found in the ABOT corpus. The focus is on the functions that humour performs as part of workplace practices, and findings from a comparative analysis of humour according to variety (British and American), gender and speaker relationship (manager or subordinate) is also reviewed. The analysis comprises all instances of humour identified in transactional as well as relational encounters, but particular attention is paid to the role of humour in transactional talk.

As the discussion above of relational talk in the ABOT corpus has shown, much relational talk involves the use of humour, but humour also occurs during transactional talk. I examined 60 instances of humour in the corpus: 30 from British and 30 from American data, which includes the majority of all instances I was able to identify in the fully transcribed corpus. These instances of humour were from 38 conversations involving 27 different speakers, and included the following types of humour:

1 situational humour

2 teasing

3 self-deprecation

4 word play and punning

5 amusing narratives or funny anecdotes

6 joke-telling

Situational humour 'is a play frame created by the participants, with a backdrop of in-group knowledge' (Boxer and Cortés-Conde 1997, p. 277). It is thus different from telling an amusing narrative or a joke, which are quite conventionalized forms of verbal performance. Teasing and self-deprecating (or self-denigrating) humour are both forms of situational humour. However, whereas teasing and self-deprecating (or self-denigrating) humour require the 'butt' of the joke to be present, other types of situational humour do not. Teasing is humour directed at other participants, whereas self-deprecating humour directed at the speaker. Besides teasing and self-denigrating humour, Boxer and Cortés-Conde (1997) identify a third type of situational humour: joking about absent others. This involves not only joking about people who are not present, but any joking that does not make any of the participants the subject of the play frame. This form of humour is often used to bond with other participants as part of an in-group, over against a joked-about out-group; and Boxer and Cortés-Conde therefore include word play and punning in this category. I have retained the label 'situational humour' for this type of joking, and identify word play and punning as a separate category. Situational humour is thus the most general category, involving quips or comments arising out of the situation; whereas teasing, self-deprecation and word play and punning are all more specific sub-types of situational humour.

These types of humour all performed a variety of functions, which can be grouped into the following five categories:

1   identity: building a positive identity

2   defending: defending own positive face

3   solidarity: showing convergence

4   mitigating : negative politeness

5   criticizing: showing divergence

According to Boxer and Cortés-Conde (1997, p. 282) 'identity display' and 'relational identity display' are the two most important functions of humour. Identity display involves the performance or 'display' of individual identities, whereas relational identity display involves the negotiation of identity in relation to others. In my categorization, the identity function (category 1) is restricted to humour which presents a positive self-image, and this is frequently performed through funny one-liners, jokes or humorous anecdotes. While 'defending' also involves identity negotiation (see ibid., pp. 284–286), it is considered as a separate function here, as it was extremely frequent (the second-most frequent after solidarity). This function is most typically performed through self-deprecation. Categories 3 to 5 all involve relational identity display, that is they involve some kind of relational 'work' vis à vis other participants. Solidarity is often shown through agreement, appreciative laughter, but also through teasing, as this is a way of displaying the closeness of a relationship. Humour can also have a negative politeness function as a device for mitigating an imposition, such as a request or a question. Finally, 'criticizing' is the functional label used for humour which shows divergence by exercising power, contesting power or simply disagreeing. This category includes all instances which, based on the situation, *could* be covert criticism: sometimes it is obvious that criticism is intended, but other instances could simply involve good-natured teasing. Teasing can involve 'bonding' or 'biting', as Boxer and Cortés-Condé (ibid.) point out. There is thus a fine line between humour that is aggressive and humour that mitigates or projects solidarity, and it is not always possible to disambiguate these two functions. Moreover, humour may be multi-functional, and a humorous comment can perform more than one of the above functions simultaneously. 'Mitigation' can also be considered to be a more general function of humour, for example criticisms are frequently couched in humour in order to mitigate their force. Here, 'mitigating' refers to a more restricted function, and only includes instances of humour used for negative politeness, for instance in mitigating the imposition of a sales visit to a customer (see example 7.17).

The different types and functions of humour in the corpus are illustrated with some selected examples below.

7.6.1 Situational humour

In example 7.8, the secretaries of two different departments in a UK university discuss how to resolve a mix-up with the phone bills of their respective departments. In the context of this discussion, one of them quips:

Example 7.8

Jane: Now which ones the less, 'cause we'll have the lesser one [chuckles]

This is an example of a funny 'one-liner' (the humour is not taken up, or even acknowledged, by Jane's counterpart), and it seems to perform an identity function of self-presentation, whereby Jane projects a positive identity of herself as a person with a sense of humour.

7.6.2 Teasing and self-deprecation

In some sense all humour is situational, but more specific categories (as listed above) are also found. A common adjacency pair found in the corpus is teasing – self-deprecation (or vice versa), for example in another interaction between the two secretaries, Liz and Susan, already encountered in example 7.5 above:

Example 7.9

(1) Liz   Is that your stomach again.

(2) Susan   Ha! ... (Hehe) .hh I'm gonna go chirp ... chirp cheep cheep cheep in a minute.

Here Liz teases Susan about her grumbling stomach, which considering the close nature of their relationship, is most likely to be a sign of solidarity, and Susan responds with self-deprecating humour, as a way of defending her positive face.

Teasing in this example is a good-natured bonding device, but teasing can also have the opposite function (divergence) and show a critical stance. In example 7.10, Paul, the office manager of the British paper supplier reprimands a sales rep for getting the amount of an order wrong, but uses humour in doing so:

Example 7.10

Paul: Yeah. Your ten and a half thousand sheet order for um ... /Phoenix./ It was two and a half thousand sheet.

            [...]

Sam: No? He said ten– *ten an' half*. That's what he said to me.

Paul: An'– I– I'll find you some cotton buds soon, all right,

Paul's joking comment, that he will get some cotton buds for his sales rep so he can clean his ears, is clearly meant as a criticism of the rep, indicating that he did not hear the order correctly (*ten* and a half instead of *two* and a half thousand) and made a mistake. As Holmes (2000b) notes, humour is a way of 'doing power' less explicitly, and therefore of performing 'off-record' evaluations or criticisms.

7.6.3 Word play

There were fewer examples of word play than of the other forms of humour (only joke-telling occurred less frequently). Word play involved not just puns (there were in fact no examples of these), but any kind of humour based on lexical, stylistic or phonological choice. In example 7.11 from the American advertising firm, the humour revolves around the pronunciation of the word 'book':

Example 7.11

Chris: Okay I don't have my/buːk/ with me.

Amy: Go get your /buːk/.[2] And I'll find mine

Chris and Amy are in trying to arrange a time for a meeting, and 'book' here refers to their diaries. In order to understand why speakers are pronouncing 'book' in this way, and why this is funny, some knowledge of local accents is necessary. The company is located in the state of Minnesota, and one of the distinctive features of this accent is the way the sound /ʊ/ is pronounced. So humour here involves making fun of the local accent. Chris seems to initiate the phonological word play here as a defensive strategy for not having his diary with him in a situation (they are in a meeting) where he would normally be expected to have brought it along. By echoing his pronunciation, Amy affiliates with him and thus shows solidarity. An example of word play involving lexical choice was seen in example 7.3 above (which is from the same American company), where the speakers joke and laugh about describing an order as 'clogged'.

7.6.4 Comparative findings

The frequencies of both type and function of humour were very similar in the American and British data. Situational humour and teasing were the most frequent types in both varieties, and solidarity was by far the most frequent function, which is consistent with Holmes and Marra's (2002) finding that supportive humour was more frequent overall across the different workplaces examined than contestive humour. There were no instances of humour with a mitigating function in the American sub-corpus, but there were also not many in the British data; therefore, this is not a significant difference (no statistical comparisons were made due to the small number of instances). This is not to say that there are no differences in the humour of the two varieties. What people find funny and the way humour is done may differ, but humour performs similar functions in both varieties, in particular in relation to the workplace tasks carried out.

The differences are greater when comparing type and function of humour according to gender, although, again the numbers are relatively small, making generalization difficult. But the results do correlate to a large extent with the findings of other studies of humour and gender. There were 34 instances of women and 26 of men initiating humour in single-sex as well as mixed gender groups.[6] Figure 7.2 shows the types of humour used by women and men respectively as a percentage of the total uses of humour by each gender. Women used situational humour most frequently, whereas men used

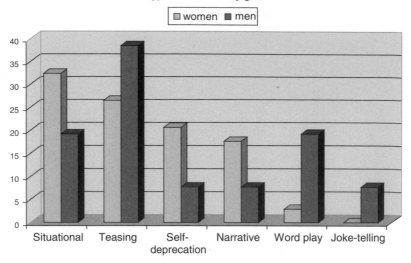

FIGURE 7.2 *Types of humour by gender in the ABOT Corpus*

teasing the most. Almost 40 per cent of all instances of humour initiated by men involved teasing, whereas women used teasing in just over 25 per cent of instances, which was still the second most frequent type of humour initiated by women. Self-deprecation and narrative were used much more frequently by women than men. Similarly, Boxer and Cortés-Conde (1997) found that men used more teasing than women, whereas women used more self-denigration. Women used humour to enact solidarity functions much more frequently than any other function, whereas men used humour for solidarity and criticizing equally frequently.

The relationship between the participants (whether the humour was between a manager and a subordinate or between peers) and the 'direction' of humour, that is who initiated it, was also examined quantitatively. Managers and subordinates initiated humour about equally, subordinates even slightly more, which may be due to the fact that self-deprecating humour (the second most frequent type) was used more by subordinates (see example 7.13). It is also important to remember that in many instances of humour, particularly if they occur during small talk, the institutional relationship may not be relevant, regardless of whether or not it is asymmetrical.

Interestingly, subordinates used humour to perform a 'criticizing' function as frequently as managers. This highlights the 'subversive' role humour can play (see Holmes 2000b, Holmes and Stubbe 2003, Taylor and Bain 2003), as shown in the following extract which occurs later in the meeting between Chris and his sales manager Joe (shown in Example 7.3):

Example 7.12

(1) Chris   No actually the problem is, that we tried to send out to *many* of them at once. (That's all)

(2) Joe   ⌊↑ Oh! So it's *your* fault!

(3) Chris   /Oh no/⌊No *no* no no!

(4) Joe   ⌊Hehehehchchcheh

(5) Chris   It wasn't my idea,

(6) Joe   ⌊Wait till I– wait till I tell 'em! Hehehehehch

(7) Chris   ⌊Hehehehehehehe

Here Joe 'gets his own back' for being criticized for the low level of sales in his department, by jokingly accusing Chris of being responsible for the problem and threatening to tell his sales team ('wait till I tell 'em!').

7.6.5 *Humour in transactional talk*

Although humour occurs most frequently in relational talk, it is also prevalent in task-oriented talk where it often serves a particular purpose in relation to the task at hand. As the above examples show, humour is a very useful device for performing certain actions which would otherwise be face-threatening, such as criticizing (example 7.12) and defending oneself against criticism (example 7.14). Self-deprecation is also often used as a defensive strategy in situations where speakers may feel they are not living up to the expectations of their job, as shown in example 7.13, which involves Ann training a new employee, Meg (see also example 7.11 above):

Example 7.13

Meg: Yeah. an' I immediately forgot everything you told me about–

Ann: ⌊That's okay.

Humour also occurs in problematic or difficult situations to defuse tension or awkwardness. An interesting example of this occurs in the American advertising company during a meeting where two senior managers, Amy and Chris, discuss how to solve some problems with the accounts, for which Amy is responsible. An interruption by Amy's assistant, Becky, occasions a relational episode in which Amy comments on a seemingly unrelated non-workplace issue: the fact that Becky has been experiencing problems trying to buy a house:

Example 7.14

(1) Amy   Will you close on your freakin' house? I think *that's* →

(2) Chris   ⌊ Heheh

(3) Amy   → hangin' over all of our heads.

(4) Becky   Maybe *that's* it. Heheheheh

(5) Amy   ⌊ Heheheheh

Here Amy humorously implies that Becky's problems with the purchase of her new house is somehow responsible for the current problems they are experiencing at work; thereby relativizing these problems and temporarily detracting attention from her own predicament (see also Koester 2006, pp. 142–144).

Such attempts to defuse difficult situations through the use of humour are, however, not always successful, as example 7.15 from the British printing company shows. In this example, Sid, the owner, and his office manager, Val, have been talking about how to resolve a dispute with a customer, with the discussion having become increasingly heated, as Sid rejects each of Val's suggestions of how to deal with the problem. At this point in the discussion, Val attempts to lighten the tone with a humorous comment, which however falls flat, as Sid becomes even angrier, and the conflict escalates as a result:

Example 7.15

(1) Val   Mmm … She's only– she– she-you're probably both the same *star* sign Sid, =

(2) Sid   = ↑ How can– how can I jump into– What?

(3) Val   I said you're both probably the same *star* sign.

(4) Sid   Oh God help us.

(5) Val   You– you're not *Tau*rus, are you?

(6) Sid   ⌊ Why– w– well why do you put me– No.

(7) Val: (Oh)

(8) Sid   Why do you put me– ↑Why is it every time we have a conflict
  →

(9) Val   ⌊ ↑ No but–

(10) Sid   → here, that I'm partly responsible for it.

(11) Val ⌊ ↑ No because you're *both* standing your ground!

(12) Sid I'm an innocent party in this, totally– I've done what I was asked to do.

(13) Val No–

(14) Val I'm just saying that you're both– you're both standing your ground. So where do you *go.* other to– other than to arbi*tr*ation!

Here Val teases Sid that his dispute with the customer is due to their being the same star sign. In addition to being an attempt to lighten the atmosphere, this constitutes an indirect criticism of her boss for being so inflexible. Sid, however, does not join in the humorous frame, but challenges her, forcing Val into voicing her criticism directly:

(11) Val ⌊ ↑ No because you're *both* standing your ground!

Holmes and Marra's (2002) study indicates that humour is used most frequently between colleagues who work together closely (see section 7.5 above), but humour can also contribute to building a relationship which is not yet well-established, for example with new customers or between people who do not work together on a regular basis. Boxer and Cortès-Condé (1997) note that humour for social bonding often takes place between interlocutors of medial social distance, in contrast to high-risk teasing, which typically occurs between intimates. A meeting between the office manager of a British paper seller and one of his suppliers, who do not have regular contact, provides a good example of how the nature of the humour develops in the course of the interaction, thus showing relationship-building in action. First, solidarity is established through banter in the initial small talk, as Angus, the supplier visiting the company, jokes about the difficulty he had finding the branch, as the building is 'very anonymous' (It is in an old farm building in a rural area):

Example 7.16

(1) Angus: You're very anonymous aren't you.

(2) Paul: Uh I like to be. yeah.

(3) Angus: Heheheh

(4) Paul: You been here before?

(5) Angus: Yea:h. Luckily, [Paul: Yeah] You wouldn't know though would you.

Humour occurs again when Angus explains the purpose of his visit:

Example 7.17

(60) Angus: An' I was saying well how can I: you know, get more business out of um: [name of company], 'cause it's been growing, it's been doing very well [Paul: Mm.] So he said well first thing is to get off your back side an' go round an' see the– see the branches, so I'm doing a grand tour of the: [name of company] branches

(61) Paul: The worl– that'll keep you busy for a week or two

Here Angus uses self-deprecating humour as a way of mitigating the imposition of his visit:

- 'get off your back side' (referring to himself)
- 'I'm doing a grand tour'

and Paul reciprocates with good-natured teasing, thus showing solidarity:

- 'that'll keep you busy for a week or two'

Thus the function of humour in the early part of the meeting is clearly one of establishing solidarity. However, later in the conversation, the humour has a more biting edge when Paul mentions a competitor, whom Angus then refers to as 'an enemy':

Example 7.18

(102) Angus: Ah. Yes. Well we see them as an enemy as well

(103) Paul: ⌊ Yes yes I thought you might yeah

(104) Angus: Yes heheheh ↑ Thank you. Anything else you wanted to mention.

(105) Paul: No no no no. ↑ I mean we– you– we– you know we're not proud [...]

This teasing (describing a competitor as 'an enemy') is somewhat more risky than that used at the beginning of the meeting, as it could imply criticism of Paul doing business with a competitor. It is more typical of the type of ribbing that takes place between close colleagues. The fact that Angus attempts this kind of teasing, and that Paul teases him back, seems to indicate that both speakers are trying to build a closer relationship. The way in which the type and function of humour change in the course of one meeting provides a tangible example of relationship-building as it occurs.

7.7 Conclusion

This chapter has demonstrated that relational talk in general, and humour in particular, are integral, rather than peripheral, to workplace discourse. Both forms of talk are used by speakers to 'do' important work in relationship-building, identity negotiation, carrying out politeness functions and exerting or resisting power. Humour was shown to be particularly useful strategy in carrying out potentially face-threatening or risky discursive actions. While the studies reviewed here show that the most important function of humour is bonding and building or consolidating relationships, it can also perform important work in difficult or sensitive areas of workplace interactions, including defusing tension, performing indirect evaluation or criticism and subverting authority.

It was suggested that, according to Wenger's work, relational aspects of interaction are central to a workplace community of practice. This is borne out through a comparative analysis of relational talk across the workplaces from which the ABOT Corpus was drawn, and of humour in four organizations from the Language in the Workplace database (Holmes and Marra 2002). The exploration of types and functions of humour found in the ABOT Corpus further enriches the picture of the role of humour in the workplace. The analysis shows that relational talk and humour are part of the practice of all the workplace communities examined, but differences in the frequency and nature of these forms of talk, as well as participants' views of these, also revealed differences in workplace culture. Such a comparative analysis across different workplace environments lends further support to seeing small talk and humour as key components of workplace practice, as already attested by many studies of individual workplaces. By examining relational talk and humour across a range of workplace settings, it is possible to gain a comprehensive and differentiated picture of the role played by relational forms of talk in workplace discourse.

This chapter has explored the link between relational talk, including humour, and workplace culture. But relational talk is also an important site for invoking and reinforcing other forms of culture, including regional and national culture (as found, for instance in the word play involving regional accent in example 7.11). What happens, however, when the participants do not share the same culture or mother tongue? This is one of the topics which looks at workplace and business encounters across cultures, where people from different cultural backgrounds and different countries interact using English as a second language or 'lingua franca'.

Notes

1 See also King and Sereno (1984) on the effect of relationship history on communication, Norrick (1993) on customary joking relationships and Koester (2004 and 2006) on relational talk in workplace encounters.

2   For most of the recordings made for the ABOT corpus, the researcher rather than the participants controlled the tape recorder, therefore any phatic communication that occurred was usually recorded. Its absence cannot usually be explained by participants simply not switching on the recording equipment because they did not think it was important.

3 See Koeter (2006) for a further discussion of identity negotiation in manager-subordinate encounters.

4 See Norrick (1993, pp. 43EUR1) on customary joking relationships between colleagues.

5 But note that definitions of humour in the literature abound and do not always converge EUR, for example humour may be defined more from the speaker's or from the other participants' point of view (see Holmes 2000b for an overview).

6 This does not necessarily mean that women used humour more than men did, as the corpus was not balanced for gender (there were slightly more women than men), or for the amount of talk produced by each. See also Holmes et al. (2001) for a comparison of humour used by men and women.

8

Development of medical discourse

Britt-Louise Gunnarsson

In this chapter I will sketch an exemplary picture of the emergence and development of medical written discourse. I will analyse and compare medical articles published in scientific journals during three centuries – the eighteenth, nineteenth and twentieth centuries – and discuss my results in relation to the varied contextual frameworks in which these texts were written. Socio-historical changes in relation to text patterns and linguistic expressions of evaluation will thus be related to different scientific stages: the pre-establishment stage, the establishing stage and the specialized stage.

My analysis in this chapter takes as its theoretical basis the constructivist approach. In the first part of this chapter, I briefly recapitulate what a constructivist view entails for medical language at cognitive, social and societal layers. As an illustration of what scientific language was like at different periods, I cite in the second part selected excerpts from medical articles published in the eighteenth, nineteenth and twentieth centuries. In the third part, I return to the history of medical science and outline its development in relation to three scientific stages. Part 4 presents the study of scientificality in medical articles and discusses its results in relation to the content and content structuring of the texts (8.4.1), the formal organization of the texts (8.4.2) and the linguistic expressions of evaluations (8.4.3). In part 5, I return to the scientific stages and place the analysed articles on developmental axes. Part 6 includes my conclusions.

8.1 A constructivist approach to medical discourse

My claim in this chapter is that a constructivist approach[1] deepens our understanding of the historical development of medical language and communication in its rich and varied totality. Medical scientific discourse has emerged in a cooperative and competitive struggle among scientists to create the knowledge base of their field, to establish themselves in relation to other scientists and to other professional groups, and to gain influence and control over political and socio-economic means. In order to grasp the dynamic processes we should therefore include the cognitive as well as the social and societal layers in our analysis.

If we begin by considering the *cognitive layer*, we find that the medical profession has a certain way of viewing reality, a certain way of highlighting different aspects of the world around it. Socialization into the medical profession means learning how to discern the relevant facts, how to view the relationships between different factors. The medical practitioners and scientists are taught how to construct and use a grid or a lens to view reality in a professionally relevant way. Language, texts and spoken discourse help them in this construction process. They use language in the construction of medical knowledge. Medical terminology, medical text patterns, and medical text and discourse content have developed as a means of dealing with reality in a way that is appropriate for medical purposes.

Secondly, where the *social layer* is concerned, the medical group, like other social groups, is also formed by the establishment of an internal role structure, group identity, group attitudes and group norms. The use of medical scientific language during different periods is thus related to the type and level of the medical scientific community (the social group), its size, structure, degree of professionalization, degree of internationalization, degree and nature of mutual contacts, existence of publications, etc.

Thirdly, as regards the *macrosocial* or *societal layer*, the medical professional group also stands in a particular relationship to the society in which it operates: it exerts certain functions and is given a certain place within that society. The members of the medical profession play a role in relation to other actors in society, and the professional group acts in relation to other groups.

It is through language that medical professionals exert their societal function. If medical practitioners and scientists are going to play a role on the political scene, they have to construct their communicative behaviour in a way that serves that purpose. Their relationship to written texts and spoken discourse and to different genres is also important. The medical scientists adapt to established genres but are also involved in forming new genres, which means that the way in which language is used within medical science during different periods is linked with the relationship of the scientist and the scientific community to society in general. The societal layer is thus related to economic and political factors. It is related to power and status patterns in the particular society, e.g. the nation state, as well as on the global scene.

The cognitive, social and societal layers are strongly related to the emergence and continuous re-creation of professional language, and they are a part of the construction of professional language and discourse. Historically, language is constructed in relation to all these layers. The cognitive establishment of the field takes place at the same time as the professions are fighting for their place in society and to strengthen their group in relation to other groups.

8.2 Excerpts from medical articles from different periods

As an illustration of the emergence of the scientific use of language within medicine, I will cite selected excerpts from three medical articles. The excerpts have been selected to express the tendencies that were found more generally in the large medical corpus, comprising 60 articles, which will be analysed in this chapter. The articles cited below were written by Swedish scientists and published in the Swedish medical journal of the time. I present the excerpts in an English translation.

The first three excerpts are taken from an article from 1782 which was published in the Annals of the Swedish Academy of Sciences. The article deals with a method intended to cure tuberculosis, the so-called cowshed cure, which can be briefly described as requiring the patient to live and reside in a cowshed

Text 1[2]

(1) Mr. *READ's* little Treatise on the Cowhouse Cure has attracted much attention from those suffering from tuberculosis in this Country since Dr. SCHÜTZERCRANTZ published and translated the work in Swedish in 1768. Many became curious and attempted this cure, and did so more often than not with blind trust that far exceeded those bounds to which common caution should have confined them: bounds that it would be harmful for a healthy person to transgress, let alone invalids.

(2) In the month of September, the mistress moved into this room. By now the disease of tuberculosis had quite possessed her. [...] Her lack of breath was now so stifling that she had to spend both night and day sitting in her bed; and she

was moreover aff licted with a permanent colicky diarrhoea and swollen legs. Dr. SCHÜTZERCRANTZ and Mr. *NATHORST* had, like me, given up every hope of her recovery.

This new accommodation seemed fairly strange to the sick lady to begin with. Unaccustomed to the noise of cattle, caused by the rubbing of their f lanks and the contact of their horns with the mangers, for several nights she was unable to sleep, for as soon as she dozed off this clamour awoke her and that more often than not with some amazement. No less repugnant did it seem to her to eat in such a disagreeable room, with an open drain full of cattle dung. But she gradually accustomed herself to this new regime. She could see her husband's concern for her; she thought about her small children, of whom she was so fond; she contemplated her weak and decrepit condition; she could endure anything if only she could regain her health. I visited her daily as her physician; her husband and friends spent the best part of the day with her, and gradually she became used to this way of life, was merrier, undertook small chores, and hardly had a month passed before I fancied I could see clear signs of some recovery in the abatement of her diarrhoea and the improvement of her breathlessness, that she was able to do without a cushion or two to support her back to maintain her sitting position.

(3) Moreover we know what exemplary effect a mild diet, of milk, vegetables, white meat etc., may have in improving the f luids. Today we have dissociated ourselves completely from the erroneous theories Doctors once embraced about the efficacy of Balsams on internal ulcers, they are scarcely used now externally, except in healthy wounds, as we could well do without them there too. /.../ In this form of consumption the cowshed cure can provide no visible gain, but rather worsens the condition with its irritating and softening qualities.

In his introduction (1), the author expresses explicit criticism, addressed directly to those beguiled into testing the method. This criticism is also aimed indirectly at those who introduced the method, Mr. Read and perhaps to some extent the translator, Mr. Schützercrantz. The author then goes on to describe three cases which he links to 'three personages of respectable rank, who, in each of their houses, made fitting arrangements in order to carry out this cure with every caution and with all seemliness that could be contrived'. The first case, excerpt (2), was that of the consumptive wife of a wealthy citizen in the southern part of Stockholm. What we can note is that the text very carefully describes observations of a single medical case. It provides a good deal of detail, also in relation to the individual patient and it contains dates. Another striking feature is of course its use of straightforward language. We can also note that there are no headings or references. Apart from the personal style and vivid description in excerpt (2), we can also observe that the author refers by name to two colleagues, 'Dr. SCHÜTZERCRANTZ and Mr. NATHORST', to corraborate his own judgement of the patient's condition. We can also note the subjective way in which the author describes his own assessment: 'before I fancied I could see clear signs of her recovery'. In the third excerpt (3), we can observe, among other things, the author's explicit and highly critical evaluation of previous medical theories: 'Today we have dissociated ourselves completely from the erroneous theories Doctors once embraced.'

The following three excerpts, (4) – (6), are taken from an article from 1842, which was published in the medical journal *Hygiea,* the predecessor of today's *Läkartidningen,* the Swedish medical journal. The article deals with asthma, or more specifically asthma thymicum. It discusses the research of other doctors and presents original findings.

Text 2[3]

(4) As this disease is still little known in this country, we have come to the conclusion that a more detailed description of its form is not superf luous, particularly in view of the fact that no such account exists in Swedish apart from the extract from *HIRSCH'S* thesis published in the Journal for Physicians and Pharmacists 1836, p. 261. Our intention will have been achieved if we can thereby also succeed in prompting among our own countrymen studies of this, in many respects, less widespread form of illness.

(5) The child awakes violently from sleep and emits a shrill squeaking noise, like the sound of inhalation during whoopingcough, but much shriller, higher and more superficial *(HIRSCH),* or even more like the sound caused by spasms of the bosom in hysterical women suffering from heart ailments. On closer examination one finds that this emanates from some obstruction to breathing; for the child becomes agitated, moves violently, and makes every effort to gasp in air, its face turns red, its eyes stare fixedly and immediately after the attack the patient has the appearance of terror and bursts brief ly into tears.

(6) With regard to the *nature* and *essence* of the disease, on the whole two different opinions prevail. [...] But given the current state of the science it is, however, difficult to provide a satisfactory account of all the circumstances surrounding the disease. The increased size of the gland cannot here function mechanically by exerting pressure as notwithstanding that this pressure is continuous, during the first phases no sign of illness can be observed in the child between the paroxysms.

In his introduction (4), the author justifies his account by referring to the necessity of collecting information: 'Our intention will have been achieved if we can thereby also succeed in prompting among our own countrymen studies of this, in many respects, less widespread form of illness.' In excerpt (5), we can note that also in this article from 1842, the descriptions of the course taken by the illness are vivid. The perspective is, however, that of the watching doctor and not, as in the article from the eighteenth century, the patient. The author also refers to other colleagues, e.g. 'Hirsch'. The article on the whole contains a relatively extensive discussion of previous findings and the author identifies a large number of researchers and sources, and as excerpt (6) shows, the author does not merely list earlier findings uncritically but also adopts a standpoint to them.

Excerpts (7) – (10) are taken from a co-authored article published in 1980 in the Swedish medical journal *Läkartidningen*. The article deals with a method for the treatment of pneumothorax.

Text 3[4]

(7) The twofold aim of the treatment is both to re-expand the collapsed lung and also to prevent a relapse. What was recommended previously was a period of waiting for 4–6 weeks if there was no valvular pneumothorax (Becker, Müller 1970) or puncture with exsuff lation (Schott, Viereck 1972). In recent years a more active attitude has been adopted with the introduction of chest drainage combined with continuous suction, known as the Bülau-drainage treatment (Becker, Müller 1970).

(8) *Materials and methods*
Between January 1977 and March 1978, 36 cases of pneumothorax, in 29 patients, were treated using a Heimlich valve (Table II).

The indications for the application of chest drainage were: 5–7 apical pneumothorax on a standing radiograph during expiration, or less severe, symptom-producing or persistent pneumothorax. All patients meeting these criteria were admitted to IVA.

(9) Removal of the Heimlich valve took place with the patient ambulant after drainage had been closed with the help of forceps for 4–6 hours and it had been determined that pneumothorax had not recurred with an X-ray.

(10) The combination of a short period of treatment with suction drainage and the Heimlich valve is a simple, reliable and effective treatment of various forms of uncomplicated pneumothorax. The treatment involves considerably less pressure on medical resources, mainly in Intensive Care Units. As fewer patients are confined to their beds for much of the treatment period, the method also involves a reduction of the total time spent in care.

In excerpt (7), we can observe how the accounts of the research of others have acquired their modern impersonal form, with attributions to articles in parentheses instead of explicit references to individual researchers. Here criticism is expressed implicitly: 'What was recommended previously'; 'In recent years a more active attitude has been adopted'. It is also veiled to a greater extent: 'The effect of the treatment on the function of the lungs seems to be fairly insignificant'. Excerpt (8) provides an example of how the authors can introduce their own research. Patients are viewed as quantifiable material. Methods are described using specialist terminology. There is an abundance of numbers and names of drugs and devices. We also find headings, tables and diagrams in the text. As excerpt (9) shows, the illnesses are described from the perspective of the physician, or more correctly of the researcher. Here experimental results are being analysed, not, as previously, cases being described. The article concludes with the adoption of an explicit stance on behalf of the method (10): 'a simple, reliable and effective treatment', 'involves considerably less pressure', 'the method also involves a reduction'. The author does not emerge here either, however, but the conclusion is presented as the logical deduction from the facts presented.

8.3 Stages in the development of medical science

All three articles cited above belong to the same genre, the medical scientific article genre. They were all written by medical scientists and for medical expert readers. Of more relevance for our discussion in this chapter is that the three articles were constructed in different contextual frames.

If we now turn to the history of medical science, we find that medical knowledge and practice took a great step forward in the seventeenth and in particular in the eighteenth century. However, it was only gradually that it developed into a science in the modern sense. Since the eighteenth century, all societies have undergone radical change. Changes have also taken place within the medical scientific community: (1) Medical knowledge has grown immensely; (2) Science in general and the philosophy of science have undergone changes. Statistics and empirical methods have developed. Positivism has become the only accepted view in many sciences; (3) The medical profession has gradually become increasingly established and recognized. Today, doctors are considered highly valuable professionals, and medical scientists and medical research are considered highly important to society; (4) The medical scientific community has become much larger. The number of doctors, medical scientists and students of medicine has increased, as has the number of medical journals and conferences.

Important changes have thus taken place relating to medical science, science in general, the medical profession and the medical scientific community. As the following discussion of results will show, language and discourse are essential elements in the construction of medical science, in profession-building and in the shaping of a medical scientific community. It will further show how academic genres play important roles in this process of construction – of scientific knowledge, of the role of scientist in society, and in the growth and strengthening of the social network among scientists.

In this chapter, I will discuss changes involving language and text patterns in relation to three scientific stages: the pre-establishment stage, the establishing stage, and the specialized stage. For each layer – the cognitive, social and societal – the three stages can be summarized on a developmental axis:

Cognitive layer
Individual findings – Accumulation of findings – Integration into theory.

Social layer
Isolated researchers – Academic grouping – Advanced scientific community.

Macrosocial/societal layer
Scientists function within society – Scientists function within society and academic groupings – Scientists function within the scientific community.

8.4 Scientificality in medical articles from 1730 to 1985

The empirical results which will be referred to in this chapter are based on studies of Swedish medical language carried out at Uppsala University. The medical corpus which will be focused on here consists of 60 scientific articles: 10 from each of the 6 periods: I 1730–1799; II 1800–1849; III 1850–1880; IV 1895–1905; V 1935–1945; VI 1975–1985. All these articles come from scientific journals and deal with pulmonary diseases (30 articles) or skin diseases (30 articles).[5] The analysis has focused on different textlinguistic levels – the cognitive, the pragmatic, and the macrothematic – and also on vocabulary and terminology. My discussion below will be organized in the following way: in 8.4.1 I will focus on the content and content structuring of the texts, in 8.4.2. on the formal organization of the text, and in 8.4.3. on the linguistic expressions of evaluations.[6]

8.4.1 Content and content structuring of the texts

First, I will here relate the content and content structuring of medical articles to the stage reached by the domain of medical science, in terms of degree and type of scientificality, and also to the role of scientists in society.

The cognitive analysis examined the content of the text in relation to five *cognitive worlds*: a 'scientific world', a 'practical world', an 'object world', a 'private world' and an 'external world'. Within each of these, two or three *aspects* were discerned: within the scientific world 'theory', 'classification' and 'experiment', within the practical world 'work' and 'interaction', within the object world 'phenomenon-focused', 'part-focused' and 'whole-focused', within the private world 'experience' and 'conditions' and within the external world 'conditions' and 'measures'. The cognitive analysis also comprised an analysis of text content in relation to four time *dimensions*: 'cause', 'phenomenon', 'process' and 'result'.

Each proposition in the articles was categorized in relation to *world*, *aspect* and *dimension*. We could thus calculate the proportions of the total number of propositions representing each world, each aspect and each dimension in texts from different periods.

The analysis showed a very clear increase in the proportion of each text devoted to the scientific world, i.e. to the presentation of 'theory', 'classifications' and 'experiment' over the periods. On the other hand, there was a clear decline in the role of the external world in particular, i.e. in the proportions of texts dealing with 'conditions' and 'measures' of a political, economic and social nature. There was also an increase in the proportion of 'experiment/observation' within the scientific world and a drop in the proportion of 'measures' within the external world. The analysis further showed that the proportions of each text devoted to describing 'causes' and 'phenomena' have decreased over time, while the proportions devoted to 'processes' and 'results' have increased.

Another part of the analysis focused on the macrothematic structure. The content of the medical articles were then categorized in relation to the four *superthemes*: 'introduction', 'theme development', 'discussion' and 'conclusions'. This analysis revealed an increase in how much of each text is devoted to the superthemes 'introduction' and 'theme development' (i.e. to a description of materials, methods, results). The proportion devoted to 'discussion' and in particular to 'conclusions', on the other hand, had declined.

A third analysis, which aimed at a description of the pragmatic character of the texts, i.e. the types of *illocution* present, pointed to an increase as regards 'informative' and 'explicative' illocutions and a decrease in 'expressive', 'argumentative' and 'directive' illocutions.

To sum up, the changes in the content and content structuring of Swedish medical articles from 1730 to 1985 show the following tendencies: more 'scientific world' – less 'external world'; more 'experiment' – less social, political and economic 'measures'; more 'process' and 'results' – less 'cause' and 'phenomenon'; a larger proportion of 'theme development' – a smaller proportion of 'discussion' and 'conclusions'; more 'informative' and 'explicative' illocutions – fewer 'expressive' and 'directive' illocutions.

These findings relating to changes in the medical article genre point, for one thing, to a development in medical science. The knowledge structure of the texts appears to have changed to include more emphasis on experiment and on process and results. There is also a trend towards a genre of a more purely descriptive character, in which the main part of the text is devoted to developing the theme, i.e. to description of the experiment, observations etc. These are features which could be related to a positivist scientific ideal. All these results can be related to the cognitive layer of the construction of academic discourse.

These results reveal the role played by scientists in society. In terms of text content, the proportion devoted to the external world and external measures has decreased, as has the proportion devoted to conclusions and directives. Such results can be discussed in the light of the specialization and professionalization of society. Compared with earlier periods, scientists today are acting to a greater extent in a discourse community of their own. Science in general and medical science in particular is accepted and highly esteemed in modern society. Considerable funding is given to medical research. The role of large-scale experiments has increased.

The discourse changes can be related to this endeavour among medical scientists to become specialists with a profession of their own and their own exclusive domain to deal with. A high degree of scientificality in spoken and written discourse imparts prestige.

A more purely scientific genre has emerged. Scientist-writers have turned towards their own group, and the medical article genre has become a within-science genre. The popularization of medical findings is undertaken by others – by trained journalists. Scientists can write for their own group without having to bother about a growing gap between the lay public and the experts. The article genre has become more exclusively internal and less concerned with reaching out to other sectors of society.

These results can also be interpreted in the light of the interplay between the cognitive and societal layers. The role played by the medical profession in society interrelates with the presentation of scientific content.

8.4.2 Formal organization of the text

Secondly, I will relate the formal organization of the texts and their rhetorical patterns to the stage reached in the development of the medical scientific community. A robust scientific community reveals itself in firm genre conventions: in more homogeneous texts and also in explicit indications of group affiliation.

The number and types of headings in the Swedish modern articles vary over time. The use of section headings has increased dramatically. The type of heading has also changed. In the early periods, headings relate to the content of the article, while in modern articles they relate to its structure: Material, Methods, Results, Discussion, Conclusions. The modern headings thus structure the presentation in a general scientific way, which also reflects a more homogeneous organization of the texts.

An increasing homogeneity is also found in relation to the thematic article structure.[7] The articles from the period around 1980 (1975–1985) were clearly more homogeneous in terms of their linear text structure than earlier articles. Similarly, the introductions in articles from different periods revealed a gradually greater homogeneity. This homogeneity can also be seen in a contrastive perspective, i.e. the Swedish pattern has come to resemble that of the English scientific article, as this is described in Swales (1990).

Another finding relates to the information flow of the text. An analysis of the connection between content structure and graphical disposition in articles from different periods showed that each sentence has become more independent with regard to the surrounding text. It introduces a new angle, which means that it becomes less integrated with its neighbouring sentences (Melander, 1993). We thus find a change towards a fact-listing or 'catalogue' style in the modern article.

This tendency towards a catalogue style can be seen as another feature reflecting firmer genre conventions. When texts are organized in a homogeneous and predictable way, there is less need to elaborate on the details. Readers know where in the text they will find different types of content. The tendency towards a more catalogue-like article could also be seen as indicating a strengthening of the scientific community. The knowledge of this community is well established among the specialist readers, and need not be elaborated on.

Other analyses reveal that the number of references per article has increased over time, and that their presentation has become more homogeneous. Another tendency relates to the changed use of personal pronouns. In the articles from the eighteenth century, the pronoun 'I' was used quite frequently although it has more or less totally disappeared in the articles from the latter part of the twentieth century. The pronoun 'we', on the other hand, which was quite unusual during the first two periods, had a similar low rank in the medical texts until the last period (1975–1985). The author's explicit marking of article relevance has also changed over time. We here find a shift from a societal orientation in earlier periods to a more internal orientation in the last period.[8]

To sum up, the changes in formal text organization and the rhetorical patterns show the following diachronic tendencies: more headings; more homogeneous text organization; more homogeneous article introductions; more fact-listing; more references; less use of the personal pronoun 'I'; more relevance marking relating to the group.

The medical article has developed towards greater homogeneity – relating to the use of headings, the superthematic text structure, the rhetorical structure of introductions etc. –, a homogeneity that indicates a strengthening of genre conventions. The medical article has become more established as a genre, and its genre conventions have become firmer and thus more homogeneous. This strengthening of the academic article genre, however, is also a sign of a growing and stronger medical discourse community. For the medical discourse community, as for most scientific discourse communities, writing plays an essential role as a group marker, and the establishment of firmer conventions for written text genres is part of the growth and strengthening of this community. The trend towards a more fact-listing and catalogue type of article can also be seen as a sign of a stronger discourse community, in the sense of a more homogeneous and closed community. It is a well-known fact within sociolinguistics that communication within a dense group or network needs to be less explicit and elaborated than communication within an open and less dense one.

The modern habit of giving references to the works of colleagues is another sign of a strong discourse community, a discourse community with a clear group feeling. When the group is essential to its members, it becomes important to indicate one's sense of belonging and one's relationship to other group members. Problems relating to the group also become more important than those relating to the world outside the group. The modern tendency to list references, to use 'we' instead of 'I', and to mark relevance in relation to one's own group can be viewed from this social perspective. I would suggest that these text features are part of the construction of an increasingly close-knit (dense) medical discourse community.

There is also a connection between these features and the role of medical scientists in society, i.e. the strengthening of the professional group is paralleled by a process of gradual specialization of the professions. These features are thus also part of the construction of a role for the medical community within society. We can thus see how the social and societal layers interact. Strengthening of the internal group structure is interrelated with the underlining of a role for the group in society.

8.4.3 Linguistic expressions of evaluations

Thirdly, I will relate the linguistic expressions of evaluation and its variation over time to the positioning of the scientist/author on the developmental axes for the three contextual dimensions.

The study referred to was based on an analysis of 30 Swedish scientific medical articles from six periods. All articles dealt with pulmonary diseases. The study, which comprised an analysis of evaluations linked to descriptions of the subjects studied, the diseases and treatments, the introduction of the author's own initiatives, and descriptions of the research and findings of others, focused on three main aspects: (1) what is being evaluated, (2) through whom the evaluation is taking place and (3) how the evaluation is being made.[9]

In articles from all periods, the object of the study and the initiatives of other researchers are evaluated. The author also refers to his own initiatives in most articles.

From a diachronic perspective, however, it is more interesting to consider the second aspect, through whom the evaluation is taking place (author's own voice, author through others, author through facts). A comparison of the medical texts from the eighteenth, nineteenth and twentieth centuries shows that in the earliest texts the evaluation is made by the author himself, using his own voice, whereas in later articles it is allowed to emerge indirectly via facts from others, e.g. in references to articles by others.

A change over time is also found in relation to the third aspect, how the evaluation is being made. When articles from the eighteenth century are compared to articles from the twentieth century, we find increasing temperance with the evaluations in articles from 1730 being expressed more severely. A more obvious change, however, relates to the degree of certainty. Here we find a discernible increase in the use of hedges and other expressions of caution over time.[10]

We thus find a progressive moderation of the author's own voice in the medical articles and increasingly the focus is placed on facts. There is another clear change in the author's relationship to facts, which is revealed in an increase in the frequency of markers of epistemic modality.

These tendencies were also found in analysis of word frequencies. As mentioned earlier, there is a change in the use of the personal pronouns 'jag' [I] and 'vi' [we] in the articles over time. The occurrences of the pronoun 'I' decline by half between period I (eighteenth century) and period IV (1895–1905) and disappear completely during period VI (1975–1985). To some extent the pronoun 'I' is replaced by the pronoun 'we' in the last period. In this case, however, the increased use of 'we' is not mainly explained either by the use of reader-inclusive 'we' or by co-authorship. It could rather be linked to the progressive phasing out of authorial identity in scientific prose.

A comparison of the frequencies of a number of markers of modality in the Swedish medical corpus, revealed an increase over time. All nine markers – 'torde' [is probably], 'tyder' [suggests], 'tycks' [seems], 'tänkbar' [conceivable], 'tveksam' [doubtful], 'sannolik' [likely], 'sannolikhet' [likelihood], 'möjlig' [possible], 'möjlighet' [possibility] – revealed a linear increase in the frequency over the six periods.

This increasing tendency to be cautious can of course be seen as a sign of the progressive extension of medical knowledge, i.e. it can be related to the author's placement on the knowledge axis. The greater the body of collective knowledge, the more aware authors are of its relativity. But it could also be linked to circumstances within the social group, in this case the medical community. In order to survive in a competitive society, which is what the world of medical research undeniably is, one must be careful not to lose face and take care not to threaten the face of others. Ideas of this kind are proposed in Myers (1989). Myers claims that in order to survive in the competitive academic world modern scientists adopt pragmatic politeness strategies and that Brown and Levinson's concepts of 'face saving' and 'face threatening' are relevant also in the analysis of scientific texts (Brown and Levinson, 1987). Scientists tread a narrow path between the need to emphasize their own achievements, on the one hand, and to criticize those of their peers, on the other.

It may well be that the difference in the wording results from the increased knowledge scientists now possess about illnesses and their treatment, i.e. that the difference can be linked to the cognitive dimension. Or it may result from greater awareness of the importance of politeness in a large and well-developed scientific community, i.e. the difference can be linked to the social dimension; doctors/researchers admittedly make evaluations, but they avoid expressing them subjectively and straightforwardly and choose greater objectiveness, thus showing more caution.

8.5 The relationship between text and context for scientific medical writing

In this part of the chapter, I will return to the three scientific stages distinguished earlier (in 8.3) and relate my results more systematically to each one of them. I will also place medical articles from the centuries discussed here, i.e. the eighteenth, nineteenth and twentieth centuries, on developmental axes related to each of the three layers: the cognitive, the social and the societal. Figure 8.1 illustrates the relationship between text and context for medical scientific articles during three centuries.

In the articles from the eighteenth century, e.g. Text 1 cited in part 8.2, we encounter a number of different individuals – the author himself, his colleagues and his patients – and their experiences and judgements are described. The typical article is full of explicit, severe and assured evaluations which concern the object of the study – the illness and method – and also the advocates of the method, its naïve practitioners. In the way the author writes, he places himself fairly obviously towards the left of all three contextual axes in

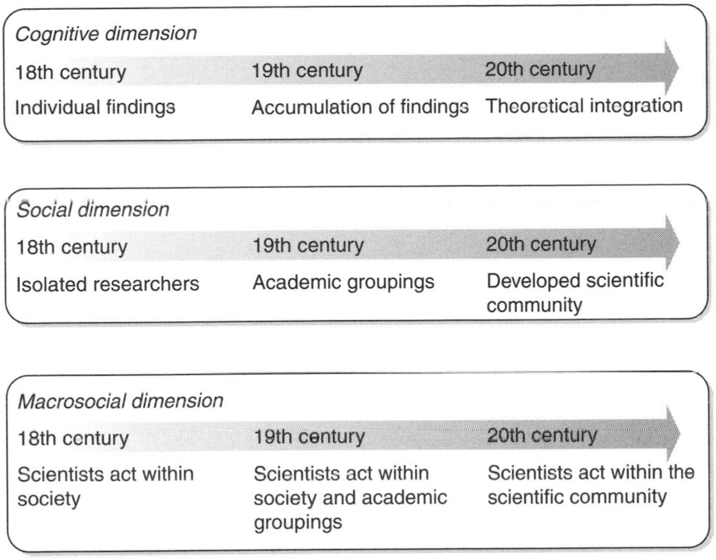

FIGURE 8.1 *Text and context during three centuries (Gunnarsson, 2001a: 136)*

Figure 8.1: he treats individual findings as if they exist *per se*, he describes himself and his colleagues as isolated researchers and he seems to act within society rather than the scientific community.

In the articles from the nineteenth century, e.g. Text 2, the typical author adopts a considerably more analytic attitude to the research of others. The author himself figures as an evaluator. He also explicitly adduces the opinions of other researchers. The evaluations are of medium severity and the author marks his doubts in different ways. The author is fair and square in the middle of the contextual axes.

In the articles from the twentieth century (around 1980), e.g. Text 3, the typical author does not express himself in his own voice or explicitly through others. Evaluations take the form of the presentation of facts, supported by references to other works. Summaries of the research of others form an integral part of the description of the illness/method. What characterizes this and other articles in the sub-corpus from this period is above all the attitude adopted to facts. The evaluations are not few in number, but they are weak to medium severe rather than severe and they are presented throughout as less certain – in other words these authors should be placed to the right on the contextual axes.

8.6 Conclusions

Language constructs science in relation to the cognitive layer (the scientific content), the societal layer (the scientists' role in society) and the social layer (relations within the group). This construction process has been in progress since the first doctors tried to establish themselves as medical scientists and it is still continuing. In Sweden this process began in the seventeenth century. However, it was not until the middle of the eighteenth century that Sweden became a national writing community. Before 1740, the language of the learned was Latin, but in the Era of Liberty, from the middle of the eighteenth century, Swedish was gradually accepted as a scientific language, and the construction of medical science and the medical scientific community was related over a long period to the development of the Swedish medical article as a genre. This article has focused on this phase in the Swedish medical history, an account which ended in 1985.

What has taken place since then is an accelerating Anglicization of the academic writing community in Sweden. English is now used in medicine as the medium for Ph.D. theses, for conference abstracts and papers, and for articles presenting original research (Gunnarsson, 2001b). *Läkartidningen*, the Swedish medical journal, still exists, but is no longer the prime forum for presentations of new findings. The Swedish medical scientists of today choose to present their research in English in international medical journals. When they write in *Läkartidningen*, the Swedish journal, they have other aims than to present original research findings. The Swedish medical scientific community has thus become diglossic, i.e. English is used for certain purposes and Swedish for others. In the Swedish medical journal, articles offer surveys and present research relating to basic diseases but it is no longer a journal for the original presentation of new research (Gunnarsson et al., 1995).

A development of the kind described here is not country specific. The shift from Latin to the national language took place around the same time in most western countries, and the modern extension of English as a scientific language is universal (Ammon, 2001; Carli and Ammon, 2007). The Anglicization of the medical scientific community and the accelerating use of the Internet as a communicative tool has led to intensified globalization and also homogenization of science and scientific language. From a socio-historical perspective this development is most interesting and will certainly in the future lead to important investigations.

Notes

1 A constructionist perspective on the emergence of scientific discourse and text genres are found within the sociology of science tradition (e.g. Knorr-Cetina, 1981, Latour and Woolgar, 1986). Bazerman (1988) studied the rise of modern forms of scientific communication, focusing on the historical emergence of the experimental article. A social constructivist approach in

relation to written texts is also found in Bazerman and Paradis (1991) and in Gunnarsson, Linell and Nordberg (1997).

2 Bergius, P. J. (1782), 'Anmärkningar öfver Fähus-Curen för lungsiktiga', in *Svenska Vetenskapsakademiens Handlingar.* Stockholm, pp. 307–318.

3 Collin, J. G. (1842), 'Underrättelser om Asthma thymicum', *Hygiea*, 6, 256–271.

4 Lindström, F. and Schildt, B. (1980), 'Förenklad behandling av pneumotorax med Heimlich-ventil', *Läkartidningen*, 999–1001.

5 The Uppsala LSP corpus, which consists of 360 articles from three disciplines (medicine, technology and economics), is presented in Gunnarsson and Skolander (1991).

6 This chapter draws on an article in *Encyclopedia in Language and Linguistics* (Gunnarsson, 2005).

7 In Gunnarsson (1993), this study is presented in more detail.

8 In Gunnarsson (1998), this study is presented in more detail.

9 See Gunnarsson (2001a), for a detailed presentation of the study.

10 Compare Salager-Meyer (1994) and Valle (1999).

9

Instructional discourses

Ken Hyland

While research discourses have gathered considerable celebrity and attention, genres concerned with the more work-a-day functions of teaching and learning have, until quite recently, been of less interest to researchers. Lectures, classroom teaching and textbooks, however, are the bread and butter of university life. Not only are they the genres which students are most likely to encounter, but they occupy much of the working lives of academics in preparation and delivery. Concerned with disseminating knowledge rather than constructing it, these genres function to establish both the content and the discourse of a discipline for students, acculturating newcomers into the schema of their fields.

When students enter university they are faced with a range of adjustments to the ways they are expected to learn, behave and understand the world. Among the most challenging of these is the need to extend their linguistic competence to deal with new demands of reading, listening, interpreting, recording and understanding required by university study. This not only involves the ability to work in a general academic register, but to cope with the demands of individual disciplines. Ballard and Clanchy made this clear many years ago.

> Just as modes of analysis vary with disciplines and with the groups that practise them (physicists, psychologists, and literary critics), so too does language. For the student new to a discipline, the task of learning the distinctive mode of analysis ... is indivisible from the task of learning the language of the discipline ... One area of development cannot proceed without the other.
>
> (1988: 17)

Competence in a discipline means understanding its concepts, its ways of working and its language, and this is largely achieved through the instructional discourses of the academy, particularly lectures, seminars and textbooks.

9.1 University lectures

The large formal lecture is perhaps *the* prototypical genre of information-transfer. Emphasizing transmission over negotiation and monologue rather than dialogue, it is seen by universities as the most practical and cost-effective way of imparting subject content *en masse* to growing intakes of undergraduate students. Critics point out that lecturing is mainly a one-way form of communication, an institutionalized extended holding-of-the-floor that does not involve significant audience participation. But while teacher-led monologic sessions may be the traditional form of lecture, it is just one type of class session which can include small lectures, seminars, tutorials, 'labinars' and discussion sessions. A survey of 900 lecturers in four US universities by Ferris and Tagg (1996), for example, found a range of practices across different disciplines and graduate/undergraduate levels, with lecturing styles apparently evolving towards less formal, more conversational interactive styles.

Academic speech genres have been largely neglected by discourse analysts until recently, however, and we know very little of how they vary within or between each other. This is, at least in part, because university lectures have not traditionally been available to outsiders. It was only a few years ago, for example, that Flowerdew (2002: 110) complained about the lack of spoken corpora for academic purposes, a situation Nesi (2003) blames for discouraging research into spoken texts and for hindering the development of authentic lecturing materials for EAP students. This situation is now beginning to change, however, and this section highlights what we know of academic lectures. I restrict the term 'lecture' here to a classroom learning event of 40 students or more primarily led by a lecturer, although it may well involve contributions from students.[1] I begin with a brief consideration of students' perceptions and experiences of the genre.

i. Comprehension and perceptions

The centrality of lectures to undergraduate teaching and learning has long been recognized. It is also widely acknowledged, however, that listening to lectures can present a considerable processing burden to students, especially those working in a foreign language (e.g. Flowerdew, 1994). Comprehending lectures is challenging for students as it requires two main cognitive operations:

First, academic listening involves 'bottom-up' processing of language input in real time, requiring students to attend to data in the incoming stream of speech signals. Second, it also draws on 'top-down' analysis of what is being said by utilizing prior knowledge and expectations to create meaning (Rost, 1990).

Research shows that among the most significant demands affecting students' effective comprehension of lectures are:

- The speed of the lecturer's delivery

- The failure of humour to cross cultural boundaries

- A lack of understanding of phonological structuring of discourse organization

- Difficulties of engaging in the participatory style of lecture preferred by western lecturers

- The lecturer's use of unknown vocabulary and specialist terminology

- Maintaining concentration for 50 minutes or longer

- Identifying the topic, main themes and ideas of a lecture and how these are connected

- Taking effective notes of the main points

- Coping with the demands of simultaneous visual and verbal inputs

(List compiled from Flowerdew, 1994; Flowerdew and Miller, 1996; Thompson, 2003). Lectures are therefore both linguistically and cognitively demanding, and L2 students are likely to experience greater difficulty with each of these skills.

One reason for these difficulties is that students often have little idea of what to expect when their studies begin, typically anticipating a dry, monologic delivery of core material and basic facts, where the tutor is 'the main giver of information' (Furneaux, *et al.*, 1991: 80). Such expectations can be a major obstacle to comprehension for learners, as 'not only the language forms (vocabulary, syntax, etc.) but also the underlying cultural grammar and interpretive strategies my be initially unknown' (Benson, 1994: 181).

Flowerdew and Miller (1996), for example, found this was particularly problematic for undergraduates in Hong Kong, where there was a serious mismatch in both perceptions and behaviours between the students and their British lecturers. While most lecturers talked about using lectures to help develop students' judgements and thinking skills, the students simply saw them as a way of getting the core facts from the course. They regarded the lecturer as an uncontested authority and lectures as a means of effecting a one-way transfer of information. The authors attribute this to a clash of academic cultures, forcefully expressed by one of their lecturers in this way:

> They [the students] sit there like goldfish with their mouths open waiting for me to pour information into them.... They only experience a system which requires them to learn the 'right' answer and to regurgitate it. The concept of evaluation, analysis etc. appears to be totally lacking.
>
> (Flowerdew and Miller, 1996: 125)

Other studies have focused on particular features of lectures and students' responses to these. Simpson (2004), for instance, points to the potential difficulties for students caused by high-frequency multi-word clusters such as *the thing is, you could say* and *look at it like*, which can be used to focus the discussion, negate a point or introduce complexities. Similarly, discourse markers such as *right, well* and *OK*, which indicate shifts in the exposition (Swales and Malczewski, 2001), and 'phonological paragraphing',[2] which chunks spoken discourse into paragraph planning units (Thompson, 2003), appear to be crucial to understanding lectures. Finally, research also shows how schematic knowledge of the different ways of structuring a lecture is vital to comprehension. Listeners must create a mental map of the organization of the lecture as a 'sequential-hierarchic network-structure' (Givon, 1995: 64) in which information is not only received linearly but where topics and sub-topics are structured and connections made. In other words, without a familiar framework for situating information, students find it extremely difficult to follow a lecturer's argument (Allison and Tauroza, 1995).

Lectures themselves, however, are often aware of students' difficulties and employ various strategies to assist comprehension. In their Hong Kong data, for instance, Flowerdew and Miller (1997) observed lecturers adopting these techniques:

- *Features of language*: attention to micro-structuring and verbal labelling of main points

- *Interpersonal*: attempting to make lectures less threatening, personalization, checking

- *Structuring*: use of narrative thread, macro-signals of organization, rhetorical questions

- *Other media*: use of visual aids, pre- and post-reading material and tutorial discussion

These strategies, however, are rarely found in materials designed to prepare students for university study. Textbooks typically depart from an authentic lecture experience, for example, by requiring students to listen and take notes from short extracts which contain no visual material and involve a speaker reading from a script (Tauroza, 2001; Thompson, 2003). The emphasis, in other words, is limited to practising discrete, bottom-up listening skills, while more global and interactive features are largely neglected. One reason for this is that textbooks are frequently informed by research conducted in controlled, non-naturalistic conditions which fail to capture either the spoken features of face-to-face monologic discourse or replicate the student lecture experience.

ii. Informality and information

The development of spoken academic corpora in the last few years has provided greater access to authentic academic speech[3] and begun to both increase our understanding of lecture discourse and inform EAP pedagogy.[4] Perhaps the most striking feature revealed by these analyses is that, at least at first glance, lectures appear to depart from our general impressions of academic discourse and contain many linguistic characteristics that seem closer to conversation. This example from the MICASE corpus gives some idea of this (dots denote micro pauses):

1 Darwin's not the only one who, notices that. lots of competing theorists are noticing the same thing, that in ... that organisms seem to ... match with ... adapt to their environments. what Darwin does that's different, from the other theories of evolution, is propose that the mechanism by which that adaptation occurs and the mechanism that he proposes is natural selection. *<PAUSE: 05>* now I wanna spend a little bit of time talking about natural selection because, but f- first I'll just read this definition which is any inherited characteristics, that increase the likelihood of survival in reproduction are selected for, if it helps you it's gonna be selected for, and any that decrease the likelihood of survival, are selected against. now uh, one of the things that's ... hard to get about natural selection is often ... people think about natural selection as being this sentient knowledgeable all-knowing guided planful ... thing out there ... as though ... nature natural selection has a grand plan for each of us ... and it's gonna determine what things are good and what things are bad. um in fact last night I was watching with Michael we were flipping through the Discovery Channel and they had a program on, about.... these guys who were diving down to three hundred feet underneath the water trying to find a species of fish ...

This extract from an *Introduction to Psychology* lecture given to 250 students illustrates the colloquial character of much impromptu lecturing.

We see, for example, the hesitations, false starts, fragments and repetitions typical of online production, as well as filled pauses, contractions (*gonna* and *wanna*), vagueness (*thing, a little bit*) and informal constructions (*what Darwin does is, one of the things that's hard to get, these guys*) familiar from casual conversation. There is also considerable effort invested in directly acknowledging and engaging with a live audience, as the speaker takes care to set out what she will do, anticipates how the students might react to the idea of natural selection and provides a personal example involving watching TV with her partner. Finally, turning to grammar, we might note the clausal structure of the piece and see how the text is composed of a series of conversation-like short clauses rather than the phrasal syntax of textbooks (e.g. Biber, 2006).

But while lectures tend to have many of the features of conversation, they also follow the conventions of an academic register. Research tells us, for instance, that lectures are heavily hedged, particularly in humanities and social science disciplines, although this is not always for the traditional reasons of uncertainty or modesty. Poos and Simpson (2002) observe that the high frequency of '*sort of/sorta*' and '*kind of/kinda*' in arts and social science lectures often serve to socialize undergraduate students into the discipline by highlighting the negotiability of relatively vague terms such as *culture* and *communication*. Lectures also tend to be highly reflexive (Mauranen, 2001) with an abundance of metadiscursive expressions used to structure on-going speech. As we can see from the extract above, lecturers like to heavily signpost their presentations. Framing constructions (*now I wanna spend a little bit of time talking about natural selection*), and what Swales and Malczewski (2001) call 'new episode flags' (*OK, now, right*), which mark shifts in the discourse, can help enormously in guiding students through a lecture (Crawford Camiciottoli, 2004).

The extract also suggests the importance of definitions and examples in lectures. In a study of 16 lectures, for instance, Flowerdew (1992) found there was a definition about every 2 minutes as lecturers introduced terms on the fly, as in these examples from MICASE:

2   what is a false reference blank? okay <u>that is</u> any reference blank that <u>that is</u> incorrectly designed and it happens in research all the time

if the cation is a hydrogen ion H-plus, then <u>we'll be calling it</u> an acid if it's got O-H-minus <u>we call it</u> a base, and if it's got oxygen O-two-minus, <u>we call</u> it an acid-anhydride.

Swales (2001) and Simpson (2004) also note the high frequency of formulaic expressions in lectures which function to manage the discourse and highlight key information, much like in written academic genres (Hyland, 2008):

3 Sun, just two years ago by default wouldn't compile ANSI-C you had to tell them specially, compile ANSI-C for me. so, <u>the point is</u> these, slight differences among versions of the language, do impact us in a practical way.

but actually <u>it turns out that</u> the blood stream is not a particularly hospitable place, for cancer cells and in fact very few cancer cells, actually survive the trip.

but <u>the thing is,</u> it's perfectly elastic, so it was it had become a correspondence that C-F could be anything, as long as, number one holds.

Such similarities with written academic texts are a consequence of the need to construe experience in ways which encourage learners to think about content not just as facts, but as complex systems. It is a language suited to talking about thinking itself and about sets of complex relationships. This involves presenting material in certain conventional ways which require, in part, speakers and writers to explicitly label their discourse structure and direction, highlight key points and rework utterances to offer a reformulation or concrete instance of what they have said.

iii. Interaction and evaluation

Perhaps counter intuitively, the most distinguishing feature of academic lectures is their relatively high levels of involvement and interactivity: the ways they bring the speaker and audience closer and so add a dimension that is absent from most textbooks. Interactive lecturing, where the lecturer speaks from notes or visuals, for example, seems to be growing in popularity in the UK (Flowerdew, 1994).

In part, interactivity is achieved by the kinds of explicit signalling of intent I mentioned above as speakers frame stretches of talk to actively engage listeners, but we can also see how other features contribute to learner involvement in this short extract from a MICASE biology lecture. Here, through the informal label 'folks', inclusive pronouns, questions and the adoption of a personal stance, the speaker takes the trouble to address his audience directly:

4 okay folks. I think I'm gonna, bring us back now. um, so I wanna talk now about micro-evolution, which is usually defined as the mechanism of evolution. um I first wanna make clear a couple of things. um first of all what is it exactly that evolves? I mean we've all talked about how our ideas are evolving or our, our um, our relationships evolve but as biological beings ... individual organisms do not evolve.

Woven into the ideational content concerning how the concept of evolution should be understood are statements which call attention to the discourse itself and its possible reception. These statements provide information about how the lecture will be organized and about the relationship the speaker wants to establish with her audience.

One of the most obvious mechanisms a speaker can use to establish a relationship with an audience is pronominal reference. Walsh (2004) adopts Goffman's (1981) notion of 'footing' to make the point that while the relationship between lecture participants remains relatively fixed at the level of speech event, the speaker can vary this at utterance level by adopting different allegiances and projecting different roles onto students. This is most easily done in English by exploiting the vagueness of pronoun reference; shifting the scope of *you* and *we* to more directly engage students in both the material and the learning process. This is clear in the use of 'inclusive we' in acts of discourse framing to involve students in the unfolding speech event:

> **5**   and yes this is up on the web <PAUSE : 15> are <u>we</u> okay? oh we have time to do this okay. now, <u>let's</u> do the Marxist over here first, because this is what <u>we've</u> just done and then I wanna contrast it with liberal pluralists.

We and *you* play a key role in creating an atmosphere of interaction and involvement in lectures and are often used to include students in the community of experts, drawing them into the processes of disciplinary research and the questions which motivate them:

> **6**   what <u>we</u> want to know is which is the most parsimonious cladogram. that's what <u>you</u> would be, that's the question that <u>you're</u> asking, in doing a particular analysis. the first thing <u>you</u> wanna do is <u>you</u> have a bunch of traits that <u>you've</u> observed, on these organisms, then <u>you</u> want to know how to analyze these traits. the first thing <u>you</u> have to do since <u>you</u> only want to look at shared derived features, features that are not primitive, and features that are shared, is that <u>you</u> have to determine polarity. how do <u>you</u> know whether something's a primitive trait or a derived trait?

Second person pronouns also function to involve students when discussing the occurrence or existence of something. They can, for example, be used to replace more predictable passive or *there* structures (Example 7), or to assign students roles in hypothetical worlds of action to bring alive examples or cases (Example 8):

7 so just because <u>we</u> can't see bacteria, doesn't mean <u>we</u> can't study them scientifically, because <u>we</u> have microscopes and other machines that can help <u>us</u> see bacteria

8 if there was a wrongful death, so <u>you</u> could go to the government, and <u>you</u> could petition, the shogun, <u>you</u> could petition the government and say, I wish to have a license to go and kill somebody as a vendetta, and they would grant <u>you</u> that.

In addition to inclusive pronouns, evaluative language helps to create and negotiate interpersonal relations between the speaker and an audience. Bamford (2004), for instance, points to the importance of signalling nouns such as *problem* which is often used in lectures to prospectively or retrospectively frame a stretch of talk in the judgments of the discipline, alerting students to the shared norms and understandings of the field.

9 and, another <u>problem</u> is, that he's often misrepresented and simplified, by both folks who … are Marxist or claim to be Marxist and by folks who, oppose Marxism.

so they therefore are not totally respectful of the idea of other people owning land. so that's another <u>problem.</u>

Perhaps more explicitly, evaluations function interactively in cases where the lecturer takes a clear stance towards the propositional content of his or her talk using modal verbs and stance adverbs (Biber, 2006). In Biber's data, modals frequently signalled upcoming information or future topics (*we will look at, I'd like you to*), but they are also widely used to express possibility in the MICASE lectures, particularly *would* and *might*. Lecturers also frequently use stance adverbs, sometimes to identify information as factual and beyond dispute (Example 10), but more generally to express likelihood and convey something of the tentativeness of academic discourse (Example 11):

10 … this high frequency is <u>definitely</u> not due to the fact that this allele confers any advantage.

… and <u>in fact</u> if you look, one or two days after you've injected those cancer cells in the lungs, you will find lots of cancer cells, lodged in the lungs.

11 <u>presumably,</u> this is not a five-H-T two-A receptor. but, some other one is. and it's, <u>probably</u> postsynaptic.

… the blood vessel they're, li- most <u>likely to</u> invade into is gonna be a very tiny capillary cuz it's got the thinnest wall.

Finally, a word about questions. Successful interaction depends on a sense of co-occupation of the same social space and questions are a frequent means of making the shared here and now a salient feature of the discourse. In fact, questions in lectures play both textual and interpersonal roles, organizing the flow of information and indicating a desire for a more dialogic discourse. Not all questions expect a response however, and the majority of questions in lectures fail to open the floor to students at all. Instead, they tend to be either rhetorical, pulling students along with the monologue, or act as comprehension checks, ensuring that students are following the line of argument. This extract from a MICASE management lecture gives some flavour of these uses:

> **12** There are three questions you wanna ask, when you wanna know, if people are motivated or not. The first one is direction right? Where is their effort directed? What tasks are getting done? Right? This, basic thing, where is their effort directed? The second, is amplitude right? How much effort are they devoting, to a particular task? How much of a task is getting done? That's the second diagnostic question when we wanna figure out if people are motivated, or not, to do something that we want, that we want them to get done. Finally persistence, right? How long does their effort last? How long are they doing a particular task? Okay those are the three, questions for, detecting whether in fact, what we want to motivate, is being motivated right?

Overall, it is clear that not everything which occurs in a lecture works to convey information. Speakers not only seek to ensure that the information they present is intelligible, but also that it is understood, accepted and, hopefully, acted upon. Students must be drawn in, engaged, motivated to follow along, and perhaps be persuaded by the discourse and to do this speakers attempt to shape their texts to the anticipated expectations and requirements of receivers.

9.2 Seminars

Although lectures tend to predominate at lower levels of university instruction, classes often become smaller and the interaction in them more frequent as students progress. Seminars seek to further the disciplinary acculturation of graduate and advanced students and are often based around texts, groupwork activities (Northcott, 2001) or student presentations (Basturkmen, 2002; Weissberg, 1993). Essentially, however, they can be seen as relatively informal, small group, tutor-led events at which everyone present is asked to participate. This overt participation is highly regarded by students and appears to make instruction more effective (Morell, 2007). It can also encourage greater involvement by non-native English speaking students (Kang, 2005), although interaction may simply increase the cognitive demands of an already difficult listening task (Northcott, 2001). Once again, however, we know very little about how this genre works or its impact on learning, although research allows us to say something about its key features.

i. Interactivity and personalization

Clearly, explicit interactivity is a defining feature of seminars. The MICASE statistics, for example, show that students contributed 35 per cent of the total words in the seminar corpus compared with just 6 per cent in the large lectures. Class size and students' knowledge of the subject will obviously influence how far participation is possible, but equally important is the skill of the tutor in facilitating it. Interactivity in spoken discourse requires speakers to demonstrate their involvement in the flow of talk and engagement in a shared context. They do this largely by expressing a personal stance to the topic and by referring to themselves and addressees, which means that we find seminars contain more of the features identified by Morell (2004) as characteristic of interactive lectures: personal pronouns, discourse markers, elicitations, questions and negotiation.

One way we can see the distinctiveness of seminars is to make use of the Wordsmith KeyWords[5] tool, which highlights statistically significant differences between corpora. This shows us that the words which best distinguish seminars from large lectures in MICASE are those which also characterize the interactivity of informal conversation, that is *I, yeah, mhm, know, like, right, um*. More helpfully, we can see the distinctiveness of seminars by comparing the extensive use of personal pronouns in this genre. Table 9.1, for instance, shows that the MICASE seminars contain almost 50 per cent more cases than the large lecture corpus. While these findings may be skewed by low frequencies,[6] they indicate some key differences between the two genres and something of the interaction that occurs in them.

It is not surprising to find fewer cases of *we* in the seminars, for example. Audience inclusive *we* tends to be the predominant form in spoken academic

TABLE 9.1 *Personal reference in seminars and large lectures (per 1,000 words)*

	I	Me	You (Subject and object)	We	Us	Let's	Totals
Seminars	29.5	1.7	28.7	7.9	0.8	0.6	69.2
Large lectures	13.8	1.3	21.6	10.2	0.8	1.0	48.7

TABLE 9.2 *Main collocates of 'you' in MICASE seminars and lectures*

Seminars				Lectures			
you know you	81	and you know	49	you have to	81	you have a	44
you knowl	75	that you know	48	you can see	79	that you can	43
you know the	72	you know that	42	you look at	55	so if you	40
uh you know	65	do you know	40	if you look	48	and if you	38
um you know	52	you know uh	37	and you can	47	you know you	38

discourse (Fortanet, 2004), and I noted above that in lectures it largely works to reduce the distance between speaker and audience to promote awareness of a common purpose. The greater social and physical proximity of the graduate seminar, however, perhaps makes such explicit structuring of involvement less urgent. In most seminars there tends to be greater overlap of knowledge and more opportunities provided by the context for participants to see how they might contribute to the discussion.

Something of the immediacy and interactivity of the seminar is also shown by the more frequent use of *I* and *you* in the seminars, and this also points to the different ways that speakers tend to engage with each other in these events. Table 9.2, for example shows that the pronoun *you* collocates principally with cognition verbs such as *think* and *know* in the seminars and with verbs of perception and ability like *look, see* and *can* in the lectures. At first glance, this might suggest that perhaps there is more emphasis on speaker stance and direct participant involvement in the seminars and more concern with the management of learning in lectures.

Essentially, as we noted above, *you* is often used by lecturers to orientate listeners to the discourse and focus students' attention on the topic. The clusters (or frequently occurring sequences) shown in Table 9.2 are common ways of doing this:

13 ... you have to convert, to capital X and capital Y. okay?

... you can see you just get slightly different results.

... so if you look in your guide, you'll see that some plants, are rated, for their hardiness

In the seminars, however, *you* occurs principally with the verb *know*, which on closer study is only partly due to the speaker attributing understanding to others. More often, it occurs in the unplanned speech of student contributors to buy time as they organize their thoughts:

14 Student: then like the other one is like, totally strong and <u>you know</u> but, Offred is like, she's more like what a Christian woman should be because she's not like, <u>you know</u> too extreme or too evil

Student: uh well you <u>know you</u> can claim that the, overall picture <u>you know</u> could be, uh <u>you know</u> that it's correlated with many things and and that there's not necessarily a causal relationship

The frequency of this pattern as a floor holding strategy in the seminar discourse indicates the online planning and direct orientation to interlocutors typical of less formal oral genres and illustrates the very different patterns of a more egalitarian discourse than found in the lectures.

The most striking difference between the seminars and lectures, however, is in the use of the first person, with twice as many examples in the seminars (see Table 9.1 above). The pronoun I often occurs in cetain fixed patterns or clusters and helps confirm Biber *et al's*. (2004) observation that classroom teaching contains far more stance clusters than either conversation or written academic genres. In the seminar corpus where clusters with *I* overwhelmingly convey attitudes or assessments of relative certainty:

15 Student: mhm. Although <u>I think that</u> Benjamin himself doesn't, necessarily see all the advantages and disadvantages.

Student: so, you know <u>I think that</u> that's, that's an incomplete solution, and <u>I don't think</u> it's, the cure all that you're, you're claiming it is.

In fact, by far the most frequent 3-word *I* cluster in the seminar data is *I don't know*. This is a collocation which can express the speaker's unfamiliarity or uncertainty with a topic, but which more often helps oil the interactional wheels. This is typically achieved either by interjecting a personal note into an academic comment, or by hedging a statement to tone down its impact on the hearer, as in this exchange:

16 Student: um, yeah, famille d'yeux <u>I don't know</u>, that's a good question. cuz I saw this being a, a poem very much between, the narrator and les yeux des pauvres, and not, the narrator and this woman

Tutor: um, <u>I don't know</u>, I feel like it would, it would kinda cheat, the s- the strength of the satire. Okay? So unless you mean, something like, well actually within this novel, we see instances of, real service or you know, um, persecution that should be borne, right? Unless you mean that, uh <u>I don't know</u>, I don't quite, I don't quite follow why, you are, objecting the way you are.

Such strategies are useful to both lecturers attempting to maintain social cohesion by reducing the privileged status of their contributions and students wishing to avoid appearing too unfashionably swotish.

ii. Turns and exchanges

I have, until now, illustrated aspects of spoken discourse as isolated example utterances, but we have to remember that seminars are dialogic, or often multi-logic, in that the discourse is jointly constructed and multi-authored. While often including lengthy monologic episodes, they typically evolve through the taking of successive, relatively short, turns by different participants. These may be unsolicited questions and comments by students to the tutor or student presenters, but more often they are orchestrated by a tutor-led discussion following some initial presentation or group work.

Questions are important here. Unlike their role in managing the flow and understanding of information in lectures, questions in seminars are oriented to content and function to raise issues, introduce information and get responses. The hierarchical relationships of the lecture remain however, as most questions come from the seminar leader, either thrown out generally or through nomination:

17 Tutor: what do you think? [S4: um] things you would change? If any?

Tutor: Jeremy, why don't you start and, tell us what your, thoughts were about this.

Tutor: does anyone else wanna tease anything else out of that poem?

Tutor: uh does the audience have any questions they want to ask either of the teams? Yeah, Harry?

While questions are typically designed to elicit the knowledge and experience of the students, they also serve to guide the interaction and structure the discourse.

In her study of student-to-student discussions following case-study presentations in MBA seminars, for example, Basturkmen (2002) found that the most frequent pattern of interaction was the simple Initiation– Response– Feedback sequence. This was originally identified by Sinclair and Coulthard (1991) as the basic exchange unit in school classrooms, as here:

Initiation	Teacher:	Where does he live?
Response	Student:	Rome
Follow-up	Teacher:	Rome, yes

The remaining interactions in the seminars involved an elaboration of this pattern, with the first speaker using the follow-up move to re-initiate another sequence. Basturkmen notes that this typically occurred when the speaker was dissatisfied with a response, with the exchange continuing until reaching an acceptable outcome. In the MICASE data however, such extended chains of utterances are the spine of the discourse. This is a key way in which this genre develops as the seminar leader works to draw more students into the discourse and create a discussion.

Ultimately, then, interlocutors work together to jointly construct and negotiate meaning through a dialogic process in which ideas and views emerge. This example is typical of this process:

18 Initiation: Tutor: what do you think?

   Response: S13: don't you need to you have to do
                          undergrad before you do PhD.

   Follow up/initiation: Tutor: yeah, so?

   Response: S13: so if there's less people going to
                          undergraduate school then there's less people
                          available to go, get a PhD.

   Follow up/initiation: Tutor: absolutely there's a, uh you know that's
                          right, fewer people and what what else might
                          happen? why are these things like you didn't
                          actually link it [S12: right] specifically in your paper
                          but, they're they are linked, yeah.

   Response: S2: there'll be uh a skew in, in the type of
                          information that is produced and in the type of
                          research perhaps that is uh, that they partake in.

   Follow up/initiation: Tutor: why would that be?

   Response: S2: well if you, if there's a decrease in minorities
                          for instance, in the undergraduate and then
                          therefore there's a decrease in minorities then
                          in the PhD program, there's less, research just
                          by the the the trends, that have been taken. uh
                          more people tend to do research that is pertinent
                          to themselves.

While tutor questions help drive the discussions, not all contributions are explicitly solicited. Individuals respond to each other, or more usually the tutor, to express a view or comment on what has been said. Interestingly, these utterances rely heavily on concession and the interpersonal paraphernalia of spoken interaction, with due care given to the protection of personal face and the maintenance of group solidarity. Making a contribution to a seminar is an assertion of power and so calls for mitigation. Here, for example, we see some of the ways that students mark their interventions with appropriate tentativeness and humility:

> **19** He also <u>sort of</u> attributes that conformity to um, the fact that, like Haussmann and um, the emperor were <u>basically just, sort of</u> in bed with the same five, real estate companies right?
>
> Another thing there is, <u>I don't know exactly how that works</u> but, but <u>I thought</u> it was interesting the way that all those, <u>um,</u> new apartments, had, <u>like</u> the, the side that faced the, the street was, the living room and the dining room and so, <u>in a sense like,</u> the, the everyday life is also uniformed in its relation of the public and private, areas.
>
> … but, but <u>I don't think</u> she is though. <u>I think that</u> her, it could be interpreted that way but <u>I don't think</u> that's the way she <u>uh</u> …

Finally, seminar discourse is also fashioned through student questions. These are largely requests for clarification on certain points of content and, interestingly, they are often prefaced with an explicit labelling of the speech act, possibly to reduce the abruptness of an intervention or any suspicion that the contribution might be seeking to challenge what has gone before. These examples are typical:

> **20** S8: can I ask a quick <u>question?</u> um, are the percentages, what are can you just, explain the percentages again to me?
>
> S3: okay my <u>question</u> is, how do we know that the numina does not already have these, processes already involved?
>
> S3: I have a <u>question</u> [Tutor: yeah] so the main difference between the- this hypothesis and the other one is that the action of, the serotonin is either presynaptic or postsynaptic?

Such requests are common in the MICASE seminar data and once again underline the role that negotiation of meaning plays in this instructional discourse, allowing different participants to work together to arrive at a mutual understanding of their utterances and the topic.

This overview is clearly very preliminary and there are many other features of this genre worthy of study. We might, for example, profitably explore the role of humour and irony, rephrasing and elaboration, topic management, the expression of evaluation and the oral style of student presentations themselves. I hope to have shown, however, that the graduate seminar is a rich and interesting discourse which will amply reward further study.

9.3 Undergraduate textbooks

Textbooks are indispensablo to academic life, facilitating the professional's role as a teacher and constituting one of the primary means by which the concepts and analytical methods of a discipline are acquired. They play a major role in the learners' experience and understanding of a subject by providing a coherently ordered epistemological map of the disciplinary landscape and, through their textual practices, can help convey the values and ideologies of a particular academic culture. This link to the discipline is crucial for novices seeking to extend their competence into new areas of knowledge and trying to cope with the specific demands of a new interpretive community. Thus students, particularly in the sciences, often see textbooks as concrete embodiments of the knowledge of their field.

University textbooks, however, are, once again, something of a neglected genre. Little is known about their rhetorical structure, their relationship to other genres, or the ways that they vary across disciplines. This section looks at this important genre to examine the ways that textbook authors speak to students, and indirectly to their peers, in constructing a plausible vision of their disciplines.

i. Authority and intertextuality

Textbooks are widely regarded, particularly by undergraduate students, as repositories of codified knowledge and disciplinary lore: places where the accepted theories of a discipline are defined and acknowledged fact represented. Brown refers to this as canonizing discourse:

> At any point in time, the canon is fixed in that it represents as conventional wisdom that any competent member of the discipline would except as uncontroversial. In this way the canon presents a view of the discipline that epitomizes and underscores the disciplines own sense of identity and intellectual tradition.

(1993: 65)

The canon then, is a dominant perspective that helps construct a coherent conception of what the discipline is and what it stands for. It is an ideological representation of stability and authority. Bakhtin (1981: 427) refers to this as 'undialogized' discourse, privileged in its absolute definition of reality, thus the textbook represents an attempt to shape and order the disputes, controversies and variety of a field, reducing the mulitivocity of past texts to a single voice of authority.

So textbooks are both evidence of a paradigm (Kuhn, 1970) and examples of intertextuality. That is, the property that texts have of being comprised of 'snatches of other texts, which may be explicitly demarcated or merged in, and which the text may assimilate, contradict, ironically echo, and so forth' (Fairclough, 1992: 84). Textbooks are, by definition, composed of other texts. Their value depends on them representing the issues, ideas, current beliefs and chief findings of the discipline by borrowing and incorporating these from their original sources. Other texts are adopted for a new audience and developed through commentary, tasks, examples or analyses, with the original words of their authors being recast as bullet points, sidebars, flowcharts, paraphrases, summaries or otherwise worked into a new discourse and recoverable from it.

In addition to such explicit intertextuality, however, textbooks also borrow interdiscursively from the conventions, values and practices of their fields. Most obviously, there are differences in the form and presentation of textbooks. Those in business studies, for example, often resemble coffee-table books and display marketing norms in their use of colour and glossy presentation, while the taxonomies and electron micrographs common in biology textbooks help represent and construct a knowable, objective world. More importantly, writers draw on the genres, models and beliefs of their communities in constructing their material, representing their field in particular ways. They are not concerned only with presenting an accessible introduction to subject matter, but with providing students with a framework for understanding the field. In economics, for example, the repetition of patterns which move from general statements about economic processes to historical or hypothetical examples helps acculturate students into a disciplinary schema (Bondi, 1999). Similarly, the structure of geology textbooks, based on the cycle of past processes producing present geological features which in turn provide evidence for these processes, reflect the basic taxonomic principles of the discipline (Love, 1993).

Textbooks thus both contain evidence of other texts and of the 'ways of seeing' of their disciplines. They are also creatures of their communities in other ways, and in particular in the roles they play in different fields. In hard knowledge fields the discipline appears to be defined in its textbooks, embodying its truths and current areas of professional activity. So, in the sciences and hard social sciences, certitude, abstract nominalizations, thematic structure and style, seem to reinforce existing paradigms. In philosophy and composition, on the other hand, textbooks are altogether more circumspect and are often important vehicles for presenting original research (e.g. Gebhardt, 1993). The regular publication of new editions of textbooks in communication theory and marketing, for example, both updates fast changing information and disseminates new work.

ii. Audiences and literacies

For many students textbooks do not only represent the knowledge and methods of a discipline but also provide a model of literacy practices: how the discipline discusses what it knows. But while students attempt to acquire the specialized narratives of their community along with its subject knowledge, the language used in setting out a canon is very different from that of arguing for new claims (e.g. Hyland, 2004b). In concealing much of the argumentative nature of science, the textbook reshuffles its discourse to replace the novel and provisional with the familiar and accredited.

For one thing, authors feel less need to explicitly reference earlier work. Because they are attempting to weave currently accepted knowledge into a coherent whole rather than construct academic facts, tying ideas to their sources is less imperative. This absence of acknowledgment itself bestows an implicit acceptance on what is reported and establishes a very different representational context. While students in the soft fields are more likely to encounter argument structures which reach outside the text by citing the source of claims, evidence in the sciences is largely presented in terms of general experimental work or unassigned activity in the field:

21 Surface structures of the pathoge\nic Neisseria have been <u>the subject of intense microbiological investigations for some time.</u>

(Biology)

<u>A great amount of research has been carried out in the past years</u> to improve the toughness of ceramic materials.

(Physics)

<u>Experiments indicate that</u> such behavior does indeed occur for impact velocities in excess of the critical impact velocity, and....

(Mechanical Engineering)

It has also often been noted that textbooks contain far more unmodified assertions than other forms of academic writing, disdaining the caution of research genres to underscore the factual status of propositions (e.g. Latour and Woolgar, 1979). As in these examples:

22 <u>It is a well-established fact that</u> if the mechanical resonance frequency occurs inside or near the servo bandwidth, the loop's stability is degraded ...

(Mechanical Engineering)

<u>It is generally agreed that</u> the stigma attached to divorce has been considerably reduced. This, in itself, <u>will</u> make divorce easier.

(Sociology)

Einstein suggested that this might be possible, and <u>indeed</u> this has been <u>experimentally confirmed countless times</u> and forms the basis for many important processes.

(Biology)

When qualifications are omitted the result is both greater certainty and less deference, reflecting a different attitude to both information and readers. Here is a pedagogic model where the expert is distinguished from the novice and the process of learning treated as a one-way transfer of knowledge. The student, in other words, is initiated through the text into a new world of cultural and social competence.

The textbook genre, however, is not simply a celebration of academic truths. While hedges are far more common in the soft knowledge fields (Hyland, 2004b), all writers pick their way through the information they present, sorting the taken-for-granted from the still uncertain. This is particularly the case where authors speculate about the future or distant past (Example 23), or when generalizations may attract challenges if presented baldly (Example 24):

23   ... earliest cells <u>could also have</u> obtained energy by chemoor-ganotrophic mechanisms, most <u>likely</u> simple fermentations. Photosynthesis is also a <u>possibility</u> but <u>seems less likely</u> ...

(Biology)

<u>We cannot say as yet</u> how far these extreme inequalities of gender are <u>likely to</u> become less acute in the near future. It is <u>possible</u> that there are ...

(Sociology)

24 In such systems, use of an amplifier with a differential input together with the use of input guarding will <u>probably</u> be the answer to this ground-loop problem

(Electrical Engineering)

They <u>seem to</u> be very fundamental functions of language, <u>perhaps</u> because they derive from the basic components of any interaction ...

(Applied Linguistics)

In contrast, boosters are often used to give readers a clear picture of scientific progress, distinguishing the false assumptions of the past from the assurances of the present. The manipulation of certainty can therefore help establish an ideological schema for students concerning the increasing ability of their discipline to describe the world:

> **25** <u>We now know that</u> the various components of the substrate are far from exhausted after the initial flushes of growth and sporulation. <u>What has really happened is</u> that Coprinus has seized control by suppressing most of the other fungi. Hyphae of Coprinus <u>are actually</u> ...
>
> (Biology)

This kind of authorial assuredness helps the writer gain scholastic influence among students. But it is, of course, addressed as much to colleagues as to learners, imprinting a personal stamp on what peers might otherwise see as a recounting of disciplinary orthodoxy. In fact, regarding textbooks as a purely instructional discourse simplifies a rhetorically more complex picture. While writers gain little institutional credit for producing textbooks, an activity often regarded as commercial and unscholarly by university promotion committees, they are aware that they are writing for a professional as well as student audience. It is disciplinary peers who recommend textbook adoptions and orchestrate their use in classes, and it is only with the peer audience that credibility is gained and copies sold (Swales, 1995).

Writers therefore tread a line between representing new material for learners and constructing an acceptable representation of the discipline for colleagues, and this helps to account for the intrusion of personal attitudes and evaluation in this genre. The explicit presence of the writer marks out an individual perspective on the discipline and announces a confident and expert guide in full control of the material, as these examples suggest:

> **26** <u>I am convinced, for my part, that</u> no ontology – that is to say, no apprehension of ontological mystery in whatever degree – is possible ...
>
> (Philosophy)

> <u>My own view is that</u> Krashen's hypotheses do not, on closer inspection, conform to the three linguistic questions.
>
> (Applied Linguistics)

> <u>What is most interesting is that</u> we can also subtract n (or add -n) by moving the arrow 16 – it positions clockwise.
>
> (Electrical Engineering)

Textbook authors, then, appear to be very alive to both the role of textbooks in introducing neophytes to the practices of their disciplines and to the judgements of their fellow professionals.

iii. Arguments and asymmetries

While textbooks express something of the literacy practices of their disciplines and their writers' desire to gain professional credibility among their peers, they are principally instructional discourses. The use of both *interactive* resources, which help guide the reader through a text, and *interactional* features, designed to involve the reader in the discourse underline this goal (Hyland and Tse, 2004). We see in these choices a complex array of motives, but most centrally a didactic model concerned with laying out disciplinary content as clearly as possible and constructing the participant identities of professional and novice through the writer's assumptions about reader competence.

Looking at interactive items first, we can identify a range of features in textbooks which display writers' sensitivity to their readers' prior knowledge and processing needs. Perhaps the most obvious of these is the explicit signalling of logicality. Essentially, novices lack the domain knowledge of the expert to make connections between entities and to see the implicit cohesion of a text, and this means that writers must provide a framework which shows links between ideas more explicitly. The following two extracts dealing with lipids, the first from a research article and the second from a textbook, illustrate these different ways of structuring texts:

> **27** Steryl glucosides are characteristic lipids of plant membranes. The biosynthesis of these lipids is catalyzed by the membrane-bound UDP-glucose sterol glucosyltransferase.
>
> The purified enzyme (Warnecke and Heinz, 1994) has been used for the cloning of a corresponding CDNA from oat (*Avena sativa L*.). Amino acid sequences derived from the amino terminus of the purified protein and from peptides of a trypsin digestion were used to construct oligonucleotide primers for polymerase chain reaction experiments.
>
> (Biology)

> **28** Although the nature of the fatty acid can be highly variable, the key point is that the chemical linkage to glycerol is an ester link. By contrast, archaeal lipids consist of ether-linked molecules (see Figure 20.1). In ester-linked lipids, the fatty acids are straight chain (linear) molecules, whereas in ether-linked lipids, branched chained hydrocarbons are present. In Archaea, long chain branched hydrocarbons, either of the phytanyl or biphytanyl type, are bonded by ether linkage to glycerol molecules (see Figure 20.1).
>
> (Biology)

While the reader needs domain knowledge to infer connections in the first example, this textbook author takes considerable trouble to spell these out. Using connectives, evaluative commentary, references to examples and code glosses giving on-the-fly definitions, he attempts to link readers' existing knowledge with the new specialized terms of the discipline.

This concern with what the audience can be expected to know and what needs to be spelt out, is also apparent in the copious use of examples and, in the sciences, the constant to-ing and fro-ing between text and visuals. Lemke (1998: 87) observes that scientific concepts are typically 'semiotic hybrids, simultaneously and essentially verbal, mathematical, visual-graphical, and action-operational' so that meanings are created through the rhetorical combination of images and text. Switching the reader between these modes therefore not only highlights particular features of content, but also exposes learners to the ways that the verbal and visual interact in the sciences and the different affordances of these modes. Thus constant exposure, to examples such as these, help induct learners into the discourses of their fields.

29 The radial-vane design <u>shown in Figure 3.14</u> is just such a variation and does in fact have a nearly linear scale.

(Electrical Engineering)

<u>Figure 10.49</u> compares the thermal conductivities of many ceramic materials as a function of temperature.

(Physics)

The use of visuals in textbooks, therefore, represents important conventions of field-specific argumentation. By requiring students to interpret and orient to this way of representing reality this contributes towards their acquisition of a new literacy.

Textbooks also take more care than research articles to keep readers informed about where they are in the unfolding text and where they are going. The use of frame markers (Hyland, 2004a and 2005) to announce discourse goals, indicate topic shifts and label text stages, however, not only helps the reader to process information but can simultaneously construct the writer as an expert guide and the reader as a passive novice following the trail laid down:

30 <u>Finally, one must consider</u> the effects of the measurement methods used to obtain data for repeatability and accuracy.

(Mechanical Engineering)

<u>This chapter discusses</u> the characteristics of the different types of meter movements used to measure alternating current (ac).

(Electrical Engineering)

<u>We shall see in this section that</u> these differences in emphasis imply quite different analyses of the role and functions of the capitalist state.

(Sociology)

The writer speaks here as an authority, an expert knower possessing superior knowledge in an interaction which simultaneously constitutes the reader as less expert.

This differentiation of status is equally clear in the use of interactional features, and particularly in the heavy use of second person pronouns, which are rare in peer-to-peer genres such as research articles. By explicitly acknowledging the readers' presence, *you* is ostensibly the most interactive of pronouns. But as it clearly distinguishes writer and reader it also differentiates categories of knowledge and competence, allocating participants into different groups:

31 Perhaps now <u>you can understand</u> why <u>I and many other teaching mycologists</u> ask our classes to put their culturally determined attitudes on hold, …

(Biology)

<u>You should encourage your</u> local engineering chapters, such as Tau Beta Pi, to invite outside lecturers to discuss these topics with you. It is important that <u>you learn how to protect yourself</u> from being found guilty by a judge or jury for a 'dangerous product design'.

(Mechanical Engineering)

Watch for the answers to the following questions <u>as you read</u> the chapter. They should <u>help you understand</u> the material presented.

(Electrical Engineering)

Once more, then, there is a clear implication that the writer is an expert in full command of the topic and the audience. The texts establish clear role relationships, with the writer acting as a primary-knower in assisting novice readers towards a range of values, facts and practices that will enable them to interpret and employ academic knowledge in institutionally approved ways.

Perhaps the most obvious manifestation of how writers negotiate an asymmetrical relationship of competence, however, is through the use of directives, which expressly emphasize correct courses of action or thought through imperatives and necessity modals:

32 <u>It must be noted that</u> sometimes the molecular weight distribution can be important in ways that are not obvious.

(Physics)

Here are the introduction and instructions <u>you should read</u> to respondents, <u>practice reading</u> them beforehand until they sound fairly conversational.

(Sociology)

As you read this excerpt, <u>pay particular attention</u> to how the teacher sets up the structure of the student–student interaction.

(Applied Linguistics)

While directives are also heavily used in research papers in the sciences, they are more common and often more personal in the textbooks, explicitly positioning readers through choices which assume an inequality that is closer to classroom than peer interaction.

Textbooks are therefore a distinctive form of academic discourse. In framing disciplinary knowledge through selecting and sequencing content, writers commit themselves to a perspective on their fields. At the same time, they build both an authoritative picture of their discipline for learners, and an uncontroversial depiction of its central features for peers. By asking (mainly rhetorical) questions, varying their certainty, evaluating ideas, issuing directives, providing definitions and leading readers to particular interpretations, writers massively intervene in these texts to construct themselves as experts and establish a knowledge-transfer perspective of teaching. At the same time, however, textbooks are not blandly uniform and in various ways represent the discourse of their parent cultures, helping students to gain some understanding of the ways that meanings are encoded in their disciplines.

9.4 Conclusions

Although collected here under the heading of 'instructional discourses', it is clear that the three genres examined in this chapter vary considerably in the ways they map disciplinary knowledge, negotiate information and establish participant relationships. It is also the case that contextual factors such as discipline, student level, mode of learning and so on, will play a significant part in how students experience these genres as part of their courses. Most obviously, however, it would be wrong to understand any of these three genres in terms of straightforward information-transfer, as participant relations and complex interactional patterns lie at the heart of each of them.

Textbooks seem to have a very conservative role and are often depicted as representations of disciplinary orthodoxy established through writers' attempts to construct an expert–novice relationship, while large lectures seem to offer few opportunities for interaction. Corpus data, however, suggests an increasing tendency for these genres to recognize that students need to be actively involved in learning. We have seen, in fact, that lecturers, seminar leaders and textbook writers go to some lengths to establish connections with their students to encourage engagement and facilitate learning. This is because it is by no means certain that employing rhetorical choices which distance one-who-knows and one-who-doesn't can be the basis for successful learning (Bourdieu and Passeron, 1996). Vygotsky (1978), for example, has stressed that learning is not simply a passive transference of knowledge from the more to the less competent but involves an interactive process in which learners increasingly participate in a community of social practice (Lave and Wenger, 1991). Explicit interaction and negotiation, long established in seminars, are therefore beginning to find their way into lectures, with questions, discourse markers and personal pronouns becoming particularly prominent.

Another feature of instructional genres, emphasized in my discussion of textbooks in particular, is that while they principally address the informational needs of the uninitiated, they are also embedded in the rhetorical and social conventions of their discipline. Learning a disciplinary culture and learning its language are inseparable, as this is the only context in which the language has meaning. Students, in other words, do not learn disciplinary knowledge independently of language but become competent through an understanding of how language constitutes and is constituted by interaction within a discipline. Instructional discourses are a key way through which this is achieved.

Notes

1 This follows the MICASE classification of academic speech events at the University of Michigan.

2 There is some disagreement about which phonological features are important here, but most analysts accept that a basic requirement is that the speaker ends a phonological paragraph with low termination followed by a jump up to relatively high pitch on the onset syllable of the next unit, sometimes with a pause between them.

3 Both the MICASE and BASE corpora are publicly available and openly accessible through online software.

4 The main spoken academic corpora are:

- TOEFL 2000 Spoken and Written Academic Language Corpus (T2K-SWAL)
- Hong Kong Corpus of Spoken English (HKCSE) http://www.engl.polyu. edu. hk/department/academicstaff/Personal/ChengWinnie/HKCorpus_ SpokenEnglish.htm

- Michigan Corpus of Academic Spoken English (MICASE) http://quod.lib.umich.edu/m/micase/

- British Academic Spoken English (BASE) corpus http://www2.warwick.ac.uk/fac/soc/celte/research/base/

5 This program identifies words and phrases that occur significantly more frequently in one corpus than another using a log-likelihood statistic. This offers a better characterization of the differences between two corpora than a simple comparison of individual words ranked for frequency as it identifies items which are 'key' differentiators across many files, rather than being dominated by the most common words in each corpus.

6 The version of MICASE used here contains 31 large lectures of 257,300 words and 8 seminars of 151,000 words.

10

Images in the news

Monika Bednarek and Helen Caple

10.1 Introduction

This chapter focuses on still and moving images in the news, including the kinds of images that get taken up in the news and their role within news discourse. This means examining the communicative functions of images, which have been largely influenced by the historical contexts underpinning news discourse. We will focus in this chapter on the ways this relates specifically to photography. Historically, print news has been somewhat text-dominated, and where images have been used, little attention has been given to their position or function within news discourse (see also Caple 2010b). However, as can be seen in Figure 10.1, news story structure has shifted and images now tend to dominate the verbal text: indeed, in some cases, it is the image that is propelling a story into the news.

FIGURE 10.1 *Story packaging – the evolution of news print from text-dominance to image-dominance*

New ways of telling stories online, such as on news homepages or in multimedia sections, also incorporate both verbal and visual elements. The organization of such verbal–visual texts and the relations between the verbal and the visual thus deserve further attention. In this chapter we examine the ways in which words and images relate to each other within a particular news story, be it in the newspaper, on television or online. Our objectives for this chapter are to enable readers to understand:

- the communicative functions of images in the news
- the historical context underpinning the use of news images
- the position of images in the organization of news
- relationships between words and still and moving images.

10.2 The communicative functions of news images

While illustrations have appeared in news print since the very beginnings of the mass news media, their position and prominence have been somewhat (but not totally) contingent on the development of technologies capable of clearly rendering them on the printed page and on the screen. We will refer to these technological developments throughout this section, but for ease of reference Table 10.1 offers a timeline of major shifts in the technological advancement of photography, film and printing as they relate to and impact on the use of images in the news.

More importantly though, when and how images have been used in the reporting of news events has been very much contingent on the prevailing attitudes towards photography (see Barnhurst and Nerone 2001 for a comprehensive historical review). These attitudes are evident in both the professional rhetoric on the role of images in the news and in academic theorizing. They range from viewing images as mere *illustration* and therefore adjunct to the more important verbal descriptions of news events, to seeing them as reflecting reality (giving them the function of *evidence*), or as *sensation*, as visible in the early tabloid press. Images also have the ability to function as *icons*, symbolic representations of key moments in history;[1] and, more recently, they have been viewed as functioning *evaluatively* (carrying emotional appeal) and *aesthetically* (showing concern for composition). In the following paragraphs we discuss each of these communicative functions and make reference to the role of technological developments (as outlined in Table 10.1) in this process. Given its long history in news discourse, we focus primarily on press photography.

TABLE 10.1 Timeline of technological advancements in relation to photographic reproduction

1800s	**1839:** Daguerreotype: one of the earliest photographic methods to produce a single positive image exposed directly onto a silver-coated plate.
	1842: *Illustrated London News* (UK), *L'Illustration* (France) relied on the reinterpretation of the daguerreotype using woodcut engravings; reporting on events such as ceremonies, royal visits and even a fire in Hamburg.
	1851: The (wet plate) collodion process is invented and photography becomes mobile: Roger Fenton took 360 photographs of the Crimean War between 1853 and 1856 and Mathew B. Brady similarly photographed the American Civil War.
	1881: The half-tone process is invented: it converts different tones into dots of varying size. This allowed for the simultaneous and more accurate reproduction of photographs in newspapers.
	1888: Kodak camera introduced – reducing the size and weight of camera equipment dramatically.
	1890s: Roll film was introduced, allowing for multiple exposures of an event to be taken in quick succession. Flash powder also allowed for photography in poor light conditions and was used to freeze the action in scenes where there was a lot of movement, such as horse racing.
1900s	**1902:** British Pathé, established in London, is credited with producing the first newsreel – a compilation of moving images depicting news stories that was screened in movie theatres before the main film.
	1920s: Newsreels became 'talkies' from the 1920s on when movie companies like Fox Movietone, Paramount, Universal, Warner-Pathe and Hearst Metrotone in the United States added sound. Newsreels continued to be screened in cinemas until the beginning of the 1970s.
	1925: The Leica 35 mm roll-film camera was introduced. Wide-aperture lenses meant that exposure time was drastically reduced, allowing for more active, narrative type images to emerge; indoor photography using available light became possible.
	1935: Kodachrome perfected the art of colour photography.
	1940s–1950s: Single lens reflex cameras introduced and shortly after this a range of detachable lenses were developed to allow photographers to take all manner of shots from extreme wide angle (using a fish-eye lens) with maximal distortion, to extreme long shots (using a telephoto lens) with maximal compression, and capable of capturing images from hundreds of metres away.
	1950s on: Television sets mass produced with the aim of having one in every living room. Graphic footage of the Vietnam War led to massive political activism.

(Continued)

TABLE 10.1 (Continued)

	1980s: Offset lithography printing introduced in newspaper production allowing for premium quality photographic reproduction. **1981:** IBM launches home computers (the PC) and the digital race begins. **1988:** Fuji FILM introduces the world's first digital camera, complete with removable media, known as the DS-1P. **1990s:** The internet provides a way for computers to communicate with each other through a global system of interconnected computer networks; while the world wide web allows anyone with internet connection to view, share and upload hyperlinked documents, including images and videos.
2000s	**2000s:** Fully digitized news capture, design and production.

10.2.1 Image as illustration

The role of the press photograph in news discourse was initially seen as being an illustrative adjunct to the more important verbal reporting of newsworthy events. This probably had much to do with the fact that during the 1800s photographs were reinterpreted in woodcut engravings giving them more of an art feel. They were also mostly static portraits of prominent individuals (see Caple 2010b for examples). The verbal text took control of all of the description. However, to view portraiture (particularly of prominent figures in society) as merely illustrative would be a mistake. Portraiture became, and still is, a dominant means of establishing a rapport between the reading public and key figures in society. As noted by Welling (1987), putting a face to the names that frequently appear in the news helps the public not only to identify such figures, but also to humanize them, and then to empathize with them (we have talked about this with respect to the news value of Personalization). As early as 1860 Abraham Lincoln suggested that he was able to sway the public in the presidential election that saw him take office through the wide distribution of visiting cards, or carte-de-visite as they were called then, which were like small business cards that carried a portrait of the person (Welling 1987). This means that as well as having this illustrative function, such images also have the capacity to play a significant role in engaging both the public and their representative governments in ways that may bring about significant social, political and cultural change. At the same time, however, the professional rhetoric around the role of news images has remained sceptical, as noted by Zelizer:

For most journalists, news images have always taken a back seat to words. Since the photograph's inception in the mid-1800s, pictures have long been seen as the fluff of journalism, the stuff that **illustrates** but is adjunct to verbal descriptions. (Zelizer 2004: 118, bold face ours)

10.2.2 Image as evidence

The evidence status of press photography is tied to the notion that a photograph is a way of truth-telling and that indeed, the photograph 'never lies'. With this view we also encounter the notion of objectivity. This notion of objective truth is encapsulated in Barthes' (1977: 44) description of the photograph as record:

> In the photograph – at least at the level of the literal message – the relationship of signifieds to signifiers is not one of 'transformation' but of 'recording', and the absence of a code clearly reinforces the myth of photographic 'naturalness': the scene is *there*, captured mechanically, not humanly (the mechanical is here a guarantee of objectivity). (Barthes 1977: 44, italics in original)

This truth-telling role is also reflected in the Media/Journalism Studies literature, which describes press photographs as authoritative, as mirrors of the events they depict – what Zelizer refers to as 'photographic verisimilitude' (2005: 171). Examples can be seen in the documentary photography of the late nineteenth century, which was used to help galvanize governments to take action on social issues. Photographers in New York, Glasgow and London began photographing slum conditions in these cities and 'straight' photography, introduced by P. H. Emerson in 1889, showed images in sharp focus and free of manipulation or reinterpretation (Welling 1987). With this the notion of truthful, objective photography emerged and through such realistic images, governments began to take note of social and environmental conditions and how they impacted upon their citizens. Such work has continued throughout the twentieth century in the images of photographers such as Robert Capa, Dorothea Lange or Nick Ut. However, we can again see at least two functions present in such images. On the one hand, they do stand in evidence of the existence of dire situations, but on the other hand, they also have the capacity to elicit strong affective responses in the viewer (see Section 2.5 'Image as evaluation'), responses that have the potential to prompt governments to take steps towards remedying such situations.

10.2.3 Image as sensation

The notion of image as sensation is tied closely to the emergence of the tabloid and picture press of the early to mid-twentieth century. Tabloid newspapers like the *Daily Mirror* in the United Kingdom and the *Daily Graphic* in the United States emerged as newspapers that relied exclusively on photography to relay news (Gernsheim 1955). The tabloid press placed great emphasis on photography in newspapers, using large, sensational images that usually revolved around the themes of violence, sex, scandal and accidents. Photography historian Robert Taft labelled the reproduction of such photographs in the tabloids as 'trite, trivial, superficial, tawdry, salacious, morbid or silly' (1938, cited in Becker 1992/2003: 133). Thus the early twentieth century press photograph earned its reputation as sensational journalism, which made it increasingly difficult to view photography as a credible medium for serious news reporting. This view shifted considerably though, when images became central to the reporting of war.

10.2.4 Image as icon

Iconic images are images that function as symbolic representations of key moments in history. This iconic status comes through most clearly in war photography, with the many wars of the twentieth and twenty-first centuries providing key critical moments that have since become embedded in the national psyche, symbols of nationalism and even at times used for propaganda purposes. Iconic images of the twentieth century that came to represent an entire historical period/event include Joe Rosenthal's 'Raising the Flag on Iwo Jima' (World War II) and Nick Ut's image of Phan Thi Kim Phúc, as a naked 9-year-old girl fleeing a napalm attack during the Vietnam War. Both of these images won Pulitzer Prizes. 'The Tank Man', an image taken by Jeff Widener of the Associated Press, shows a man defiantly standing in front of army tanks in Tiananmen Square in Beijing, China, in June 1989. This is another example of an image that has come to symbolize an entire historical event. Ken Jarecke's shot of a dead Iraqi soldier, charred and ashen, still at the wheel of his vehicle stands as an iconic reminder of the first Gulf War in the early 1990s, while Richard Drew's '9/11 Falling Man' is an iconic image from a more recent event. Again, iconic images of this nature can be deployed to galvanize a particular social group to support or resist a particular action. For example, some of the most memorable and terrifyingly authentic images to come out of the Vietnam War were instrumental in swaying public opinion and fuelling antiwar protests around the world (Sontag 2003; for a comprehensive account of the role of press photography in bearing witness see Zelizer 2004).

However, this potential to provoke strong reactions may also mean that photographs are sometimes deliberately withheld. This was the case in 2011 when the president of the United States of America, Barack Obama, decided not to release images showing the body of Osama bin Laden, who was killed by US Navy Seals on 2 May 2011. His reason for doing so was based on the fear that they would become a propaganda tool. White House press secretary Jay Carney said, 'it is not in our national security interests to allow those images, as has been in the past been the case, to become icons to rally opinion against the United States' (as reported in Cowan 2011).

10.2.5 Image as evaluation

The ability for iconic images to have an enduring effect on our visual memories is not only because they capture a critical moment in the unfolding of an event, a moment that comes to represent the entire event, but also because such images carry huge emotional appeal. This strong emotional engagement with the viewer can be achieved in the capturing of dramatic, graphic or emotionally confronting images. Examples of such images in the news today can be seen in the winning portfolios in competitions like World Press Photo. In 2011, press photographer Daniel Morel won first prize in the category for 'spot news stories' for his images of the dramatic rescue of victims (with the dead alongside the living) of the Haiti earthquake. Guang Niu, of China, won second prize in the category 'general news' for his graphic depiction of the mass cremation of victims of an earthquake in Qinghai province, and Javier Manzano's emotionally confronting image of the head of a man by the roadside near Ciudad Juarez in northern Mexico gained third prize in the same category.

From a semiotic perspective, both Economou (2006) and Caple (2009a) have argued that news images, in combination with verbal text and layout, can function to establish an evaluative stance on the events retold in the story (Caple 2009a) or that they instantiate different evaluative 'voices' or 'keys' in relation to their role in the news discourse as record or interpreter (Economou 2008: 255).

10.2.6 Image as aesthetic

Aesthetics in news photography is somewhat of a controversial issue. At various points in recent history, academics have denied press photographers a hand in the aesthetic appeal or even composition of their images. For example, Bignell (2002: 98) suggests that 'photogenia and aestheticism **are rarely** seen in press photography' (bold face ours), and Schirato and Webb (2004: 96), in describing a photograph of a protest depicting police and protesters facing each other, make the claim that 'it is manifestly not a press photograph, because there is a concern with composition rather than action'. However, we argue in this book that press photographers are indeed concerned with composition and the choices they take up in relation to this are very much motivated by an aesthetic value. In other words, photographers are always conscious of the aesthetic potential of any news image they produce. We also believe that there is evidence of resurgence in valuing the aesthetic in news images on the part of editors.

10.3 Images and the organization of news

It has become clear in the above discussion that images perform many functions in news discourse and that these functions occur simultaneously. Images have the capacity to function as evidence at the same time as they are able to elicit strong emotional responses in the audience; and some of these images may enter the national psyche as icons.

It is important to note that considerations for page layout, the size of images on the page and the relations between the verbal and visual text are also significant in pointing to the functions of images as news discourse. Indeed, those working on a daily basis with the production of the news claim that today's newspapers are a 'designer's newspaper' (Stephen Clark, senior news designer with the Australian broadsheet the *Sydney Morning Herald*, 2006, personal communication). They suggest that stories are planned and packaged around the notion of visual design, taking into consideration how they are framed and how they relate to other stories and advertising spaces on the page. From a linguistic perspective, Bateman (2008: 157) refers to the rhetorical organization of image and text within a single page layout as 'page-flow'. He states that page-flow is of central importance for advancing the treatment of multisemiotic genres because it is the primary 'resource' that multisemiotic genres build upon (Bateman 2008: 198). Bateman further suggests that newspapers rely on the page-flow model because when we read the newspaper there are many chunks that can be read about many different topics and without any necessary order imposed (Bateman 2008: 226). How layout and typography impact on the ways in which we engage with images in the news is very clearly shown in Figure 10.2. Here we see 'screamer' headlines with capitalization, exclamation marks superimposed onto the large-size images of bin Laden allowing for maximum bleed between the image and the typography.

In the context of broadcast news, Montgomery (2007) proposes that frameworks of consumption (the fixed/closed daily news bulletin in conventional TV news programming versus the free-floating/open structures

FIGURE 10.2 *Front pages on the killing of Osama bin Laden*

of the dedicated 24-hour news channels) have different effects on news story organization. He suggests that features of the more open structure of news storytelling, such as updates, constant forward projection through time and to later moments in the programme are beginning to influence the whole of broadcast news, and as such are having a significant effect on the ways in which discourse, audience and news events interact (Montgomery 2007: 67). In relation to the visual, Montgomery (2007: 55) points to the distinct postural shifts enacted by the newsreader as s/he moves from addressing the audience to addressing the correspondent on the video screen in the studio, which are characteristic of this change in structure.

Furthermore, different rhetorical organizations and functions of images and text have emerged in new ways of reporting the news. For example, Knox (2007, 2010) investigates the role of thumbnail images in newsbites, the short headline-plus-lead-plus-hyperlink stories on newspaper website homepages. He argues that 'each home page is a complex sign, consisting of a range of visual and visual–verbal signs which function as coherent structural elements' (Knox 2007: 23). In particular, he suggests that the function of newsbites on newspaper homepages is very different to that of news texts on story pages in that they operate as 'independent texts in their unique contextual environment to construe actors and events according to the institutional goals and ideologies of the newspaper' (Knox 2007: 26). He goes on to state that:

> newsbites function to highlight the stories valued by the institution of the newspaper as most important on a given day. Their social purpose is to present the focal point of a news story with immediacy and impact. They afford the institutional authors of the newspaper the means by which to visually evaluate stories in terms of their *comparative* importance (including by size, relative positioning, headline font size and colour and inclusion of optional structural elements such as images), and are designed to attract readers to navigate to story pages in order to access longer (and/or modally different) versions of the 'same' story. Every reader's click on a newsbite provides another advertising opportunity for the newspaper. (Knox 2007: 26, italics in original)

Other new practices emerging in the online environment can be seen in the 'Multimedia' sections of newspaper websites. Here, audiences can engage with photo galleries, videos, interactives, graphics or audio slideshows that are often hyperlinked to written news stories elsewhere on the website. Audio slideshows are automated and run from the first image to the last and often include music, ambient sound and voice-over from a reporter offering commentary on elements of the story (which may or may not be depicted in the corresponding images), while interactives consist of maps or images, where readers activate the revelation of information by hovering the cursor over these figures and thus navigate their own pathway through the text; graphics are additional tables and figures that are linked to a news story elsewhere on the website. Further, major world events (e.g. The Royal Wedding of Prince William and Kate Middleton in the United Kingdom in April 2011) are not only streamed live on news websites, but are then packaged up into shorter 'themed' units (like 'the balcony kiss', 'the vows', 'the wedding procession'), for audiences to relive their favourite moments from the event. Other practices that are far less polished are also emerging where 'raw' (unedited) footage from an event is being released to the public without any verbal commentary (although with original ambient sound). This seems to be associated more with breaking news events such as the protests on the streets in Bahrain, Benghazi or Tripoli (in February 2011) or with footage taken in the aftermath of natural disasters like the massive earthquake and tsunami in Japan in March 2011, and certainly help to construe news values such as Timeliness and Negativity.

Whether or not we are looking at practices of telling news stories in print news, broadcast news or online news, any analysis of the way such stories are organized in these different media forms arguably benefits from taking into account the relations between the verbal and the visual text. Therefore, we now turn to an exploration of text–image relations in news discourse, and discuss the ways in which language and still and moving images relate to each other.

10.4 Text–image relations in news discourse

10.4.1 Overlap, displacement and dichotomy

One of the classic studies on the relations between visual and verbal text in the news is Meinhof's (1994) research into televisual news discourse.[2] This research focuses on the textual strategies deployed in TV news bulletins to elicit certain responses in the viewers. Meinhof takes as her unit of analysis three 'action components' in the news item: the actors, the activities/ events and

TABLE 10.2 Categories for analysing intersemiotic relations

Categories	Definitions
Overlap	– where the visual track and the verbal track share the same action component, either directly or metonymically
Displacement	– where the visual and verbal tracks represent different action components of the same event (e.g. text reports the causes, images the effects)
Dichotomy	– where the visual and verbal tracks represent action components of different events

the affected/effect/outcome (1994: 215–16) and proposes three categories for relating these components to each other in the form of image/ text relations: overlap, displacement and dichotomy (1994: 216–17) (see Table 10.2).

In our analysis below, we will examine the extent to which Meinhof's categories for analysing text–image relations can be applied to both still and moving news images. We begin with an investigation of moving images, before widening our discussion to include still images in print news discourse and we end with a brief look at sequenced images in online news galleries.

10.4.2 Text–image relations in moving images

The relationship between moving images and the verbal text accompanying them (e.g. in the case of TV news: the voice of newsreaders in the studio, the voice-over of reporters, and 'talent' interviewed on camera) can be analysed for the ways in which they form an intersemiotic relationship. To clarify, by *inter*semiotic relationship we mean the relations between different semiotic systems such as language and image (e.g. the relation between the voice-over and what is depicted in a shot), whereas *intra*semiotic relationship refers to relations within one semiotic system (e.g. relations between images/shots or relations between sentences/clauses).

To exemplify **inter**semiotic relationships in moving images in this section (overlap, displacement, dichotomy), we draw on shots from two video news bulletins that were published online by ABC News (Australia) and BBC News (UK) on 2 May 2011, in which the death of Osama bin Laden was confirmed.

The first category suggested by Meinhof is that of **overlap**, where the visual and the verbal track share the same action component. Indeed, news organizations are often berated for simply restating verbally what can be seen visually, although this may at times be necessary (e.g. to clarify that a group

TABLE 10.3 Examples of overlap in text–image relations in moving images (ABC *News in 90 Seconds* bulletin)

Shot Visual Track	Verbal Track	Text–Image Relations
5 [Fixed camera position. Shot duration: 56 sec.] President Obama speaking into a microphone	'Today, at my direction, the United States launched a targeted operation against that compound in Abbottabad Pakistan … We must and we will remain vigilant at home and abroad.' (President Obama)	**Overlap** Verbal track: direct speech – the words spoken by the President match the visual track Visual track: President speaking
6 [Fixed camera position. Shot duration: 15 sec.] Crowds of people waving flags, punching the air, very dark surrounding so location is vague.	**Newsreader:** The announcement sparked scenes of jubilation outside the White House with people gathering to cheer and celebrate the death of America's most wanted terrorist.	**Overlap** Verbal track: scenes of jubilation Visual track: people punching the air, waving flags

of people standing by the side of a road are victims rather than perpetrators of a crime). Such overlap can be achieved through shared reference between the verbal and visual tracks, for example, in the use of spatial deixis (*here*) and demonstrative reference (*this man*) (Montgomery 2007: 95). In Table 10.3, two shots (5 and 6) from the ABC bulletin exemplify overlap between the verbal and visual track. In shot 5, President Obama speaks directly to the camera, and the verbal track carries his exact words. In shot 6, the verbal track indicates the effect of Obama's announcement (*scenes of jubilation*) and the visual track shows people cheering, punching the air and waving flags, that is, acting out this *jubilation*.

Another way in which the verbal and visual tracks relate to each other is through **displacement** where 'film footage and text represent different action components of the same event' (Meinhof 1994: 216). Meinhof suggests that displacement can be seen in the typical cause–effect type reporting of natural disasters. The cause, an earthquake or tornado or cyclone, may be restated in the verbal text while the pictures show the devastation, destroyed buildings, debris and loss of life. Another kind of cause–effect relationship can be seen in the example in Table 10.4, which is taken from the BBC news bulletin. In shot 8, the visual track depicts the site of the attacks on the World Trade Centre in New York, while the verbal track relates the number of people killed as a result of these attacks.

TABLE 10.4 An example of displacement in text–image relations in moving images (BBC *One-minute World News* bulletin)

Shot	Visual Track	Verbal Track	Text–Image Relations
8	[Fixed camera position. Shot duration: 3 sec.] Aerial shot of the remains of the towers, after they had collapsed	… 2001 in which around three thee-thousand people were killed.	**Displacement** Verbal track: details on the number of people killed in these attacks Visual track: the smouldering ruins of the WTC

Sometimes, there may be no immediate relation between the visual and verbal track in a news bulletin. This occurs most frequently when no suitable vision is available for a story, or if archived footage is used. This can be very misleading and may lead the viewer to attempt to make connections where none are intended. Meinhof (1994: 217) uses the term 'dichotomy' to refer to instances where 'film footage and text represent action components of different events'. For instance, both the BBC and the ABC show file footage of Osama bin Laden in their reporting of his death. In Table 10.5 we can see

TABLE 10.5 An example of dichotomy in text–image relations in moving images (ABC *News in 90 Seconds* bulletin)

Shot	Visual Track	Verbal Track	Text–Image Relations
3	Osama bin Laden in a crouching position, fires a gun	**Newsreader:** … Obama has announced that Osama bin Laden was killed by US forces who now …	**Dichotomy** Verbal track: indirect speech of US president Obama on the killing of bin Laden Visual track: shows images of bin Laden alive and actively firing a gun

footage of Osama bin Laden crouching and firing a gun, very much alive and well, while the verbal text is an indirect speech act from President Obama explaining how he was killed. This is a clear example of **dichotomy**.

Apart from analysing the intersemiotic relationships that hold between visual and verbal track in moving images, it is also important to consider **intra**semiotic relations, that is, the relations between shots in the visual track (shot sequencing) and between clauses and sentences in the verbal track. Van Leeuwen (1991: 76, 2005: 229) approaches such analysis through conjunction, and puts it that just as clauses and sentences can build up a structure through temporal, comparative, causal or conditional relations, similar logical relations can also be identified for sequences of images. For example, temporal relations are enacted through the shot sequencing of one event after another and typically provide narrative progression, while the transition from a long shot to a close shot (i.e. a zoom-in) of the same subject realizes 'Detail' in van Leeuwen's (2005: 229) terms and the transition from close-up to long shot (i.e. a zoom out) realizes 'Overview'. For instance, in the news bulletin on the death of Osama bin Laden, the BBC follows a shot of the burning towers of the World Trade Centre with a zoom-in on the rubble showing details of the effects of the attacks (Table 10.6).

TABLE 10.6 An example of a zoom-in shot sequence, from Overview to Detail (BBC *One-minute World News* bulletin)

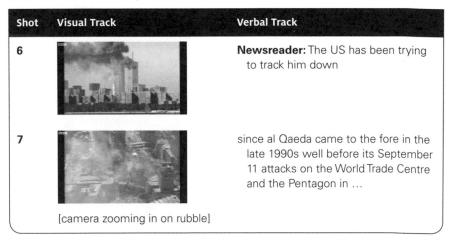

Shot	Visual Track	Verbal Track
6		**Newsreader:** The US has been trying to track him down
7		since al Qaeda came to the fore in the late 1990s well before its September 11 attacks on the World Trade Centre and the Pentagon in …
	[camera zooming in on rubble]	

In general, it seems that when engaging with moving images viewers often expect the shots to relate to each other and attempt to make sense of each shot in terms of its position in the sequence. Furthermore, synchronized editing, where the transition from one shot to another coincides with clause and sentence boundaries, may help to establish parallelism between the verbal and visual track and with this their reciprocal relevance: 'the words seem to be driving the pictures at the same time as the pictures seem to be driving the words' (Montgomery 2007: 104).

To conclude this section, when considering the relations that hold between elements in online videos or televised reports or indeed other types of news discourse where moving images are used, we need to analyse not just the relations between words and images/shots but also the relations between clauses/sentences and between shots. Hence, it might seem as if the relations that hold between text and **still** images (e.g. in print news) are less complex. However, here we can investigate the relations between images and different parts of the verbal text: the caption, headline and body text. In the following we will explore image/caption, image/headline and image/ body text relations and the extent to which categories like those suggested by Meinhof for text–image relations in **televisual** news (moving images) may be applied to similar relations in **print** news (still images).

10.4.3 Text–image relations in still images

To explore text–image relations in still images we will draw on an example story from the *Boston Herald* ('Children OK, jake injured in blaze', *Boston Herald*, 15 December 2010, p. 11; reporter: Renee Nadeau Algarin, photo by Mark Garfinkel). This story (represented in Figure 10.3) includes a press photograph with a caption and an extended story.

Before we examine the relationship between the image and caption/ headline/body text we will look at the image itself and see what is depicted here. The image focuses on the work of two firefighters (the *actors*, in Meinhof's terms): one is outside standing on a crane and is inspecting the roof of a building (*activities*) and the other, inside the building, is removing external wall panelling (*activities*). We can also see aspects of the damage caused to the building in the blackened walls (*affected/effect/outcome*). The depiction of uniformed firefighters in this image construes the news value of Prominence. As a professional elite they are trained to deal with dangerous situations, and carry with them a degree of gravitas that also construes Negativity (in the event they are attending). The walls of the building appear to be severely damaged and the inside of the room is blackened, which construe the news value of Impact. There are no flames in the image and only minimal smoke, which leads us to conclude that the major threat of the fire appears to be over.

Image/caption relations

We will now consider the relations between the image in Figure 10.3 and its caption: **HOT AND COLD:** *Boston firefighters battle a fire at 18 Boyden St. in Dorchester yesterday that caused $350,000 in damage to a day care.*

Children OK, jake injured in blaze

By RENEE NADEAU ALGARIN

A two-alarm fire sent the kids and staff at a Dorchester day care scrambling yesterday morning, but everyone made it out safely.

The fire broke out at 18 Boyden St. on the Dorchester-Mattapan line at 10:08 a.m. yesterday, said Boston fire department spokesman Steve MacDonald.

The blaze was caused by an electrical short circuit inside the walls of two-story wood-framed house.

"The fire got in the walls and just traveled throughout the house," MacDonald said.

Two adults at the Pride N Joy Day Care center on the building's first floor managed to get all 10 children out safely before the fire engines arrived at the scene, MacDonald said.

Residents of an upstairs apartment were not home at the time of the fire.

One firefighter suffered a hand injury fighting the flames. He was treated and released from Carney Hospital in Dorchester.

Damage was estimated at $350,000, MacDonald said.

— rnadeau@bostonherald.com

STAFF PHOTO BY MARK GARFINKEL

HOT AND COLD: Boston firefighters battle a fire at 18 Boyden St. in Dorchester yesterday that caused $350,000 in damage to a day care.

FIGURE 10.3 *'Children OK, jake injured in blaze', Boston Herald, 15 December 2010, p. 11, reprinted with permission of the Boston Herald*

The bold, capitalized minor clause (**HOT AND COLD**) at the beginning of this caption is a feature of caption writing that is becoming increasingly common. Briefly here, Caple (2008a: 129) has theorized this minor clause as a 'prosodic tail' in relation to its use in stand-alone stories. It is often playful and requires the reader to be familiar with the text as a whole (including the image) in order to decode its meaning. In this instance, it is possibly referring to the fact that the fire (*hot*) resulted in the children and staff inside the building having to evacuate into the *cold* December outdoors.

Turning now to the relationship between the rest of the caption and the image: In this caption the verbal text tells us who – the actors – (*Boston firefighters*) is depicted, what they are doing – the activities/events – (*battle a fire*), where this is taking place (*at 18 Boyden St. in Dorchester*) and when – the circumstances – (*yesterday*). In terms of text-image relations we can say that in general there is **overlap** between the caption text and the image. However, this may seem somewhat of a simplification of these relationships since in the verbal text we get clarification of which firefighters these are (*Boston*) and in the image we can also see their uniforms, including hard-hat, gloves, heavy boots, and the types of equipment (oxygen tank, ladders) these firefighters are deploying in their work. Thus, the text specifies who these firefighters are but the image also specifies what exactly they are wearing and the tools they are carrying and working with (attributes), which also serve to clarify that these are firefighters rather than paramedics. So this is a two-way relationship in which both words and pictures specify each other in very detailed ways. The caption text further summarizes the activities of the firefighters in the verb *battle*; however, the image offers a more nuanced depiction of one firefighter inspecting the roof section of the building from a crane and another (largely obscured) inside the building and removing wood panelling from the smoking walls. We could then say that there is **displacement** between the activities in the caption and the activities in the image, as *battle* seems to be pointing to an earlier stage in this event when the firefighters probably were battling to bring the blaze under control. The action in the image lacks the intensity implied in the verb (presumably used to increase news value), but the presence of smoke and the extent of the damage depicted in the image point to this intensity. Note also that the verbs in this part of the caption tend to be written in the simple present tense.

Sometimes, a caption may stop after the first stage of clarifying our understanding of what is going on in the image. Quite often, however, news image captions tell us more than just what is going on in the image, as is the case in the *Boston Herald* story in Figure 10.3. This leads us to the second function of the caption, which is to relate the image to the wider news event and its news value (Caple 2009b). Clauses here are also usually marked by a shift in time/tense choice. In the caption in the fire story (Figure 10.3) we get the following extra information attached to the main clause: *that caused $350,000 in damage to a day care*. In this relative clause we get a shift in tense from present (*battle*) to past (*caused*) and we get additional information relating to the financial impact/consequences of this fire event. Meinhof's category of **overlap** can again be deployed in that the damage visually depicted is specified in the verbal text. However, we also get additional information relating to the use of the building (as a *day care* centre), which cannot be recovered from the image alone. This information, then, extends the meanings presented visually. Caple (2009b: 116) terms the **function** of this part of the caption text *contextual extension*. In this sense, the second clause in this caption elaborates on the wider news context and focuses our attention on the news angle, contextualizing the story in a news sense; it answers the question 'why is this news?', justifying its place in the newspaper. This part of the caption also serves to position the event in the image in relation to other activities preceding or following it or in relation to the event as a whole. This is why such contextual extension features a shift in time/tense choice.

Image/headline relations

The relationship between headlines and images is typically a lot less direct than that between images and their captions. Indeed, in the majority of cases, the headline text has little or nothing to do with any images associated with the story. Rather, headlines are most often extrapolated from the lead paragraphs of the verbal text and hence form a very close relationship with the lead. This is also a reflection of the institutional practices of news writing, where headlines are usually written by subeditors not journalists or photographers. An example of a story where the headline and image are only tangentially related to each other can be seen in the story in Figure 10.3 from the *Boston Herald*. The headline to this story reads 'Children OK, jake injured in blaze'. The image does not depict any children and it is impossible to gauge from the image alone that this building is particularly associated with children (although readers may infer that *children* were the occupants of the building before the *blaze* mentioned in the headline). There is a further point of commonality between the headline and image in the mention of *jake* (Boston slang for firefighter) in the headline and the depiction of two 'jakes' in the image. However, neither of the firefighters in the image appears to be injured: rather, they are working. Further, the *blaze* mentioned in the headline is more or less over in the photograph, with only a little smoke still visible. Thus, we can analyse the relationships between headline and image in this story as **displacement**, as the words and the image point to different action components of the same event.

While it is rare for headlines and images to share close relationships of **overlap**, there are instances where images and headlines do attempt to do this. Examples are where a person depicted in an image is named in a headline (see Example 1 in Table 10.7) or where a facial expression is rendered verbally in the headline (also in Example 1). This verbal labelling is also used with place names: a place is visually depicted and named in the

TABLE 10.7 Examples of overlap in image/headline relations

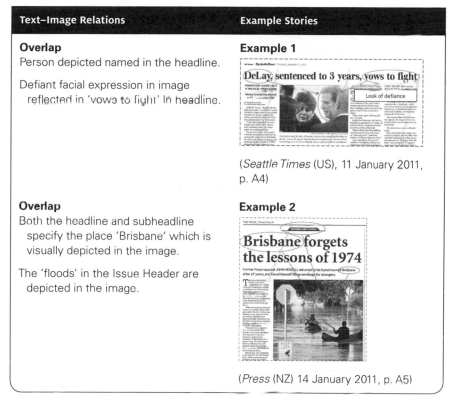

Text–Image Relations	Example Stories
Overlap Person depicted named in the headline. Defiant facial expression in image reflected in 'vows to fight' in headline.	**Example 1** (*Seattle Times* (US), 11 January 2011, p. A4)
Overlap Both the headline and subheadline specify the place 'Brisbane' which is visually depicted in the image. The 'floods' in the Issue Header are depicted in the image.	**Example 2** (*Press* (NZ) 14 January 2011, p. A5)

headline, as in *Brisbane* in Example 2, Table 10.7. Example 2 also makes use of what journalism professionals call an Issue Header. Issue headers are used when several stories on a page all relate to the same topic, in this case the *Queensland floods*. Sometimes, this header may be the main (or only) way in which connections are established between images and headline text.

To conclude, it would seem as if most news stories do not enjoy very close intersemiotic relationships between image and headline, although particular kinds of stories may do so – an example is the stand-alone (Caple 2010a). Here, we will continue our discussion of intersemiosis by examining the relationship between photographs and the body text of a news report.

Image/body text relations

We can also use Meinhof's categories of overlap, displacement and dichotomy to examine the relationships between image and body text. Indeed, it is likely that all three of these relations are present as the image will often capture a particular moment in the unfolding of an event while the story text will also relate to the happenings on either side of the captured moment as well as point to other matters of news value in the event. Let us continue with our examination of the fire story from the *Boston Herald* for image/body text relations (in Table 10.8).

We have already established above that the major threat of the fire appears to be over in this image; rather the image focuses on the work of the firefighters in inspecting the roof of the building and removing wall panelling, which reveals the extent of the damage to the building. The caption also points to the impact/consequences of the fire by putting a dollar figure to the damage depicted and the headline evaluates the situation in terms of human safety and injuries sustained. In terms of image/body text relations a clear pattern emerges in relation to time. The verbal text mostly retells action components that occurred before the one shown in the image (**displacement**) and emphasizes that the building occupants are safe; however, there was an injury sustained by a firefighter. Since the headline refers to the safety of the building occupants and the injury to the firefighter, it seems that the relationship between the headline and the body text is much closer than that between image and body text. It is possible to also state that there is limited **overlap** between the body text and image in the verbal mention and visual depiction of the building.

An unusual instance of direct **overlap** between an image and the body text of a print news story can be seen in Table 10.9. In this example, the story leads with the moment captured in the image and makes direct reference to the image in the verbal text *this is the dramatic moment....* The use of the demonstrative *this* in the lead paragraph is reminiscent of TV news reporting where shared reference between the verbal and visual track is achieved through spatial deixis, and demonstrative reference in the verbal track overlaps the visual track (Montgomery 2007: 95). Indeed, the fact that there is a photograph (originally published in colour) of *the dramatic moment* could be the reason why this story has achieved such prominence on the page (rather than being included in a simple newsbrief).

With respect to the relations in print news between image, caption, headline and body text, we may ask whether or not it is necessary to analyse all of these relations and in what order they should be analysed. This is pertinent to studies that investigate how we 'read' news stories. For example, eye-tracking studies seem to suggest that readers of print newspapers engage first with the largest headlines and image on the page, and captions to such images (especially depicting action) are also more likely to be read before the main story (Quinn and Stark Adam 2008). Thus it may be prudent to analyse the relationship between image, caption and headline first and then relate the three together to the remainder of the story text.

TABLE 10.8 Image/body text relations in 'Children OK, jake injured in blaze', *Boston Herald*, 15 December 2010, p. 11

Image/Caption	Story Text	Text–Image Relations
 STAFF PHOTO BY MARK GARFINKEL **HOT AND COLD:** Boston firefighters battle a fire at 18 Boyden St. in Dorchester yesterday that caused $350,000 in damage to a day care.	**Children OK, jake injured in blaze** A two alarm fire sent the kids and staff at a Dorchester day care scrambling yesterday morning, but everyone made it out safely.	Displacement
	The fire broke out at 18 Boyden St. on the Dorchester-Mattapan line at 10.08 a.m. yesterday, said Boston fire department spokesman Steve MacDonald.	**Displacement** (**Overlap** – mention of the building and building is pictured)
	The blaze was caused by an electrical short circuit inside the walls of two-story wood-framed house [*sic*].	Displacement
	"The fire got in the walls and just traveled throughout the house," MacDonald said.	Displacement
	Two adults at the Pride N Joy Day Care centre on the building's first floor managed to get all 10 children out safely before the fire engines arrived at the scene, MacDonald said.	Displacement
	Residents of an upstairs apartment were not at home at the time of the fire.	Dichotomy

TABLE 10.8 (Continued)

	One firefighter suffered a hand injury fighting the flames.	**Displacement**
	He was treated and released from Carney Hospital in Dorchester.	**Displacement**
	Damage was estimated at $350,000, MacDonald said.	**Displacement**

Reprinted with permission of the *Boston Herald*

TABLE 10.9 An example of overlap in image/body text relations

Text/Image Relations between Image and Body Text	Example Story
Overlap Direct reference made in the lead paragraph to the moment captured in the image in: *BLEEDING profusely from a head wound,* **this is the dramatic moment** *an alleged car thief was arrested after ramming a police car in a desperate bid to get away.*	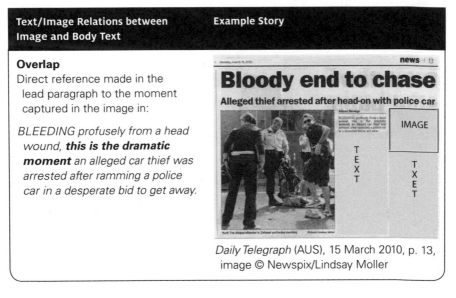 *Daily Telegraph* (AUS), 15 March 2010, p. 13, image © Newspix/Lindsay Moller

10.4.4 Text–image relations in sequenced images

The relationships described in the previous sections between headline, image and caption are also relevant to emergent online practices in which news organizations are taking advantage of the abundance of visual material to create photo galleries or online news galleries (see Caple and Knox in press).

Such galleries typically include a headline, and a caption with each image; however, they are also **sequences** of images. This means that they also have things in common with moving images where we can find sequences of shots. We briefly explore such galleries in the following section.

At their most basic, online news galleries (Caple and Knox in press) are authored sequences of images and captions constructed around a news event (e.g. Deep Water Horizon Oil Spill in the Gulf of Mexico) or according to themes (e.g. Weather) or time (e.g. This Week in Images). They are 'authored' in that photographers and editors select from a number of images and write captions (and often headlines) for these images. They are numbered and sequenced and when opened one enters the gallery at the first image. A scroll tool usually allows the viewer to move forwards or backwards once the sequence has begun. This ordering of images has led researchers like Caple and Knox (in press) to question the extent to which galleries with a *sequential* beginning, middle and end have the potential to also be guided by narrative norms with a *rhetorical* beginning, middle and end. This is driven by the fact that news reporting is often defined in terms of its storytelling nature (see for example Tuchman 1973/1997, Schudson 1978, van Dijk 1988, Bell 1991). Thus, online news galleries add to the range of possibilities for online news storytelling. Since such galleries involve image/verbiage complexes of still image and caption (and often headline) and are at the same time sequences of images, they can be analysed both for the relations that hold between each still image and its accompanying verbal text (**inter**semiotic relations), as well as for the relations that hold between images (**Intra**semiotic relations).

To illustrate this point briefly we will look at one online news gallery where both inter- and intrasemiotic relationships are employed to produce a cogent story.[3] The gallery concerns the *Oktoberfest* in Munich and was published on the *Guardian* (UK) newspaper website (www.guardian.co.uk/) on 21 September 2009. The gallery can be accessed at www.guardian.co.uk/travel/gallery/2009/sep/20/oktoberfest-festivals-munich?INTCMP=SRCH#/?picture=353206027&index=0 and we therefore do not reproduce the whole gallery here. Rather, we draw on four examples from the beginning, middle and end of the gallery to exemplify inter- and intrasemiotic relations (in Table 10.10, see Caple and Knox in press for a complete analysis of this gallery). There are fourteen images in the gallery: five from the parades, five from inside the beer tents, two from the fairground, one of drunken revellers sitting/lying on the floor, and one of a night view of the whole venue, including fairground rides, beer tents and the crowds on the street. From the ordering of these images, we can already detect a temporal and spatial progression as we move through the gallery (from day to night, and from outside to inside to outside again). The headline 'Oktoberfest starts in

TABLE 10.10 Inter- and intrasemiotic relations in the online news gallery 'Oktoberfest starts in Munich' (www.guardian.co.uk/, 21 September 2009)

Slide	Image	Caption	Text–Image Relations	Conjunctive Relations	
				Between Images	**Between Captions**
1		Children play drums and march during the marksmen's parade on the second day of the Oktoberfest beer festival at the *Theresienwiese* in Munich	Overlap	n/a	n/a
2–5	More images of people parading				
6		Visitors clink beer mugs	Overlap	Next event	Addition/ next event
7–10	More images of people drinking in the beer tents				
11–12	Visitors at the fairground				
13		After drinking, what better than a rest against a wall	Overlap	Next event	Next event
14		Crowds flock to the beer tents at night	Overlap	Next event/ overview	Next event/ conclusive event

Munich' is consistently displayed above every slide and each image has its own caption.

In terms of text–image (**inter**semiotic) relations, the caption texts remain closely descriptive of the images and there is clear **overlap** between caption and image. Indeed, all of the images and captions relate to each other in this way throughout this gallery. Turning to the (**intra**semiotic) relations between the images, sequential meaning is afforded by the mechanical requirement of clicking through the sequence of images in the gallery. This is also a temporal sequencing (i.e. relating to each other as the next event), which is reinforced by the transition from daytime to night time in the final image. Also, in van Leeuwen's (2005) terms, the shot type (long shot of the beer tents, the parade ground and the fairground rides) of the final image can be read as a conjunctive relation of Overview between the final image and **all** of the preceding images. A similar pattern emerges for the **intra**semiotic relations between the captions in this gallery. The captions are generally related by addition and/or temporally as next event. In this way, intra- and intersemiotic relations are employed to tell a cogent news story about 'things that happen' at the Oktoberfest.

10.5 Conclusion

In this chapter, we have examined the important contributions that images in and of themselves make to the ways in which readers and viewers engage with major news events, for example, as evidence, evaluation or aesthetic. We have also explored the relations between elements in news stories that include still or moving images. We have drawn primarily on Meinhof's framework and have shown how it can be applied to moving images, print news stories and online news galleries. Other frameworks that draw more explicitly on linguistic concepts such as cohesion (see n. 2) may allow a more in-depth analysis but have so far not been applied to news discourse. Our discussion has demonstrated the complexity of relations that hold between different elements of news stories and have shown the need for systematic analysis that takes into account the fact that words and images work together to create meaning. Images can be regarded as partners in the retelling of newsworthy happenings and capable of allowing for the multiplication of meaning at the intersection of words and images (Caple 2009b). We thus need to develop specific frameworks not just for analysing relations between the verbal and the visual, but also for systematic analysis of meanings made in the language and meanings made in the image so that we can bring both together.

Directions for further reading

For discussion on intersemiosis see:

Caple, H. (in press), *Photojournalism: A Multisemiotic Approach*. Basingstoke: Palgrave Macmillan. Explores inter- and intrasemiotic relations in print and online news discourse.

Royce, T. (2002), 'Multimodality in the TESOL classroom: exploring visual–verbal synergy', *TESOL Quarterly*, 36 (2), 191–205. Investigates intersemiotic complementarity from a systemic functional linguistic perspective.

van Leeuwen, T. (1991), 'Conjunctive structure in documentary film and television', *Continuum*, 5 (1), 76–114. Examines conjunctive relations between sequences of images in documentaries.

—— (2005), *Introducing Social Semiotics*. London/New York: Routledge. Chapter 11 deals specifically with 'information linking' in the multimodal environment.

For discussion of TV news and the relationship between words and images:

Meinhof, U. H. (1994), 'Double talk in news broadcasts: a cross-cultural comparison of pictures and texts in television news', in D. Graddol and O. Boyd-Barrett (eds), *Media Texts: Authors and Readers*. Clevedon: Open University Press, pp. 212–23. Investigates intersemiosis in televisual news discourse.

Ray, V. (2003), *The Television Handbook: An Insider's Guide to being a Great Broadcast Journalist*. London: Macmillan. Investigates the relationships between words and images in televisual news discourse from a professional perspective.

Notes

1 This is different to Peirce's notion of icon, where the signifier represents the signified through likeness (see Rose 2007: 83, Sturken and Cartwright 2009: 28–9).

2 In Social Semiotics, the main focus of research has been on intersemiosis (the relationship between visuals and verbal text) in a wide variety of contexts. While this research has not focused specifically on text–image relations in news discourse, it has provided the basis for other researchers investigating intersemiosis. Royce (2002: 194) bases his interpretation of ideational, or representational, meanings encoded in a multimodal text in high school science textbooks in lexical cohesion (after Halliday and Hasan 1985), including synonymy, antonymy, hyponomy, meronymy and collocation. Van Leeuwen (1991) looks at conjunctive relations both within and between the verbal and visual tracks in documentary film and television. Building on this work on conjunctive relations, Martinec and Salway (2005) develop their approach to componential cohesion in text–image relations by combining logico-semantic and status relations (Halliday 1985) with text relations (Barthes 1977). With regard to *news* discourse, social semiotic research in this area includes investigation of newspaper texts (Macken-Horarik 2003), newspaper front pages (Kress and van Leeuwen 1998), stand-alones (Caple

2006, 2008a, 2010a, in press), longer-form news features (Economou 2006, 2008), newsbites (Knox 2007, 2010) and online news galleries (Caple and Knox in press).

3 It must be noted that many galleries do not (or may not even attempt to) achieve such cogent storytelling. Indeed, it is those based on a particular news event rather than a theme that will try to tell a cogent story through the gallery (see Caple and Knox in press for further discussion of these issues).

PART THREE

Electronic discourses

11

Stance in blogs

Greg Myers

The chapter in a sentence: *Bloggers are often surprisingly careful in how they present their opinions to an audience, using a range of markers that suggest how they are making this statement.*

We expect most bloggers to give us their opinions: on the Iraq war, a new Indiana Jones movie, the cooking of asparagus, Dunkin Donuts coffee, the seats at the Old Vic theatre or space-time curvature. Nearly every sentence has some sort of evaluation, explicit or implied. Even a simple list of links, the most basic of blog forms, asserts some sense of personal preferences or interests. So why would they need to tell us, one way or another, that what they are doing is giving their own opinion? One reason is that blogs are not all just rants in which authors shout their opinions at some imagined public; most bloggers adjust the ways they express opinions to interact with the audience and convey the complexity, interest and novelty of the views they are expressing. Take this sentence in a comment by jeff (referring to astrophysicists' tendency to ignore the problem of defining 'now' as part of their theories of time):

> Personally, I think they may be making a big mistake, but I don't know how else they could proceed, objectively. (comment to *Cosmic Variance*)

Within all this careful packaging, there is an assertion that 'they are making a mistake'. But there is a modal (**may** be making a mistake); the assertion is the complement of a main clause that says 'I **think** they may ...', and that main clause is prefaced by an adverbial marking it as just jeff's opinion: '**personally**'. Then after the assertion, there is a concession, saying that jeff doesn't have an alternative.

These devices, taken together, are aspects, of **stance**, 'lexical and grammatical expression of attitudes, feelings, judgments, or commitment concerning the propositional content of a message' (Biber and Finegan 1989). Of course there are other markers in the example, including obviously evaluative words ('mistake') and words that may be implicitly evaluative for some writers and readers ('objectively'). But I will focus in this chapter on markers that separate out what Biber and Finegan call the 'propositional content' and make comment on how the writer relates to that proposition, for instance by saying 'I think'. These markers are part of a larger interactive process of *stance-taking* in interaction; here, jeff's interaction with Doug (who made the comment to which jeff is responding) and the larger audience of astrophysicists and other readers of *Cosmic Variance*.

Why should we pay attention to all this, and not just edit out all the verbiage and say that jeff says physicists are wrong? Well, for one thing, there are lots of these markers in blogs. And they do something: the passage from which this was taken would read very oddly if it had no stance makers at all. If it was just asserted, it could sound bullying and egotistical (and some blogs do indeed sound that way). Stance leads us to a more complex view of writers' opinions as more or less, certain or tentative, personal or collective. Attention to stance also leads us to a more complex view of how bloggers interact with potential readers, insisting they have something new to say, while also maintaining (usually) enough politeness to allow the discussion to continue, and to keep the blog entertaining.

The term **stance** covers features that are often discussed in other terms: modal verbs (*can, may*), some main verbs (*claim, think*), hedges (*possibly*), reported speech (*they say*), and conversational particles (*well*). I will consider the different kinds of stance-taking, and then divide the stance markers into those that use grammatical and lexical resources (such as adverbials) and those that use discourse resources (such as reported speech). In each category, I will go from features that are pretty obviously and commonly markers of stance, to constructions that are more novel and surprising, and that may stretch our conception of stance-taking. We will see that bloggers are quite careful about the ways they mark their opinions as (just) opinions.

11.1 Kinds of stance

Stance-taking can do different kinds of work; that is why it is an interesting concept. One of the big reference grammars of English, Biber et al. (1999), divides stance into three categories, epistemic (dealing with facts), attitudinal (dealing with personal perspectives) and stylistic (dealing with the way it is said). I was originally looking just for epistemic uses, and I find this categorization useful in pushing me to look at a broader range of stance-taking that is found in blogs. The next three sections deal with the differences between these kinds of stance before I look at attitudinal and stylistic stance in more detail.

i. Epistemic

Epistemology is the branch of philosophy studying how we know what we know. But we all deal with epistemological issues in our everyday lives, and epistemic stance concerns the marking certainty and uncertainty about the factual basis for statements. 'Facts are not our forte' is the wonderful motto of the *West End Whingers*, and it might serve as a motto for the entire blogosphere. The blogs I studied make surprisingly few statements of facts. But when the facts are uncertain, bloggers are generally rather careful in marking the uncertainty. For instance, *Instapundit* refers to some news reports, but raises doubts about them:

> ARE SOLDIERS **REALLY** BEING ASSAULTED <u>ON THE D.C. METRO?</u> Bob Owens looks into it and **it seems** to be mostly bureaucratic smoke-blowing – or ass-covering – based on a single incident. (*Instapundit*)

The author of *Instapundit* has very little direct access to news stories, sitting at his desk in Knoxville, Tennessee, and most of the work of his blog is in linking to various suggestions on the internet, and sorting out what he thinks can be believed from what can't. Here, he puts what might be a headline ('Soldiers are assaulted') as a question, and then puts an alternative interpretation in a report from someone else, and in a phrase introduced with 'it seems', which gives a carefully graded stance on this new view. If it turned out it wasn't mostly bureaucratic smoke-blowing, he wouldn't have misled you; he just said it *seemed* that way from what Bob Owens found, and it could well look different in the future, or even later that same day.

Unlike *Instapundit*, the author of *Thoroughly Modern Millie* has immediate access to what she is talking about here, the Passover practices of residents of her Florida retirement community.

> **I would say that** most of the population in this area either eat out or order a complete dinner and have it at home. (*Thoroughly Modern Millie*)

But she still marks it as just her perspective, by making her point the complement of a clause 'I would say that', leaving open the slight possibility that in some corner of the town she doesn't know about, a lot of Jewish residents are preparing chicken soup and matzoh balls entirely made from scratch.

Epistemic markers are relatively infrequent (compared to the other categories of stance), but they are very important, because they affect the way blogs are interpreted as part of news and political discussion.

ii. Attitudinal

The vast majority of instances of stance that I coded marked the writer's personal aesthetic preference, moral judgement or emotional response. Nearly every example later in the chapter fits in this category, so I will just give a few here, to show how much is covered by 'attitude'. Food bloggers frequently make statements that have no better support than the writer's own taste:

> **I humbly suggest that** the key to a good springtime curry is to keep things on the light side. (*101 Cookbooks*)

If this appeared without the words in bold, we would still know that this was just the *aesthetic* preference of Heidi Swanson (as she has other preferences for the less familiar grains, fresh vegetables and exotic salts). By emphasizing that it is just her suggestion, she actually strengthens it. Readers go to the blog just because they think her taste is pretty good, or is at least interesting, not because she claims any credentials to lay down the law on the authenticity of south Asian cuisine. The same sorts of statements might be made in blogs devoted to theatre, music, fashion or film, and often attention is drawn to the element of personal taste, as it is here.

Some attitudes are *judgements* based on moral or political norms, presumably shared with right-thinking readers. Here Angellos Makis, commenting on a post, presents himself as a Greek:

> **I am personally ashamed that** my country did not speak up of the Olympics been held in China. (comment to *Dr Dave*)

In this framing, the attitude is not just a matter of personal taste; he feels 'ashamed', implying that others will share his sense that Greece must be guardian of the moral and political norms of the Olympic movement, and that others will identify him as a Greek with the decision (or lack of decision) of the Greek government. Others make similar sorts of statements about parenthood, human rights, history or environmental action, implying that the issue is one that can be treated in terms of right and wrong.

Some markers of attitudinal stance convey an emotional response, rather than an aesthetic preference or a moral norm. Here *IsraeliMom* is talking about reading other blogs that in her view question the right of Israel to exist:

I confess, these posts/comments upset me. (*IsraeliMom*)

She conveys her feelings, but frames the statement with 'I confess', implying that there is something secret about these feelings, or difficult about revealing them (even though we are hardly likely to be surprised that they had this effect on her). Of course there is a moral comment here too; she is implying that the posters and commenters were wrong to threaten her country and her family. But in this sentence she conveys that judgement by talking about *affect*, about her feelings, rather than about right and wrong.

The three categories of aesthetic appreciation, moral judgement and emotional affect are useful in pushing us to look at the diversity of statements about attitudes, but like many category systems in this book, they soon get blurred. An affective response can lead us to a moral judgement (as we saw with the example from *IsraeliMom*). Similarly, a reviewer of a play who said it made her uncomfortable might use this affective response as a preface to favourable or unfavourable aesthetic stance-taking.

iii. Stylistic

When Heidi Swanson says 'I **humbly** suggest ...' she is not just embedding the comment that follows, she is telling us how it is offered. In speech, much of the work of suggesting tone of voice can be done with intonation, volume and pace. In written genres, such as blogs, it may be marked explicitly. One device that has been much commented on is the smiley, such as :-) or ;-) or :^), all of which are used by various posters and (more often) by commenters on the posts, often to soften what could otherwise seem to be a harsh comment on someone else, or to mark an ironic or self-mocking comment directed at oneself or one's family. Here a blogger is writing about her annual move from Massachusetts to Florida:

I know from experience the first few days It takes time to find the light switches, the cabinets where I keep the dishes, glasses, pots and pans. Not that I'm going to cook anything. ☺ (*Thoroughly Modern Millie*)

She scatters lots of smileys through her post, consistent with the light bantering tone.

Many examples of stylistic stance markers, especially adverbs (*seriously, honestly, frankly*) seem intended to mark a shift in tone, and not, perhaps, to describe the actual tone intended as serious or honest or frank. Let's take three examples, all from *India Uncut*. Here Amit Varma is suggesting that makers of a stuffed pastry put tandoori chicken in it to boost sales in the Punjab:

> **Seriously**, they should try it. (*India Uncut*)

I don't know about pavs, the pastry he is discussing, or about the Punjab, but I suspect this adverb signals that he is anything but serious in this suggestion. Another comment is about an ad for a vegetarian organization featuring a model wearing a lettuce bikini, saying (in Kannada) 'Turn over a new leaf':

> **Honestly**, in these circumstances that would be difficult even for a vegetarian, no? (*India Uncut*)

He does not mean that his previous comments were not honest, but more likely that we are now to read the literal meaning of the ad's slogan, and picture ourselves as males trying to turn over one of these strategically placed leaves (and presumably getting hit). In the next example, the marker of stance (unusually) follows the statement:

> To me, the Marvel superheroes just had more complexity – even more humanity, **if I may put it like that**. (*India Uncut*)

This metacomment draws attention, as a sort of afterthought, to the oddity of talking about the 'humanity' of comic superheroes who are, by definition, not entirely human. In fact, a stylistic stance marker seldom means exactly what it says:

> **With all due respect**, this sounds like a crippling way to learn an
> Asian language (i.e. a character-based language). (*Language Log*)

When one reads this phrase at the beginning of a sentence, one suspects that something potentially disrespectful (here, an unmitigated harsh evaluation of a proposed teaching method) will follow. When one is really respectful, such prefaces are unnecessary.

11.2 The grammar of stance-taking

So far I have been discussing the broad categories of functions of stance-taking. I will now take the attitudinal and stylistic categories and look more closely at the form of stance-taking devices. The categories are arranged to go from the more obvious marking of stance (a proposition in one clause and a statement of a relation to it in another clause) to less obvious means, such as adverbials and nouns.

i. Verb plus clause complement

In my data, by far the most common way of marking stance was to make the proposition the complement of a clause of thinking, speaking or wishing. A common verb in my data, and probably the prototypical verb for this purpose, is *think*. All three of the following are comments after posts that implicitly invited other opinions.

> **I think** this is a beautiful story. (comment to *Bitch PhD*)

> But **I think** everyone learns differently. (comment to *Language Log*)

> **I think** you should water your garden. (comment to *Raising Yousuf*)

Apparently the sentences would say the same thing if the first clause was left out; it is obvious that what they say is, usually, what they think. But in each of these cases, the writer is marking her or his statement as just her or his opinion, in the face of possible disagreement from other people. The first one is commenting on reports of a Chinese soldier breast-feeding survivors of the 2008 earthquake; by marking it this way, she suggests other people might not find it beautiful. The second example is responding to the assertion of a right way to teach Chinese; by marking it this way, he suggests possible opposition to earlier suggestions. In the third example, the blogger had said she wouldn't water her plant in North Carolina, in solidarity with suffering people in Gaza; by using 'I think', the commenter is marking her comment as a suggestion rather than as a directive. Some of the blogs and posts are peppered with 'I think', but only where the writers see themselves as being engaged in an argument.

If we take 'I think' as a neutral verb in the introductory clause, one can make it weaker by using a verb that does not carry the full force of *think*.

> **I wonder if** part of what I'm saying is that someone should have said to Parker, 'uh, are you sure you really want to go here?' (comment to *Bitch PhD*)

> And **I suppose** the EU laws on human rights add another layer. (comment to *BoingBoing*)

> **I guess** they'll need the cool dip after all the fire making efforts! (*IsraeliMom*)

> In fact **I rather suspect** there's a social continua of acrolect-mesolect-basilect for Mandarin and the other Chinese language-dialects in Singapore (paralleling the situation with English). (comment to *Language Log*)

It is my personal feeling that the blogosphere has elements which may change us all, when we can indulge in peering into the souls of those affected by current events. (*IsraeliMom*)

Or one can embed the introductory clause (*I think*) in another introductory clause to weaken it still further. Here Heather Armstrong is talking about giving her father her new book, which has essays about fathers so it might be expected to have personal significance for him, and finding he has used it to straighten out his toilet.

I like to think that I improved his life by those two inches. (*Dooce*)

She doesn't *think* this, she *likes to* think this, suggesting another viewer outside the speaking self who can see that this view (that she has improved his life) is a kind of wishful thinking.

Similarly, one can strengthen the stance by choice of verbs in the introductory clause:

I **hope**, wait no, I **am sure** you'll have a good time in Tokyo! (comment to *Dr Dave*)

I **truly believe** that in order to change things and arrive at a solid foundation for peace, we have to learn to accept each other narratives. (*IsraeliMom*)

Or one can present oneself as being compelled to say this, or as wanting to say the opposite, but finding themselves unable to:

If 'sacrifice' is the yardstick by which we're measuring how American one is, **I have to say** that Amilcar is a hell of a lot more American than, say, I am. (*Bitch PhD*)

devin: you know, **I wish I could say** this is intentional. (*Dr Dave*)

I must admit i had slight teary sheen to my eyes after. (*BoingBoing*)

These constructions again suggest an adversarial situation in which the writer is positioning herself or himself against an opposing view, that she would have wished to say that he is more American than Amilcar, or he would have wished to say that this obscure writing by linguists is intentionally obscure, or that he didn't have tears in his eyes after watching a satellite landing on Mars. But he or she has to say it, so the statement is all the stronger.

The introductory clause doesn't have to be something like *think* or *say*; it can present a fact as relevant. Here the author of *Going Underground* is explaining with some embarrassment her occasional eating of fast food on the London tube:

> **It's just that** you're so limited for healthy food late at night near London Underground stations, you don't get much choice. (*Going Underground*)

Her behaviour is presented as following from this self-evident fact.

Conrad and Biber (2000) have suggested that the word order of these typical statements of stance is important: in nearly all cases, the readers get the stance in the main clause, before they find out what it is a stance *on* ('I think this is a beautiful story' has a different effect from 'This is a beautiful story, I think'). That makes sense, because it is important to know how to take a statement before processing it. An exception is the use of smileys, where one gets to the end of the sentence before finding that it is meant to display humour or shock, and abbreviations like LOL (laughing out loud) that give the effect on the writer after the statement. But they may act as a kind of insurance, in case you missed what should have been an obviously joking tone.

Let's consider one case of slightly odd word order:

> When I was a kid, eating poisonous toad excretions was the sort of thing **I never thought** you'd have to warn people not to do. (comment to *Boing Boing*)

In this phrasing, we get the 'eating poisonous toad secretions' first, and are allowed to figure out for ourselves that this is a stupid thing to do, so when the stance is given, 'I never thought you'd have to warn people not to', it comes as humorous understatement. At least I *think* that's why that comment is funny.

ii. Separate sentence

In the examples so far, the stance-taking clause (*I think*) comes first, and subordinates the clause that states the stance (*this is a beautiful story*). It should work the same way to have the stance-taking in a separate sentence. But it doesn't, especially if the stance comes after the statement. Here a blogger describes the approach to her local library in the evening:

> I remember going there last spring and found the street was not well lit, the sidewalk was irregular and there is no parking lot. That's not for me. (*Thoroughly Modern Millie*)

The first sentence is evaluative enough for us to guess her stance – she's not going there. But she makes it explicit, and also marks those elements as problems for her, not perhaps for everyone. The effect of putting the stance second can be one of an ironic turnaround:

> The Whingers are feeling a tad existential today. Not that they are *quite* sure what that means. (*West End Whingers*)

In the first sentence, the bloggers present themselves as people who can use philosophical terminology in this casual way, and in the second they undercut that self-presentation.

iii. Adverbial

An adverbial is a part of a sentence that gives an extra aspect of the meaning to the clause, saying how the action was done or giving circumstances:

> **Fortunately**, adding some common houseplants to your surroundings can apparently help clean up the toxins. (*BoingBoing*)

An adverbial can be one word, a phrase or a clause. It is the one part of a clause (subject, predicate, object, complement) that can easily be moved through the sentence (and trying to move it makes a good test if you aren't sure if it is an adverbial). So the following example could be rewritten with no difference in meaning:

> So which statistics do a good job of illustrating India's progress? One very good one, **in my view**, is the divorce rate. (*India Uncut*)

> **In my view**, one very good one is the divorce rate. (rewritten example)

> One very good one is the divorce rate, **in my view**. (rewritten example)

The difference is just stylistic, and I think we'll agree that Amit Varma got it right, using the adverbial for a pause before revealing his surprising choice of statistic. Adverbials can be used to qualify or support a statement by giving one's credentials, or to qualify it by saying it is just you:

> **As an Israeli civilian who has not served in the army** I say this without moralizing or judging. (comment to *Raising Yousuf*)

> **As far as I'm concerned**, the performers and director have made a pact with you, the audience member, when you buy that seat for a show, and that pact is to *give you a good evening* [italics in original] – to entertain you. (comment to *West End Whingers*)

Adverbials can be used to give the background or circumstances of a statement, or to attribute it:

> I was so happy to find enormous piles of cherries and other stone fruits (peaches and apricots) at the farmer's market last weekend! **For some reason** I wasn't expecting them until at least June … (*101 Cookbooks*)

> **According to Bill O'Reilly**, I am using the Presidential campaign to engage in 'villainous pursuits' to promote a radical agenda. (*Black Prof*)

The 'for some reason' adds the information that she was wrong and that she isn't sure why she was wrong; the 'according to Bill O'Reilly' marks this as not the author's own view.

The most frequent use of adverbials in these blogs is to weaken or strengthen the statement:

> **Certainly**, there are going to be more rough days ahead – especially as a cornered Al Qaeda feels the need to demonstrate that it is still a major force. (*Instapundit*)

> Cyber-terrorism, **perhaps**, to mark the 60th anniversary of the Nakba? (*Raising Yousuf*)

> **Apearantly** they both are pretty good about Native American issues. (comment to *Bitch PhD*)

> Despite appearances, this **really** is just the standard cosmology, not some fairy tale. (*Cosmic Variance*)

> **Obviously** the term has gained more prominence in this election cycle because it's the first time that the choice made by superdelegates has mattered so much. (*Language Log*)

As we have seen with other adverbials in discussing stylistic functions, the uses have often become conventionalized so that the words serve as markers and no longer have their literal meanings. 'In fact', for instance, seldom has the epistemic function of saying something is a fact.

iv. Modal and semi-modal verbs

Modal verbs come before the main verb and modify its effect:

> I **might** ignore that 'makes about 48 petite bites' part and cut this sucker into pie slices. (comment to *101 Cookbooks*)

> Terror? If there were giant poisonous hallucinogenic toads roaming the streets then that **might** warrant the use of 'terror' in the headline. Idiot ingests toxin and dies does not. (comment to *DoingDoing*)

The 'might' makes the 'ignore' or the 'warrant the use' only a possibility. They mark stance because they comment on the statement being made, although in a more subtle way than an introductory clause (The commenter could have said 'It is possible that I will ignore ...'). Modal verbs are usually classified as *epistemic* (e.g., *may, might*, having to do with certainty or uncertainty), *deontic* (e.g., *should, must*, having to do with obligation or necessity) and *dynamic* (e.g., *can*, having to do with ability or inability).

> **Epistemic**: Tomorrow **may** have a slightly higher entropy than today, but not by an amount that explains the radical difference in the behavior of memory over the two intervals (comment to *Cosmic Variance*)

> **Deontic**: Black people **should** remain focused and be ourselves without worrying about what other people have to say. (comment to *Black Prof*)

> **Dynamic:** Health officials said the hardened resin, made with venom from toads of the Bufo genus, contains chemicals that **can** disrupt heart rhythms. (*BoingBoing*)

As one might expect, blogs and their comments have a lot of the deontic category, people telling others what should happen or what has to happen. Modals can also be used to create a hypothetical situation that is contrary to fact. Here Heather Armstrong has told a cab driver that she writes a blog:

> I **could** have said, 'I teach English to genius pandas,' and the look on my face **would** have been the same. (*Dooce*)

She didn't say this, but she wants us to imagine the situation.

Besides the short list of actual modal verbs, there are also semi-modals that work in similar ways, for instance to express obligation:

> It took me a long time to even get into bulgur ... I **need to** expand my horizons! (comment to *101 Cookbooks*)

> This morning, though, I **had to** check in at my neighbourhood clinic and undergo a whole series of health exams. (*Dr Dave*)

> It's always a quiet sad day, with sad songs on the radio and nothing but Memorial programs on TV (not that I **dare** watch any of them – way too painful). (*Thoroughly Modern Millie*)

These also modify the main verb to suggest the writer's stance. For instance, Millie could have said 'not that I watch any of them', but saying 'not that I dare watch any of them' she conveys the stance of avoiding them out of sensitivity, not out of boredom or disinterest.

Modal verbs have equivalent adjectives (e.g., *possible*), adverbs (e.g., *possibility*) and nouns (e.g., *possibility*), but I will stick to the verbs because they are less likely to be noticed as markers of stance.

v. Premodifying adverb

The term *adverb* sounds like *adverbial*, but they are different: an **adverb** is a class of words that modify a verb, an adjective, or another adverb. They are usually single words (there is one exception in my examples), and they cannot float around the sentence as adverbials do. Bloggers often add adverbs in a way that emphasizes their attitude to a statement.

> I'm **so** making this! (comments to *101 Cookbooks*)

> And it **totally** made viewers think that if they watched the piece they'd come away with some sort of gooey film in-between their fingers. Or a cold sore. (*Dooce*)

> but I **absolutely** know one thing – if I desperately needed help, these women would help me, no strings attached. (*Bitch PhD*)

> I've always liked Howard, but isn't this **kind of** gratuitous? (*Instapundit*)

In these examples, 'so' has to go before 'making', 'totally' before 'making', 'absolutely' before 'know', and 'kind of' before 'gratuitous', because those are the words they modify (*Kind of* is an example of a two-word adverb).

But their effect is more slippery and general than that precise word order would suggest. I still haven't figured out the use of *just*.

> **Just** one individual's thoughts. (comment to *101 Cookbooks*)

> I **just** chose to tell it from the point of view of a time coordinate that is oriented in the opposite direction from the one we usually use. (*Cosmic Variance*)

The *just* is always deletable, but it limits the effect of the noun phrase or verb, 'this and only this'. For instance 'just chose' means the same as 'chose', but the addition of the adverb stresses this is *all* he did; the implication is that a big difference arises from an apparently small choice. *Just* projects an assumed expectation onto the reader (it's only this), and then denies it (it's more).

Adverbs compress the kind of stance marker that we have seen earlier. The adverbs in the following sentence are the equivalent of 'I was disturbed that ...' and 'We were irritated that ...':

> Bourne delivers a superb performance, quite **disturbingly** convincing and – had it not been for the fact that Xavier's trousers were **irritatingly**

too short for most of the play – Andrew would have been quite moved. (*West End Whingers*)

As adverbs rather than clauses with subjects, they suggest that anyone would be disturbed or irritated, because the explicit subject (*we*) is now implicit. There is the same effect from 'the fact that', which really means 'We thought that the trousers were too short'. Of course no reader will be confused by the lack of subject; in a theatre review, which is what the Whingers are writing here, everything is the writers' opinion. But there is a difference between marking the statement as opinion and projecting it, with adverb or noun, as already what everyone thinks.

vi. Stance nouns

I have been tracing stance markers from what I think are more obvious to less obvious grammatical forms. When the stance has been compacted into a noun (called **nominalization**), it may take some unpacking to see that it is the writer's opinion. Here Annie Mole is listing the advice she gave to bloggers at a workshop:

> The **importance** of primarily writing for yourself so that ideally your enthusiasm shows through. (*Going Underground*)

She could have said 'I think it is important that you write for yourself....', but here that personal view is made into the noun *importance*, which makes it a topic one talks about, rather than an evaluation. A similar sort of compacting into a noun can happen with almost all the kinds of stance I have discussed. For instance, 'It is possible that there will be cheap shots' can be made into

> – but **the possibility** of this kind of cheap shot from media folks is one reason (among many) why I don't have them. (*Instapundit* [he's talking about blog comments])

At this stage, the explicit marking of stance with which we started has become rather attenuated, so the reader has to work to see it.

What's the point of figuring out the grammar of the stance marker? One reason is just to make yourself more aware of how many such markers there are in blogs. I didn't see how many deontic modals there were until I actually searched for them with a list. And it can be useful to note how they are distributed. There is one cautious comment in *Language Log* that uses 'I think' or 'I thought' seven times in a short paragraph. On the other hand, an angry post on *Raising Yousuf* asserting that Israeli actions in Gaza constitute genocide has no stance markers, except for a few deontic modals. Putting the stance marker in a separate clause or an adverbial makes it stand out, and signals the stance before the statement; putting it as a modal, adverb or noun makes it more taken for granted as part of the statement.

11.3 The discourse of stance-taking

i. Reported speech

The categories of stance-taking so far are tied to specific grammatical components of the clause. But there are also ways of suggesting the writer's stance by using structures that go beyond the clause, and rely on the reader's sense of how language is used in context. One way to do this is to use reported speech or thought to represent, often indirectly, one's own point of view. The examples that are relevant here dramatize a situation from which the reader can infer the writer's view. Since Heather Armstrong is particularly good at this, I will take all my examples from her blog *Dooce*. Nearly all her examples are hypothetical or modified reports that suggest what somebody would have said or could have said. Here she is describing how her father got her 4-year-old to eat pasta:

> I was all **YOU CANNOT BE SERIOUS, OUR DAUGHTER WILL NOT EVEN EAT BREAD**. And he was all, **woman, calm down, I am made of magic**, and after waving his hand and chanting a hypnotizing spell, that kid put a noodle in her mouth, I WILL NEVER GET OVER IT. (*Dooce*)

Note that there is no reporting verb (*I said, he said*); the 'I was all' and 'he was all' suggest that she is giving more or less the effect of what was said, but not that these were her words. By dramatizing it this way, she takes a very ordinary everyday scene and conveys both her shock and her father's tone. In one bravura passage (about whether her work is to be classified as a 'mummy blog') she carries on a conversation first with herself, in reported thought, and then with her father, who is directly addressed:

> When I sit down to update my website I don't think to myself, **'What will I say today on my mommy blog?'** The first thing I think is, **how can I give my father a heart attack**? And then I back up a second and go, **nah, I'd miss him too much, I will just have to write this story about Jon's Brazilian wax in my personal diary**. Dad, are you paying attention? It's because of you that the world does not get to hear about Jon's genitals. I HOPE YOU'RE HAPPY. (*Dooce*)

The first, hypothetical report is given quotation marks. The second, 'real' thought is not given quotation marks, but is given in direct speech (that is, the tenses aren't shifted). The shifts to reported speech or thought are often seamless. Here she starts describing the studio of the NBC *Today* show, and then conveys her shock at the mess backstage with a sudden shift to direct speech:

> Not that I was expecting the walls to be lined with gold, but you look at the set and see how sharp and clean it is, and then you go backstage and, **oh my god, has my daughter been playing in here**? (*Dooce*)

Again, no reporting verb; readers have to be awake to the dramatization, as they would be in conversation, where such hypothetical reports are common.

ii. Rhetorical questions

We saw the use of questions as ways of engaging with the audience. Real questions may not convey stance; they may just be requests for information. But rhetorical questions, to which both writer and reader already know the answer, always convey a stance, if only by aligning writer and reader in this way. For instance, this question conveys a view of the plays of Bernard Shaw even if you don't know enough about them to share the evaluation:

> When did you last see the words 'Shaw' and 'concise' in the same sentence? (*West End Whingers*)

You now know that the Whingers don't think Shaw's plays are concise, and think their readers have already been bored by his characters going on too long. Generally, the reader's answer is known; in the following cases, the answer is 'No':

> Can you even imagine how one would go about envisioning the laws of physics spontaneously reversing a supernova, for instance? (*Cosmic Variance*)

> Maybe we shouldn't ever leave the house, otherwise? (*Dooce*)

> That is terrific, but do you think there'll ever be a time when a gay atheist has a shot at the presidency? (*India Uncut*)

The rhetorical question presents the point of view as obvious. Occasionally, though, the writer tells us the right answer, perhaps thinking we will miss it:

> If we are in the business of trying to understand, can we ignore a large part of recorded history because we don't like it. **I think not**. (comment to *IsraeliMom*)

iii. Irony

Irony, like a rhetorical question, attributes a view to the reader. Here, for instance, the reader must know these assertions are right (at least the date of the US Constitution), so putting it in a complement clause, using an adverb to weaken it, and then taking it all back, come across as ironic:

> I was *pretty* sure the nation was founded in 1789, that there was just the one candidate, and that there was no primary the first time around, but I guess I was wrong. (*Language Log*)

The effect is to suggest that the article he is criticizing has not just made mistakes, but has made obvious mistakes. There is usually some obvious contradiction to signal the irony:

> Albert Hofman, discoverer of the lysergic acid diethylamide compound (better known under its initials) and advocate of a mature, non-repressive approach to psychedelic drug experimentation, died this week at the age of 102. Yet another tragic example of a young life cut short by the evils of drugs. (*Dr Dave*)

Here the inconsistency of 'a young life' and 'the age of 102' makes us look for an alternative meaning, a mockery of warnings about drugs.

iv. Concessions

All the discursive markers of stance so far involve holding up some possible alternative view to one's own. The most obvious way to do this is to make a concession, usually stating some opposing view first:

> I think Nottingham University, and the police, and the home office, have acted appallingly in this case, **but** it isn't helpful to have this sort of grossly inaccurate reporting. (comment to *BoingBoing*)

> Yes, many events are documented, and I have a lot of respect for history as a discipline, **but** in the end of the day, we can go on arguing forever, because each side will pick the events that best suit their narrative, emphasize some events, and ignore or play down others. (*IsraeliMom*)

> The three instructions may be 'motherhood' (ie, obvious, although even that is arguable), **but** that property is not the same as being meaningless. (*Language Log*)

The adversative conjunction (but) signals the beginning of the view one holds and wants to emphasize. The construction shows that one has rationally considered alternative interpretations (of the case, the importance of history, the instructions discussed earlier), and then arrived at one's own view.

v. Conversational devices

Blogs have a surprising number of particles and non-word sounds that don't usually appear in writing, but that can be imagined in speech. They occur most frequently in response to some earlier post or comment. Here is a typical exchange, after Israeli Mom had moved to her own URL:

> ontheface said ... So does the move mean that you're going to post more often? ;)
> IsraeliMom said ...
> **Yesssssss**! Well, **ummmm**, yes, I mean to post more often, we'll see what life has to say about it, I guess! (*IsraeliMom*)

She doesn't just say 'yes', she spells it in a way that suggests a high-pitched drawn-out conversational response. Then she gives an alternative, with 'well', a long-filled pause 'ummmm', and a plain 'yes', suggesting that her initial enthusiasm may need to be qualified. I found lots of different words and non-words, usually at the beginning of a negative response to some point or suggestion:

> **Harrumph** (*Bitch PhD*)
>
> I mean, **gee**. (*Bitch PhD*)
>
> **Um.** The intent of Memorial Day is to remember the dead. **Soooooo**
>
> ... it's not the kind of thing of which you're meant to wish for happy observance. (comment to *BoingBoing*)
>
> oh noooooooes (*BoingBoing*)
>
> GEE, DO YOU THINK? John Kerry as an imperfect messenger. (*Instapundit*)
> **Sigh**. Not much more to say. (*IsraeliMom*)

These do not just convey a response, they also set a joking tone, a shift from writing to mock conversation. We will see lots more of these in disagreements in *Wikipedia*.

What all these discourse devices have in common is that they ask the reader to imagine an interaction, typically an adversarial interaction, and then draw inferences from the way the blogger is interacting. So they work differently from the grammatical markers; they can't be identified on their own, but have to be read for a specific meaning in context.

11.4 Why stance matters

Bloggers are often accused in the media of being solipsistic ranters shouting at an empty internet. It wouldn't surprise these accusers that I have found so many opinion statements in blogs. But it might surprise them to find that these opinions are so carefully marked, in many cases, for the way the writer holds them, the way he or she says them, and their basis of lack of basis in fact. One reason to look at the categories of stance-taking is to see the wide range of ways bloggers relate to what they say. Another reason to look at these categories is to see, again, how interactive blogs must be to survive. The blogs I have analysed vary in their numbers of readers, but they all do interact with their readers in nearly every sentence. The pleasure in reading something like *Dooce*, *Instapundit*, *India Uncut*, or *Going Underground* is not just in getting the opinions – I certainly don't agree with all of them. It is also in seeing how cleverly they manage that interaction and keep it going.

11.5 What I did

For this chapter, I took the blogs, and analysed them using Atlas ti. I started with the grammatical categories from Biber et al. 1999, and added discourse categories to them. The categories of rhetorical questions and conversational devices, for instance, emerged as I went through the data. In general, there are far more markers in the readers' comments than in the bloggers' posts. As my choice of examples suggested, there are far more stance markers in some blogs than in others; I found relatively few in *Black Prof,* and huge numbers in *BoingBoing* and in the academic discussions on *Cosmic Variance.*

11.6 What I read

There is a large literature on stance. The chapter in the *Longman Grammar of Spoken and Written English* (Biber, Johansson, Leech, Conrad and Finegan 1999) can serve as a starting point, and several collections extend the concept from grammar to discourse and interaction (Hunston and Thompson 2000; Englebretson 2007). *Stance* is a rather broad umbrella term; there has been far more work on what I have treated as specific categories, such as modality (Palmer 1990; Fairclough 2003), hedging (Hyland 1998), reported speech (Semino and Short 2004) and narratives (Eggins and Slade 1997; Georgakopoulou 2007). Of course none of these studies refers specifically to blogs; you have to go back to studies of other genres of writing and speech.

12

Respellings in text messages

Caroline Tagg

12.1 Introduction

12.1 Hi NAME219 hope unis ok&u'r feelin gud Hows it bin wiv NAME227
sincc u got bac? Gud news bout the playscheme Lookin4ward 2seein
u soon hav missd u lotsa love NAME330

> Alison, in her early thirties

Text messaging is often defined, at least in the media and in much public
debate, by its spelling. The text message above encapsulates popularly held
conceptions as to what Txt looks like. Words are shortened in various ways
(*feelin, bout, hav, missd*) and some are spelt phonetically (*gud*), while other
spellings reflect how we might say the words in fast, informal speech (*bin,
wiv, lotsa*). Words may often be run together without spaces between them.
As you'll notice above, words may instead be separated by punctuation (*u got
bac?Gud news*) or by number homophones such as *2* and *4* in *Lookin4ward*
and *2seein*.

The paradox with Txt, however, is that the popular conception doesn't
always match how many people actually text. Since I started studying text
messaging, I've had several conversations which go along the lines of:

Me: Actually at the moment I'm looking at the language of text
messaging.
Interested person: Oh, I never usc text language. I write everything out
normally.

The assumption made by the 'interested person' (who is in some cases simply being polite) is that by 'language of text messaging' I mean the kind of abbreviated and unconventionally spelt language discussed above. And their response tends to be that they do not text in this way. One caveat here is the unreliability of self-reports – the possible discrepancy between what people do and what they say. Nevertheless, what these people tell me is reflected in my data. In fact, what struck me first when looking through CorTxt was the *absence* or infrequency of unconventional spellings in many text messages. Here are some examples.

12.2 Everybody had fun this evening. Miss you.

12.3 Men like shorter ladies. Gaze up into his eyes.

12.4 No, but you told me you were going, before you got drunk!

12.5 Sorry NAME352. I will be able to get to you. See you in the morning.

Admittedly, neither my data nor my conversations involve many teenagers, and it may be this age group (or younger) that tends to abbreviate. (Although, interestingly, so far the people I've encountered who are most voraciously critical of 'textese' were a group of English Literature undergraduates.) Indeed, my informants will sometimes extend the above conversation by describing what they see as the more idiosyncratic and indecipherable spelling practices of offspring, nieces and nephews. So it is useful in this context to note the similar infrequency of unconventional spellings found across studies. Thurlow and Brown (2003), for example, report that although 82% of the 19-year-old university students participating in their study claimed to use 'textisms', they found only an average of 3 per text message (which they describe as 20% of message content). According to Taylor and Harper (2003), the value placed on text messages by young people can depend on the language used, and abbreviating to avoid sending more than one message can in fact *lower* their value. It might be worth reflecting on your own practice – and your own inbox. To what extent do you, and the people you text, play with spelling conventions? (And do your practices shift to accommodate those of your interlocutors?) How do you judge messages with unconventional – and those with conventional – spellings?

Another question worth considering is how intelligible you find your friends' and family's spelling practices. One of the fears expressed in the media is that Txt is indecipherable. And it may well be – to those looking over their children's shoulders. We may all have received the odd text message (in both senses of the word) which we puzzled over. In general, however, it is fair to say that when we text we are aware of what our interlocutor will understand. Textisms are difficult for outsiders to understand precisely because they draw on intimate contextualized practices and shared knowledge between those involved. As Thurlow and Brown (2003, p. 15) point out, most textisms are 'semantically recoverable', that is, they can be understood in (or 'recovered' from) context. When people shorten a word by omitting the vowels, for example, they recognize the fact that consonants carry the greater information load: *please* can be recovered from <pls> but you would hardly recognize it if you removed the consonants and were left with <eaae>; while phonetic spellings can often be interpreted simply by reading them aloud. Spaces are often only omitted where words are broken up by numbers or punctuation: hence the alphanumeric sequences *Lookin4ward* and *2seein* described above. Ultimately, these forms emerge from interaction and are likely to be understood by the people involved: in this respect, as Thurlow and Brown put it, textisms are fairly 'unremarkable'.

Why do people sometimes choose to spell certain words unconventionally? The obvious answer is that they are abbreviating words to save time, effort and space (and hence money), and that this is encouraged by the constraining physical features of the mobile phone – the tiny keypad, the limited character allowance. As Crystal (2008, p. 20) points out, abbreviated messages in full form would tend to be longer than unabbreviated ones (as illustrated in the text messages above), suggesting that people are trying to compress longer messages, or hasten their delivery. Two points emerge here.

Firstly, if we look at the data, it becomes apparent that the need for brevity is not only motivated by technological factors. It is also dictated by communicative demands, such as the expectation that responses will be quick (Thurlow and Brown, 2003). So, abbreviations may be a response to **interpersonal** as well as technological factors. That is, when people decide how to spell, they are concerned with how their spelling will be received by their interlocutor as well as how much space, time or money they can save. The question then becomes: if people abbreviate with an eye to their audience (rather than to save space), will they not also lengthen words or play with spellings in a way that does not result in truncation? Is brevity the only result when people play with spellings? Once we accept that spelling practices may be shaped by interpersonal considerations, we can assume that spelling plays a greater role in communication than simply speeding it up. Is the need for brevity enough to explain the differences in spelling and the effect they have in these two messages, for example?

12.6 Thankyou for ditchin me i had been invited out but said no coz u were cumin and u said we would do something on the sat now i have nothing to do all weekend i am a billy no mates i really hate being single

12.7 Hi, how u? R u getting ther? I'm in bank quein up-payin in stuf4alice-who I Wrk4. We'l av2go out4drink soon-let me no if u wan2 ova nxt few days-not thur. Sux

In their study of text messaging in the UK, Thurlow and Brown posit three motivations for respelling. These are as follows:

1 'brevity and speed' (seen in lexical abbreviation including letter-number homophones; and the minimal use of capitalization, punctuation and spacing);

2 'paralinguistic restitution' (such as the use of capitals to indicate emphasis or loudness, or multiple punctuation, which compensate for the lack of such features as stress and intonation)

3 'phonological approximation' (i.e. often playful attempts to capture informal speech such as <ya> or <nope>).

Often, more than one of these motivations can be fulfilled within one spelling: <ya> for *you*, for example, serves both to abbreviate *and* recreate a spoken utterance. In other cases, however, the desire to approximate an informal spoken form may result in additional characters, as in <nope> or <okie dokie>.

In this chapter, I work within the assumption that how we spell (and 'respell') can be meaningful. It is meaningful because the way we choose to spell words contributes to the effect that a text message has and what the text message says about the person who sent it. In other words, how we spell contributes to our portrayal of social identities, as we choose to express them through text messaging. In taking this approach, I adopt a sociocultural model of orthography, one which posits spelling choices as a socially meaningful practice.

Below, I first explain what is meant by a sociocultural model of orthography and by the term respelling. I then describe the respellings which occur across CorTxt and, working within the model, try to explain their significance in terms of making meaning. They may be unremarkable – but they are not meaningless.

Conventions Used

Throughout this book, I italicize linguistic items under discussion. When I focus on a word as a respelt form, or when presenting an orthographic letter, it is framed by angled brackets, so that I can talk about alternative spellings of *what* being <wat> or <wot>. This practice draws on Sebba (2007). In contrast, representations of sounds are captured within slashes, so that I can say that the letter >c> is pronounced /s/ in *ceiling* and /k/ in *cat*.

12.2 A sociocultural model of spelling

Any guesses as to what these words have in common?

cerise, interning, semaphore, condominium, ratoon, narcolepsy, odontalgia, vivisepulture

The answer is that they are all words with which young American children bagged first place in annual spelling competitions (taken from every decade from 1926 to 2006) (see *http://www.spellingbee.com/champions-and-their-wi nning-words*). 'Spelling Bees' have been hugely popular for years in the United States, and have recently caught on in other countries, including Britain.

What do spelling bees tell us? Firstly, they remind us of what every schoolchild knows – spellings are either right or (more often, it would seem) wrong. These contests wouldn't work otherwise. Quite why spellings are viewed through the rigid perspective of right and wrong is not entirely clear. It certainly wasn't always the case. In the Middle Ages and up to the time of Shakespeare (also known as Shakespere and Shakspeare), people's spellings would reflect their local pronunciation; but more than that, there simply wasn't the belief that each word should have one spelling. The notion of correct spelling emerged as a result of the invention of printing and the establishment of mass schooling, both of which encouraged the perception that one word needed one stable form. In comparison to, say, punctuation, it is also fairly easy to standardize spelling – it is tricky to generate rules that account for the placing of commas in whatever people choose to write, but fairly easy to dictate which letters should make up each word. And dictionaries have proved an effective, popular and trusted way to codify and disseminate spellings.

Secondly, spelling bees tell us that how good someone is at spelling matters. Not being able to spell well tends to carry a stigma in literate societies – it suggests you are uneducated or even unintelligent; the flip side of this coin is that being able to spell well is a great achievement. So, correct spelling is not neutral; it is a highly evaluative activity around which cultural practices are built up. Spelling bees award good spellers, while bad spellers are met with some social opprobrium. In other words, adhering to the correct model or diverging from it, both carry social meaning – it says something about who you are and how society sees you.

Is the social meaning carried by 'incorrect' spelling always the same? Or does it depend on who is involved, where they are writing, and with what intention? Advertisers, for example, often use respellings to sell products. A prominent and enduring advertising slogan in the UK is *Beanz Meanz Heinz*, for Heinz Baked Beans (where >z> replaces >s>). If an advertiser uses unconventional spelling such as the above, can it be described as a mistake or the result of ignorance – or as an attempt to catch the eye of consumers in a memorable way? What about graffiti sprayed onto a wall or scratched into a desk, which include respellings such as in *I woz ere*. Is this so widely used because successive generations of graffiti artists are unable to spell, or because it signals through its unconventional spelling the casual and transgressive intentions of its author?

The significance and status of orthography and spelling can only be appreciated when its context is taken into account. A vivid example of this is the clash in literary practices between Spanish missionaries and local Mexican linguists as they devised orthographies for previously unwritten Mexican languages (Barros, 1995). The missionaries brought with them their assumption that reading and writing were solitary and silent practices (as they largely continue to be in many places) and so favoured alphabetic Spanish orthography. The local linguists, however, came from a society with a focus on collectivity and orality, and so they argued for 'mural texts' or 'wall-newspapers' and for a phonetic script resembling a phonemic transcription (Barros, 1995, p. 282). As Sebba (2007, p. 24) puts it, different orthographies support different literacy practices, emerging from different ways of seeing and doing things. To take another example, in the 1700s, spelling played a significant role in signalling the unity and identity of the United States and its independence from Britain. I grew up thinking that American spelling was a more 'logical' system; it turns out to be much more to do with forging an American identity.

What's the difference between: spelling and orthography?

The difference is crucial in understanding how unconventional spellings work. **Orthography** refers to the conventions of a particular written language, which determines possible letter-sequences and the sounds that written letters represent. For example, English orthography allows the lengthy consonant clusters <sch> or <ght>, but does not allow <ng> at the beginning of a word (which is possible in, e.g. Vietnamese); while the sound /u:/ can be represented by <oo> but not by <uu> . **Spelling** is the application of these orthographic principles to particular words. So, for example, although English orthographic principles would allow the spelling <gudz>, the correct spelling is <goods>.

As the above examples show, decisions by individuals or groups to spell according to prescribed usage or to depart from prescription by varying spellings can have various social meanings. The fact that unconventional or non-standard spellings can be deliberate and meaningful is captured in the term **respelling** (e.g. Sebba, 2007), which avoids the evaluative perception of incorrectness that colours the alternative term 'non-standard'.

There is, however, only a restricted set of options from which people can pick in respelling. Any variation from conventional norms must follow language-specific orthographic principles to remain recognizable to readers and thus be effective (Sebba, 2007, p. 32). That is, when people respell words, they alter spellings in line with existing orthographic principles. What this means is that respellings draw on the same orthographic conventions as conventional ones. <woz>, for example, works as a respelling of *was* because it follows the principles of English orthography. The particular principles involved here state that the vowel sound of *was* (/ɒ/) can be represented by the letter <o> (consider *cos* and *hot*); and that the sound /z/ can be written with the letter <z>. In fact, we could argue that <woz> adheres more strongly than *was* to the sound-symbol correspondences we expect to see (so that <cos> arguably works better as an abbreviation of *because* than <cause>). The spelling of *was*, in contrast, is phonetically more irregular. This is how phonetic spelling works, and how it derives the social meaning it does.

Look at two respellings of *school* scratched on a school desk. Which one is more effective, and can you explain why the other does not work?

Down with skool
Down with zguul

The second option <skool> is often used as a respelling of *school* (Ministry of Sound released the dance album *Back to the Old Skool* in 2011, *Skool Daze* was a 1980s computer game and the online site *skool UK* provides creative teaching solutions, to pluck a few examples). The phrase *Down with skool* is itself taken from the title of Geoffrey Willans' (1953) book about a boy's experiences at school (cited by Sebba, 2007, p. 31). The respelling is chosen to make a rebellious yet humorous point against schooling: yet, to do so, the choice of <skool> conforms to English sound-spelling conventions. In contrast, <zguul>, while recognizable, is not a meaningful deviation from the spelling of *school* because it does not follow English orthographic principles: <zg> is not a permitted sequence in English orthography, while <uu> is very rare (occurring in a few words like *vacuum* and *continuum*). <Zguul> has no meaning at all. This shows that respellings are neither freely nor randomly chosen but that the choice is restricted according to orthographic principles.

These ideas constitute what is known as the **sociocultural model of orthography** according to which, respellings can be both principled and meaningful. Can you think of other contexts in which people – either individuals or societies – engage in respelling? Can these examples be described as both principled and meaningful?

The context we are interested in now is that of texting. If respelling in texting adheres to the same orthographic principles as in other contexts, as indeed it must, it follows that textisms will reflect or extend existing patterns of respelling. That is, respellings that occur in texting are not unique but resemble those that occur elsewhere. Kesseler and Bergs (2003), for example, compare their corpus of valentine text messages with love letters written by lower-class 'fallen' girls at the London Foundling Hospital in the 1800s. The two are similar in that both tend to be written on the spur of the moment and combine emotion with everyday purposes. Kesseler and Bergs (2003) found that, like texting, Victorian letters contained phonetic spellings such as <bcoz> (*because*) and <luv> (*love*), graphic symbolizations of kisses (*xx*) and roses, shared metaphors and figures and grammar and spelling mistakes. They conclude that popular perceptions of an earlier, literate age are based unfairly on letters composed by highly literate, public individuals who knew their writings would be retained. The letters of lower-class writers, however, was much more an everyday practice comparable to present-day texting; and spelling variation in texting is a continuation, or development, of these earlier practices. Their findings are reflected by Shortis (2007a,b), who describes texting as extending, popularizing and legitimizing an existing yet devalued 'orthographic palette' of spelling options. The 'palette' extends the traditional binary of 'correct' and 'incorrect', and provides texters with a range of meaningful options.

So, what respellings occur in text messaging, and what do they mean? In the following section, I address these questions, using examples from CorTxt. After exploring the most frequently occurring respellings in the corpus, I look at how these can be categorized, based on both form and function. I then explore three functional categories in greater depth: colloquial contractions (which reflect spoken forms), phonetic spelling and abbreviations (the last two rely for effect solely on their visual form). In each case, I argue that the respellings say something about how the texter who used them wishes to come across.

12.3 Respellings in CorTxt: a study

Table 12.1 lists the 50 most frequently occurring words in CorTxt which also appear in a respelt form. (That is, frequent words that were not respelt, such as *I*, *a* and *me*, are not included.) The numbers to the left indicate the position of the word in the overall frequency list. *The*, for example, is the 6th most frequent word once *I* and *a* are included. What, if anything, do you notice about the list in terms of the respellings?

TABLE 12.1 The top 50 most frequent groups including respelt forms

	Headword	Respelt forms	Freq of group
1	you	u (3043), ya (256), yer (14), ye (9), uu (2)	7,884
2	to	2 (690), ot (3)	4,976
3	x	xx (833), xxx (635), xxxx (11), xxxxxx (3), xxxxxxx (2), xoxox (1), xxxxx (42)	3,689
6	the	d (21), da (6), th (8), hte (3), te (2), ze (2)	3,553
7	and	n (182), an (19), adn (10), amd (2), annd (2)	3,171
8	in	iin (2)	2,387
9	for	4 (357), fer (2)	2,057
11	have	av (8), hve (6), ave (5), hav (106)	1,993
13	be	b (375)	1,567
16	are	r (422), ar (2)	1,478
20	good	gud (40), gd (25), goodo (3)	1,265
22	see	c (248)	1,255
23	just	jus (18), jst (6), jurt (2)	1,240
24	i'm	im (280)	1,216
25	so	soo (1), sooo (5), soooo (1)	1,159
27	will	wil (12)	1,124
28	that	tht (1), dat (4), tha (2)	1,118
29	your	ur (286), yor (2), yer (9), yr (13), u'r (2), ure (1)	1,111
30	not	nt (4)	1,106
31	do	d' (12), du (5)	1,061
32	ok	okay (75), okey (27), k (33), okej (1), okie (12)	1,040
34	with	wiv (82), wid (4), wiht (3)	1,002
35	was	woz (4), ws (3)	952

TABLE 12.1 Cont'd

	Headword	Respelt forms	Freq of group
36	yes	yep (69), yeh (22), yea (15), yeah (382), yup (13)	952
39	can	cn (1)	894
40	tomorrow	tomoz (9), tomorro (6), tomorow (4), tomora (3), tomo (361), morrow (6), mora (1), tom (24), 2mora (14), tomoro (10), 2morrow (9), tmw (9), 2morow (4), 2morro (4), 2mrrw (4), 2moz (3), 2mrw (2), amoro (2), tomorrrow (2), 2moro (42)	888
41	what	wot (148), wat (37)	839
43	know	no (57), knw (1), kno (2)	776
44	about	bout (123), abt (4)	768
45	hope	hpe (2)	746
47	back	bak (38), bac (7), bck (3), bk (11), bek (2)	733
49	no	nope (19), nah (18)	714
50	now	nw (9)	713
51	going	goin (60)	710
52	its	It's (240), tis (21)	696
53	how	hw (2)	692
54	don't	dont (198), dnt (4)	671
57	i'll	ill (46), il (21), i'l (30)	628
58	this	dis (6)	598
59	when	wen (75)	589
60	there	ther (2)	588
61	night	nite (105)	586
65	from	frm (9), fm (3)	568
67	had	hd (1), ad (2)	562
68	too	2 (61)	554

	Headword	Respelt forms	Freq of group
71	come	cum (8), com (2)	537
73	well	wel (5)	520
74	one	1 (88)	514
78	sorry	sori (3), sos (12)	502
79	soon	sn (6)	499

One observation is the proportion of frequently occurring words that are respelt – of the 79 most frequent words in CorTxt, 50 occur also in a respelt form. In fact, frequently occurring words such as the above are more likely to be respelt than those further down the frequency list. One reason for this may be that common words tend to be more irregularly spelt and are thus open to being respelt phonetically (Weber, 1986, p. 418). Examples from the above list include *was* (as discussed earlier) as well as *what* and *come*. Another reason may be that respelling frequently used words also ensures recognition (between texters) of variants used. Grinter and Eldridge (2003) similarly observe that the teenage texters in their study shortened everyday words such as *tomorrow* and *school*. Here we see that texters also regularly respell common functional words such as *you* (<u>, <ya>, <ye>, <yer>), *to* (<2>) and *the* (<d>, <da>, <te>, <th> and <ze>). This is in contrast to the complex list of abbreviated phrases often found in online text dictionaries (and in Crystal 2008).

Also evident in this list is the tendency for more frequent words to be respelt in more varied ways. Of those words that have more than two respellings, most tend to be higher in the frequency list. *You*, for example, has 5 respelt forms, and *the* 6; whereas at the other end of the list words like *had*, *come* and *sorry* just have 2. (The fact that *tomorrow* stands out in the list below with 20 variant forms is perhaps due to the fact that its length renders it amenable to different forms of respelling.) In many cases, it is interesting that texters appear to have choices as to how they spell any one particular word. This is illustrated by <ya> and <u> as respellings of *you*, which are very different approaches to respelling the same word. In other words, texters have choices not only in *whether* they respell but *how* they do so. This point is returned to throughout the chapter.

Forms of spelling variation practice

The above respellings can be grouped into four categories: letter substitution, letter omission, letter appellation and letter transposition, with each subdivided into vowels, consonants and numbers. For example, <thanx> can be described as the 'substitution' of <ks> with <x>, <jst> as the 'omission' of <u>, <soooo> as the 'appellation' of <o>'s and <adn> as a transposition of <n> and <d>. (Unlike other categories, transpositions appear to be mistakes or typos.) In several cases, one respelling exhibits two or more patterns. In <plz>, for example, <s> is replaced by <z> (substitution) and the vowels <ea> are omitted (omission) (see Figure 12.1).

Letter Substitution

- Vowels

  - <o> for <a> (/ɒ/) in *wot* and *woz*;

  - <u> for <o> du (/u:/); *cum, luv* and *gunna* (/ʌ/);

  - <a> for <er> (/ə/) in *betta, numba, lata*; <a> for <ou> (/ə/) in *ya*; <a> for <ow> (/ə/) in *tomora*);

  - <e> for <ou> (/ə/) in *ye*;

  - <i> for <ee> (/ɪ/) in *bin*;

  - <o> for <au> (/ɒ/) in *cos* and *coz*; <o> for <ow> (/əʊ/) in forms of *tomorrow* (*tomoro*);

  - <u> for <oo> ((/ʊ/) in *gud*; <u> for <oul> ((/ʊ/) in *wud, cud*;

  - <er> for <our> (/ɔ:/ /ə/) in *yer*; *ur* for *your* (/jɔ:/)

  - <u> for *you*

  - <ite> for <ight> (/aɪt/) in *nite, 2nite, mite*

- consonants

  - <z> for <s> (/z/) in *coz*(24), *cuz*(3), *cz*(2), *plz*(4), *plez*(3), *howz*(8), *woz*(4)

  - <d> for <th> (/ð/) in *wid* and *dis*; <f> for <ph> (/f/) in *fone*; <v> for <th> (/ð/) in *wiv*; <x> for <ks> (/ks/) in *thanx*

  - <b> for *be*; <c> for *see*; <r> for *are*; <n> for *and*; <ne> for *any*

  - <v> for *very*

FIGURE 12.1 *Categories of respelt forms*

- numbers
  - 0 <2> for <to> (tuː) in *2morrow, 2nite, in2*
  - 0 <4> for <for> (/fɔː/) in *b4*
  - 0 <8> for <ate>, <eat> (/ ɛɪt/) in *m8* and *gr8*

Letter Omission

- vowels
  - vowel omission   (gd, hve, thx, frm, lv, plz, cld, wld)
- consonants
  - double letter reduction   (beta, tomoro, i'l, stil, wel, gona)
  - final letter omission   (an, com, goin, bac, wil, jus)
  - first letter omission (<h>, <th>)   (av, ello, em)
  - mid-position omission of h   (wat, wen, wot, te)
  - other mid-position omissions   (gona, thx)
- syllables
  - final syllable omission   (tomo, prob, num, mess)
  - first syllable omission   (k, bout, cause)

Letter Appellation

- o appellation (so → soooo)
- p appellation (yeah → yep; no → nope)
- y appellation (please → pleasey)
- doubled letter (summort, summing, untill, till)

Letter Transposition

- *adn* for *and*
- *hte* for *the*
- *ot* for *to*
- *thrus* for *thurs* (*Thursday*)

FIGURE 12.1 *Cont'd*

What sense can we make of these patterns? Transpositions, as mentioned above, may be the only category to involve non-deliberate mistakes or typos. Omissions and substitutions involve systematic replacements of less frequent spellings with what Carney (1994) describes as the 'default' or most frequent spelling for the sound. To elaborate on my previous example, <o> replaces <a> to form <wol>, <woz> and <coz> because <o> is the more frequent representation of the sound /ɒ/ (as in *pot*, *toggle*, *forgot*). Other examples are <u> which is used to represent /ʊ/ in <gud>, <wud>, and <cud>, as well as the sound /ʌ/ in <cum>, <luv> and <gunna>; <a> to represent /ə/ in <betta>, <numba>, <lata> and <tomora>. In the case of consonants, it is not frequency which governs the choice of respelling but the more marked or prototypical association of certain letters with certain sounds. The letter <z>, for example, is associated with the sound /z/ (you may think this self-evident, but in fact /z/ is often represented by the letter <s> in *realise*, *dogs* and *has*, for example); and /f/ with <f>, rather than <ph>, which is historically restricted to words of Greek origin (Carney, 1994, pp. 228–30).

Economy of expression is an obvious motivation for substitutions and omissions. This is inevitable in the case of omissions, but most substitutions also involve reductions in the number of letters used. In many cases, one letter replaces two (or three): <d> for <th> (<wid>), for example, <u> for <oo> (<gud>), or <ite> for *ight*. The only example which does not involve some reduction in letters is the replacement of <a> with <o> in <woz> (for *was*). However, the patterns do not suggest that abbreviation and the need for brevity are the only, or even the predominant, motivations. Certain substitutions, for example, show alteration in pronunciation. Replacing <th> with <d> in <with> suggests a change of pronunciation which, as we shall see, reflects a Caribbean pronunciation. The final letter omission in <goin> also reflects a regional informal spoken pronunciation; while <er> in <yer> reflects the pronunciation of /r/ in some English dialects. Nor, clearly, do appellations such as <soooo> or <pleasey > serve to abbreviate. As suggested previously, these respelt forms also function to reflect spoken forms.

The functions behind spelling variation

The functions of variation that emerge from categorizing these formal patterns can be described as in Figure 12.2 below.

- **Colloquial contractions** (Weber, 1986) in *CorTxt* include: *n, av, yer, wiv, goin, bin, allo* and *fink*.

- Other **colloquial respellings** include *goodo, pleasey, nope* and the informal variants of *yes*: *yep*; *yeah, yup*.

- **Regiolectal respellings** (Androutsopoulos, 2000) include <summat>, <summort>, <sumfing> and <summing> for *something*; and <wid> and <dis> for *with* and *this*;

FIGURE 12.2 *Functions of spelling variation in CorTxt*

- Examples of **phonetic spelling** include: *2, 4 u, b, c, gud, woz, coz, thanx, wot, nite, cum, luv, fone, cud*, and *wud*.

- **Abbreviations:** clippings include *tomo, cause* and *bout*; while the final letter is omitted from a number of words including: *are, have, will, just, all, back*;

- **Consonant writing**, in which the vowels are omitted, is evident in *gd* (*good*), *jst* (*just*), *thks, thnx* or *thx* (*thanks*), *bk* (*back*), *frm* (*from*), *wk* (*week*), *lv* (*love*), *pls* or *plz* (*please*), *cld* (*could*), *wld* (*would*), *nxt* (*next*), *txt* (*text*), and *wknd* (*weekend*).

- The **omission of apostrophes** is evident in the otherwise standard contractions: *im* (*i'm*) and *ure* (*you're*) (categorized as a type of abbreviation).

- **Visual morphemes** (Bolinger, 1946) are present in the symbol *x*, or a series of *x*'s, which occur frequently, apparently to represent kisses in order to sign messages off, sometimes alongside *o*'s, representing hugs.

- **Mistakes or mistypings** such as *thrus, iin, adn* and *jurt*.

FIGURE 12.2 *Cont'd*

In the rest of this chapter, I shall look at three of these categories: colloquial contractions, phonetic spelling and abbreviations. The forms that fulfil these functions in CorTxt are listed in Figure 12.3 below.

1 abbreviations

    a) apostrophe omission (im, its, dont ill)

    b) double letter reduction (2morow, wil, beta, gona, hapy)

    c) mid-letter(s) omission

        i. h (nigt, wat, wich, wen, tnx)

        ii. c from ck (bak)

        iii. n (thx, thks)

        iv. e (havnt), <a> (hve, yeh), ou (abt), <i> (finshed)

        v. ee (wkend), eek (w'end), vi. lea (pse)

        vii. shd

        viii. bday, b'day

    d) final letter(s) omission

        i. e (sum, luv, ar)

FIGURE 12.3 *Functions and the forms that realize them*

      ii.   h (o), k (bac), s (thur), w (kno)

      iii. rs (thu), gh (thou)

  e) final syllable(s) omission (fri, num, mess, eve, tomo, tom)

  f) initialisms (v, sth)

  g) substitutions

      i.   sos for sorry

      ii.   z for rrow (tomoz)

  h) standard abbreviations (pm, xmas, 1st)

2. phonetic spelling

  a) number homophones

      i.   1 for one (/wʌn/)

      ii.   2 for to (/tuː/)

      iii. 4 for fore (/fɔː/)

      iv. 8 for ate /ɛɪt/

  b) letter homophones

      i.   b for be (/biː/)

      ii.   c for see (/siː/)

      iii. r for are (/ɑː/)

      iv. u for you

      v.   f for ph (/f/)

      vi. ne for any (ɛnɪ)

  c) ur for you're and your (/jɔː/) – not phonetic

  d) other homophones

      i.   ite for ight (2nite, rite, mite)

      ii.   y for why (/waɪ /)

      iii. yt for ight (/aɪt/) (myt)

      iv. no for know (/nəʊ/)

  e) schwa (/ə/) represented (see section 12.4 on the sound 'schwa')

      i.   a for er (/ə/) (lata, afta, ova, betta, numba)

  f) letter o

      i.   o for <a> (/ɒ /) (wot, wots, wot's, woz, coz, cos)

      ii.   o for ow (/əʊ/)

  g) letter u

      i.   u for au (/ɒ/)

FIGURE 12.3 *Cont'd*

     ii.   u for \<o\> (/ɒ/)

     iii.   u for \<o\> (/uː/) (du)

     iv.   u for \<o\> (/ʌ/) (cumin, cum, luv, dun)

     v.   u for oo or oul (/ʊ/) (gud, cud, wud, shud)

  h)   other vowel sounds

     I.   ar for \<a\> (/ɑː/) (arvo)

     ii.   or for ough (/ɔː/) (thort)

     iii.   or for our (/ɔː/ /ə/) (yor)

 i)   consonants

     i.   x for \<ks\> (/ks/) (thx)

     ii.   z for \<s\> (/z/) (coz, cuz, plz)

     iii.   doubled letter (m) (summat, which shortens the previous vowel sound)

 j)   eye dialect or clipping (tho, although)

3. colloquial contractions

  a)   first letter omitted

     i.   h (ad, ell, ere, avin)

     ii.   th (em)

     iii.   a (n)

  b)   first syllable omitted (though, cos, till, bout, k, morrow, mora)

  c)   mid-syllables omitted (satdy)

  d)   mid-letters omitted (probaly)

  e)   weak sounds represented

     i.   schwa (/ə/)

        1.   a for \<e\> (/ə/) (da)

        2.   a for ou (/ə/) (ya)

        3.   a for ow (/ə/) (tomora)

        4.   a for to (amora)

        5.   d for th (/ð/) (d, dat, wid)

        6.   e for ou (/ə/) (ye)

        7.   er for our (/ɔː/ /ə/)

     ii.   /ɪ/

        1.   i for ee (/ɪ/) (fil, bin)

  f)   f for ph (sumfing)

FIGURE 12.3 *Cont'd*

g) t for th (/q/ /t/) (tank)

h) z for th (ð) (ze)

i) v for f (/f/) (arvo)

j) final letter omitted

   i. d (an, n)

   ii. e (th, d)

   iii. g (avin, goin, mornin, somethin)

   iv. t (jus, tha, tex)

k) final syllable omitted (prob, morn, mo, avo, arvo)

l) tis

m) something (summort, summat, summing)

FIGURE 12.3 *Cont'd*

In the following sections, I explore the three functional categories in greater depth. I look at their use in historical and other written texts, and consider how and why they are used; and then I begin to speculate on their use in CorTxt.

12.4 Colloquial contractions

In this section, before turning to CorTxt, I outline what colloquial contractions have been seen to 'mean' in other written texts. *Colloquial contractions* such as <ya> or <gonna> are reduced or contracted written forms which reflect informal pronunciation as well as suggesting various emotions (Weber, 1986, p. 420; Androutsopoulos, 2000, p. 521). These contractions can involve word shortenings (<you> to <ya>) or combine two words (<going to> to <gonna>). Although, as Crystal (2003, p. 275) points out, many now have established written forms, they differ from standard contractions (such as *I'm* or *can't*) in not being formally recognized in dictionaries or schools, not using apostrophes and involving at times just one word. Colloquial contractions are largely limited to written discourse representing direct speech: comic strips and jokes, dialogue in prose fiction, advertisements, and pop and rock songs such as 'I wanna hold your hand' (The Beatles) and 'Never gonna happen' (Lily Allen).

Colloquial contractions 'mean' by evoking aspects of identity and register through writing. Their function is **indexical**. Indexical reference describes the way in which features of language relate directly to personal or social characteristics of the language user. For example, if I say *'im* instead of *him*, it is likely that this says something to a particular community about my social background or level of education. In other words, reflecting a certain pronunciation is not the ultimate purpose of respelling; what is important is what this means for readers regarding the level of formality and/or speaker identity (Jaffe and Walton, 2000).

This is evidenced by the use of **eye dialect**, such as *wot* for *what* and *sez* for *says*. Eye dialect is the respelling of a word in a more straightforward yet unconventional way; in Sebba's (2007, p. 34) words, '[u]sing sound-symbol correspondences which are conventional for the language, but are the wrong ones for the particular word': eg, <thort> for <thought>'. Unlike colloquial contractions, eye dialect does not alter the pronunciation of a word. For example, <thort> and <thought> are both pronounced the same, unlike <you> and the colloquial contraction <ya>. So, eye dialect forms like <thort> or <wot> represent a standard pronunciation in a non-standard way – rather than representing an informal or non-standard way of speaking. However, through their unconventional form, they can tap directly into a particular social identity. They often indicate an act of transgression or difference (discussed in the next section), or they suggest a lack of education, in that the phonetic spellings can be interpreted as mistakes made by people who write what they hear. *Down with skool*, for example, can be interpreted as signalling a schoolboy's rebellion against the school, as well as the school's failure to teach him to spell.

Eye dialect and colloquial contractions are thereby often used to characterize or ridicule people of low educational, economic or social status and/or those with strong regional accents. For example, the coarse language used by the porter in Macbeth is accompanied by respellings suggesting colloquial contractions which contrast with that of the **unmarked** voices of other characters – unmarked in the sense that they embody common, expected, default features. In contrast, the features in the example below are **marked** – unusual, unexpected, informative.

> Knock, knock, knock! Who's there, i'th'name of Belzebub? Here's a farmer that hang'd himseld on th'expectation of plenty: come in time; have napkins enowa about you; here you'll sweat for't.
>
> (The porter, Act II, Scene III)

Colloquial contractions can also be used in self-representation (rather than the portrayal of others), and in these cases are used overwhelmingly in positively affirming community values and identities (Jaffe, 2000, p. 508). We can see this in Irvin Welsh's (1993) *Trainspotting*, in which spellings reflect the characters' Scottish pronunciation, as well as in Roddy Doyle's Dublin-based novels. The extract below illustrates Doyle's portrayal through respelling of the speech of an Irish working class family in *The Snapper* (first published 1990).

> Jimmy Jnr walked back in.
> —What's *tha'*? A rat?
> —It is not a rat, Jimmy Rabbitte, said Tracy. —It's a dog.
> —It's a dog, *righ'*, said Linda.
> It was warm and quivering. Jimmy Snr could feel its bones.
> —*Wha'* sort of a dog is it but? he asked.
> —Black, said Tracy.
> —Go *'way*! said Jimmy Jnr.
> —I'm your new da, Jimmy Sr told it. They all laughed.
> —*An*, look it. There's your mammy *makin'* the tea.
>
> Doyle (1998, p. 165)

Caribbean poets often use respelling reflecting pronunciation of their creoles.

> wi feel bad
> wi look sad
> wi smoke weed
> an if yu eye sharp,
> read de vialence inna wi eye;
> wi goin smash de sky wid wi bad bad blood
>> *Dread Beat an Blood* (Johnson, 1975, cited in Crystal, 2003, p. 348)

Androutsopoulos (2000, p. 528), to take a final example, describes colloquial spelling variation in German underground music magazines as establishing informal, intimate arenas between writers and readers. The difference between these fanzines and the derogatory descriptions of 'others' is that, with the former, the respellings do not contrast with conventional surrounding text (often the language of educated or higher-standing persons) but occur throughout the fanzines in an unmarked manner. Fanzines and Caribbean poetry show that, while colloquial and regional respellings used to represent others are contrasted unfavourably with the conventional language of educated persons, colloquial respellings can also affirm group boundaries, evoking shared identity and intimate, personal and informal relationships. This performance of intimacy and informality also occurs in texting.

As we saw above, colloquial contractions are widely used throughout CorTxt. They include the omission of final letter <g> from progressive verbs such as in *goin*; and of <d> after <n> in <an> and <n>. The drop-ping of <h> can be seen in <ad> and <avin> and other shortenings seen in *ok* (<k>), *because* (<cause>, <cos>, <coz>) and *about* (<bout>). The letter <a> is used to represent **schwa**, in <ya>, <da>, <tomora> and <amora>, as well as <gonna>, <gunna>, <gona>. Schwa is a vowel sound that occurs only on unstressed syllables in a word and unstressed words in a sentence: *tomorrow, about, computer, I'm going to pick up the kids*. As you can see, it can be represented by various letters and letter combinations (<o>, <a>, <er>), but in respelling it tends to be represented by <a>. (Although in the Middle and Early Modern English periods, schwa was often represented by <e>.) Like other colloquial contractions, the respelling of schwa serves to create an informal and speech-like feel, which is exploited to good commercial effect in the 1950s advertising slogan: *Drinka Pinta Milka Day* (Carney, 1994, p. 447). Other examples of colloquial contractions in CorTxt are the deletion of <t> in <jus>, <tha> and <tex>, for example, which we saw in the novel dialogue above, 'What's tha'? A rat?' (Doyle, 1998). In general, although Txt may seem to comprise 'new' spellings, they in fact repeat or extend existing functional patterns.

The implications are that colloquial contractions used in texting not only reflect those seen in other texts, but that texters also fulfil functions which are historically and widely fulfilled by these contractions: namely, they are striving to set the tone of the message, indicate emotions or construct identities through their texting practices, and they adopt and exploit well-established linguistic devices for doing so. As in other texts, therefore, the effect created is of intimacy, informality and, at times, a certain nonchalance.

Text messages which include colloquial contractions, and other attempts to capture spoken forms, include the following. Other kinds of respellings such as letter homophones <r> and <u> also occur – these are explored below.

12.8   Hello beautiful r u ok? I've *kinda ad* a row *wiv* NAME99 and he walked out the pub?? I wanted a night *wiv* u Miss u xx

12.9   Thought *praps* you meant another one. *Goodo*! I'll look tomorrow xx

12.10   NAME79 says that he's quitting at least5times a day so i wudn't take much notice of that. *Nah*, she didn't mind. Are you *gonna* see him again? Do you want to come to taunton tonight? U can tell me all about NAME79!

12.5 Phonetic respellings

Phonetic respelling involves substituting letters in irregular conventional spellings for those which more regularly correspond to the particular sound.

They are thus found with common words more likely to be irregularly spelt. As mentioned above, one use of phonetic respelling is eye dialect: where the respelling serves (often derogatorily) to indicate an individual's social identity and speech.

In other contexts, phonetic respelling creates modern, dynamic, eye-catching effects, through the visual effect of its deviance from expected spellings. Many brand names involve what Androutsopoulos (2000) calls 'grapheme substitutions': the substitution of one letter for another such as in *Beanz Meanz Heinz*. Back in the early 1900s, Pound (1925) identified a 'Kraze for K', which has not disappeared: *KitKat, Kwik Save, Kleenex*. Many phonetic respellings are shorter than corresponding conventional variants, due to a tendency to reduce vowel pairs and consonant clusters: studies of trademark respellings by Jacobson (1996) and Praninskas (1968) include *Protex* (where <x> replaces <ks>), *Tru-Blu, Fre-Flo, Mildu* and double-consonant reduction – *Hot-Stuf, Chil-Gard, Fly-Kil*. Use of letter and number homophones is noted by Carney (1994, p.448), who cites *Spud-U-Like, U2, INXS* and *IOU*. Another well-established example in advertising is the reduction of *ight* to *ite* (Moon, 2008) as in *Miller Lite*.

What impact are advertisers after? (Think back to your earlier musings on *Beanz Meanz Heinz*.) The aim of phonetic respelling in advertising is ultimately to attract consumers. It achieves this through respelling because distinct, unexpected spellings contrast with the surrounding text, disrupt readers' scanning and so catch their eye (Jaffe, 2000, p. 510). In other words, the impact of these respellings lies in their divergence from expected norms.

Another example of the impact of phonetic respelling is the fanzines explored by Androutsopoulos (2000). Use of <x> to represent <ks>, <cks> and <gs> in English and German words produces <punx>, <thanx>, <sonx> (*songs*), <lyrix> and <demnaxt> (*demnachst* = *soon*) positions the fanzines in the subculture and marks them as radical, tough and original (Androutsopoulos, 2000, pp. 527–8). However, their phonetic respelling not only affirms group identity but also creates deviance by marking the subculture as distinct or opposed to mainstream ideology: the two functions of convergence and opposition operate simultaneously. Similar observations have been made of the texting practices of teenage groups, in that parents and other adults are often unable to penetrate what they describe as a secret code known only to members of the texting circle (e.g. Ling and Yttri, 2002). Despite not being teenagers, the texters in this study can be seen as similarly adopting respellings to affirm close relationships and cement shared practices in a way that inevitably excludes those who do not share the code.

As with colloquialisms, phonetic respelling in CorTxt reflects existing patterns of variation. Texters use number and letter homophones, as in other domains, often combining the two: <b4>, <m8>, <cu> and <ur> (*you are*). Other grapheme substitutions include <ite> for <ight> (in <mite>, <2nite>, <rite> and <lite>); the more unusual <yt> in <myt> (*might*), which appears to extend the spelling of / aɪ/ with <y> in *my* and *dry*; and consonant substitutions <x> for <ks> in <thx> and <z> for <s> in <coz>, <cuz> and <plz>. As mentioned above, these consonant forms are the most salient spellings of particular phonemes, rather than the most frequent spellings. Vowels used in phonetic spelling include <o> for <a> in <wot>, <woz> and <coz>; <u> for <o> in <cum>, <cumin>, <luv>, <dun>; and <thort> for *thought*. Most are familiar from other domains: ite from advertising; <woz> and <wot> from graffiti; <gud> and <luv> from informal personal writing; <x> from Androutsopoulos's fanzines. Other forms in CorTxt which seem less familiar extend existing patterns or practices: representations of schwa in respellings like <betta>; <u> for <oo> or <oul> in <cud>, <wud>, and <shud>; <cumin> (*coming*) and <myt> (*might*).

There are respelt forms in CorTxt which are less well-documented elsewhere. These include <ne> (*any*) with 8 occurrences and <y> (*why*) with 7 occurrences. Below are some examples.

12.11 Ive only ever been 2 1 that 1 lol. Don't think there r *ne* others. U goin 2 cardiff 2morow?

12.12 Mam said dont make *ne* plans for nxt wknd coz she wants us to come down then ok (ps u still havnt got the hang of txtin ppl back have u!) x

12.13 Love u loads! *Y* didn't u take new phone and charger with u? Aah, we need 2 check they fit! My day is slow but ok, voda sorted, running out of time now ;-(c ya

12.14 Had some letters bout stuff i need to take and confirming my start dat, not really. Tried2ring woman2day2see if she cud recommend some reading, but think they're al on holiday at mo, which is y my start date was to far off.

Use of <ur> in respelling *your* is interesting in that it is not strictly phonetic – yet it occurs more often in place of *your* (286 occurrences) than it does of *you are* (177 occurrences). Below are randomly selected occurrences of <ur> as the possessive *your*.

12.15 Hi will be thinking about u tomorrow and hope u can sit down in *ur* dress!! Have a good day xxx

12.16 Hello. Gd joke, by the way! So wots *ur* plan4the rugby tomo, apart from winnin ... I will mostly be watchin bonobos shaggin ... One of them stole my watch 2day, ripped it right off my arm, damn animal. I get back at 3 on wed, u around for coffee? If im not too travel smelly …! hav gd weekend X

12.17   I admire *ur* commitment. Save me some x

In personal correspondence with one contributor to my corpus, she suggested that she 'probably substituted the *u* for *you* and then added the *r* to make it *your*' – a complex practice which starts with a phonetic respelling.

Text messages in CorTxt using phonetic respelling (and other respellings) include the following.

12.18   *Thnx* dude. *u* guys out *2nite*?

12.19   Ok that would *b* lovely, if *u r* sure. Think about *wot u* want to do, drinkin, dancin, eatin, cinema, in, out, about … Up to *u*! *Wot* about NAME408? X

12.20   Hey! Congrats *2u2*. id *luv 2* but ive had *2* go home!xxx

12.6 Abbreviations

It is perhaps abbreviation with which texting is most often associated. It may surprise you to consider the long history of abbreviation, and the variety of formal and informal contexts in which it occurs. Handwritten medieval manuscripts from across Europe were heavily abbreviated (Bradley, 1919, p. 4) for two main reasons: because at that time spelling had not been standardized and to fit words on the page. Elizabethan scribes were paid by the inch and thus invented lengthier versions of words (*pauvre* for *povre*, for example) (Scragg, 1974, p. 52 in Baron, 2000, p. 98). These practices continued with the development of technology. Although early printing, for instance, played a leading role in standardizing spelling and punctuation, Elizabethan printers also varied spellings due to space constraints and cost. The need to justify the right-hand margin of printed pages and to ensure text fit the page, for example, prompted the use of an elaborate system of abbreviation and variable spelling: *busy* could be spelt <busie>; *here* as <heere> (Baron, 2000); *on* as <onn>, <hon> and <ho> and *say* as <sai>, <say>, <saie> and <sei> (Bennett and Smithers, 1968 in Baron, 2000, p. 104). Other strategies employed by printers included increasing or decreasing gaps between words, and substituting words for phrases, or vice versa.

The pragmatic flexibility of these practices is not dissimilar to those used in texting. A more recent example than pre-standardization printing is the nineteenth-century telegram, the cost of which was calculated according to the number of words it contained, encouraging highly abbreviated styles

(Crystal, 2003: 425). However, abbreviated forms occur in greater number across a wider range of current texts than might be thought. In 2001, the *Acronyms, Initialisms & Abbreviations Dictionary* listed over 586,000 entries (Crystal, 2003, p.121), and the extent to which abbreviations such as laser, DVD-ROM, scuba and NATO have entered our lexicon is often illustrated by ignorance as to what the full terms of some are.

Abbreviation fulfils functions other than that of shortening. Other reasons include the value often placed on linguistic economy or attempts to achieve concise styles, the desire to convey social identity or be part of the social group to which the abbreviation belongs. EFL, ESOL, IATEFL, CELTA and TOEFL, for example, belong to the British English language teaching community, while abbreviations abound in science, technology and specialist fields such as cricket, computing and the armed forces. As argued in this book, abbreviation in texting is not chiefly motivated by any need to be brief but instead contributes to texting identity through performances of brevity and informality and through acts of divergence or separation from mainstream norms.

Abbreviations tend to follow certain formal patterns and can be categorized into the following types (see Figure 12.4).

- **Initialisms**—Phrases which are shortened to the first letter of each word (or syllable): BBC, BA, EEC, TV, PhD.

- **Acronyms**—Initialisms which are pronounced as single words, such as NATO, laser and UNESCO.

- **Clipping**—Words formed through either the beginning, end or middle of a longer word being clipped: *demo, exam, bus, plane, fridge, flu, maths, specs.*

- **Blends**—Words made by blending other words together, such as *brunch, heliport, smog, Eurovision.*

FIGURE 12.4 *Types of abbreviation*

While colloquial contractions mirror contracted spoken forms, abbreviations are largely driven by attempts to alter the written form. In cases where written abbreviations correspond to spoken phrases, the spoken shortenings arise from the written abbreviation rather than the other way around. Interestingly, in saying web addresses, people tend to use the written abbreviation *www,* which in spoken form is longer than *World Wide Web.* Abbreviating tends to reduce the written form, not the spoken. (Although the spoken form is relevant in distinguishing between initialisms and acronyms.)

Examples of familiar patterns of abbreviation in CorTxt include consonant writing, with the omission of <a>(<tht>, <bck>, <lst>), <e> (<txt>, <nxt>, <snd>), <ea> (<pls>, <spk>), <o> (<2mrw>, <nt>, <hpe>) and <ou> (<cld>, <wld>, <shld>). Other abbreviated forms in the text messages depart in marked ways from respellings elsewhere. However, as with other functional categories we have looked at, in most cases unusual forms emerge from extending or combining existing patterns. For example, double-letter reduction, producing <stil> (*still*), <gona> (*gonna*) and <beta> (*betta = better*), although appearing unusual, has been seen to occur not only as a medieval printers' trick but in advertising slogans such as *Hot-Stuf* (Carney, 1994:447), and the omission of other final letters such as <e> in *hav* and *sum* can be explained as part of phonetic spellings: *sum* represents the phoneme /ʌ/ better than *sume* where, by English orthographic conventions, the <e> lengthens the vowel.

To take another example, although the following forms are unconventional in that they are not widely used elsewhere: <kno> (*know*), <bac> (*back*), <thou> (*though*), <mess> (*message*), <thu> (*Thursday*), <tomo> and <tom> (*tomorrow*), they can be described as extensions of the practice of clipping. It may be the case that clippings are favoured by the predictive text devices particular to mobile phones, whereby the phone predicts the most likely letter sequence as you type. Pressing the 8 key (tuv) and then the 6 key (mno) produces *to*, the third press suggests *too* as the most likely sequence, but by the fourth, *tomo*. Another example may be the final letter reductions in <i'l>, <stil>, <wel>, <com>, <hav> and <jus>, where the phone has apparently recognized the word before the last letter has been typed and thus affords a convenient abbreviation.

Other unfamiliar forms include <sos> for *sorry* and <tomoz> for *tomorrow*. <Sos> is a variant of <soz>, with both <soz> and <tomoz> recent, largely online abbreviations of, respectively, *sorry* and *tomorrow*. Omission of certain mid-letters is similarly unusual: <h> from *nigt, wat, wich, wen, tnx*; <c> from *bak*; <leas> from *pse*; and <n> from *thx* and *thks*. In these examples users seem to rely on the *shape* of the word, rather than the sound, to convey meaning. The use of <x>'s to represent kisses, a common feature of personal correspondence (Kesseler and Bergs, 2003), is similarly a visual device. This is important, because it reminds us that texting is not simply about sounding speech-like, but that texters are also aware of and play with the visual appearance of words.

Text messages with abbreviated forms include the following. Again, abbreviations tend to combine with other kinds of respellings.

12.21 V skint too but fancied few bevies.waz *gona* go meet
NAME211&*othrs* in spoon but *jst* bin *watchng* planet earth&sofa is
v comfey; If i *dont* make it *hav gd* night

12.22 Ok. Can be later showing around 8–8:30 if you want + *cld* have drink before. *Wld* prefer not to spend money on nosh if you don't mind, as doing that *nxt wk*.

12.23 That's a shame! Maybe *cld* meet for few *hrs tomo*?

12.7 One implication: choice in texting

As mentioned towards the start of this chapter, it is evident that many words can be respelt in varied ways. *You*, for example, can be spelt conventionally as <you> (4560 times in CorTxt); or with the letter homophone <u> (3043 times), or <ya> (256), <ye> (9) and <yer> (14), used to reflect regional or informal spoken forms. Other examples include those listed in Figure 12.5. What, if anything, strikes you about the choices that texters seem to make?

av (8), hve (6), ave (5), hav (106)
gud (40), gd (25), goodo (3)
jus (18), jst (6),
tomoz (9), tomorro (6), tomorow (4), tomora (3), tomo (361), morrow (6), mora (1), tom (24), 2mora (14), tomoro (10), 2morrow (9), tmw (9), 2morow (4), 2morro (4), 2mrrw (4), 2moz (3), 2mrw (2), amoro (2), 2moro (42)
wot (148), wat (37)
2nite (45), tonite (10), 2night (12), 2nigt (3),
thanx (32), thx (5), tank (2), sanks (2), thnx (2), thks (1), thanxs (1), tnx (2),
cud (48), cld (19),
luv (46), lv (4), lov (4)
wud (38), wld (22)
cos (226), coz (24), cause (4), cuz (3), cs (2), cus (2), cz (?)
pleasey (4), plez (3), pls (35), plse (3), plz (4), pse (2) gunna (11), gona (6)
sth (9), somethin (8), summort (3), sumfing (2), summat (2),
summing (2) msg (7), mess (8)

d (21), da (6), th (8), te (2), ze (2)
n (182), an (19)
havin (24), avin (6)
mornin (23), morn (18)
l8r (20), lata (5), l8er (2)
mite (9), myt (6)

FIGURE 12.5 *'Competing' respellings*

Some competing respellings illustrate how one function (say, abbreviation) can be achieved in different ways. The various ways in which words can be colloquially contracted is illustrated in <ya>, <ye> or <yer>; and in <havin> (where the <g> is dropped) or <avin> (where the <h> is also dropped), as well as in *and*, contractions of which are captured by <an> or <n>. Respellings of *something* show several regional pronunciations: <summort>, <sumfing>, <summat> and <summing>. Contrasting forms of eye dialect of *later* are <l8r> and <lata>; and of *might*, <mite> and <myt>. Others seem to indicate choices open to texters in reducing the number of characters used, depending perhaps on how much they wish to abbreviate: <thurs> or <thu>, for example, and <pls>, <plse> or <pse>. The choice between clipping or consonant writing in some examples may depend on texters' use of predictive texting. *back*, for example, is abbreviated either as <bac> or <bk>; *give* as <giv> or <gv>; *have*, as <hav> but also as <hve> and as <av> (8); *tomorrow* as <tomo> or <tmw>.

Other examples suggest choices between two functions of respelling, that is, forms of abbreviation or attempts to reflect speech: the aforementioned variants of *you* (<ya> and <u>) are echoed in the spoken chatty form of *please* as <pleasey> versus the brief abbreviated <plz>. Elsewhere, eye dialect forms contrast with consonant writing in, for example, *would*, which occurs both as eye dialect, <wud>, and as consonant writing, <wld>. Similarly *could* is spelt either <cud> or <cld>; and similar examples include *good* (<gud> or <gd>); and *love* (<luv> or <lv>).

The choice of <wot> or <wat> as variants of *what* is interesting as an example of conventional versus apparently new spelling forms. <wot> is a phonetic respelling used in graffiti, as in 'Wot, no butter?' (Crystal, 2003, p. 275). 'Wot no … ?' was a popular post-war graffiti in Britain, accompanied by the picture of a figure peering over a wall which commented on the lack of various items in the aftermath of the World War II. According to Crystal, it occurred in similar forms in other countries.

Whether the less conventional form, <wat>, is a competing form of phonetic respelling or simply an attempt to cut down on characters is difficult to determine. The form is reflected also in <wen>, for *when*. A similar process may be in evidence with *come*, which occurs both as the conventional eye dialect form *cum* but also as the less conventional clipping *com*.

12.8 What do 'textisms' mean?

In this chapter, I have given some indication of the meaning-making potential of respellings in texting. Two initial observations were made: that most spelling variation in CorTxt follows or extends English orthographic principles; and that it thus reflects historical and current spelling practices. By choosing to spell in principled ways which deviate from expected conventions, texters use respellings in meaningful ways. The fact that texters make choices, vividly illustrated through 'competing' respellings such as <u>, <ye> or <ya> for *you* implies texters actively and creatively choose how to present themselves, albeit constrained by situational factors and orthographic principles.

It is naturally not possible from the text messages alone to determine what texters intend to mean through respellings, nor how the respelt forms are interpreted by interlocutors, but research into other writing domains (such as fanzines or graffiti) allows us to speculate on what spelling in texting may mean. As in other attempts to reflect spoken or regional pronunciations, colloquial contractions and respellings are likely to fulfil an indexical function and to create and sustain an arena for participant relationships which, as in spoken interaction, are informal and intimate. A sense of informality is thus constructed by texters drawing on their awareness of features of everyday, face-to-face conversation. However, texters also draw on existing patterns of abbreviation which contrast with the speech-like language described above and so add what could be described as illusions of brevity to otherwise lengthy, expressive messages. The purely visual device of phonetic spelling also disrupts the relaxed intimacy with unconventional and eye-catching forms which evoke the originality and radicality of advertising, graffiti and underground subcultures. Through signalling deviance or divergence from expected, mainstream norms, these respellings affirm both group identity and distinguish the group from other social groups. Putting all this together, we can see that texters can express attitudes and emotions, define relationships and construct texting identities simply through the choices they make when spelling.

12.9 Some notes on methods

To conduct this investigation of respelling, I generated a word frequency list, and used it as the basis for the grouping of respellings around headwords, using the corpus analysis tool *WordSmith Wordlist*. *Wordlist* must be purchased as part of the *Wordsmith* set of tools; AntConc is free, accessible online and can similarly be used to generate a word list. Of course, an analysis of respelling in text messaging does not have to be as wide or as thorough as mine: it can work just as well on a small number of text messages which you can process manually.

The categorization of respellings into groups requires several decisions to be made. One problem is ambiguous respellings with more than one referent, such as <2> (which can refer to *to, too* or the numerical value) and <prob> (*problem* or *probably*). These cannot be handled simply by looking at a frequency list but must be checked through sorting concordance lines, and adjusted manually. Other ambiguous respellings constituted the standard form of another word (<ill>, for example, as a respelling of *I'll* and a word meaning to be sick; <no> as a shared respelling of *know* and *number*, and as a negative marker). Elsewhere, respellings proved difficult to identify and label. For example, it was difficult to know whether *wk* in the following referred to *work* or *week*.

5.11   Hi, wkend ok but journey terrible. *Wk* not good as have huge back log of marking to do

12.10 Further reading

Urban Dictionary (www.urbandictionary.com) is a great resource for looking up the meaning and origin of slang and newly coined words. The dictionary is compiled by its users, who contribute definitions and examples – an understanding of word's complex usage and meaning builds up through these sometimes contradictory entries.

13

The language of tweets

Michele Zappavigna

Alongside comment on the discourses of social media in general, my more particular focus throughout this book will be on the language used in microblogging. Microblogging is a form of length-delimited (hence 'micro') communication using a social networking service. These services allow short posts to be published online and users to subscribe to feeds of other users' updates. The services are syndicated and may be accessed via an official website or third-party applications, often running on mobile devices such as smartphones. The first part of this chapter gives an overview of microblogging as a semiotic activity. The second section begins an analysis of the main linguistic patterns in the HERMES corpus.

Because of the character limitations imposed on microposts, they are interesting data to observe how meaning can be made in constrained environments. The brevity encouraged by the medium affords frequent and continuous updating, and consequently, jokes abound about the egocentricity of telling the world the minutiae of personal experiences that constitute your everyday life. Generally, however, microblogging has been positively portrayed in the press (Arceneaux and Schmitz Weiss 2010) and is a social phenomenon experiencing rapid increase.

Unlike other social networking services, microblogging services generally allow asymmetrical relationships between accounts. While Facebook requires that both parties explicitly consent to becoming 'friends' via an explicit link, microblogging services generally allow the user to subscribe to another user's feed of microposts without any binding expectation of reciprocation. In the case of Twitter this subscription practice is referred to as 'following', and a user who has subscribed to your tweets is termed a follower. I may choose to follow an individual who posts content that I find interesting without a social bond being inferred. By way of contrast, declining a Facebook friend request is viewed as an act of social rejection and in 'choosing who to include as Friends, participants more frequently consider the implications of excluding or explicitly rejecting a person as opposed to the benefits of including them'. (Boyd 2010, p. 44).

A micropost may have a wide range of social functions realized by different microgenres, though it is not yet clear whether the linguistic patterning seen is best described through the lens of genre. In SFL, genres have generally been explored using more extended texts (Martin and Rose 2008). It is yet to be understood whether or how the intersection of different textual timelines that constitute a user's stream of posts can be modelled in terms of genre theory. However, Myers (2010) uses genre to explore blogging which may be argued to be an antecedent to microblogging. As I will note later, some kind of visualization support is likely required to perceive the patterning and better ways of approaching texts as processes rather than static products (Zhao 2010). As Russell (2011, p. 10) suggests, 'Because the social web is first and foremost about the linkages between people in the real world, one highly convenient format for storing social web data is the graph'.

Users may confess their personal thoughts and feelings with emotional language, complain about their everyday existence, contribute to a micro-meme, engage in humour or express political opinion. In all these cases the act of microblogging has enough semiotic pull that the user has stopped whatever he or she may have been doing to post a thought. This will have been undertaken with varying degrees of deliberation, depending on the context. In some cases, 'Similar to fashion, there is a self-consciousness and self-reflection when deciding what to share' (Subramanian and March, 2011), and in others the post may be hurried, embedded in ongoing activity while out and about with a mobile device.

The phatic dimension of microblogging

Some studies claim that microblogging has a phatic function. Malinowski introduced the notion of 'phatic communion' as a way of describing communication in the service of establishing or solidifying bonds of companionship rather than serving 'any purpose of communicating ideas' (2004, p. 250). This notion may be extrapolated to relationships formed via social media as part of an overall 'phatic media culture', where 'content is not king, but "keeping in touch" is' (Miller 2008, p. 395):

> More important than anything said, it is the connection to the other that becomes significant, and the exchange of words becomes superfluous.

Thus the text message, the short call, the brief email, the short blog update or comment, becomes part of a mediated phatic sociability necessary to maintain a connected presence in an ever expanding social network. (Miller 2008, p. 395)

If conceived in this way, microblogging functions as what Makice (2009) describes, using a computer metaphor, 'linguistic ping'.[1] Just as a computer on a network can be pinged, we may think of microbloggers declaring to their ambient audience, 'I'm still here!'. This kind of phatic function is complementary to the more ideational description of Web 2.0 as driven by user-generated content. The extent of this function across microblogging platforms is likely to vary since, for example, status updating on Facebook within a semi-private network of peers encourages different forms of expression to the more public networking seen with Twitter (Page 2011).

It is unlikely that this phatic dimension with all its interpersonal potential was anticipated in the original design of Twitter (with its origins in a concept for status updating via SMS). The first paragraph of the service's self-description on Twitter's About page, privileges the ideational function of communication, referring to itself as an information network:

Twitter is a real-time information network that connects you to the latest information about what you find interesting. Simply find the public streams you find most compelling and follow the conversations. (Twitter 2010)

The social importance of information sharing influences the content of tweets, and, as we will see in this chapter, the marker identifying a hyperlink is the fifth most common lexical item in HERMES, showing the extent to which users share web links with each other. Nevertheless, there is much accompanying evidence that interpersonal meanings are also critical, and in any case, the ways in which information is shared is always subject to tenor variables, such as power relations.

The distinction between an ideational focus on information and an interpersonal emphasis on social connection should not be conceived in binary terms since language makes multiple kinds of meaning simultaneously. As mentioned earlier, Halliday and Matthiessen (2004) refer to this concurrent meaning potential, as metafunctions: an ideational function of enacting experience, an interpersonal function of negotiating relationships and a textual function of organizing information. Thus, a tweet may have both an information-sharing and a bonding function, as the following example illustrates:

http://www.loftcube.net/ Why do we all live in these big homes ... how cool is this!!

Here a hyperlink to an architectural website is offered to the putative audience alongside evaluation of its content, drawing upon both ideational and interpersonal resources for making these meanings.

As with social media research in general, work on microblogging is generally interdisciplinary or cross-disciplinary, spanning areas as diverse as library science (Murphy 2008; DeVoe 2009; Cuddy 2009; Aharony 2010; Hricko 2010; Kushin and Yamamoto 2010), language learning (Borau et al. 2009) and spam detection (Moh and Murmann 2010) to name but a few. There has been a tendency in the research to taxonomize the functions of microposts based on user intention. Java and colleagues (2007) suggest that 'daily chatter', 'conversations', 'sharing information/ URLs' and 'reporting news' are the most common reasons people use Twitter. They identify three main kinds of users in terms of this classification: 'information sources', 'friends', and 'information seekers'. Naaman and colleagues (2010) extend this work, arguing, via content analysis, that users can be categorized into 'meformers', largely concerned with self, and 'informers', interested in sharing information. Many similar content-oriented studies of microblogging categorize posts or types of users by topic, for example, by most frequent topic (Ramage et al. 2010). Complementary to this content-based perspective is a more functional orientation considering how microposts make meaning and requiring detailed linguistics analyses.

Microblogging as conversation

Descriptions of microblogging usually imply that it is a form of conversation involving some kind of 'conversational exchange' (Honeycutt and Herring 2009). It is variously described as 'lightweight chat' (Kate et al. 2010, p. 242), as 'prompting opportunistic conversations' (Zhao and Rosson 2009, p. 251), as 'a specific social dialect, in which individual users are clearly singled out and engaged in a conversation' (Grosseck and Holotescu 2009) and as constituted by 'dialogue acts' (Ritter et al. 2010, p. 172). Yardi and Boyd (2010) suggest that the conversational exposure afforded by Twitter may have an edifying impact on the general population of users:

> Twitter affords different kinds of social participation. In the same way a reader has to skim the front page of a physical newspaper to get to the comic section, most Twitter users will be exposed to varied slices of news. Thus, many people may be witnessing diverse conversations and also participating in topics they otherwise may not have. (p. 325)

Indeed, Twitter's About page invites users to 'follow the conversations' to locate information of interest to them (Twitter 2010). Businesses are advised to 'be where the conversations are' (Bradley 2010). This commercialization of conversation sees microblogging interaction used to develop personal branding (Marwick 2010), to publicize professional blogs, to generate word-of-mouth interest in a product and to generally create buzz around something for profit.

Most studies do not offer a theoretical basis for the description of microblogging as a form of conversation, though they often invoke a sociological definition. This disciplinary orientation is different to that which would be adopted by a linguist:

> Sociologists ask 'How do we do conversation?', and recognize that conversation tells us something about social life. Linguists, on the other hand, ask 'How is language structured to *enable* us to do conversation?', and recognize that conversation tells us something about the nature of language as a *resource* for doing social life. (Eggins and Slade 1997, p. 7)

The kinds of structural configurations possible with microblogging are mediated by the nature of the channel, and this is also true of face-to-face conversation. However, as I am working with a randomized corpus of tweets, it is not possible to retrieve extended sequences of exchanges between users; so I will make little comment on conversational structure, aside from the few general observations made here.

Most definitions of conversation presuppose some version of 'turn taking'. This is a concept for theorizing how exchanges are managed in interactions, usually attributed to Sacks et al. (1974). Sacks argued, 'For socially organized activities, the presence of "turns" suggests an economy, with turns for something being valued – and with means for allocating them, which affect their relative distribution, as in economies' (Sacks et al. 1974, p. 696). The field of conversation analysis takes the notion of an adjacency pair as the fundamental unit of conversation. Other perspectives, such as that of Martin (2000b) and Eggins and Slade (1997), employ a more elaborated framework that considers how exchanges work within the genres in which people are called to operate. This perspective also demonstrates the value of accounting for the role that the prosodic patterning, particularly of evaluative language, plays in negotiating meaning (Martin 2000b).

There are a number of significant problems in directly applying the idea of turn-taking to microblogging. I have already mentioned that microblogging services generally allow asymmetrical relationships, where reciprocation of a follower is not obligatory, nor is non-reciprocation interpreted as rejection. Similarly, there is little social expectation that users reply to a given micropost, and even where a direct address is made to a particular user, the obligation to reply is relatively weak. Oulasvirta and colleagues (2010, p. 244) refer to this as a kind of 'dilution of conversational obligations'. In addition, a different kind of attention seems to be at work, with microblogging involving a kind of 'information snacking', where users are not obligated to complete a conversational exchange. In this way, given the asynchronous nature of Twitter CMC, 'Twitter usage is akin to a radio-like information source, turned on or dialled into as needed to pragmatically address "in the moment" curiosity or information needs' (Brooks and Churchill, 2010 p. 4).

Another issue is that since posts are persistent, available for viewing and reply long after they were originally produced, users will drop in and out of an exchange, and exchanges will overlap. Fast-paced multicast (many-to-many broadcast) problematize the concept of an adjacency pair so fundamental to traditional conversation analysis. This property of CMC has long been recognized in studies of email and Listservs (Harrison 1998). Boyd (2010, p. 47) notes with concern the potential for conversation to be 'consumed outside of its original context' given the persistence afforded by social networking technologies.

The back channel as shadowing conversation

Microblogging can be used as a form of 'back-channel communication' (McNely 2009; Yardi 2006). The back channel is supplementary media running in parallel to some main form of communication. As such, it forms a kind of 'intangible, clandestine community' (Sarita 2006, p. 852) and allows novel forms of ancillary participation in events. Back channelling may act as a kind of 'conversational shadow' to live media events, such as the 2008 US presidential election (Shamma et al. 2010). Other contexts in which back channelling may occur include collaborative learning environments (Yardi 2006), education (Ebner et al. 2010), conferences (McCarthy and Boyd 2005; Reinhardt et al. 2009; Grosseck and Holotescu 2010), question-and-answer sessions (Harry et al. 2009) and other kinds of large events, such as fashion trade shows (Bisker et al. 2008). In addition, the back channel has been incorporated into mainstream television, with feeds of tweets sometimes appearing in news broadcasts or during programmes involving audience commentary, such as chat shows. Anstead and O'Loughlin (2010) term the emergence of viewers who engage with new media as they respond to broadcasts 'the rise of the Viewertariat – a section of the audience that, aided by emerging technologies such as Twitter, comments on events on the screen, responds and gives meaning to the broadcast in real time'.

Atkinson (2010, pp. 58–9) suggests a number of functions for the back channel: reporting information by posting informational highlights, enhancing information by adding additional material and commenting on information by offering an opinion. In addition, he suggests that the back channel offers new ways in which conference participants may engage with each other: monitoring what others are saying (reading posts), amplifying what others are saying (retweeting a post), helping others (e.g. posting a message to assist with a technical problem) and arranging face-to-face meetings (pp. 60–1). Indeed, academic and technology conferences will often adopt a designated hashtag that conference participants may follow. For example, #ISWS2009 was used at the 8th International Semantic Web Conference (Letierce et al. 2010). Other examples are #Online09 at the Online Information 2009 Conference (Ebner et al. 2010).

Some conferences will also implement a live feed running in the background of a conference presentation (Ebner 2009). While a feed may support a presentation with additional useful material, it can lead to distraction from the main content, as occurred with Dana Boyd's presentation at Web 2.0 Expo 2009. In this case the back channel disrupted the speaker because the live feed was not visible to her, and she was unable to contextualize audience response. As she later explained on her blog,

> I walked off stage and immediately went to Brady and asked what on earth was happening. And he gave me a brief rundown. The Twitter stream was initially upset that I was talking too fast. My first response to this was: OMG, seriously? That was it? Cuz that's not how I read the situation on stage. So rather than getting through to me that I should slow down, I was hearing the audience as saying that I sucked. And responding the exact opposite way the audience wanted me to. This pushed the audience to actually start critiquing me in the way that I was imagining it was. And as Brady went on, he said that it started to get really rude so they pulled it to figure out what to do. But this distracted the audience and explains one set of outbursts that I didn't understand from the stage. And then they put it back up and people immediately started swearing. More outbursts and laughter. The Twitter stream had become the center of attention, not the speaker. Not me. (Boyd 2009)

This incident is an example of how important interpersonal meaning is to microblogging and the consequences that arise when the technology is deployed as if it had only an ideational function. The back channel here took on more than a supplementary function of elaborating information given in the presentation and interfered with the interpersonal dynamics of the academic conference presentation genre itself.

Microblogging and heteroglossia

While first-generation microblogging services have not been designed to directly support conversation, perhaps with the exception of Jaiku's message-threading capabilities, there is a social need among users to engage with the other voices that they encounter despite the speed at which microblogging streams unfold in time. Indeed, as we have seen in the previous section, the phenomenon of back channelling is in general a collaborative endeavour. Hence, in the case of Twitter, we see creative use of punctuation to address other users and to tag common topics. Consider, for example, the following tweet:

RT @user: **#**wordsthatcanstartawar mariah carey thinks she's still 20

This text references other voices through various types of grammatical resources, such as projection via a mental process (Mariah carey thinks). These resources, form part of the ENGAGEMENT, a discourse semantic system for adopting a stance in relation to other potential positions (Martin and White 2005). Alongside making use of these resources, the text deploys two typographic conventions, shown in bold, that leverage the affordances of electronic text and that have emerged through grass-roots use. These conventions centre around three linguistic markers:

- addressing and referencing other users with @;
- republishing other tweets with RT;
- labelling topics with #.

Address and @mentions

The first convention marks address with the @ character when a user wishes to explicitly direct a micropost at another user. In these instances @ will be deployed as a deictic marker, as in the following example:

@User Thanks for the #FF

Used in this way, the @ character indicates that the user name[2] which it precedes is directly addressed in the tweet. As such, it functions to mark a vocative, often occupying initial position in a clause, though it also can occur in medial or final position. When not in initial position, @+user name is more likely to indicate a reference to a user rather than to explicitly inscribe an address. For example:

Talking to **@User1** about how I've known her for over 11 years! I am getting old, but like Dorian Gray, she remains young.

This tweet is not directly addressing User1 and instead indirectly refers to this user with what is termed a 'mention'.

Mentioning a user with the @ character in this way is a kind of amplified reference and potential tool for self-promotion since, depending on privacy settings and the evolving functionality of Twitter,[3] other users who follow this user may view the mention. The @mention is also amplified in the sense that the @ character is searchable. Mentions can be aggregated, and other users can search for particular instances. It is possible to retrieve all instances of @ mentions to a given user (within a particular time window) with the Twitter search interface or using metadata and the Twitter API.

Considering @ more generally in electronic discourse, Honeycutt and Herring (2009, p. 4) provide an overview of the various uses of the character (examples added):

1   Addressivity – e.g. @user I really like you.

2   Reference – e.g. I really enjoyed @user's talk today.

3   Emoticons – e.g. @_@

4   Email – user@email.com

5   Locational 'at' – Eating pizza @ Mimmo's

6   Non-locational 'at' – I'm doing two things @ the same time.

7   Other – This is so @#%*ing stupid!

Taking into account current Twitter usage, the @ character seems to have undergone an evolution toward being an increasingly interpersonal resource. This follows a general trend in the evolution of punctuation identified by Knox (2009), namely, an evolution from textual functions toward a more interpersonal functions.

Retweeting

Another way of bringing external voices into a tweet is to republish another user's tweet within your own tweet. This is known as retweeting and is usually marked by the initialism RT to indicate that the body of the tweet is quoted text. In other words, RT marks grammatical projection, economically standing for 'User X has posted the following'. In most instances RT will be followed by the @ character to attribute the retweeted text to its original author. The following tweet uses this structure to indicate that @User2 is the source:

RT @User2: Perhaps having people grow gardens shows them that it's a little harder to grow food than they think. #agcast

Thus retweeting 'allows members to relay or forward a tweet through their network' (Nagarajan et al. 2010, p. 295), marking the quoted text as notable and effectively recommending it to their followers.

Retweeting can significantly amplify the reach of a tweet, particularly when a user with a large body of followers, such as a celebrity, chooses to retweet something. Beyond rebroadcasting, retweeting 'contributes to a conversational ecology in which conversations are composed of a public interplay of voices that give rise to an emotional sense of shared conversational context' (Boyd et al. 2010, p. 1). The convention marks a tweet as worth the attention within this conversational context. The emergent convention allows the retweeter to display a stance toward the retweeted text and project it as inherently valuable to the community. This kind of evaluative appendage has also been noted by Page (2011), who, approaching media from the perspective of narrative, has suggested the role of retweeting in new 'co-tellership practices' and noted the tendency of celebrities to append evaluative assessment to their retweets as a means of aligning with their audience.

Hashtagging

Lastly, hashtags are a convention for marking an annotation of the topic of a tweet. As the name implies, a hashtag involves a hash (otherwise known as a pound) symbol marking the label appended to the tweet, for example #linguistics. Where there is more than one word assigned, it will usually be represented without spaces (e.g. #Iheartlinguistcs). Hashtag are a form of conversational tagging (Huang et al. 2010). The hashtag is a form of metadata that emerged through community use on Twitter. Its use may derive from internet relay chat (IRC) conventions for naming channels (#channelname), where a channel is the essential mechanism that people use to communicate with each other during an IRC session. As used on Twitter, the # character is used to mark a label that the user has assigned to a tweet. For example, #python in the following indicates that the tweet is about the programming language Python:

Oh well at least the next Chapter should be fun 'Objects and Object Orientation' :) #python

The label means that that other users interested in Python can find the tweet even though this lexical item does not occur in the body of the tweet. They may do this by searching for the tag via the search interface that Twitter provides, or, if they are likely to have an ongoing interest in the tag, they may elect to subscribe to a feed of tweets containing this tag: a process known as following the tag.

The kind of collaborative tagging evolving with community use in social media is often referred to as a practice of folksonomy (Vander Wal 2007), or social tagging. This community-based metadata is very different to the top-down hierarchical approaches developed by subject classification in libraries. Whereas document classification involves experts, social tagging engages communities of general users. For example, it is used heavily on photo-sharing sites, such as Flickr, where it functions as a cooperative form of verbal indexing involving a bottom-up approach to the kind of classification previously achieved by reference librarians. Indeed hashtags have been likened to the concept 'better known to librarians as a subject heading' (Ovadia 2009, p. 203). The tags assigned provide 'access to the reader's view of aboutness in a way which was previously possible only on a small scale through elicitation experiments' (Kehoe and Gee 2011). A popular social-tagging site at the time of writing was Delicious, a service that encourages users to assign tags in the form of social 'bookmarks' describing the content of their favourite websites so that they can share these resources publically. Consensus and divergence in vocabulary choice for tags have been one of the main areas of research from an information science perspective. Some studies, for example, Schifanella and colleagues (2010, p. 279), look at consensus in terms of the patterning of the social network itself. This study looked at lexical and topical alignment in social networks and found that there was a local alignment in tag vocabularies among users even where the social-tagging system (e.g. Flickr) did not have a globally shared vocabulary.

Microblogging and communities of value

Microblogging, and social media in general, affords new insight into aspects of everyday life that have hitherto not been readily made public. Personal expression of routine experiences has never been subject to real-time mass dissemination in the way that we are currently witnessing. Microblogging services provide a forum where these routine experiences may be almost instantaneously broadcast, whether to share a positive moment or to satisfy the very human need to complain. Microposts frequently provide an opportunity for bonding around the quotidian, affording the private realm of daily experience a public audience.

The increasing pervasiveness of this form of personal disclosure arises from the history of online journaling and blogs, where authors often use their own lives as the focus of their material. The microblogger is engaging in a practice that 'centers on making the ordinary visible to others' (Oulasvirta et al. 2010, p. 238). A social need to remain in the collective consciousness of the social stream as it unfolds in time seems to motivate this kind of disclosure:

> What needs to be explained is somebody's willingness to stop the current activity, take out the phone, and expend effort to actively create such a 'peephole' for others. The key is to understand that a microblogger 'exists' through a staccato of one-liners, organized in reverse chronological order such that the most recent one fixes others' interpretation of his or her most current doings. (Oulasvirta et al. 2010, p. 248)

In this way microblogging can be seen as an ongoing performance of identity. Perhaps another significant explanatory factor is the human desire for affiliation: we exist within communities of other voices with which we wish to connect. The stances we adopt and observations and evaluations we share all exist relative to the meaning-making of the other members of our social network and to all other potential networks of meaning. In other words, we perform our online identities in order to connect with others.

The range of potential bonds that may be offered in a micropost is vast. A common bond around which users may affiliate is appreciation of a microcelebrity (Marwick 2010), a form of celebrity, distinct from traditional celebrity, that arises out of connection with an ambient audience via a kind of 'amping up' of popularity using social media (Senft 2008, p. 25). An example is the popular blogger Dooce, whose internet fame began when she was fired for writing about her colleagues on her blog. Alongside her blog content, this user produces additional content about her life and family via Twitter, where she commands an audience of followers of over 1.5 million.

Traditional celebrities also populate Twitter, attracting communities of fans who engage in public performances of affiliation (Marwick and Boyd 2011). The most frequently parodied community developing around one of these celebrities is that which concentrates around the singer Justin Beiber, who at the beginning of 2011 had a follower base of more than 7.5 million users, exceeding that of the US president at the time. These users are often mocked as 'beliebers', a reference to their apparent emotional fanaticism and manifest in expressions of Bieber-targetted affect (e.g. user names such as UserLuvBieber). Such a large user base means that Beiber frequently precipitates trending topics. For example, the following tweet by Beiber rapidly elevated the phrase Latin girls to a trending topic on 27 February 2011:

> shoutout to all of Latin America … i got love for all my Latin Girls

As one user quipped:

> Beliebers run Twitter. Hater or not. You have at least 1 belieber following you.

This user humorously comments on the way Justin Beiber fandom polarizes opinion on Twitter, with public appreciation of celebrities creating both an in-group rallying around positive values targeted at the public figure and an out-group who mock those values. For example, the following tweet is an example of the discourse of the latter:

> Attention all **#Beiber** fans! I am not a fan, in fact I hate the spastic! Don't follow me thinking I am, I'm not! I repeat, I am not!!

Hashtags play a role in coordinating such mass expression of value by focusing it around a particular ideational target (e.g. #Beiber). In other words, hashtags align users into 'overlapping communities of attitudinal rapport' (Martin 2004, p. 323).

Time and microblogging

Time is an important variable in microblogging. As part of the real-time web, microposts tend to disseminate material at the time it was generated and '[t] he stories told in Twitter prioritize the present moment (as signaled through the use of temporal adverbs like today, tonight and tomorrow)' (Page 2011, p. 161). Two different types of time are in play in microblogging: the unfolding of meaning in a text, that is, 'text time', and the 'real time' associated with the unfolding stream of posts. Meaning unfolds in a text 'dynamically as currents flowing through a stratified semiotic system' (Halliday 1991, p. 40). Halliday (Halliday and Martin 1993) described three kinds of semiotic change, or semogenesis: logogenesis, the unfolding of text, phylogenesis, the evolution of culture, and ontogenesis, the development of the meaning-making potential of a human over time. Once contiguity relations are added to a model of language such as SFL that primarily considers paradigmatic relations, the linguist is 'taking on a dynamic commitment' (Halliday 1991, p. 40). As such they are involved in modelling semiotic change.

Alongside logogenetic text time, there is the common time in which tweets unfold in the Twitter stream. This is captured as temporal metadata by Twitter and also displayed to users as a time stamp via the Twitter-web interface. Updates to the Twitter stream are almost instantaneous from a mobile device, meaning that this text time bears a close relationship to the

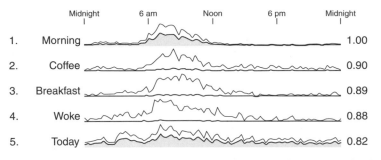

FIGURE 13.1 *Words having a positive time correlation with "morning" (Clark 2009)*

lived experience of time by users. To adequately account for both kinds of time, discourse analysts require support in order to make plain the complex patterns generated as language patterns in microposts that emerge over time. This support should assist them in understanding how the linguistic features they are interested in increase or diminish in frequency and change over time. A likely technology for achieving this is text visualization (Zappavigna 2011). The patterns may be within single user's Twitter stream, across groups of users or across the entire microblogging feed.

Twitter metadata allows exploration of collocation in the traditional corpus linguistics sense of the term to be extended diachronically. It affords a view of how particular couplings of meaning shift and change, enabling us to consider relationships between linguistic features in time series. For example, Figure 13.1 shows words that have a positive time correlation with a time series of word counts for 'morning' in the Twitter stream. The collocation of 'coffee' and 'morning' was a pattern present in HERMES, for example:

> @User That is hilarious! I needed a good laugh with my **morning coffee**! thx. ;)

> wow, a **coffee** in the **morning** is the best thing ever !!!

> partaking in my **morning coffee** and dose of Sportscenter. then spending the rest of the morning writing w/ @User. afternoon plans?

> @User I need **coffee** in the **mornings**! It's my picker upper!!

These tweets offer coffee appreciation as a potential rallying point for users who are concurrently engaging in practices of complaining about being up too early in the morning or of having to go to work. Figure 13.1 allows us to see the time dependency of the association between morning and coffee and the fact that, unsurprisingly, the relationship between these two words peaks in the early part of the day (which will clearly be different depending on the geographical location of the microbloggers).

In this book I use the text visualization software Twitter StreamGraph (Clark 2009) to show snapshots of lexis unfolding over short time periods in the Twitter stream. Streamgraphs are an example of a text visualization technique that does not efface logogenesis, the unfolding of text over time (Zappavigna 2011). The visualization 'shows the usage over time for the words most highly associated with the search word' (Clark 2009). While an area graph usually shows a single data series, streamgraphs are a form of stacked area graph that represent multiple data series by stacking one on top of the other and presenting the series as unfolding 'streams'. Smooth curves are generated for these streams by interpolating between points to produce a flowing river of data. In a stacked area graph the height of the curve at a given point represents the total frequency of all features at that point, and thus each data series should be read as starting at zero rather than at the accumulative height.

This streamgraph technique is most useful to a linguist interested in the general trend of a data series or, in other words, the qualitative ebb and flow of features over the time series. It is also a useful technique for appreciating the relationships between the data series as they unfold by the overall impression of the relative amount of colour. The technique has been used to visualize box office revenues changing over time (Byron and Wattenberg 2008), changes in music-listening habits (Byron 2008), shifts in lexical themes in corpora with time (Havre et al. 2002) and changes in word association in Twitter status messages (Clark 2009).

In the case of microblogging texts and, in particular, Twitter, StreamGraphs allow multiple lexical items in tweets to be depicted as coloured streams flowing with the time series on a single graph. For example, Figure 13.2 shows a Twitter StreamGraph[4] for the lexical item 'coffee'. To generate the StreamGraph in Figure 13.2, the user has entered the search term 'coffee'. The coloured streams displayed represent lexis that collocates with coffee in the twitter stream over an interval of time (17:50 to 18.29) close to the time at which the query was made. The stream representation allows us to see how the frequency of a lexical item varies over time at the same time as other co-occurring items. For example, the stream selected in red is the word 'morning', and we can see its association with the search term coffee and with other words such as Starbucks, drink, and cup. The local association of these terms is apparent within a single tweet; for example, the following tweet was part of the dataset used to generate the graph (a sample of which is shown under the graph in the figure):

+ I'm drinking my morning coffee. Is there anything better? :)

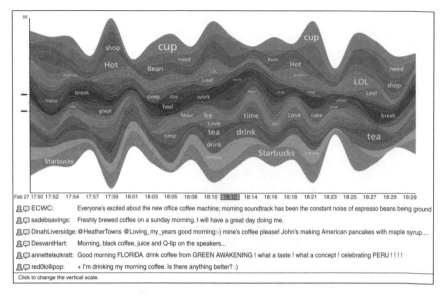

FIGURE 13.2 *Twitter StreamGraph for 'coffee' (Clark 2009)*

The streamgraph representation provides us with a view of more global patterns of collocational flow over time. While current automatic text-processing techniques mean that we are largely restricted to considering lexis rather than more complex discourse semantic features, the visualization offers some initial guidance to the discourse analyst attempting to understand the unfolding complexity of streams of microposts.

Linguistic patterns in the HERMES

In order to understand the linguistic tendencies seen in microblogging, I will look at some of the most common patterns in the HERMES. We will begin with a top-down approach by inspecting a word-frequency list. Following this broad view I will consider some frequent n-grams that reveal common syntagmatic patterns in the corpus. N-grams are used within corpus linguistics to look at clusters of words in texts of different lengths (e.g. a 3-gram is a 3-word cluster, where n is equal to 3). The general principle is that previous n − 1 words in a sequence can be used to predict the next word as part of models trained on very large corpora. These techniques are not employed as an end in themselves but instead to guide close discourse analysis of specific instances of texts.

Table 13.1 shows the 20 most common words in the corpus as a ranked frequency list. Three items which would not be expected to occur in a

TABLE 13.1 The 20 most frequent words in the Twitter corpus

N	Word	Frequency	%
1	@_word_	4,037,829	4.04
2	THE	3,358,659	3.15
3	TO	2,379,223	2.23
4	I	2,236,470	2.10
5	A	1,674,654	1.57
6	HTTP	1,631,187	1.53
7	AND	1,545,943	1.45
8	OF	1,217,398	1.14
9	#_word_	1,253,853	1.25
10	YOU	1,194,631	1.12
11	IS	1,120,058	1.05
12	IN	1,118,227	1.05
13	RT	990,287	0.93
14	ON	906,996	0.85
15	FOR	891,100	0.84
16	THAT	871,925	0.82
17	MY	858,657	0.81
18	IT	853,209	0.80
19	THIS	678,193	0.64
20	ME	676,702	0.63

frequency list for a traditional, non-CMC corpus have been highlighted in grey in the table. These are

- @ – The 'at' character is usually used to address as tweet to another user.

- *HTTP*– The characters HTTP (Hyper Text Transfer Protocol[5]) appear at the beginning of weblinks in HERMES followed by a colon which the Wordsmith system has interpreted as a word break. Nevertheless, HTTP acts as a marker indicating that the full sequence included a weblink and, as such, is useful in counting the number of weblinks that occurred in the HERMES.

- # – The hash character is used to mark a hashtag, typically to indicate the topic of a tweet.

- *RT* – Two characters that refer to a 'retweet', the act of republishing another tweet within your own tweet.

All of these items are examples of resources for bringing voices from other texts into a tweet (theorized as associated with the engagement system). It is interesting that these three items in this frequency list that are dependent on the mode of communication (i.e. the microblogging service) are items that work in the service of interactivity. This interpersonal orientation is an important pattern that will be illuminated further in this chapter as we look at common n-grams that characterize HERMES.

Word lists as stand-alone entities are of limited utility and are more useful when compared with lists derived from other corpora, particularly reference corpora. However, determining an appropriate reference corpus for use with HERMES is a problematic task given that it is larger than most available traditional corpora. In addition, we are dealing with a corpus of 'international' English, and many traditional corpora focus on a single kind of English, for example, the British national corpus. Further, building corpora of computer-mediated communication is an emergent area, and so appropriately balanced corpora are difficult to access. A candidate reference corpus was the 25-billion-word USENET corpus (Shaoul and Westbury 2011); however, the large size of this corpus was beyond the computing power of this project and would have required a cluster of computers to generate analyses such as n-grams.

We might compare the HERMES frequency list with frequency lists from the 410-million-word Corpus of Contemporary American English (COCA). American English is frequent in HERMES since the majority of Twitter users reside in the United States. A significant limitation of the comparison is that COCA does not include a CMC in its constituent registers (spoken, fiction, magazine, newspaper, academic). Table 13.2 shows the 20 most frequent words in COCA alongside those in HERMES.

TABLE 13.2 Comparing the 20 most frequent words in the Corpus of Contemporary American English (COCA) with those in HERMES

	COCA			HERMES	
N	**Word**	**Frequency**	**N**	**Word**	**Frequency**
1	THE	22,038,615	1	*@word*	**4,037,829**
2	BE	12,545,825	2	THE	3,358,659
3	AND	10,741,073	3	TO	2,379,223
4	OF	10,343,885	4	I	2,236,470
5	A	10,144,200	5	A	1,674,654
6	IN	6,996,437	6	**HTTP**	**1,631,187**
7	TO	6,332,195	7	AND	1,545,943
8	HAVE	4,303,955	8	OF	1,217,398
9	TO	3,856,916	9	*#word*	**1,253,853**
10	IT	3,872,477	10	YOU	1,194,631
11	**I**	**3,978,265**	**11**	IS	1,120,058
12	THAT	3,430,996	12	IN	1,118,227
13	FOR	3,281,454	13	**RT**	**990,287**
14	YOU	3,081,151	14	ON	906,996
15	HE	2,909,254	15	FOR	891,100
16	WITH	2,683,014	16	THAT	871,925
17	ON	2,485,306	17	MY	858,657
18	DO	2,573,587	18	IT	853,209
19	SAY	1,915,138	19	THIS	678,193
20	THIS	1,885,366	20	ME	676,702

The most common item in HERMES, @ symbol, was most often used as part of an @mention. Its frequency indicates the prominence of dialogic interaction in the corpus, a point also recognized by Honeycutt and Herring (2009), who note the conversationality of Twitter stemming from the addressivity afforded by @. In addition, at first glance, Twitter discourse appears more focused on the self, given the higher ranking in HERMES of *I* (4 in HERMES; 11 in COCA), *me* (20 in HERMES; 62 in COCA), and *my* (17 in HERMES; 44 in COCA). However, we should also note the higher ranking in HERMES of *you* (10 in HERMES; 14 in COCA), suggesting Twitter's dialogic function where people use the service to interact and converse (the variant *u* was not tracked in this count but would likely increase the ranking). The dominance of the interpersonal will also be seen in the most common n-grams in the corpus explored in the next section.

Syntagmatic patterns in HERMES

While a word list offers an interesting starting point for discourse analysis, its utility is limited since meanings are made logogentically as texts unfold via complex, multidimensional syntagmatic and paradigmatic patterns. I will now consider some of the most frequent syntagmatic patterns in HERMES. The technique used throughout this book for inspecting these patterns is n-gram analysis (otherwise known as cluster analysis), where n is the number of items in the cluster. N-grams were computed automatically using the software application Wordsmith. Table 13.3 shows the 20 most frequent 3-grams in HERMES. The most common 3-gram, 'Thanks for the', will be considered in detail in this chapter.

However, in keeping with a systemic functional approach to language, I will also assume a paradigmatic perspective on the corpus by using concordance lines. Bednarek (2010, p. 239) suggests that concordance lines offer the potential for such a dual lens along paradigmatic and syntagmatic axes. For example, following her logic, we can inspect 'thanks for the' (the most common 3-gram in the corpus) along both axes. Along the syntagmatic axis, we can see the collocates of this structure (marked by the border around the first entry in the concordance lines in Figure 13.3). Along the paradigmatic axis we can see that ff could be substituted by RT, tip and support, affording a perspective on the choice of collocates. This paradigmatic gaze is shown in grey in the figure. These two kinds of approaches to patterning are employed in the next section, which explores this 3-gram in more detail.

TABLE 13.3 The 20 most common 3-grams[6] in HERMES

N	Word	Frequency	%
1	THANKS FOR THE	26,498	0.02
2	I HAVE TO	21,230	0.02
3	I HAVE A	20,919	0.02
4	I WANT TO	18,835	0.02
5	GOING TO BE	18,480	0.02
6	I NEED TO	18,443	0.02
7	ONE OF THE	18,158	0.02
8	WE ARE THE	18,026	0.02
9	I'M GOING TO	17,516	0.02
10	TO GO TO	17,096	0.02
11	A LOT OF	16,904	0.02
12	ARE THE WORLD	16,071	0.02
13	TRY IT HTTP	14,999	0.01
14	I THINK I	14,947	0.01
15	IS GOING TO	13,713	0.01
16	I LOVE YOU	13,415	0.01
17	OF THE DAY	12,892	0.01
18	TO BE A	12,765	0.01
19	LOOKING FORWARD TO	12,755	0.01
20	CHECK IT OUT	12,615	0.01

@User	**Thanks for the**	ff babe x
@User Hi -	**thanks for the**	RT. Much appreciated :)
@User	**thanks for the**	follow hun
	Thanks for the	RTs @User @User2 @User3 @User4 Happy #FF!
@User	**thanks for the**	Tip. i guess i expect that software with millions of users to work properly :)
	thanks for	Support, love ya @User @User2 :)

FIGURE 13.3 *The dual affordance of concordance lines*

The most frequent 3-gram in HERMES: 'Thanks for the'

Inspecting common clusters in HERMES provides the first significant clue pointing to the importance of interpersonal meaning in microblogging. The most common 3-gram, 'Thanks for the', is a pattern indicating interpersonal reciprocity. The pattern is an example of Twitter users directing a message of thanks to other users and was most usually accompanied by the @ character, rendering it a direct address. It occurred in the following tweet, for example, where an author thanked another user for retweeting one of his or her microposts:

@user **Thanks for the** RT. Hope you are having a wonderful week.

The most frequent target of thanks was a Follow Friday (FF) mention, for example:

@User Thanks for the FF :)

'FF', refers to Follow Friday, a Twitter meme[7] with the function of 'promoting other people on Twitter – anyone you think your followers should also be following for any reason' (Horovitch 2010). The concept centres upon users mentioning in a tweet people worthy of such subscription each Friday. For example (positive evaluation in bold):

#followfriday @User – always **inspiring** art and a **nice** guy!

This tweet invites the audience to follow @User, deploying the hashtag #followfriday to indicate allegiance with the meme. Users tracking this hashtag will automatically see this tweet, or, alternatively, a user can search by using the hashtag as a query.

Being the most frequent 3-gram in HERMES and inherently dialogic in this way, the cluster strongly suggests that microblogging is more than simply posting about the day's activities. The pattern provides some initial evidence that an important facet of microblogging is reciprocation of social bonds. Users are typically thanking each other for providing some form of interpersonal recognition or support. Processes of thanking also have a politeness function (Brown and Levinson 1978). Table 13.4 shows examples of the most common items that occupied R1, the position directly to the right of the cluster, giving an indication of the targets of the thanks. The first four of these items in R1 (FF, RT, follow and RTs) refer to social practices that have emerged on Twitter for recognizing other users.

The second most common item in R1 was RT. As explained earlier, this typographic convention indicates that the post involves a retweet, republication of another tweet within your own, as in the following example:

#followfriday **RT @User2**: want to get my followers up to 30.000, it's been stuck at 28,794 for too bloody long, converts come forward!

User2's original post has been republished in this tweet along with the Follow Friday hashtag to indicate that the person posting this tweet endorses the appeal for a wider body of followers made by the original poster. This is an example where the @ symbol is functioning as an attribution marker, working in tandem with the RT to specify the original authorship of the tweets. The

TABLE 13.4 Examples of the most frequent occupants of R1 for the 3-gram 'thanks for the'

N	R1	Example
1	FF	@User Thanks for the ff babe x
2	RT	@User Hi – thanks for the RT. Much appreciated :)
3	follow	@User thanks for the follow hun
4	RTs	Thanks for the RTs @User @User2 @User3 @User4 Happy #FF!
5	tip	@User thanks for the tip, i guess i expect that software with millions of users to work properly :)
6	support	Thanks for the support, love ya @User @User2 :)

pattern 'thanks for the RT' involves users expressing appreciation for this rebroadcast:

@User Hi – thanks for the RT. Much appreciated :)

As this example suggests the thanks is usually accompanied by positive evaluative language. Examples 5 and 6 in Table 13.4 are typical of a second function of 'thanks for the', namely, expressing gratitude for some service rendered. Lexis that occupied this R1 slot also included *hugs, concern, time, offer to help*, and *feedback, input, link, heads up, article*. The former group are examples of emotional support and counsel, while the latter group tend toward an offer of information (although this category is fuzzy and blurs into 'advice').

Thus the two main functions of 'thanks for the' appear to be offering appreciation for public acknowledgement received and showing gratitude for counsel. The target of the thanks being social processes rather than goods accords with the highly interpersonal nature of Twitter and the value placed on social relations. Looking at the frequent collocates of 'thanks for the' in COCA, this latter kind of gratitude for some kind of material object (e.g. thanks for the book) is much more frequent in HERMES. Tweets are highly dialogic and part of a heteroglossic (Bakhtin 2008) Twitter stream in which an important social process is showing reciprocity by public thanking of other users. These users are clearly doing more than broadcasting the personal, self-indulgent or mundane details of their daily routine. They are producing more than a kind of monoglossic, self-indulgent stream of consciousness that is oblivious to other texts. This is not to say, however, that microposts are not highly self-promoting (Page 2011). The act of thanking someone for a RT or FF is a means of demonstrating a high perceived status in the community and displaying one's place within the social network.

Notes

1 Ping' in networking refers to a way of detecting if there is a valid communication path between two or more computers: one computer sends out a message and the other replies with an identical copy.

2 In All user names in this book have been anonymized.

3 In September 2010 Twitter began to release New Twitter, a reworked version of Twitter.com that includes a number of changes in functionality, in particular, being able to view multimedia without leaving the site and a redesign of the user interface. At the time of writing, commercial features such as sponsored 'promoted' trending topics had begun to appear on Twitter.

4 The interactive application is available at www.neoformix.com/Projects/ TwitterStreamGraphs/view.php.

5 IHyper Text Transfer Protocol (HTTP) is the network protocol governing data communication on the web

6 I have excluded n-grams generated by automated non-human services such as: I just took 'How will you win justin bieber's heart?' and got With your passionate side! Try it: http://bit.ly/9iwUcl

7 A Twitter meme is a form of internet meme that spreads virally through social media networks. Often humorous, social media memes are any form of media that self-propagates across the network from user to user. A common example is amusing YouTube videos.

References

Ackroyd, S. and Thompson, P. (1999), *Organizational Misbehaviour*. London: Sage.

Aharony, N. (2010), 'Twitter use in libraries: an exploratory analysis', *Journal of Web Librarianship* 4 (4): 333–50.

Allison, D. and Tauroza, S. (1995), 'The effect of discourse organisation on lecture comprehension', *English for Specific Purposes* 14 (2): 157–73.

Ammon, U. (ed.) (2001), *The Dominance of English as a Language of Science. Effects on Other Languages and Language Communities*. Berlin and New York: Mouton de Gruyter.

Androutsopoulos, J. K. (2000), 'Non-standard spellings in media texts: the case of German fanzines'. *Journal of Sociolinguistics* 4 (4): 514–33.

Anstead, N. and O'Loughlin, B. (2010), Emerging Viewertariat: Explaining Twitter Responses to Nick Griffin's Appearance on bbc Question Time. In *PSI Working Paper Series*: School of Political, Social and International Studies, University of East Anglia, Norwich, UK.

Arceneaux, N. and Weiss, A. S. (2010), 'Seems stupid until you try it: press coverage of Twitter, 2006–9', *New Media & Society* 12 (8): 1262–79.

Åstedt-Kurki, P. and Isola, A. (2001), 'Issues and innovations in nursing practice – humour between nurse and patient, and among staff: analysis of nurses' diaries', *Journal of Advanced Nursing* 35 (3): 452–8.

Atkinson, C. (2010), *The Backchannel: How Audiences Are Using Twitter and Social Media and Changing Presentations Forever*. Berkeley, CA: New Riders.

Bakhtin, M. (1981). *The Dialogic Imagination*. Edited by M. Holquist. Austin, TX: University of Texas Press.

—(2008), *The Dialogic Imagination : Four Essays*. Edited by M. Holquist. Vol. 1, University of Texas Press Slavic series. Austin: University of Texas Press.

Ballard, B. and Clanchy, J. (1988), 'Literacy in the university: an anthropological approach', in G. Taylor, B. Ballard, V. Beasley, H. Bock, J. Clanchy and P. Nightingale (eds), *Literacy by Degrees*. Milton Keynes: Open University Press, pp. 7–23.

Bamford, J. (2004), 'Evaluating retrospectively and prospectively in academic lectures', in J. Bamford and L. Anderson (eds), *Evaluation in Oral and Written Academic Discourse*. Rome: Officina Edizioni, pp. 15–30.

Barnhurst, K. G. and Nerone, J. (2001), *The Form of News: A History*. New York: Guilford.

Baron, N. (2000), *Alphabet to Email: How Written English Evolved and Where it's Heading*. London: Routledge.

Barros, C. D. M. (1995), 'The missionary presence in literacy campaigns in the indigenous languages of Latin America', *International Journal of Educational Development* 15 (3): 277–87.

Barthes, R. (1977), *Image, Music, Text.* London: Fontana.

Barton, E. L. (1995), 'Contrastive and non-contrastive connectives'. *Written Communication* 12 (2): 219–39.

Basturkmen, H. (2002), 'Negotiating meaning in seminar-type discussion and EAP', *English for Specific Purposes* 21 (3): 233–42.

Bateman, J. (2008), *Multimodality and Genre: A Foundation for the Systemic Analysis of Multimodal Documents.* Basingstoke: Palgrave Macmillan.

Bazerman, C. (1988), *Shaping Written Knowledge. The Genre and Activity of the Experimental Article in Science.* London and Madison, WI: University of Wisconsin Press.

Bazerman, C. and Paradis, J. (eds) (1991): *Textual Dynamics of the Professions. Historical and Contemporary Studies of Writing in Professional Communities.* Madison, Wisconsin: The University of Wisconsin Press.

Becker, K. E. (1992/2003), 'Photojournalism and the tabloid press', in L. Wells (ed.), *The Photography Reader.* London: Routledge, pp. 291–308.

Bednarek, M. (2010), 'Corpus Linguistics and Systemic Functional Linguistics: interpersonal meaning, identity and bonding in popular culture', in M. Bednarek and J. R. Martin (eds), *New Discourse on Language: Functional Perspectives on Multimodality, Identity, and Affiliation.* London and New York: Continuum.

Beechener, C., Griffiths, C. and Jacob, A. (2004), *Modern Times.* Oxford: Heinemann.

Bell, A. (1991), *The Language of News Media.* Oxford: Blackwell.

Bennett, J. and Smithers, G. (eds) (1968), *Early Middle English Verse and Prose.* Oxford: Clarendon Press.

Benson, M. (1994), 'Lecture listening in an ethnographic perspective', in J. Flowerdew (ed.), *Academic Listening: Research Perspectives.* Cambridge: Cambridge University Press, pp. 181–98.

Benwell, B. (2005), '"Lucky this is anonymous!" Ethnographies of reception in men's magazines: a "textual culture" approach', *Discourse and Society* 16: 147–72.

Benwell, B. and Stokoe, E. (2006), *Discourse and Identity.* Edinburgh: Edinburgh University Press.

Bernstein, B. (1975), *Class, Codes and Control, Vol. 3: Towards a Theory of Educational Transmissions.* London: Routledge & Kegan Paul.

—(1990), *The Structuring of Pedagogic Discourse. Class, Codes and Control, Vol. IV.* London and New York: Routledge.

—(2000), *Pedagogy, Symbolic Control and Identity. Theory, Research, Critique* (rev. edn). Lanham, MD; Boulder, CO; New York and Oxford: Rowman and Littlefield.

Biber, D. (2006), 'Stance in spoken and written university registers', *Journal of English for Academic Purposes* 5 (2): 97–116.

Biber, D. and Finegan, E. (1989), 'Styles of stance in English: lexical and grammatical marking of evidentiality and affect', *Text* 9 (1): 93–124.

Biber, D., Conrad, S. and Reppen, R. (1998), *Corpus Linguistics: Investigating Language Structure and Use.* Cambridge: Cambridge University Press.

Biber, D., Johansson, S., Leech, G., Conrad, S. and Finegan, E. (1999), *Longman Grammar of Spoken and Written English.* London: Longman.

Biber, D., Conrad, S. and Cortes, V. (2004), 'If you look at … : lexical bundles in university teaching and textbooks', *Applied Linguistics* 25: 371–405.

Bignell, J. (2002), *Media Semiotics: An Introduction* (2nd edn). Manchester: Manchester University Press.

Bisker, S., Ouilhet, H., Pomeroy, S., Chang, A. and Casalegno, F. (2008), Re-thinking fashion trade shows: creating conversations through mobile tagging. In *CHI '08 extended abstracts on human factors in computing systems*. Florence, Italy: ACM.

Blommart, J. (2005), *Discourse*. Cambridge: Cambridge University Press.

Bloor, T. and Bloor, M. (2004), *The Functional Analysis of English: A Hallidayan Approach* (2nd edn). London: Hodder Arnold.

Board of Studies (1997), *1996 H.S.C. Sample Answers, 2/3 Unit Modern History*. North Sydney, Australia: Board of Studies.

Bolinger, D. (1946), 'Visual morphemes', *Language* 22: 333–40.

Bondi, M. (1999), *English across Genres*. Modena: Edizioni Il Fiorino.

Borau, K., Ullrich, C., Feng, J. and Shen, R. . (2009), 'Microblogging for language learning: using Twitter to train communicative and cultural competence', in M. Spaniol, Q. Li, R. Klamma and R. Lau (eds), *Advances in Web Based Learning – ICWL 2009*. Berlin and Heidelberg: Springer.

Bourdieu, P. and Passeron, J.-C. (1996), 'Introduction: language and relationship to language in the teaching situation', in P. Bourdieu, J.-C Passeron and M. de Saint Martin (eds), *Academic Discourse*. The Hague: Mouton, pp. 1–34.

Boxer, D. and Cortés-Conde, F. (1997), 'From bonding to biting: conversational joking and identity display', *Journal of Pragmatics* 27: 275–94.

Boyd, D. (2009), Do You See What I See?: Visibility of Practices through Social Media. Paper read at Supernova and Le Web, 1 and 10 December 2009, at San Francisco and Paris.

—(2010), 'Social network sites as networked publics: affordances, dynamics, and implications', in Z. Papacharissi (ed.), *A Networked Self: Identity, Community, and Culture on Social Network Sites*. New York: Routledge.

Boyd, D., Golder, S. and Lotan, G. (2010), *Tweet, Tweet, Retweet: Conversational Aspects of Retweeting on Twitter*. Computer Society Press 2010. Available at www.danah.org/papers/TweetTweetRetweet.pdf.

Bradley, H. (1919), *On the Relations between Spoken and Written Language with Special Reference to English*. Oxford: Clarendon Press.

Bradley, P. (2010), 'Be where the conversations are: the critical importance of social media', *Business Information Review* 27 (4): 248–52.

Brooks, A. L. and Churchill, E. (2010), Tune In, Tweet On, and Twit Out: Information Snacking on Twitter. Paper read at Workshop on Microblogging at the ACM *Conference on Human Factors in Computer Systems*, 10–11 April 2010, at Atlanta, Georgia.

Brown, P. and Levinson, S. (1978), 'Universals in language usage: politeness phenomena', in E. Goody (ed.), *Questions and politeness*. Cambridge: Cambridge University Press.

—(1987), *Politeness: Some Universals in Language Usage* (Studies in Interactional Sociolinguistics 4). Cambridge: Cambridge University Press

Brown, V. (1993), 'Decanonizing discourses: textual analysis and the history of economic thought', in W. Henderson, T. Dudley-Evans and R. Backhouse (eds), *Economics and Language*. London: Routledge, pp. 64–84.

Bunton, D. (1999), 'The use of higher level metatext in PhD theses', *English for Specific Purposes* 18: S41–S56.

Butt, D., Fahey, R., Feez, S., Spinks, S. and Yallop, C. (2000), *Using Functional Grammar: An Explorer's Guide* (2nd edn). Sydney, NSW: National Centre for English Language Teaching and Research (NCLTR Macquarie University).

Byron, L. and Wattenberg, M. (2008), *Stacked Graphs – Geometry & Aesthetics*. Lee Byron 2008. Available at www.leebyron.com/else/streamgraph/

Cameron, D. (2001), *Working with Spoken Discourse*. London: Sage.

Caple, H. (2008), 'Intermodal relations in image-nuclear news stories', in L. Unsworth (ed.), *Multimodal Semiotics: Functional Analysis in Contexts of Education*. London: Continuum, pp. 125–38.

—(2009a), 'Multisemiotic communication in an Australian broadsheet: a new news story genre', in C. Bazerman, A. Bonini and D. Figueiredo (eds), *Genre in a Changing World: Perspectives on Writing*. Fort Collins, CO: WAC Clearinghouse and Parlor Press, pp. 243–54. Available at http://wac.colostate.edu/books/genre/.

—(2009b), 'Playing with words and pictures: intersemiosis in a new genre of news reportage', Ph.D. Thesis, Department of Linguistics, University of Sydney. Available at http://ses.library.usyd.edu.au/handle/2123/7024.

—(2010a), 'What you see and what you get: the evolving role of news photographs in an Australian broadsheet', in V. Rupar (ed.), *Journalism and Meaning-making: Reading the Newspaper*. Cresskill, NJ: Hampton Press, pp. 199–220.

—(2010b), 'Doubling-up: allusion and bonding in multi-semiotic news stories', in M. Bednarek and J. R. Martin (eds), *New Discourse on Language: Functional Perspectives on Multimodality, Identity, and Affiliation*. London and New York: Continuum, pp.111–33.

—(in press), *Photojournalism: A Multisemiotic Approach*. Basingstoke: Palgrave Macmillan.

Caple, H. and Knox, J. (in press), 'Online news galleries, photojournalism and the photo essay', *Visual Communication*.

Carli, A. and Ammon, U. (eds) (2007), 'Linguistic inequality in scientific communication today', *AILA Review*, volume 20. Amsterdam and Philadelphia: John Benjamins.

Carney, E. (1994), *A Survey of English Spelling*. London: Routledge.

Carter, R. (1987), *Vocabulary: Applied Linguistic Perspectives*. London: Allen and Unwin.

Christie, F. (1999), 'The pedagogic device and the teaching of English', in F. Christie (ed.), *Pedagogy and the Shaping of Consciousness*. London: Continuum, pp. 156–84.

Clark, J. (2009), *Temporal Correlation for Words in Tweets* 2009 [cited 20 March 2011].

Clark, R. J. (1995), 'Developing critical reading practices', *Prospect* 10: 65–80.

Coates, J. (1983), *The Semantics of the Modal Auxiliaries*. Beckenham: Croom Helm.

Coffin, C. and Derewianka, B. (2009), 'A multimodal analysis of history textbooks', in G. Thompson and G. Forey (eds), *Text-Type and Texture*. London: Equinox.

Collinson, D. (1988), 'Engineering humour: masculinity, joking and conflict in shop floor relations', *Organization Studies* 9 (2):181–99.

Conrad, S. and Biber, D. (2000), 'Adverbial marking of stance in speech and writing', in S. Hunston and G. Thompson (eds), *Evaluation in Text*. Oxford: Oxford University Press, pp. 56–73.

Cook-Gumperz, J. and Messerman, L. (1999), 'Local identities and institutional practices: constructing the record of professional collaboration', in S. Sarangi and J. Roberts (eds), *Talk, Work and Institutional Order: Discourse in Medical, Mediation and Management Settings*. Berlin: DeGruyter, pp. 145–81.

Coupland, J. (ed.) (2000), *Small Talk*. Harlow: Pearson Education.

Coupland, N. and Ylänne-McEwen, V. (2000), 'Talk about the weather: small talk, leisure talk and the travel industry', in J. Coupland (ed.), *Small Talk*. Harlow: Pearson Education, pp. 163–82.

Cowan, J. (2011), 'Obama won't release bin Laden photo', *ABC News*. Available at www.abc.net.au/news/stories/2011/05/05/3208049.htm? section=world, accessed 5 May 2011.

Crawford Camiciottoli, B. (2004), 'Interactive discourse structuring in L2 guest lectures: some insights from a comparative corpus-based study', *Journal of English for Academic Purposes* 3 (1): 39–54.

Crismore, A., Markkanen, R. and Steffensen, M. (1993), 'Metadiscourse in persuasive writing: a study of texts written by American and Finnish university students', *Written Communication* 10 (1): 39–71.

Crystal, D. (2003), *The Cambridge Encyclopedia of the English Language*. Cambridge: Cambridge University Press.

—(2008), *Txtng: The Gr8 Db8*. Oxford: Oxford University Press.

Cuddy, C. (2009), 'Twittering in Health Sciences Libraries', *Journal of Electronic Resources in Medical Libraries* 6 (2): 169–73.

Danet, B. (1980), '"Baby" or "fetus": language and the construction of reality in a manslaughter trial', *Semiotica* 32 (1/2): 187–219.

DeVoe, Kristina M. (2009), 'Bursts of information: microblogging', *The Reference Librarian* 50 (2): 212–14.

Doyle, R. (1998) *The Barrytown Trilogy: The Commitments, The Snapper, The Van*. London: Vintage

Ebner, M. (2009), 'Introducing live microblogging: how single presentations can be enhanced by the mass', *Journal of Research in Innovative Teaching* 2 (1): 108–19.

Ebner, M., Lienhardt, C., Rohs, M. and Meyer, I. (2010), 'Microblogs in Higher Education – a chance to facilitate informal and process-oriented learning?' *Computers and Education* 55 (1): 92–100.

Economou, D. (2006), 'The big picture: the role of the lead image in print feature stories', in I. Lassen, J. Strunck and T. Vestergaard (eds), *Mediating Ideology in Text and Image: Ten Critical Studies*. Amsterdam: John Benjamins, pp. 211–33.

—(2008), 'Pulling readers in: news photos in Greek and Australian broadsheets' in P. R. R. White and E. A. Thomson (eds), *Communicating Conflict: Multilingual Case Studies of the News Media*. London: Continuum, pp. 253–80.

Eggins, S. (1994), *An Introduction to Systemic Functional Linguistics*. London: Pinter.

—(2004), *An Introduction to Systemic Functional Linguistics* (2nd edn). London: Continuum.

Eggins, S. and Slade, D. (1997), *Analysing Casual Conversation*. London and New York: Cassell.

Englebretson, R. (ed.) (2007), *Stance-Taking in Interaction*. Amsterdam, John Benjamins.

Fairclough, N. (1989), *Language and Power*. London: Longman.

—(1992), *Discourse and Social Change*. Cambridge: Polity Press.

—(1995), *Critical Discourse Analysis*. London: Longman.

—(2003), *Analyzing Discourse: Textual Analysis for Social Research*. London: Routledge.

Fairclough, N. and Wodak, R. (1997), 'Critical discourse analysis: an overview', in T. A. van Dijk (ed.), *Discourse as Social Interaction*. London: Sage, pp. 258–84.

Ferris, D. and Tagg, T. (1996), 'Academic oral communication: what subjectmatter instructors actually require', *TESOL Quarterly* 30 (1): 31–58.

Flowerdew, J. (1992), 'Definitions in science lectures', *Applied Linguistics* 13 (2): 202–21.

—(ed.) (1994), *Academic Listening: Research Perspectives*. Cambridge: Cambridge University Press.

—(2004), 'The discursive construction of a world-class city', *Discourse and Society* 15: 579–605.

Flowerdew, J. and Miller, L. (1996), 'Lectures in a second language: notes towards a cultural grammar', *English for Specific Purposes* 15 (2): 121–40.

—(1997), 'The teaching of academic listening comprehension and the question of authenticity', *English for Specific Purposes* 16: 27–46.

Flowerdew, L. (2002), 'Corpus-based analyses in EAP', in J. Flowerdew (ed.), *Academic Discourse*. Harlow: Longman, pp. 95–114.

Fortanet, I. (2004), 'The use of "we" in university lectures: reference and function', *English for Specific Purposes* 23 (1): 45–66.

Foucault, M. (1972), *The Archeology of Knowledge*. London: Tavistock.

Francis, W. N. and Kučera, H. (1982), *Frequency Analysis of English Usage: Lexicon and Grammar*. Boston: Houghton Mifflin.

Furneaux, C., Locke, C., Robinson, P. and Tonkyn, A. (1991), 'Talking heads and shifting bottoms: the ethnography of seminars', in P. Adams, B. Heaton and P. Howarth (eds), *Socio-Cultural Issues in English for Academic Purposes*. Hemel Hempstead: Phoenix ELT, pp. 75–88.

Gebhardt, R. C. (1993), 'Scholarship, promotion, and tenure in composition studies', *College Composition and Communication* 44: 439–42.

Gee, J. (1999), *An Introduction to Discourse Analysis*. London: Routledge

Georgakopoulou, A. (2007), *Small Stories, Interaction, and Identities*. Amsterdam, John Benjamins.

Gernsheim, H. (1955), *The History of Photography*. London: Oxford University Press.

Givon, T. (1995), 'Coherence in text vs coherence in mind', in M. Gernsbacher and T. Givon (eds), *Coherence in Spontaneous Text*. Amsterdam: John Benjamins, pp. 59–116.

Goffman, E. (1981), *Forms of Talk*. Philadelphia, PA: University of Pennsylvania

Greatbatch, D. and Dingwall, R. (1998), 'Talk and identity in divorce mediation', in C. Antaki and S. Widdicombe (eds), *Identities in Talk*. London: Sage, pp. 121–32.

Grinter, R. E. and Eldridge, M. (2003), 'Wan2tlk?: everyday text messaging', *Proceedings of the CHI'03 Conference on Human Factors in Computing Systems* (Fort Lauderdale).

Grosseck, G. and Holotescu, C. (2009), 'Indicators for the analysis of learning and practice communities from the perspective of microblogging as a provocative sociolect in virtual space', in *5th International Scientific Conference eLSE – eLearning and Software for Education*. Bucharest.

—(2010), 'Microblogging multimedia-based teaching methods best practices with Cirip.eu', *Procedia – Social and Behavioral Sciences* 2 (2): 2151–55.

Gunnarsson, B.-L. (1993), 'Pragmatic and macrothematic patterns in science and popular science: A diachronic study of articles from three fields', in, M. Ghadessy (ed.), *Register Analysis: Theory and Practice*. London and New York: Pinter Publishers, pp. 165–79.

—(1998), 'Academic discourse in changing context frames: The construction and development of a genre', in P. Evangelisti Allori (ed.) *Academic Discourse in Europe. Thought Processes and Linguistic Realisations*. Rome: Bulzoni, pp. 19–42.

—(2001a), 'Expressing criticism and evaluation during three centuries', *Journal of Historical Pragmatics* 2 (1): 115–139.

—(2001b), 'Swedish, English, French or German – the language situation at Swedish universities', in U. Ammon (ed.), *The Dominance of English as a Language of Science. Effects on Other Languages and Language Communities*. Berlin and New York: Mouton de Gruyter, pp. 229–316.

—(2005), 'Medical Discourse: Sociohistorical Construction', in *Encyclopedia of Language and Linguistics*, (2nd edn) Vol 7, eds. K. Brown. Oxford: Elsevier, pp. 709–716.

Gunnarsson, B.-L. and Skolander, -B. (1991), *Fackspråkens framväxt: terminologi och ordförråd i facktexter från tre sekler 1. Projektprosentation och materialbeskrivning*. FUMS rapport nr 154. Uppsala: Uppsala University.

Gunnarsson, B.-L., Bäcklund, I. and Andersson, B. (1995), 'Texts in European writing communities', in B.-L. Gunnarsson and I. Bäcklund (eds), *Writing in Academic Contexts*. TeFa nr11. Uppsala: Uppsala University, pp. 30–53.

Gunnarsson, B.-L, Linell, P. and Nordberg, B., eds., (1997), *The construction of professional discourse*. London and New York: Longman.

Halliday, M. A. K. (1973), *Explorations in the Functions of Language*. London, Edward Arnold.

—(1985), *An Introduction to Functional Grammar*. London: Edward Arnold.

—(1991), 'Towards probabilistic interpretations', in E. Ventola (ed.), *Functional and Systemic Linguistics: Approaches and Uses*. Berlin and New York: Walter de Gruyter.

—(1993), 'On the language of physical sciences', in M. A. K. Halliday and J. R. Martin (eds), *Writing Science: Literacy and Discursive Power*. London: Falmer Press, pp. 54–68.

—(1994), *An Introduction to Functional Grammar* (2nd edn). London: Edward Arnold.

—(2002), 'The construction of knowledge and value in the grammar of scientific discourse: Charles Darwin's The Origin of the Species', in J. Webster (ed.), *Linguistic Studies of Text and Discourse. The Collected Works of M.A.K. Halliday Vol 2*. London: Continuum.

—(2004), 'On the language of physical science', in *The Language of Science, Collected Works of M. A. K. Halliday, Vol. 5*. (ed. J. Webster), London: Continuum, pp. 140–58.

Halliday, M. A. K. and Hasan, R. (1985), *Language, Context and Text: Aspects of Language in a Social-Semiotic Perspective*. Geelong: Deakin University Press.

—(1989), *Language, Context, and Text: Aspects of Language in a Social Semiotic Perspective*. Oxford: Oxford University Press.

Halliday, M. A. K. and Martin, J. R. (1993), *Writing Science. Literacy and Discursive Power (Critical Perspectives on Literacy and Education)*. London and Washington, DC: Falmer Press.

Halliday, M. A. K. and Matthiessen, Christian M. I. M. (2004), *An Introduction to Functional Grammar* (3rd edn). London: Arnold.

Harrison, S. (1998), 'E-mail discussions as conversation: moves and acts in a sample from a listserv discussion', *Linguistik Online* 1 (1).

Harry, D., Green, J. and Donath, J. (2009), Backchan.Nl: Integrating Backchannels in Physical Space. In *Proceedings of the 27th International Conference on Human Factors in Computing Systems*. Boston, MA: ACM.

Havre, S., Hetzler, E., Whitney, P. and Nowell, L. (2002), 'ThemeRiver: visualizing thematic changes in large document collections', *IEEE Transactions on Visualisation and Computer Graphics* 8 (1): 9–20.

Hay, J. (2000), 'Functions of humour in the conversations of men and women', *Journal of Pragmatics* 32: 709–42.

Holmes, J. (2000a), 'Doing collegiality and keeping control at work: Small talk in government departments', in J. Coupland (ed.), *Small Talk*. Harlow: Pearson Education, pp. 32–61.

—(2000b), 'Politeness, power and provocation: how humour functions in the workplace', *Discourse Studies* 2 (2): 159–185.

—(2006), *Gendered Talk at Work: Constructing Gender Identity through Workplace Discourse*. New York and Oxford: Blackwell.

Holmes, J. and Marra, M. (2002), 'Having a laugh at work: how humour contributes to workplace culture', *Journal of Pragmatics* 34: 1683–700.

Holmes, J. and Stubbe, M. (2003), *Power and Politeness in the Workplace*. London: Pearson Education.

Holmes, J., Marra, M. and Burns, L. (2001), 'Women's humour in the workplace: a quantitative analysis', *Australian Journal of Communication* 28 (1): 83–108.

Honeycutt, C. and S. Herring. (2009), Beyond Microblogging: Conversation and Collaboration in Twitter. Paper read at *Proceedings of the Forty-Second Hawai'i International Conference on System Sciences (HICSS-42)*, at Los Alamitos, CA.

Hood, S. and Forey, G. (1999). Research to pedagogy in EAP literature reviews. Paper presented at TESOL Convention, March 1999. New York.

Horovitch, D. (2010), *#FF Follow Friday explained. Tweet Basics: Day 4* 2009 [cited 17 February 2010]. Available at www.teachmetotweet.com/news/ff-foll ow-friday-explained-tweet-basics-day-4/

Hricko, M. (2010), 'Using microblogging tools for library services', *Journal of Library Administration* 50 (5): 684–692.

Huang, J., Thornton K. M. and Efthimiadis, E. N. (2010), Conversational Tagging in Twitter. In *Proceedings of the 21st ACM conference on Hypertext and hypermedia*. Toronto, Ontario, Canada: ACM.

Huckin, T. N. (1997), 'Critical discourse analysis', in T. Miller (ed.), *Functional Approaches to Written Text: Classroom Applications*. Washington, DC: United States Information Agency, pp. 78–92. Available at http://eca.state.gov/education/engteaching/pubs/BR/functionalsec3_6.htm, accessed 19 August 2011

—(2002), 'Textual silence and the discourse of homelessness', *Discourse and Society* 13: 347–72.

Humphrey, S. and Droga, L. (2002), *Getting Started with Functional Grammar.* Berry, Australia: Target Texts.

Hunston, S. (2000), 'Evaluation and the planes of discourse: status and value in persuasive texts', in S. Hunston and G. Thompson (eds), *Evaluation in Text.* Oxford: Oxford University Press, pp. 176–206.

—(2002), *Corpora in Applied Linguistics.* Cambridge: Cambridge University Press.

Hunston, S. and Thompson, G. (2000), *Evaluation in Text. Authorial Stance and the Construction of Discourse.* Oxford: Oxford University Press.

Hutchby, I. (1996), 'Power in discourse: the case of arguments on a British talk radio show', *Discourse and Society* 7: 481–97.

Hutchby, I. and Wooffitt, R. (2008), *Conversation Analysis: Principles, Practices and Applications* (2nd edn). Cambridge: Polity Press.

Hyland, K. (1998), *Hedging in Scientific Research Articles.* Amsterdam: John Benjamins.

—(1999), 'Disciplinary discourses: writer stance in research articles', in C. Candlin and K. Hyland (eds), *Writing: Texts, Processes and Practices.* Harlow: Longman, pp. 99–121.

—(2000), *Disciplinary Discourses: Social Interactions in Academic Writing.* London: Longman.

—(2001a), 'Bringing in the reader: addressee features in academic articles', *Written Communication* 18 (4): 549–74.

—(2001b), 'Humble servants of the discipline? Self-mention in research articles', *English for Specific Purposes* 20 (3): 207–26.

—(2004a), 'Disciplinary interactions: metadiscourse in L2 postgraduate writing', *Journal of Second Language Writing* 13: 133–51.

—(2004b), *Disciplinary Discourses: Social Interactions in Academic Writing.* Ann Arbor, MI: University of Michigan Press.

—(2005), *Metadiscourse: Exploring Interaction in Writing.* London: Continuum.

—(2008), 'As can be seen: lexical bundles and disciplinary variation', *English for Specific Purposes* 27 (1): 4–21.

Hyland, K. and Tse, P. (2004), 'Metadiscourse in academic writing: a reappraisal', *Applied Linguistics* 25 (2): 156–77.

Ivanic, R. (1998), *Writing and Identity: The Discoursal Construction of Identity in Academic Writing.* Amsterdam: John Benjamins.

Jacobson, S. (1996), *Unorthodox Spelling in American Trademarks.* Stockholm: Almqvist & Wiksell.

Jaffe, A. (2000), 'Introduction: non-standard orthography and non-standard speech', *Journal of Sociolinguistics* 4 (4): 497–513.

Jaffe, A. and Walton, S. (2000), 'The voices people read: orthography and the representation of non-standard speech', *Journal of Sociolinguistics* 4 (4): 561–87.

Java, A., Song, X., Finin, T. and Tseng, B. (2007), Why We Twitter: Understanding Microblogging Usage and Communities. In *Proceedings of the 9th WebKDD and 1st SNA-KDD 2007 Workshop on Web Mining and Social Network Analysis.* San Jose, CA: ACM.

Johnson, L. (1975), 'Dread Beat an Blood'. Available at www.last.fm/music/ Linton+Kwesi+Johnson/_/Dread+Beat+An%27+Blood, accessed on 25 April 2012.

Kang, S. (2005), 'Dynamic emergence of situational willingness to communicate in a second language', *System* 33: 277–92.

Kate, S., Leysia, P., Hughes, A. L. and Sarah, V. (2010), Chatter on the Red: What Hazards Threat Reveals about the Social Life of Microblogged Information. In *Proceedings of the 2010 ACM Conference on Computer Supported Cooperative Work*. Savannah, GA: ACM.

Kehoe, A. and Gee, M. (2011), 'Social tagging: a new perspective on textual "aboutness"', in P. Rayson, S. Hoffmann and G. Leech (eds), *Studies in Variation, Contacts and Change in English Volume 6: Methodological and Historical Dimensions of Corpus Linguistics*. Helsinki: University of Helsinki.

Kelly, N., Rees, R. and Shuter, J. (1997), *Living through History*. Oxford: Heinemann.

Kesseler, A. and Bergs, A. (2003), 'Literacy and the new media: vita brevis, lingua brevis', in J. Aitchison and D. M. Lewis (eds), *New Media Language*. London: Routledge, pp. 75–84.

King, S. W. and Sereno, K. K. (1984), 'Conversational appropriateness as a conversational imperative', *Quarterly Journal of Speech* 70: 264–73.

Knorr-Cetina, K. (1981), *The Manufacture of Knowledge*. Oxford: Pergamon Press

Knox, J. S. (2007), 'Visual/verbal communication on online newspaper home pages', *Visual Communication* 6 (1): 19–53.

—(2009), 'Punctuating the home page: image as language in an online newspaper', *Discourse & Communication* 3 (2): 145–72.

—(2010), 'Online newspapers: evolving genres and evolving theory', in C. Coffin, T. Lillis and K. O'Halloran (eds), *Applied Linguistics Methods: A Reader*. London and New York: Routledge, pp. 33–51.

Koester, A. (2004), 'Relational sequences in workplace genres', *Journal of Pragmatics* 36: 1405–28.

—(2006), *Investigating Workplace Discourse*. London: Routledge.

Korner, H., McInnes, D. and Rose, D. (2007), *Science Literacy*. (NSW Department of Education and Training, Adult Migrant Services, Quality Language and Literacy Services, Series Editor H. de Silva). Sydney: NSW Adult Migrant Education Service.

Kotthoff, H. (2000), 'Gender and joking: on the complexities of women's image politics in humorous narratives', *Journal of Pragmatics* 32: 55–80.

Kress, G. (1991), 'Critical discourse analysis', *Annual Review of Applied Linguistics*, 11: 84–99.

—(1994), 'Text and grammar as explanation', in U. Meinhof and K. Richardson (eds), *Text, Discourse and Context: Representations of Poverty in Britain*. London: Longman, pp. 24–46.

Kress, G. and van Leeuwen, T. (1996), *Reading Images: The Grammar of Visual Design*. London: Routledge.

—(1998), 'Front pages: (the critical) analysis of newspaper layout', in A. Bell and P. Garrett (eds), *Approaches to Media Discourse*. Oxford: Blackwell, pp. 186–219.

Krzyzanowski, M. and Wodak, R. (2008), 'Multiple identities, migration and belonging: "Voices of migrants"', in C. R. Caldas-Coulthard and R. Iedema (eds), *Identity Trouble: Critical Discourse and Contested Identities*. Basingstoke, UK: Palgrave Macmillan, pp. 95–119.

Kuhn, T. (1970), *The Structure of Scientific Revolutions* (2nd edn). Chicago: University of Chicago Press.

Kushin, M. J. and Yamamoto, M. (2010), 'Did social media really matter? College students' use of online media and political decision making in the 2008 election', *Mass Communication and Society* 13 (5): 608–30.

Latour, B. and Woolgar, S. (1979), *Laboratory Life: The Social Construction of Scientific Facts*. Beverly Hills, CA: Sage.

—(1986), *Laboratory Life. The Construction of Scientific Facts*. Princeton, NJ: Princeton University Press.

Lave, J. and Wenger, E. (1991), *Situated Learning: Legitimate Peripheral Participation*. Cambridge: Cambridge University Press.

Laver, J. (1975), 'Communicative functions of phatic communion', in A. Kendon, R. Harris and M. Key (eds), *The Organization of Behaviour in Face-to-Face Interaction*. The Hague: Mouton, pp. 215–38.

Lemke, J. L. (1998), 'Multiplying meaning: visual and verbal semiotics in scientific text', in J. Martin and R. Veel (eds), *Reading Science*. London: Routledge, pp. 87–113.

—(2002), 'Multimedia semiotics: genres for science education and science literacy', in M. J. Schleppegrell and M. C. Colombi (eds), *Developing Advanced Literacy in First and Second Languages. Meaning with Power*. Mahwah, NJ: Erlbaum, pp. 21–44.

Letierce, J., Passant, A., Breslin, J. G. and Decker, S. (2010), Using Twitter during an Academic Conference: The #iswc2009 Use-Case. Paper read at Proceedings of the Fourth International AAAI Conference on Weblogs and Social Media, 23–26 May, at Washington, DC.

Ling, R. and Yttri, B. (2002), 'Hyper-coordination via mobile phones in Norway', in J. Katz and M. Aakhus (eds), *Perpetual Contact: Mobile Communication, Private Talk, Public Performance*. Cambridge: Cambridge University Press, pp. 139–69.

Love, A. M. (1993), 'Lexico-grammatical features of geology textbooks: process and product revisited', *English for Specific Purposes* 12: 197–218.

McCarthy, M. (2000), 'Captive audiences: small talk and close contact service encounters', in J. Coupland (ed.), *Small Talk*. Harlow: Pearson Education, pp. 84–109.

McCarthy, J. F. and Boyd, D. (2005), Digital Backchannels in Shared Physical Spaces: Experiences at An Academic Conference. Paper read at *Conference on Human Factors and Computing Systems (CHI 2005)*, 2005, at Portland, Oregon, USA, 2–7 April.

McKenna, B. (2004), 'Critical discourse studies: where to from here?' *Critical Discourse Studies* 1: 9–39.

McNely, B. (2009), Backchannel Persistence and Collaborative Meaning-Making. Paper read at *Proceedings of the 27th ACM international conference on Design of communication*, at Bloomington, Indiana, USA.

Macken-Horarik, M. (2003), 'A telling symbiosis in the discourse of hatred: multimodal news texts about the "children overboard" affair', *Australian Review of Applied Linguistics*, 26, (2), 1–16.

Makice, K. (2009), Phatics and the Design of Community. In *Proceedings of the 27th International Conference Extended Abstracts on Human Factors in Computing Systems*, Boston, MA: ACM.

Malinowski, B. (1923), 'The problem of meaning in primitive languages', in C. K. Ogden and I. A. Richards (eds), *The Meaning of Meaning*. London:

Routledge & Kegan Paul. Excerpt reprinted as 'Phatic communion', in J. Laver and S. Hutcheson (eds) (1972), *Communication in Face to Face Interaction*. Harmondsworth: Penguin, pp. 146–52.

—(1935), *Coral Gardens and Their Magic, Vol. 2*. London: Allen and Unwin.

—(2004), *Magic, Science and Religion and Other Essays 1948*. Lavergne, TN: Kessinger. Original edition, 1948.

Mallinson, C. and Brewster, Z. W. (2005), '"Blacks and bubbas": stereotypes, ideology, and categorization processes in restaurant servers' discourse', *Discourse and Society*, 16: 787–807.

Martin, J. R. (1992), *English Text: System and Structure*. Amsterdam: John Benjamins.

—(1997), 'Analysing genre: functional parameters', in F. Christie and J. R. Martin (eds), *Genres and Institutions: Social Processes in the Workplace and School*. London: Pinter, pp. 3–39.

—(2000a), 'Close reading: functional linguistics as a tool for critical analysis', in L. Unsworth (ed.), *Close Reading: Functional Linguistics as a Tool for Critical Discourse Analysis*. London: Cassell, pp. 275–303.

—(2000b), 'Beyond exchange: APPRAISAL systems in English', in S. Hunston and G. Thompson (eds), *Evaluation in Text: Authorial Stance and the Construction of Discourse*. Oxford: Oxford University Press.

—(2004), 'Mourning: how we get aligned', *Discourse & Society* 15 (2–3): 321–44.

Martin, J. R. and Rose, D. (2003), *Working with Discourse*. London: Continuum.

—(2008), *Genre Relations : Mapping Culture, Equinox Textbooks and Surveys in Linguistics*. London and Oakville, CT: Equinox Pub.

Martin, J. R. and White, P. R. R. (2005), *The Language of Evaluation : Appraisal in English*. New York: Palgrave Macmillan.

Martinec, R. and Salway, A. (2005), 'A system for image-text relations in new (and old) media', *Visual Communication*, 4, (3), 337–71.

Marwick, A. (2010), *Status Update: Celebrity, Publicity, and Self-Branding in Web 2.0*, Department of Media, Culture, and Communication, New York University.

Marwick, A. and Boyd, D. (2011), 'To see and be seen: celebrity practice on Twitter', *Convergence: The International Journal of Research into New Media Technologies* 17 (2): 139–58.

Matthiessen, C. (2005), 'Frequency profiles of some basic grammatical systems: an interim report', in S. Hunston and G. Thompson (eds), *System and Corpus: Exploring Connections*. London: Equinox.

Mauranen, A. (2001). 'Reflexive academic talk: observations from MICASE'. In R. Simpson and. J. Swales (eds), *Corpus linguistics in North America*. Ann Arbor, MI: University of Michigan Press, pp. 165–78.

Mautner, G. (2005a), 'Time to get wired: using web-based corpora in critical discourse analysis', *Discourse and Society* 16: 809–28.

—(2005b), 'The entrepreneurial university: a discursive profile of a higher education buzzword', *Critical Discourse Studies* 2: 95–120.

Meadows, B. (2009), 'Nationalism and language learning at the US/Mexico Border: an ethnographically-sensitive critical discourse analysis of the reproduction of nation, power, and privilege in an English language classroom', Ph.D. dissertation, University of Arizona.

Meinhof, U. H. (1994), 'Double Talk in news broadcasts: a cross-cultural comparison of pictures and texts in television news', in D. Graddol and O. Boyd-Barrett (eds), *Media Texts: Authors and Readers*. Clevedon: Open University Press, pp. 212–23.

Melander, B. (1993), *From Interpretation to Enumeration of Facts: On a Change in the Textual Patterns of Swedish LSP Texts during the 20th Century*. TeFanr 7. Uppsala: Uppsala University.

Miller, V. (2008), 'New media, networking and phatic culture', *Convergence: The International Journal of Research into New Media Technologies* 14 (4): 387–400.

Moh, T.-S. and Murmann, A. J. (2010), 'Can you judge a man by his friends? – Enhancing spammer detection on the Twitter microblogging platform using friends and followers', in S. K. Prasad, H. M. Vin, S. Sahni, M. P. Jaiswal and B. Thipakorn (eds), *Information Systems, Technology and Management*. Berlin: Springer

Montgomery, M. (2007), *The Discourse of Broadcast News: A Linguistic Approach*. Abingdon and New York: Routledge.

Moon, R. (2008), 'Lexicography and linguistic creativity', *Lexikos* 18: 1–23.

Morell, T. (2004), 'Interactive lecture discourse for university EFL students', *English for Specific Purposes* 23: 325–38.

—(2007), 'What enhances EFL students participation in lecture discourse? Student, lecturer and discourse perspectives', *Journal of English for Academic Purposes* 6 (3): 222–37.

Morgan, N. and Pritchard, A. (2001), *Advertising in Tourism and Leisure*. Oxford: Butterworth-Heinemann.

Murphy, J. (2008), 'Better practices from the field: micro-blogging for science & technology libraries', *Science & Technology Libraries* 28 (4): 375–78.

Myers, G. (1989). 'The Pragmatics of Politeness in Scientific Articles', *Applied Linguistics*, 10:1, pp. 1–35.

—(2010), *The Discourse of Blogs and Wikis*. London: Continuum.

Naaman, M., Boase, J. and Lai, C.-H. (2010), Is It Really about Me?: Message Content in Social Awareness Streams In *Proceedings of the 2010 ACM Conference on Computer Supported Cooperative Work*. Savannah, GA: ACM.

Nagarajan, M., Purohit, H. and Sheth, A. (2010), A Qualitative Examination of Topical Tweet and Retweet Practices. Paper read at *Fourth International AAAI Conference on Weblogs and Social Media*, at Washington, DC.

Nesi, H. (2003), 'Editorial', *Journal of English for Academic Purposes* 2 (1): 1–3.

Northcott, J. (2001), 'Towards an ethnography of the MBA classroom: a consideration of the role of interactive lecturing styles within the context of one MBA programme', *English for Specific Purposes* 20. 15–37.

New South Wales Board of Studies (1991), *Science and Technology Syllabus K-6*. Available at http://k6.boardofstudies.nsw.edu.au/go/science-and-technology, accessed 25 April 2012.

—(2003), *Science Syllabus Years 7–10*. Available at www. boardofstudies.nsw. edu.au/syllabus_sc/pdf_doc/science_710_syl.pdf, accessed 25 April 2012.

Norrick, N. R. (1993), *Conversational Joking: Humor in Everyday Talk*. Bloomington: Indiana University Press.

—(2003), 'Issues in conversational joking', *Journal of Pragmatics* 35: 1333–59.

Norrick, N. R. and Chiaro, D. (eds) (2009) *Humor in Interaction*. Amsterdam: John Benjamins.

O'Halloran, K. (2007), 'Mathematical and scientific forms of knowledge: a systemic functional multimodal grammatical approach', in F. Christie and J. R. Martin (eds), *Language, Knowledge and Pedagogy. Functional Linguistic and Sociological Perspectives*, London and New York: Continuum, pp. 205–38.

Omoniyi, T. (1998), 'The discourse of tourism advertisements: Packaging nation and ideology in Singapore', *Working Papers in Applied Linguistics* 4 (22): 2–14.

Oulasvirta, A., Lehtonen, E., Kurvinen, E. and Raento, M. (2010), 'Making the ordinary visible in microblogs', *Personal Ubiquitous Computing* 14 (3): 237–49.

Ovadia, S. (2009), 'Internet connection: exploring the potential of Twitter as a research tool', *Behavioral & Social Sciences Librarian* 28: 202–5. Available at http://dx.doi.org/10.1080/01639260903280888 doi: 10.1080/01639260903280888.

Page, R. E. (2003), '"Cherie: lawyer, wife, mum": contradictory patterns of representation in media reports of Cherie Booth/Blair', *Discourse and Society* 14: 559–79.

—(2011), *Stories and Social Media: Identities and Interaction*. London: Routledge.

Painter, C. (2003), 'Developing attitude: an autogenetic perspective on appraisal', *Text* 23 (2): 183–210.

Palmer, F. (1990), *Modality and the English modals* (2nd edn). London: Longman.

Poncini, G. (2002), 'Investigating discourse at business meetings with multicultural participation', *International Review of Applied Linguistics* 40: 345–73.

—(2004), *Discursive Strategies in Multicultural Business Meetings*. Bern: Peter Lang.

Poos, D. and Simpson, R. (2002), 'Cross-disciplinary comparisons of hedging: some findings from the Michigan Corpus of Academic Spoken English', in R. Reppen, S. Fitzmaurice and D. Biber (eds), *Using Corpora to Explore Linguistic Variation*. Amsterdam: John Benjamins, pp. 3–23.

Pound, L. (1925), 'The Kraze for "K"', *American Speech* 1 (1): 43–4.

Praninskas, J. (1968), *Trade Name Creation: Processes and Patterns*. The Hague: Mouton.

Pullin Stark, P. (2007), 'An investigation into social cohesion in workplace meetings'. Unpublished Ph.D. thesis, University of Birmingham, Department of English.

—(2009), 'No joke – this is serious! Power, solidarity and humour in business English as a lingua franca (BELF)', in A. Mauranen and E. Ranta (eds), *English as a Lingua Franca: Studies and Findings*. Newcastle-upon-Tyne: Cambridge Scholars Press.

Quinn, S. and Stark Adam, P. (2008), *Eye-Tracking the News: A Study of Print and Online Reading*. St Petersburg, FL: Poynter Institute, Eyetrack07. Available at http://eyetrack.poynter.org/index.html#contact, accessed 2 May 2011.

Ragan, S. L. (2000), 'Sociable talk in women's health care contexts: two forms of non-medical talk', in J. Coupland (ed.), *Small Talk*. Harlow: Pearson Education, pp. 269–87.

Ramage, D., Dumais, S. and Liebling, D. (2010), Characterizing Microblogs with Topic Models. Paper read at *Fourth International AAAI Conference on Weblogs and Social Media*, at Washington, DC.

Reinhardt, W., Ebner, M., Beham, G. and Costa, C. (2009), How People Are Using Twitter during Conferences. Paper read at *Proceedings of the 5th EduMedia*

Conference: Digital Creativity and Innovation in the Web 2.0, at Salzburg, Austria, 4–5 May.

Resende, V. M. (2009), '"It's not a matter of inhumanity": a critical discourse analysis of an apartment building circular on "homeless people"', Discourse & Society 20: 363–79.

Ritter, A.,Cherry, C. and Dolan, B. (2010), Unsupervised modeling of Twitter conversations. In Human Language Technologies: The 2010 Annual Conference of the North American Chapter of the Association for Computational Linguistics. Los Angeles, California: Association for Computational Linguistics.

Rodrigues, S. B. and Collinson, D. L. (1995), '"Having fun?" Humour as resistance in Brazil', Organization Studies 16 (5): 739–68.

Rogers, R. (2004), 'Setting an agenda for critical discourse analysis in education', in R. Rogers (ed.), An Introduction to Critical Discourse Analysis in Education. Mahwah, NJ: Laurence Erlbaum, pp. 237–54.

—(ed.) (2011), An Introduction to Critical Discourse Analysis in Education (2nd edn). London: Routledge.

Rose, G. (2007), Visual Methodologies: An Introduction to the Interpretation of Visual Materials (2nd edn). London: Sage.

Rost, M. (1990), Listening in Language Learning. London: Longman.

Rothery, J. (1994), Exploring Literacy in School English. Write it Right: Resources for Literacy and Learning. Sydney, NSW: Disadvantaged Schools Program, Metropolitan East Region, Department of School Education.

—(1996), 'Making changes: developing an educational linguistics', in R. Hasan and G. Williams (eds), Literacy in Society. London: Longman.

Russell, M. A. (2011), Mining the Social Web. Beijing and Farnham: O'Reilly.

Sacks, H., Schegloff, E. A. and Jefferson, G. (1974), 'A simplest systematics for the organization of turn-taking for conversation', Language 50 (4): 696–735.

Salager-Meyer, F. (1994), 'Hedges and textual communicative function in medical English written discourse', English for Specific Purposes. 13 (2), pp. 149–170.

Schegloff, E. (1997), 'Whose text? Whose context?' Discourse and Society 8 (2): 165–87.

Schenkein, J. (1978), 'Identity negotiations in conversation', in J. Schenkein (ed.), Studies in the Organization of Conversational Interaction. New York: Academic Press, pp. 57–78.

Schifanella, R., Barrat, A., Cattuto, C., Markines, B. and Menczer, F. (2010), Folks in Folksonomies: Social Link Prediction from Shared Metadata. In Proceedings of the Third ACM International Conference on Web Search and Data Mining. New York: ACM.

Schirato, T. and Webb, J. (2004), Reading the Visual. Crows Nest, NSW: Allen & Unwin.

Schnurr, S. and Holmes, J. (2009) 'Using humour to do masculinity at work', in N. R. Norrick and D. Chiaro (eds), Humour in Interaction. Amsterdam: John Benjamins, pp. 101–24.

Schudson, M. (1978), Discovering the News: A Social History of American Newspapers. New York: Basic Books.

Scragg, D. (1974), A History of English Spelling. New York: Barnes and Noble Books.

Sebba, M. (2007), Spelling and Society. Cambridge: Cambridge University Press.

Semino, E. and Short, M. (2004), Corpus Stylistic: Speech, Writing and Thought Presentation in a Corpus of English Writing. London: Routledge.

Senft, T. (2008), *Camgirls: Celebrity and Community in the Age of Social Networks*. New York: Peter Lang.

Shamma, D. A., Kennedy, L. and Churchill, E. F. (2010), Conversational Shadows: Describing Live Media Events Using Short Messages. Paper read at *Proceedings of the Fourth International AAAI Conference on Weblogs and Social Media*, 23–26 May, 2010, at Washington, DC.

Shaoul, C. and Westbury, C. (2011), *A USENET Corpus (2005–2009)*. University of Alberta 2010 [cited 17 March 2011]. Available at www.psych.ualberta. ca/~westburylab/downloads/usenetcorpus.download.html.

Sherrard, C. (1991), 'Developing discourse analysis', *Journal of General Psychology* 118 (2): 171–9.

Shortis, T. (2007a), 'Gr8 Txtpectations: the creativity of text spelling', *English Drama Media Journal* 8: 21–26.

—(2007b), 'Revoicing txt: spelling, vernacular orthography and "unregimented writing"', in S. Posteguillo, M. J. Esteve and M. L. Gea (eds), *The Texture of Internet: Netlinguistics,* Cambridge: Cambridge Scholar Press.

Simpson, R. (2004), 'Stylistic features of academic speech', in U. Connor and T. Upton (eds), *Discourse in the Professions*. Amsterdam: John Benjamins, pp. 37–64.

Sinclair, J. (1981), 'Planes of discourse', in S. Rizvi (ed.), *The Two-Fold Voice: Essays in Honour of Ramesh Mohan*. Salzberg: Salzberg University Press, pp. 70–89.

Sontag, S. (2003), *Regarding the Pain of Others*. London: Hamish Hamilton.

Stokoe, E. H. (2003), 'Mothers, single women and sluts: gender, morality and membership categorization in neighbour disputes', *Feminism & Psychology* 13: 317–44.

Stubbs, M. (1996), *Text and Corpus Analysis*. London: Blackwell.

—(1997), 'Whorf's children: critical comments on critical discourse analysis (CDA)', in A. Ryan and A. Wray (eds), *Evolving Models of Language*. Clevedon: Multilingual Matters, pp. 100–16.

Sturken, M. and Cartwright, L. (2009), *Practices of Looking: An Introduction to Visual Culture* (2nd edn). New York/London: Oxford University Press.

Subrahmanyam, K., Greenfield, P. M. and Tynes, B. (2004), 'Constructing sexuality and identity in an online teen chat room', *Applied Developmental Psychology* 25: 651–66.

Subramanian, S. and March, W. (2011), *Sharing Presence: Can and Should Your Tweets Be Automated?* ACM, 10–15 April 2010 [cited 24 March 2011]. Available at http://cs.unc.edu/~julia/acceptedpapers/chi2010_microblogging_workshop_subramanian_march.pdf

Swales, J. M. (1990), *Genre Analysis. English in Academic and Research Settings*. Cambridge: Cambridge University Press.

—(1995), 'The role of the textbook in EAP writing research', *English for Specific Purposes* 14 (1): 3–18.

—(2001), 'Metatalk in American academic talk: the case of *point* and *thing*', *Journal of English Linguistics* 29 (1): 34–54.

Swales, J. M. and Malczewski, B. (2001), 'Discourse management and new episode flags in MICASE', in R. Simpson and. J. M. Swales (eds), *Corpus Linguistics in North America*. Ann Arbor, MI: University of Michigan Press, pp. 145–64.

Tauroza, S. (2001), 'Second language lecture comprehension research in naturalistic controlled conditions', in J. Flowerdew (ed.), *Research Perspectives on English for Academic Purposes*. New York: Cambridge University Press, pp. 360–74.

Taylor, A. S. and Harper, R. 2003. '"The gift of the gab"?: a design-oriented sociology of young people's use of "mobilze"!', *Computer Supported Cooperative Work* 12 (3): 267–96.

Taylor, P. and Bain, P. (2003), '"Subterranean worksick blues": humour as subversion in two call centres', *Organization Studies* 24 (9): 1487–509.

Teo, P. (2005), 'Mandarinizing Singapore: a critical analysis of slogans in Singapore's "Speak Mandarin" Campaign', *Critical Discourse Studies* 2: 121–42.

Thomas, S. and Hawes, T. (1994), 'Reporting verbs in medical journal articles', *English for Specific Purposes* 13: 129–48.

Thompson, G. (2001), 'Interaction in academic writing: learning to argue with the reader', *Applied Linguistics* 22 (1): 58–78.

—(2004), *Introducing Functional Grammar* (2nd edn). London: Hodder Arnold.

Thompson, G. and Thetela, P. (1995), 'The sound of one hand clapping: the management of interaction in written discourse', *Text* 15 (1): 103–27.

Thompson, S. (2003), 'Text structuring metadiscourse, intonation and the signalling of organisation in academic lectures', *Journal of English for Academic Purposes* 2: 5–20.

Threadgold, T. (2003), 'Cultural studies, critical theory and critical discourse analysis: histories, remembering and futures', *Linguistik Online* 14 (2). Available at www.linguistik-online.com/14_03/threadgold.html, accessed 25 April 2012.

Thurlow, C. and Brown, A. (2003), 'Generation txt? Exposing the sociolinguistics of young people's text-messaging', *Discourse Analysis Online* 1 (1).

Toolan, M. (1997), 'What is critical discourse analysis and why are people saying such terrible things about it?', *Language and Literature* 6: 83–103.

Tracy, K. and Naughton, J. M. (2000), 'Institutional identity-work: a better lens', in J. Coupland (ed.), *Small Talk*. Harlow: Pearson Education, pp. 62–83.

Trautner, M. N. (2005), 'Doing gender, doing class: the performance of sexuality in exotic dance clubs', *Gender and Society* 19: 771–88.

Tuchman, G. (1973/1997), 'Making news by doing work: routinising the unexpected', in D. Berkowitz (ed.), *Social Meanings of News: A Text-Reader*. London: Sage, pp. 173–92.

Tversky, A. and Kahneman, D. (1973), 'Availability: a heuristic for judging frequency and probability', *Cognitive Psychology* 5: 207–32.

Twitter (2010), *Streaming API Documentation* 2010 [cited 17 February 2010]. Available at http://apiwiki.twitter.com/Streaming-API-Documentation.

Unsworth, L. (2000), 'Investigating subject-specific literacies in school learning', in L. Unsworth (ed.), *Researching Language in Schools and Communities. Functional Linguistic Perspectives*. London and Washington, DC: Cassell, pp. 245–74.

Valle, E. (1999), *A Collective Intelligence. The Life Sciences in the Royal Society as a Scientific Discourse Community 1665–1965*. Anglicana Turkuensia No 17. Turku: University of Turku.

van Dijk, T. (1988), *News Analysis: Case Studies of International and National News in the Press*. Hillsdale, NJ: Erlbaum.

—(1998), *Ideology*. London: Sage.

van Leeuwen, T. (1991), 'Conjunctive structure in documentary film and television', *Continuum* 5 (1): 76–114.

—(2005), *Introducing Social Semiotics*. London and New York: Routledge.

van Noppen, J.-P. (2004), 'CDA: a discipline come of age?' *Journal of Sociolinguistics* 8: 107–26.

Vande Kopple, W. (1985), 'Some exploratory discourse on metadiscourse', *College Composition and Communication* 36: 82–93.

Vander Wal, T. (2007), "Folksonomy Coinage and Definition". Available at http://vanderwal.net/folksonomy.html, accessed 24 April 2012.

Veel, R. (1997), 'Learning how to mean – scientifically speaking: apprenticeship into scientific discourse in the secondary school', in F. Christie and J. R. Martin (eds), *Genre and Institutions. Social Processes in the Workplace and School*. London: Continuum, pp. 161–95.

Ventola, E. (1987), *The Structure of Social Interaction: A Systemic Approach to the Semiotics of Service Encounters*. London: Pinter.

—(1995), 'Generic and register qualities of texts and their realization', in P. Fries and M. Gregory (eds), *Discourse in Society: Systemic Functional Perspectives*. Norwood, NJ: Ablex, pp. 3–28.

Vygotsky, L. (1978), In M. Cole, V. John-Steiner, S. Scribner and E. Souberman (eds), *Mind in Society: The Development of Higher Psychological Processes*. Harvard, MA: Harvard University Press.

Walsh, B. (2001), *GCSE Modern World History*. London: John Murray.

Walsh, P. (2004), 'A complex interplay of choices: first and second person pronouns in university lectures', in J. Bamford and L. Anderson (eds), *Evaluation in Oral and Written Academic Discourse*. Rome: Officina Edizioni, pp. 31–52.

Weber, R. (1986) 'Variation in spelling and the special case of colloquial contractions', *Visible Language* 20 (4): 413–26.

Weissberg, B. (1993), 'The graduate seminar: another research-process genre', *English for Specific Purposes* 12: 23–35.

Welling, W. (1987), *Photography in America: The Formative Years, 1839–1900*. Albuquerque: University of New Mexico Press.

Welsh, I. (1993) *Trainspotting*. London: Secker & Warburg.

Wenger, E. (1998), *Communities of Practice: Learning, Meaning and Identity*. Cambridge: Cambridge University Press.

White, H. (1973). Metahistory: *The Historical Imagination in Nineteenth-Century Europe*. Baltimore, Maryland: John Hopkins University Press.

White, P. (2003), 'Beyond modality and hedging: a dialogic view of the language of intersubjective stance', *Text – Special Issue on Appraisal* 23 (2): 259–84.

Widdowson, H. G. (1998), 'Review article: the theory and practice of critical discourse analysis', *Applied Linguistics* 19: 136–51.

—(2004), *Text, Context, Pretext: Critical Issues in Discourse Analysis*. Oxford: Blackwell.

Willans, G. (1953), *Down with Skool! A Guide to School Life for Tiny Pupils and Their Parents*. London: Pavilion.

Wodak, R. (1997), 'Das Ausland and anti-Semitic discourses: the discursive construction of the Other', in S. Riggens (ed.), *The Language of Politics and Exclusion*. London: Sage, pp. 65–87.

Yardi, S. (2006), The Role of the Backchannel in Collaborative Learning Environments. In *Proceedings of the 7th International Conference on Learning Sciences*. Bloomington, IN: International Society of the Learning Sciences.

Yardi, S. and D. Boyd. (2010), 'Dynamic debates: an analysis of group polarization over time on Twitter', *Bulletin of Science, Technology & Society* 30 (5): 316–27.

Zappavigna, M. (2011), 'Visualizing logogenesis: preserving the dynamics of meaning', in S. Dreyfus, S. Hood and M. Stenglin (eds), *Semiotic Margins: Meaning in Multimodalites*. London: Continuum, pp. 211–28.

Zelizer, B. (2004), 'When war is reduced to a photograph', in S. Allan and B. Zelizer (eds), *Reporting War: Journalism in Wartime*. London: Routledge, pp. 115–35.

—(2005), 'Journalism through the camera's eye', in S. Allan (ed.), *Journalism: Critical Issues*. Maidenhead: Open University Press, pp. 167–76.

Zhao, S. (2010), 'Intersemiotic relations as logogenetic patterns: towards the restoration of the time dimension in hypertext description', in M. Bednarek and J. Martin (eds), *New Discourse on Language: Functional Perspectives on Multimodality, Identity, and Affiliation*. London: Continuum, pp. 195–218.

Zhao, D. and Rosson, M. B. (2009), How and Why People Twitter: the Role That Micro-Blogging Plays in Informal Communication at Work. In *Proceedings of the ACM 2009 International Conference on Supporting Group Work*. Sanibel Island, FL: ACM.

Zwicky, A. (1997), 'Two lavender issues for linguists', in A. Livia and K. Hall (eds), *Queerly Phrased*. Oxford: Oxford Studies in Sociolinguistics, pp. 21–34.